AFTER ALL

THE AUTHOR

AFTER ALL

THE AUTOBIOGRAPHY

OF

NORMAN ANGELL

NEW YORK

FARRAR, STRAUS AND YOUNG, INC.

PRINTED IN GREAT BRITAIN

PREFACE TO THE AMERICAN EDITION

PART of the background of this story is a frontier America that has now vanished; an America as seen by an English youngster of seventeen who left a Continental university to become a boy emigrant because he thought Europe was strangling itself in insoluble problems. He hoped to find in the New World a society freed from the social and political curses of the old.

What follows is here told. Though life as American farm hand, cowboy, prospector, homesteader, and later as reporter, taught me that the New World too has baffling problems, differing in form but having much the same roots as those of the Old World, it was in no mood of bitter disillusion concerning America that I returned to Europe at the end of the last century. I had, however, come very early to the conviction—a conviction confirmed by the years—that the freedom which as a boy I sought so hopefully in the United States cannot be achieved by this country in disregard of the Old World and its problems, any more than it can be achieved by Europe or Asia in disregard of the United States.

As a result, the work I have tried to do this sixty years or so in journalism and pamphleteering, in British politics, in Parliament, in international affairs, in educational experiments, has been as much concerned with the United States as with Europe. Indeed, much of that work has been done in America, where twenty years of my life have been passed; a similar period having been passed in France, and a somewhat longer period in Britain.

The years in America have been distributed over three generations (I have had as student in the middle of the twentieth century the grandson of a man I worked with out West in the last decade of the nineteenth) and among social surroundings as various as those of the ranch bunk-house and the American university faculty; the dire penury of the nineteenth-century frontier farm and the opulence of the twentieth-century city business man.

This is in the main the account of a sixty-year attempt to answer the question: "How may we achieve peace without sacrificing freedom?" and the closely related question: "How can the modern state best fulfil the economic functions into which it will be forced, whether it calls itself socialist or not, without sacrificing the individual in the process?"

The problem indicated by those two questions has become for this atomic generation the first of all problems. To its solution the United States is destined to make probably the major contribution. It is that fact which makes this book so largely an American story.

N.A.

NEW YORK
September 1951

CONTENTS

viii AFTER ALL

PART IV
A PERSONAL BALANCE SHEET

PART V
AT THE END

AFTER ALL

FOREWORD

WHAT KIND OF AUTOBIOGRAPHY?

WHEN, at the club or the pub, you run into a man who is in the habit of buttonholing you to recount at length his personal experiences, you commonly find you have an urgent appointment with the dentist. Why it should be different in the case of a man who offers personal experience in a longish book is not very clear. And sometimes, perhaps, the difference is not great.

Yet publishers both in Britain and America have urged me to tell this story; partly, perhaps, because my attempts during nearly sixty years to awaken the public to the nature of some of the illusions and fallacies which helped to produce two wars are an experience that has a bearing on the problem of preventing a third war; partly because the personal circumstances behind those attempts are unusual and may also have their lessons—or warnings—for those who would reach the public mind in our day.

In any case it is a mixed bag of experiences here related : that of the boy from a conventional Victorian English home who finds himself listening to the disputations of Continental revolutionaries in Switzerland, and, as a result, decides that Europe has landed itself in problems so complex that it is utterly incapable of solving them; and so, still in his teens, seeks escape by emigration to America, where he becomes a migrant farm hand, cowboy, prospector, settler on the frontier when it was still a frontier; and after some years as a manual worker, discovers that this world of the illusory simple life in the open spaces has its obstinate problems too, and turns, with knowledge gained as a manual worker, once more to writing and journalism; first in San Francisco, then in St. Louis, then in Paris, becoming in Paris the editor, then the ' owner ' of a daily newspaper; then a decade of close association with Northcliffe; during that association, awakening to the fact that Europe is heading for war, produces a political pamphlet which, at first ignored, shortly sets going a

ix

movement in Britain, the United States, France, Germany, aimed
at preventing or delaying the catastrophe; after the failure
of the movement to do either, returns to America; makes
contacts with President Wilson and his associates, discussing with
them new principles of international life; then turns to the British
Labour Party as on the whole the best available instrument for
future peace; is elected to Parliament; develops doubts as to the
Leftish approach; works for the League, for the collective defence
of the democracies; and then, despite the beginnings of international institutions, witnesses once more the spectacle of a whole
world drifting in nightmare fashion to a second war; and now,
after that second war, the prospect of still a third, this third being
the outcome of Marxist theories which he has challenged
during the whole of his writing life, as this record relates; theories
no doubt rooted originally in high purposes of social betterment,
but transformed by unforeseen, ill-recognized forces into a
doctrine of human enslavement, threatening, like some evil
pestilence, the peoples of the earth. To discover the nature of the
human motives which explain that satanic metamorphosis has
been the purpose behind many of the activities here related.

Indeed, this story might be regarded as a tale of adventures in
search of a sort of moral and intellectual North-West Passage; an
attempt to find, amidst the fogs and gales of passionate pre-
judgments and distorted education, the best road to the mind of
the millions (who of course include the man who writes this and
the man who reads it) with truths indispensable to welfare and
freedom; indispensable indeed now, perhaps, with our ever-
increasing knowledge of atomic and biological warfare, to the
continuation of any life at all upon the planet of which we have
made such poor use.

This, then, is no success story; one much more of failure than
success, in a venture where we have all—the reformers, the
teachers, the diplomats, the statesmen and peoples alike—had
more of failure than success. The personal errors and mistakes
that belong to the story have not been minimised. But a dilemma
presents itself to the writer. If the experiences in the search
for a method are to convey any useful lesson to those attempting
to reach the public mind with truths that alone can save us,
then it will not suffice to record merely the mistakes and the
failures. It is equally important to note the successes. Yet to do so

exposes one to the charge of a quite shameless vanity. That is a
risk I have to take. In this problem of getting ideas in international politics and economics before the public, the methods
followed, and here described, did in certain cases have surprising
success. It would be a silly affectation on my part to pretend
otherwise, and would deprive the story of sincerity—and of
practical value—if I did so pretend.

On a point of method, I have been warned against that
adopted in the first chapter, in which I write of the child and
adolescent with whom the chapter deals in the third person. I
do so because when one is dealing with one's childhood and early
youth that method makes for detachment, objectivity, the truth.
But the reader is duly warned of this jump to the third person,
which applies, however, only to the first chapter.

A word as to the conditions in which this book has been
written. The house on the small island where nearly all the
letters, manuscripts, documents, papers accumulated during more
than sixty years were stored, was badly bombed during the war.
(Why should a lonely house on a remote island have been worth
some of Jerry's expensive bombs?) Only a few of the papers
were actually destroyed, but all were mixed and scattered. I
spent two months trying to sort out the mess, living meantime in
a house without windows, without water and with very little roof.
The wearisome business of attempting to go through literally tens
of thousands of letters and documents usually meant that, while
at the beginning of the day most were 'retained for further treatment,' towards the end of the day, from sheer weariness of spirit
and a feeling that I was swamped and smothered in *paperasse*,
most were rejected. (I kept repeating to myself, 'One of these
days I will have all this stuff indexed and put in order.' I have
been saying it for thirty years, meantime adding to the pile,
mainly with the view to its being a substitute for a diary which
I never kept.) Nevertheless, most of what follows has been based
upon material (letters, notes, memoranda,) dating from the time
with which it deals.

An old American friend, William Allen White, who made of
his little country paper, the *Emporia Gazette*, a national organ,
prefaced his autobiography (in which he relates some of the
experiences we had together at the Paris Treaty-making of 1918)
with these words :

' This autobiography, in spite of all the pains I have taken and the research I have put into it, is necessarily fiction. The fact that names, dates, and places seem to correspond with such things that may have occurred in real life, does not guarantee the truth of these stories. So, in all candour, I wish to warn the reader not to confuse this story with reality. For God only knows the truth. I am hereby trying, in my finite way, to set down some facts which seem real and true to me. At best, this is only a tale that is told.'

No honest biographer could say other.

CHAPTER I

YOUTH AND THE VICTORIAN AGE: DEBIT AND CREDIT

BEING then all of seventeen years of age, the man felt desperately world-weary as he lay under the trees near his Lincolnshire home, reading, once more, John Stuart Mill's *Essay on Liberty;* and eating chocolate creams. The seventeen-year-old was taking stock of his life, its disillusions and disenchantments. He had, he reflected, seen men and cities—or at least some men and, well, say, three cities. And he had found everywhere not merely vanity and vexation of spirit, but shame and wrongs and crying injustices to which people like those of his family seemed indifferent; or too indifferent. His brothers and their friends had more than once made it quite plain that his eloquence on those grave subjects either bored them stiff or made them extremely embarrassed and uncomfortable. Usually they desired, above all, that he would please shut up. And his efforts in a wider field, as a 'rising journalist,' to set the world to rights had encountered most disconcerting snags. Yes, he could speak of being 'a rising journalist.' By his fifteenth birthday he had already written for newspapers. At fifteen and a half (having, while still at school, taught himself shorthand) he had taken a job as reporter, copy-reader, proof-reader, make-up man, and nearly everything else, on a country weekly at Weymouth. He worked hard and successfully for six months. He had then, on the basis of that wide experience and his knowledge of French (part of his schooling had been in France), been engaged to edit a bi-weekly English paper published in Geneva. He had been particularly glad to get that job because it would enable him to attend lectures and classes at the University, and consort with Russian and other revolutionaries who foregathered there. (He deemed himself a revolutionary.) For a year he held the position on the paper and put in a good deal of study at the University, met Russian and other radicals, joined a revolutionary club, wrote

B   I

a revolutionary pamphlet, took part in amateur theatricals as actor, manager, producer. He was—but for one thing—successful in his job and could have held the position indefinitely. Indeed the proprietor had held out the prospect of ultimate partnership. But the sixteen-year-old editor insisted on using the columns of the paper to air his revolutionary ideas in economics, politics and religion.

Now the paper depended for such circulation as it had upon tourists, holiday-makers and the members of English-speaking colonies in Switzerland, mainly church-going; and upon the advertising patronage of hotels financed by capitalists and dependent upon members of the English-speaking bourgeoisie, not likely to take kindly to revolutionary ideas in economics, sociology, or theology. The objection of the Scots proprietor to this use of his columns led repeatedly to ' words,' which finally ended in the editor's resignation on the ground that his editorial freedom had been curtailed in the interest of Philistine prejudice and capitalist exploitation. His journalist conscience would not permit him thus to ' prostitute his talents.'

On his return to England after a year or a little more in Geneva, he was offered the editorship of an evening paper then published in Ipswich. The paper sold mainly on the basis of its racing and football news : ' all the winners.' He made up the paper, tipped the winners (having not the slightest knowledge of or interest in horse-racing), wrote the leaders, and merely repeated his Geneva experience.

In a letter to his elder brother Harry[1] the boy editor tells of a characteristic difficulty with the manager (described as the boss des bosses) : ' In my notes one day I quoted a letter in which the extravagance of General Booth (of the Salvation Army), in travelling like a prince, in contrast with the penury of the humble members of the S.A., etc., was pointed out. At the end of the letter I added as a note : "Christ rode into Jerusalem on an ass. Mr. Booth drove into Kimberley in a carriage and four white horses. The first S.A. didn't pay as well as the present one." ' Well, for that truly not very witty, but certainly not very dreadful paragraph, the ignoramus of a manager kicked up the deuce of a shine. He said it was *impiety*—" No gentleman could 'er

[1] H. Angell Lane, M.R.C.S. (Eng.)., D.P.H. (Camb.), Barrister-at-Law.

written it. It was *shockin*. Ef I couldn't do better'n that I'd better *gow*." I said if reflections on Mr. Booth's extravagance were to be accounted impiety, I thought I should do well to *gow*. After a few more forcible remarks on both sides the matter dropped....'

But the same difficulty cropped up again. A leading article on 'The Mistakes of Moses' (with much plagiarism from Robert Ingersoll whom he read avidly) resulted in a still more terrific row with the Methodist manager. And once more, resignation, on the ground of editorial dignity and journalistic probity.

It has to be recorded that it did not occur to this insufferable young prig that he was entirely in the wrong on both occasions. He had been engaged for a specific purpose: in the Geneva case to produce a non-political paper likely to have some interest for visitors and tourist holiday-makers of all parties and creeds; and in the English case to produce an evening sports sheet likely to appeal to workers who had a bob both ways on a horse in the day's racing. He disregarded with a quite unconscious arrogance the fact that, instead of doing what he had been engaged to do, he had used the occasion to air heresies which, however sound they might be in themselves, had no relevance in that particular context, and were no part of his contract. It was as though, having been engaged to edit a trade journal of ironmongering, he had insisted on filling its pages with speculations on the cause of cancer. Though he could quote whole pages of Mill on Liberty, it was clear that he had missed the essence of much of that great Englishman's doctrine. This particular apostle of Mill had by implication denied the liberty of people to be interested in racing or mountaineering, their right to buy papers devoted to those things, and to get what they paid for; even though what they bought seemed to the ardent reformer, Ralph Norman Angell Lane, inexpressibly trivial and mischievous; as, indeed, it very often was. He had as little questioned his own competence to be judge of those things as he had respected the right of newspaper owners to differ; and to cater to the public preference, which usually the owners shared.

In after years, looking back, the man who grew out of that boy was to be astonished at the tolerance with which these early intolerances of his had been accepted; how little difference it seemed to make to the affection and regard shown him by his people and their friends. True, on one occasion, after a dinner-table talk which had much distressed his very orthodox mother, the eldest brother of the family, Tom, had delivered himself somewhat in this wise:

'One more quotation from John Stuart Mill, Herbert Spencer or Darwin, and in the interest of family peace I'm going to give you a first-class hiding. I think the time has come for it. I suppose it has never occurred to you that here you are, the youngest of the family, laying down the law to all of us. Our ideas are all wrong. We must give up our religion, our church, our party, our property. Nobody is right but you. You are infallible. You have read Mill, Darwin, Huxley, Herbert Spencer; we haven't; we are Philistines, and barbarians. In fact, according to you, the whole country is made up of Philistines and barbarians. You argue hotly with your mother. You try to show that what she has believed all her life is all nonsense; you put nothing in its place and cause the best mother in the world great misery. Is this what Mill and Spencer and Darwin have been teaching you? I too, of course, am an ignoramus. I'm just a farmer, and a tradesman selling seeds; but I know what Mother has done for us all and you don't seem to.'

The seventeen-year-old man of the world was near to tears at this onslaught; partly because there was so much truth in Tom's indictment; partly because there was so much failure to understand what had moved this young heretic and reformer and made him such a turbulent rebel.

His rebelliousness was now prompting a step which distressed him, yet which he knew he would end by taking; and this added to the sting of the outburst to which he had just listened. He had virtually decided to leave home and emigrate to the United States, to get away from the artificialities of the Old World and its problems, to the open spaces and simpler life of the New, earning his bread by the simple labour of his hands. He knew the decision would sorely distress his people; and might be completely misunderstood. He had the grace to admit to himself how deeply he would be wounding his family, and the decency not to like the prospect. He was not really clear as to precisely what it was that impelled or compelled this decision; he knew only that he would end by keeping to it; that his mother would strongly oppose the step and that his father, although disliking it perhaps, would, in his quiet and unobtrusive way, be on the boy's side. It was not so much the outcome which was in doubt as the family situation which would be created by it.

What had provoked this decision and this present mood? What does provoke the strange moods of sophisticated men of the world of seventeen years of age? No, as he himself reflected, it was not drink; nor women; nor conditions of poverty. He had known men whom drink and women had knocked endwise, and had always felt a deep contempt for their weaknesses—since he himself was not subject to them. (He had never found the strict Puritanical code of his Victorian upbringing hard to bear, and women, and all that the term implies, had not so far greatly troubled him.)

What then was the reason? The question has some interest these days, since the restlessness of youth, though not peculiar to this present mid-twentieth century, is a more serious problem now than it was then, if only because most of the problems of the Atomic Age are themselves more serious, and because to-day's youngsters will play so large a part in the settlement of to-morrow's problems or in the failure to settle them.

As the young nineteenth-century reformer lay under the trees, he reviewed the years of his life. He had almost said ' tragic life,' but some remaining glimmer of common sense and proportion told him that this would hardly do. He admitted (momentarily) that so far as external circumstances went, he had been far more fortunate than most. One of a large family, he had wanted for nothing, and the family, as families went, was tolerant and united. Though not rich, the household was well-to-do, and each of the children had been given a good start. Harry had gone into medicine and would soon qualify, Alec into engineering; Will was doing so well with his land agency and auctioneering that he had taken offices in London and would soon take a house there; Tom would take over the farms and specialize in seed-production, while Carrie—surely the best and most beautiful sister a man ever had—had married the schoolmaster fellow; the

Pater, in his retirement from running the group of shops he had set up in Lincolnshire, would now be able to read his French classics in peace and, as a magistrate, see that a little humanity tempered the justice which the Bench dispensed.

He was long to remember the attractive old Queen Anne house in which he had been born (one of the best in the little Lincolnshire town and known as the Mansion House); to remember his childhood fascination for its enormous cellars with great stone flags, each a yard or two square, which must have been brought from great distances because the surrounding marsh land had no stone at all. In the largest of these cellars was an eighteenth-century mangle, of strange and elaborate construction : an enormous box like an enlarged coffin, eight or ten feet long, two or three feet deep, filled with stones; under this box a dozen wooden rollers, which could be removed.

The family income after the retirement of the father from business could not have been more than four or five hundred pounds a year. Yet on that sum the family kept a horse and carriage, and several servants. There was little pretension : not even late dinners, but high teas of the English middle-class fashion. But there was plenty and comfort.

For the father of the family—‘ the Pater ’—the boy had always had deep respect and admiration and an abiding affection.

Thomas Angell Lane was one of those curious characters exercising moral influence by means which it was always difficult to define. He had no pretension to any sort of moral superiority. He could tell a somewhat ‘ broad ’ story even to his sons in their teens. He was not a highly educated man ; had not been to the university, came indeed of an order whose members did not usually go on to the university. His schooling (which had been mainly at the grammar school Horatio Nelson had attended) had consisted, so far as one could gather, in a little elementary arithmetic, a little elementary Latin and still more elementary Greek. He had somewhere or other learned French; read the French classics in the original and had a discriminating taste in literature. He had started out in life quite penniless, was apprenticed early to what in America would be called a department-store, evidently made fairly rapid headway, and had soon his own business which he developed into chain stores in a small way ; so that he was able to retire, as already related, at a relatively early age, and live

the kind of life commonly led in Victorian times by small country
land owners. He was a magistrate, chairman of local governing
bodies, governor of the grammar school, and so on.

His early retirement had probably been at the instigation of
his wife, whose character differed greatly from his own. She was
what the Victorians would have called indubitably a good
woman, but sharp-tempered at times, disposed to be a little
hysterical in her tempers, conventional, wanting her sons to
observe all the conventions too, very conscious of social distinctions, with not much regard for intellectual attainments unless
they could be translated into material and social advantage. Her
husband, on the other hand, did not care two hoots about social
distinction, or distinctions. He was no snob either in the direct
sense of dearly loving a lord or in the inverted sense of resenting
lords. He neither kow-towed to the socially prominent nor sought
their company; nor did he take a challenging or aggressive
attitude towards them. He had some secret by which, without
wealth or brilliance, he became quite the most respected (which
is so different from being the most respectable) man in that small
country town. If his neighbours had been in the habit of giving
precise expression to their feelings they would have said that the
man impressed you with his probity and integrity. He often disregarded, rather than defied convention, and even orthodoxy.
The whole family attended church, but whenever it came to a
recitation of the Athanasian Creed with the whole congregation
rising and turning to the east, this particular local bigwig
remained silent and seated: the 'damnation clauses' were too
much for him. As he once put it: 'If as a magistrate I had to
deal with the case of some man who had come before me because
he had refused to agree to something he could not understand,
I should dismiss the case. I am asked to believe that the All-
merciful will condemn millions to everlasting torment for just
that alleged offence. I refuse to assent to so horrible a proposition.'

The fact that he began life in retail trade might normally at
that period have excluded him from the company of men belonging to what would then have been described as the upper middle
class. But in the social contacts of the town he was never excluded.
He moved freely among all men of whatever social order with
whom he might have come into contact, and as to his sons, his
main concern obviously was that they should choose for them-

selves the life which each preferred. The eldest son—Tom, of the incident above described—ultimately took over the family farms, farmed them, and made a great success of his farming both on the technical and on the financial side. At a time when nearly all the farmers in England were bemoaning their financial condition, Tom was usually making a very considerable income. His son Eric—the third generation—has in turn taken over those farms, added to them and brought to their management a knowledge of agricultural science learned at Cambridge, and as a result pays tax and supertax on a very sizeable income.

The boy with whom we are concerned—he of the chocolate creams and the revolutionary philosophy—had learned from his father to pay very little attention to the legends concerning 'the Angell estates' upon which the family in some vague way were supposed to have, or have had, claims. One member of the family seems to have taken some trouble to trace the story; but no one paid much attention to it.[1]

Not at that moment, but in after years, the prospective emigrant was to ask himself, and to give some sort of answer to, the question of what it was in his very bourgeois, and, on the whole, comfortable environment that had made him such a rebel, and why, being a rebel, he had decided to emigrate to America. For if he really wanted to give his life to reform and revolution, then Europe was the place for that, not America.

If the boy himself had been asked for an explanation of his radicalism, he would have said that it was the result of the exposure of the world's injustices, miseries, and follies, to be found in the writings of Voltaire, Tom Paine, Mill, Kingsley, Morris, Carlyle, Huxley, Spencer, Bradlaugh, J. M. Robertson, Ingersoll, and Walt Whitman, which he swallowed so avidly, and to which the world in his view seemed to remain so blind, so insensitive. But the twist which had been given to what he read, the mood

---

[1] The member in question reports: 'The maiden name of the mother of Thomas Angell Lane was Caroline Angell, whom the records show pretty clearly to be a descendant of Robert Angell of Pecarck, a Captain in the time of Henry VII. Another member of the family, William Angell, was 'Seriant of the Catery to Charles II and James II.'

It is a curious coincidence that Battle Abbey, once owned by Benedict John Angell, has now as tenant a niece of Norman Angell, the daughter of the Carrie mentioned in these pages, the Abbey being a girls' school of which the niece is principal.

which differed so much from that common in his family and those among whom he moved, may have had its roots in one of those incidents of childhood to which modern psychology pays perhaps too much attention; but to which the Victorian age paid too little.

In the child's preparatory school there had blazed up some scandal concerning one of the masters and a matron. The child was too young even to understand what it was all about, or why it should be important. But he had been accused of falsehood in some connection with it, and the Head, as punishment, had forbidden any other boy in the school to speak to him for a whole month. (How little, sometimes, do those who deal with children understand the ferocity of some of the punishments they inflict.) The boys of the school of course delighted in making the punishment as complete and merciless as possible. The victim was morally flayed alive every day for weeks, for some offence he could not even understand. The punishment began on a Friday, a date which for several years afterward the boy kept as a private, secret, personal day of mourning; letting no one know why, on that day, he kept silently to himself. Religiously minded at that time, he recalled snatches of the prayer book: Crucifixion day was a Friday, and this was his crucifixion. This strange bit of dramatization, this private and secret fast-day of his own, lasted for at least four or five years. He could not even share this trouble with his sister who, fifteen years older than himself, had during his babyhood been—much more than his mother—his guardian and his refuge. But he could no longer turn to her as he would once have done, for she was now married, with problems of her own.

Her influence during his young childhood may have had something to do with the way in which he had taken the incident at the preparatory school; the sensitiveness he had then shown.

At three or four years of age, he had looked upon his sister as the most beautiful girl in England; (she was certainly one of them, with a mass of golden hair so long that she could tread upon it) as loveliness incarnate; the embodiment of all beauty. Seventy or more years afterwards he was to recall little incidents of the time when at three—possibly four—years of age he shared his sister's room. On one occasion she was to find him sobbing bitterly; and he refused to tell her what it was about. He had just had a puppy given him, and Carrie, for its misbehaviour, had turned it out of doors, at night-time; all by itself; in the dark. Such cruelty, coming from Carrie, had seemed impossible, incredible; his moral world had fallen to pieces. He could not explain all this, and he had finally to invent a non-existent pain in order to stop the girl's questioning; she never knew why the child sobbed that night. (The end of the puppy, by the way, was tragic: a careless groom drove the trap over it. Two days later Carrie woke her young brother early, before breakfast and before the household was up and about. Then the girl and child went out, in the quiet dawn, for a solemn burial under the laburnum tree in the garden.)

The man who grew out of the child was to wonder at times how far and in what way his sister had influenced him. The sister herself was to write sixty years after the incident just recounted that she had made no effort to direct her child-brother along any given line. 'I certainly loved you very dearly,' she writes on the occasion of her golden wedding celebration, 'but have no recollection of *consciously* influencing you in any direction. Your clear thinking, and strong love of peace were inherited from dear old Father. He was a much more brainy and intellectual man than most people knew and I, being older than most of you and remembering him in his best days, realized this better than you younger ones could.'

It is curious how in long stretches of forgotten things, incongruous matters of behaviour and conduct continue to stick out. One incident which may interest the psychologists, or ought to, bears on motives controlling child behaviour. Playing in the garden one day when the gardener was burning rubbish, this particular child brought a contribution of what he regarded as rubbish to the bonfire. That contribution included some wild flowers, or, it may have been, flowers from the garden pulled up as weeds and thrown on to the fire. The gardener said to the child severely, 'You must never burn living flowers. It is a wicked thing to do and God will punish you.' For a very long time after that, the child regarded the burning of living plants as an offence quite comparable to that of murder. It might have been a little more serious perhaps to have thrown his younger, baby brother on to the fire, but not so very much more serious. The gardener, who was evidently on intimate terms with God (he was probably of the Scotch Wee Free Kirk), had condemned it in the same tone as he would have condemned murder, fratricide, theft; and the child believed him. Why shouldn't he? The child had not yet any personal experience by which to establish a scale of values, an order of wickedness. He could do nothing but accept the scale laid down by those who knew; and he did accept it without question. It was perhaps a year or two before he began to see that perhaps to burn a dandelion was not quite on the same plane of importance as burning his baby brother.[1] (The taboos of many primitive peoples have often been of a kind which would make the former offence graver than the second.)

Yet it was quite early in the boy's development that there came doubts of some of the dogmas which had accompanied the religious feeling that had marked the time of his confirmation. For this, by the way, he had been prepared by Ralph Ram, the clergyman headmaster of the grammar school to which the boy had been transferred from the preparatory school where had occurred the infantile tragedy just recounted. Ralph Ram was a man of culture, sensitiveness, and understanding, of very different quality from the head of the preparatory school. Ram's influence was to leave in the mind of his young pupil a lifelong respect for whatever element it was in the Church of England which could produce that type of character.

But the dogmatic beliefs of the confirmation period did not long remain unqualified. One of the influences which made for doubt was the very ' literal ' acceptance, by his mother, of certain aspects of the Christian mythology. He was to recall her account of the fall of Satan, who had been one of the archangels, and was cast out of heaven—' thrown over the battlements '—for leading a revolt. The story was related, not as a symbolical legend, but as historical fact; and it made the boy extremely uneasy.

Two other incidents (also connected with the attitude of women to religion) impressed him. Out walking one Sunday afternoon with some younger boys, Mrs. Ram, the headmaster's wife, in charge of them, had sharply reproved several for collecting horse chestnuts (for use, of course, as ' conkers ') ' on the Sabbath.' It

[1] Who was later to die in boyhood, giving rise in the subject of this memoir to a depth of sorrow never since experienced.

was sinful to do such worldly things ' on Sunday.' Now the boy
with whom we are concerned had read his Bible and recalled very
clearly what Christ's attitude had been when, walking through
the fields on the Sabbath, His disciples had gathered a few ears
of grain. The Pharisees had reproved Him for tolerating ' de-
secration' of the Sabbath by ' labour.' Christ had poured scorn
upon this distortion of the Sabbath's purpose and meaning. Yet
here was a Christian woman, nearly two thousand years later,
guilty of the same Pharisaical distortion. Even the boy's own
mother would not allow skating on a Sunday. ' It should be spent
in reading "good" books.' These little details, even at a very
early age, made him doubt, not so much the Christian dogma,
as the effect of such dogma on the minds of those who subscribed
to it : people became blind to the plainest meaning of the religion
they accepted. Later on at the *lycée* where he read Mill these
doubts and questionings were to acquire a sharper edge.

The doubts when they did come were a source of both grief and
irritation to the mother, who was a good mother in the sense of
looking after the material welfare of the children and the household, but, contrary to the usual generalization as to women's
intuitions, was less sensitive to the boy's feelings than was the
father. She could not understand the father's insistence that the
sending of the boy to Coventry, as he had been sent at the preparatory school, was sufficient grounds for withdrawing him from
the school. She argued that the boy had not been ' hurt '; the
Head had not even thrashed him. She was apt to be infuriated at
the way in which the boys and the servants in the family had
such deep regard for her husband, who could often manage them
when she could not. She attributed it to the fact that he
' indulged ' or spoiled them. When her nerves were taut she
could say lacerating and searing things, and the memory of
occasional ' scenes ' in which the mother was involved gave the
boy during his whole life a deep loathing of bickering and
quarrelling.

The father's habit of treating the boys as adults may have been
his method—if he had a ' method ' at all—of teaching ' the facts
of life.' He would discuss cases that had puzzled him as a magistrate : a young girl accusing a man of criminal assault. ' I believe
the girl is lying, making herself important, the centre of
enormous interest. But I shall never persuade the others on the

bench that that is possible and the end will be that some poor devil will have his life blasted for an offence he did not commit.' This insight was finally revealed as sound and the man completely exonerated—thanks to the interest and, at a later stage, the intervention, of this particular magistrate. He had a few good stories of his own or his colleagues' experiences: of the town drunkard who, asked by this magistrate, 'How, with all this drunkenness, do you manage to support yourself?' replied, 'Well, usually I leans against a fence.'

The eldest brother Tom was a great amateur actor (a really good one) and whenever a road company was in the town (their shows were given in the 'Assembly Rooms' where the magistrates' court, church bazaars, political meetings were also held) would have the whole company in to supper at Mansion House. The father enjoyed these occasions immensely. But he had friends; and sometimes also the local brewer. On one occasion the company got to discussing, of all things, the work of certain Italian artists. The host expressed regret that perhaps we could not equal those artists in England. The brewer broke into the discussion with beery impatience. 'But, hang it all, we could buy up the whole lot of 'em!' The boy's father, relating the incident to his son, said, 'When I broke out into a loud guffaw, C. (the brewer) could not understand in the least why I found his remark so comic.'

One story of the father's concerning a Hyde Park orator was to stick in the boy's memory a long time. This particular orator, related the father, was attacking the Monarchy (indicative of the widespread republicanism of the time), and demanded rhetorically, 'What, after all, is this Queen? She ain't nothing but a bloody German whore.' A policeman standing near-by cocked an eye in the direction of the speaker whom he evidently knew: 'Oh I sye, Smith, draw it mild, draw it mild.' Whereupon the speaker, shaking his fist at the Queen's guardian of the law, retorted: 'Yus, and you ain't nothing but one of her bloody bullies.' And then the policeman walked away.

The boy—not yet arrived at his republican and revolutionary development—was shocked to the depths of his eleven-year-old soul, and asked why the man was not arrested. The father asked: 'Is what the speaker said true?'

'No,' replied the boy, 'it's utterly false.'

'Then,' said the father, ' I think it was best to leave it alone, and that the policeman was wise to walk away.'

When the boy later caught the then current republicanism, he happened to be visiting a neighbouring vicarage with his mother, who remarked, *à propos* of something or other, to the Scots gardener who was showing his roses, ' You know, my son does not believe in kings. He is a great republican.' ' Weel,' replied the Scotsman, ' he won't like it when he gets to heaven— for the kingdom of God is no republic. He will then, like all republicans, be subject to the King of Kings '—a consideration which had not occurred to the still loyal member of the Church of England.

Such were the memories which passed through the mind of the boy with the chocolate creams *and* John Stuart Mill's essay, as he weighed the pros and cons of emigration. He knew that he would have a tussle with his mother and with Tom. Both his parents had talked of his going to Cambridge and his mother particularly desired it. She had tried to reason with him. ' You are such a contradictory boy,' she pleaded somewhat complainingly. ' I wanted you to learn music, and you just won't learn, the teacher says. Yet you can read all those clever books, and even as a little boy you could teach yourself shorthand. So certainly you could learn to play the piano if you really wanted to. But you don't want to, though you know it would please me and give pleasure to others. And now you won't go to Cambridge. You persist in this absurd notion that you must be a farm labourer or something of that sort.'

Of course he could not explain it to his mother. He could hardly explain it to himself. Perhaps that childhood incident of being sent to Coventry for an offence he had not committed had something to do with it; had stirred emotions of revolt against his particular world. Such a feeling in any case was sharpened by an experience of a different kind at the *lycée*.

How well he recalled those *lycée* experiences : the journey, quite by himself, from London to St. Omer : how at St. Omer station he had found waiting for him a very ancient horse-drawn conveyance, in which he had been driven through the narrow streets of a French provincial town until it stopped at a large building with what appeared to the boy an enormous door; how a man came out of the building, took the boy inside and along great stone corridors to a room in which, behind an ornate desk, sat a large bearded man who immediately began to speak with great rapidity, at great length, in a language of which the boy understood not one single word.

And then there followed an incident which was to colour his whole life.

The *lycée* at that time housed about two hundred boarders and the boy who stood before the desk was then the sole English inmate of the institution of which the man behind the desk was head. (Two other English boys were to appear later.)

At the close of the completely incomprehensible discourse there appeared a middle-aged woman who led the boy away to some distant sitting-room. The woman, who had a few words of English, managed to convey to the boy that supper would not be ready for some time, and that she would get him a piece of chocolate. A very thick and solid piece was produced. The boy, finding he could not break it, produced from his pocket a knife which had been a parting gift on leaving England. He placed the thick block of chocolate on his lap, pushed the blade with all his might and with such good effect that it went through the chocolate, through the trousers and through most of the leg inside the trousers as well. Result: floods of blood all over the floor, panic shouts, bells ringing, and immediate transfer to the school hospital where this patient, who had managed to injure himself severely, stayed a week or two alone, unable to speak the language of the doctor who sewed him up, or the nurse who attended him.

During days of inactivity in bed, he had nothing but French to read and French was still a dire labour. He begged for something in English—any English book. Finally the doctor brought him one with the intimation that this was the only English book available. It was, of all things for a boy of twelve, John Stuart Mill's *Essay on Liberty*. In other circumstances, the boy would doubtless have failed to get beyond the first paragraph. But driven by loneliness, by home-sickness, by the absence of anything else whatsoever in the way of distraction; and finding that to read a 'light' book appropriate to his age in a half-known tongue demanded continuous reference to the dictionary and was thereby more of a labour than the reading of a 'heavy' book in a language with which he was familiar, he persisted in the reading of that supreme masterpiece of English political literature. With the result that before he was half-way through the reading of the book, that English boy was in a state of intense intellectual excitement, with a new world of thought and speculation opened before him.

Coming from a Conservative, English-Tory circle, he found challenged in that book many assumptions which he had been taught or had supposed were unchallengeable. He had been taught (at least by his mother) that 'pernicious' or 'mischievous' opinions should not be listened to. But here in this book it was shown, beyond possibility of dissent, that you could not possibly know whether an opinion *was* pernicious unless you had listened to it, and had considered it; that many of the opinions from which the world had profited most had at one time been condemned as mischievous and pernicious; that minorities should be allowed to express their views not merely or mainly because it is their right, but because the majority needs to be corrected by opposing and dissenting opinion, and cannot long remain right without it; that freedom of discussion is not merely or mainly a 'right' which men ought to possess, but a necessity of intellectual health without which there can be no sound judgment; that the mind of man is of such a nature that without this discipline it cannot know the truth and will almost surely fail of wisdom; that, in fact, liberty of thought, of discussion, is merely what we now call the scientific method, the method of doubt, inquiry, verification by inductive reasoning, applied to the domain of politics and social life.

It was strong meat for a young boy, and in other circumstances his intellectual digestion might have rejected it. But there was something in the experience which preceded it—the loneliness, the isolation, the strange surroundings, the absence of all other distraction, the English obligation in the midst of it all to keep a stiff upper lip—which made absorption of this strong meat possible. If ever a man's intellectual life is to be explained in terms of one experience, the life that followed for that boy is to be explained in terms of that experience.

On recovery from his injury the boy discussed the essay with his teachers, to be told that it was most unsuitable literature for one of his age; and that before he indulged in 'speculation' he must learn 'facts,' get 'information.'

Now the boy had learned enough from the essay itself to know that opinions about facts are usually more important than the facts themselves, since it is upon the opinions about facts—very often quite erroneous opinions—that men act in shaping their conduct and the world about them. And Mill had at least taught him that whether men interpreted the facts correctly or not depended upon their way of thought. Being English in a French community, he saw the truth of this all about him : the French view of certain facts of English life and history was entirely different from the English view of those facts ; just as the English view of certain facts of French life and history differed greatly from the French view. Both interpretations could not be right. Later, at a Swiss university, he even got a third view. There developed in him a certain distrust of the academic approach, a distrust which was to grow when he became a manual labourer in the Far West, a farm hand, a cowboy, a miner, and later still himself a teacher in universities.

One trouble the boy encountered in acquiring a very academic French at the *lycée* was that he was always so much more interested in the matter of what was being taught than in the manner of expressing it. This was at times embarrassing to the professors, as, instead of learning a lesson by rote and repeating it, which was what they, of course, preferred, the young English pupil would want to argue the point and probably disagree with the author under study by the class.

The religious arrangements of the *lycée* were a little puzzling. The Third Republic of the late eighties was extremely *laïque*, and yet there was grace at meals and some of the classes opened with prayer. (It depended upon the religious colour of the professor.) The chapel attached to the *lycée* was a magnificent old building, and on certain high days the English Protestants went to the services ; and the boy was always glad to do so. Otherwise Protestant religious instruction was given by a pastor who came once a month or thereabouts. But the boy could never recall anything of what the pastor was supposed to teach.

At the *lycée* he was constantly making comparisons between the relative freedom of English school life and the regimentation of the French school, though he began to learn then, as he was

c

to learn again and again later in life, to distrust easy generalizations about national character. The boys slept in very large dormitories, twenty or thirty beds to a room. A *maître* ('*pion*'—*espion*) occupied a bed on a raised platform in the middle of the dormitory; there to keep order and to create a feeling of the school being also a supervised prison.

The washing arrangements consisted of a long trough in the middle of the room, with tiny taps that ran a trickle of water. One washed by turning on a tap and allowing a little water to run over one's hands or one's toothbrush. It was the first morning, probably, that the boy stripped to the waist in order to perform his morning ablutions, to be pounced upon immediately by the *maître* for gross indecency. That sort of thing might do in barbaric Britain, but it would not do in a civilized country like France. The boys had to wash in their undershirts. The arrangements for bathing were non-existent. Once a month the boys were marched *en crocodile* to the public baths in town and compelled to take baths.

A little later, when his French became more fluent, he was able to talk high political philosophy with the older boys in the *lycée*, walking up and down the quadrangle. This was a time, by the way, when French *lycées* had no sports, virtually no games. The introduction of football from England into France was just beginning and had not yet reached the school. The only thing in the nature of games was occasional leapfrog in the quadrangle. The boys were precocious intellectually, perhaps because they had no games and recreation meant walking up and down quadrangles discussing politics—and women.

The only boys that were allowed to go out freely into the town unattended on sortie days (Thursdays and Sundays) were the three English. (This freedom positively amazed the French, boys and masters alike.) One week-end, when for some reason or other two sortie days occurred together, the boy decided to walk to Dunkirk by himself and stay there the night. His reason for wanting to do this was the desire to get away from the company of the two other English boys, who ever since their arrival had insisted upon spending their sorties with him. And he found there were times when he wanted solitude. Dunkirk was forty miles or so from St. Omer—quite a walk. Yet he did it. Arrived in Dunkirk he faced the question of where to spend the night. He went into an *estaminet* on the quayside (its seediness did not deter him) and asked the rotund lady behind the bar whether she could give him a room. For a moment or two the *patronne* did not reply, her breath a little taken away by the small figure in a *lycée* uniform making such a request in doubtful French. But after a pause she beckoned to him and showed him into a room which was decent enough—probably her best spare room; and, telling him he could have a meal whenever he wanted it, departed. When she had closed the door it suddenly burst on the boy that he had now what he had been desiring for much of his young life spent with five intrusive brothers, or in dormitories shared with scores of others—privacy and solitude. This was now *his* room, *his* castle. No one could enter save by his permission; and he was free of the two English barbarians he had come to loathe. This momentary emotion stands out more vividly than all else in that particular adventure.

Just before the brief Easter holidays his father wrote suggesting that, as an interesting exhibition was going on in Paris, he had better spend a few days there, taking it in instead of coming home to Lincolnshire; he enclosed a cheque for ten pounds which ought to see him through. When he went to the *proviseur*—the headmaster—with this letter, that functionary said : ' I simply cannot believe that parents who care for the welfare of their children should allow a young boy to go to Paris all by himself. I have a son of eighteen, much older than you, and I should not dream of allowing him to go on holiday to Paris by himself.' Despite this official protest the boy went and spent a short week in Paris all by himself. He even made friends with an elderly French officer (who mistook his *lycée* uniform for that of St. Cyr, the military academy) and met the officer's family, dining with them one night.

There were no doubtful adventures, and the boy yielded to none of the much advertised temptations.

It is quite evident therefore that the Victorianism of this household was not incompatible with a great deal of freedom. Yet the restlessness remained. One effect of the early reading of Mill was to increase his distaste for the disciplines of his home and immediate surroundings. Some of the Victorian standards—in such things, for instance, as 'no skating on Sundays'—to which he had been obliged to conform, seemed to him now more than ever silly and senseless. He had supposed conformity to be a duty. Yet his intellectual hero had demonstrated—or seemed to the boy to have demonstrated—that conformity was no virtue.

Letters which the boy wrote to his brother Harry, then a medical student, and disinterred by the latter after more than half a century of burial in attic trunks, throw some light— an unpleasant light—on the prospective emigrant's psychology at that time, and on his desire to get away. They make exceedingly distasteful and embarrassing reading for the man the boy became, revealing as they do all the priggishness and superciliousness of his seventeen years. But since they reveal also some of the more obscure undercurrents of feeling in a Victorian household; are not something which a novelist imagines a seventeen-year-old would feel and write in those circumstances, but something one Victorian youngster actually did write and therefore have their value as psychological data—for these reasons some extracts are here reproduced, though the reading of them some sixty years later was to set the author's teeth on edge. The boy writes to his brother in London:

You are right when you say that those of us who get away from home are the happiest. I am happier away. For the home atmosphere, social and climatic, poisons me. (By the way, these last few days the old trouble has assaulted me terribly, although I have had a lot of exercise in the shape of tennis.)

As an individual, and not a member of the family, I am happy enough. It is only fulfilling my part as a member of the family which brings dissatisfaction. For I have to relinquish the pursuit of that which really gives me the greatest happiness, in order, for the Mater's sake, to acquire a share of what is vulgarly known as success. I draw my appreciation of life from within and not from without. I could be perfectly happy without either wealth or reputation. If you ask me from what I do derive my satisfaction in life I can only reply: From living. Beyond that I cannot explain. Except, and this is perhaps true, the contemplation of Beauty and the search for Truth. I can quite believe Renan when he says: 'J'ai goûté dans mon enfance et dans ma première jeunesse, les plus pures joies du croyant, et je le dis du fond de mon âme, ces joies n'étaient *rien* comparées à celles que j'ai senti dans la pure contemplation du beau et la recherche passionnée du vrai.'

I suppose if I were religious I should term all this my ' conversion.'

When will you hear the result of your exam? The Mater at least, I think, is half prepared in case of failure. As to your disappearing I should not advocate that. If you really feel strongly about not spending any more of the common fund, I'll tell you what you can do.

And then there follow details of a plan by which both are to pool their earnings and be independent of the family, immediately.

Another letter reveals the attitude of the boys to their parents. The emigrant-to-be urges his brother to write to their mother:

It appears you promised to and have not done so. Ergo: Irritation. She has talked a great deal about you. She's sure you're hard up, and thinks you've pawned your overcoat and can't get it out and so catch cold. (The letter goes on to explain the very different reaction of the father.) It's really wonderful how little it affects the Pater, or rather how little he allows anyone to see it. I have such deep admiration for a silent character. One feels that a sentiment is often vulgarized by speech. I like to feel a man does not show all of himself.

The boy reveals a curious admixture of penetrating analysis of his parents and what must have been intolerable superciliousness towards his mother. He writes of the mother's talk concerning Harry; how she expressed the view that ' Harry had been a disappointment.' Which, comments the boy,

sounded very much as though you had been a speculation— something in the stocks. You know the Mater's nervous style. You had failed, you had had fads. Your friends had not been any use to you, etc., etc., etc. It is impossible to make a woman understand a man. I made a poor hand at attempting to explain that to devote one's whole attention to one study during the years of one's life when ' formative influences' act most powerfully, is to induce a sort of monomania and to starve much that is best in a man. She put me down as a visionary and one who did not recognise what you owed to your parents.

The letter goes on:

Last night she opened fire on me with respect to my theological opinions by reading me extracts from that commonplace little gospel-monger Spurgeon. And the worst of it was that Tom and Pater were there. I had hoped to be left in peace before the Pater. But he was wise, he walked out of the room. But there, I respect the old Mater for her little worrying; she does it from a sentiment of maternal duty and I'm a grumbling dyspeptic *ingrat* who wants kicking. In my letters to you, you see me in all my naked ugliness; I don't do any moral poses to *you*. This is a private soliloquy.

Evidently the medical student had been having a shot at reducing a little the younger brother's ego, but, it must be recorded, without much success. The younger admits his opinions are unusual. If they were not,

they would not be opinions but imitative superstitions. Most men acquire their life opinions in youth. It was at school, in his quick and eager youth, that Bacon rose up in scorn against the scholastic course of study and planned the first step of the *Novum Organum*, at college that Descartes became painfully conscious of the incompetence of the Aristotelian method, at school that Locke grew impatient of the quibbling pedantries that passed as philosophy. Bacon was thirteen, Comte fourteen, when this reforming spirit awoke in each.

(In passing, one may note that the little humbug had certainly not read the authors he wrote about.)

It was perhaps in a letter from Geneva that the boy got nearest to describing the root of his restlessness and the main motives for his contemplated emigration. To his father he wrote:

I believe that the happiest people are going to be those who make things with their hands. A carpenter, a cabinet-maker or a mechanic gets an idea, or desires to make something, sets about it and if he succeeds he has a sense of achievement and satisfaction. If he does not succeed he can try again in a different way. Nobody hates or abuses him. It is not at all the same when you make plans about society. If you try to improve things you are abused and hated by the very people who might benefit. If they won't listen, how can they learn to make things better? The owner of the paper makes difficulty when I want to discuss it in his paper. The club at the University to which I belong has asked me to do a pamphlet on it and I think I will.

The pamphlet was duly written and published, for in a letter to his brother the boy writes: 'My old friend the German professor has translated my brochure into French for the benefit of the members of the Cercle des Sociologistes of which I am a member.' Still later the boy writes that he proposes to enlarge it into a book, the theme of which would be that improvement in the material conditions of life do not produce any corresponding improvement in life's quality, in happiness. ' We improve everything except ourselves,' he writes to his brother.

Some of the high-falutin' these letters reveal may have been reaction from a curious and none too pleasant experience of the boy towards the end of his stay in Geneva. A raddled old woman of sixty or thereabouts, who had been associated in some way with Madame Blavatsky and was full of dubious Oriental mysticism (and possibly also of drugs or gin or both), had seriously proposed a sort of partnership to the boy in the establishment of a new cult, for which a ' Temple' had already, the old harridan asserted, been established in Cairo. She insisted that in this new cult there would be both 'lots of fun and lots of money.' She accompanied the proposal by amorous advances which both sickened and terrified the youngster. The episode may have sharpened his distaste for the Old World and his desire to get away from it; added to his growing sense of hopelessness concerning the world's major problems, and an equally deep conviction that he could do nothing about them. He did not want to be led into further futile efforts to set the world to rights, with the emotional frustrations which such efforts involved.

It has its comic aspect of course, this spectacle of a seventeen-year-old coming so solemnly to the conclusion that the folly of the world was incorrigible and beyond his power to correct. But, comic or not, the feeling which prompted the decision was genuine and is probably much commoner among adolescents than those who have forgotten what moved them in youth are apt to suppose. It was an effort to escape, prompted by motives not very different from those which led the saints of old to escape into the desert; as old as the oldest monastery; as new as the newest Communist Party attracting to itself those who seek certitudes; who can cast away their doubts, are willing to be told the path to follow, and to be kept to it by all the disciplines of the party line. Many youngsters of his age found their escape in cynicism or dissipation, in indulgence of the senses, in the trivia of sport.

To that young journalist of 1890 neither monasteries nor Communist Parties were available as avenues of escape; and whatever his childhood, in the care and under the influence of his
beautiful sister, had done for him, or his boyhood under the
influence of his father and his tutor Ralph Ram, they had at
least closed any road of escape into crude sensuality, into
cynicism, or absorption in 'sport.'

The open spaces of the New World beckoned him. There he
would find a simpler life, fewer of the problems bequeathed by
old established privilege and tradition. By the honest, actual,
physical sweat of his brow, not by the feverish imaginings of his
mind, would he earn his bread.

Motives of course are mixed. It would be quite untrue to
represent this tiresome young prig as moved merely by the kind
of impulse which sent the saint of old into the wilderness. Mixed
with this desire to escape responsibility for moral and intellectual
decisions which life in the complicated society of the Old World
demanded, was the hope that in that new western world he might
make one of the fortunes which seemed so common. If he could
do that he would be independent of newspaper proprietors who
put 'profit before reform.' He would be able to write as he
pleased and tell all the Philistines where they got off.

Meantime he had to get the consent of his people to this
adventure. He did not want to 'run away,' with its implication
that he had wanted to get rid of his family, or they of him. To
get their consent, however, would not be a simple matter. His
mother had set her heart on his going to Cambridge and his
father had rather hoped he would. He himself was indifferent.

The boy knew that he could not trust himself to discuss the
matter calmly with his mother; that he would get excited and
emotional. As he had been asked to stay a day or two with a
friend in London, he took refuge in the device of waiting until
he could put the matter by letter from London. Which was
perhaps a wise decision.

On his return from London the Pater announced that this
experiment of emigration had been agreed to, and added:

> At your age I would have gone to America myself. I've always
> admired the Americans with their self-reliance and inventiveness.
> But you go as agreed on your own resources. I will let you have

fifty pounds for your fare and a few pounds in hand. After that you are on your own.

And then, when it was settled and he was leaving all that he had known in his childhood, that past did not seem so bad. And indeed it was not so bad. He had not been insensitive to the evils of that Victorian era; indeed his deep consciousness of them was one of the impelling reasons for his desiring to find a different kind of world to the English world of that day. But later on in his life, when he was able to make comparisons of Victorian England with the new America of the West and with the more radical and revolutionary France, he felt that too often the post-Victorian reformers had thrown out the baby with the dirty bath-water; and as babies go, the Victorian one was passable. The French, among whom he was to live for nearly twenty years, had not, despite their readiness to blow up the old institutions and start afresh, despite the continual change, not merely of governments but of régimes and constitutions, been able to give the people anything like the extent of the welfare services or the social and political stability which 'reactionary' Britain had managed to achieve. Similarly when in later years he came to manage newspapers in Paris he was to make such discoveries as that the real wages of printers in London were in some cases nearly double the wages of corresponding workers in Paris.

The picture so often drawn of that Victorian age as one dominated by stuffy, conventional, whiskered, overbearing fathers, laying down the law to submissive families, as a generation full of sham and hypocrisy and snobbery, of ironclad class distinction, merciless oppression of the working classes, who were then supposed to have no rights, is a picture which, the boy came to learn in his later years, left out altogether too many of the facts.

The French had never had a 'Victorian age' in the Anglo-Saxon sense, an age, that is, of 'primness, propriety and conservatism.' They were much less convention-bound; relations between the sexes were in a sense freer. Yet woman suffrage and women's legal rights as understood in England did not come to France until they had been gained by English women for a whole generation.

This boy knew from his own observation that the Victorian age in England was a period, even in an obscure Lincolnshire country town, of very intense and very free political and social discussion. Close by the house where he lived was a small shoe factory that employed about a dozen workmen. They worked in a ground-floor shed, and in hot weather would throw open the doors at the end of it. As a child, the subject of this sketch would stand and watch them at work making the shoes, and listen to their talk. The talk, quite early, helped to indoctrinate him with political radicalism. The shoemakers were radicals, re-publicans, almost to a man, and took no trouble at all to disguise the fact. (Republicanism, in the sense of opposition to the British monarchy and royalism, was far commoner then than it is now.) One of the shoemakers was a great reader of Carlyle. When the boy first listened to this talk it was doubtful if he took in much of its meaning. But after having gone away to the preparatory school and grown a little in mind, he came back and renewed his acquaintance with one or two of these workmen, and became quite close friends for a time (much to his mother's distress) with a dark, black-haired, gipsy-like character, extremely voluble and very revolutionary in his ideas. The notion that these men felt themselves under any fear or oppression in the discussion of revolutionary politics would have been ridiculous to anyone who heard them and was in touch with them, as the boy was. Yet this was not in an industrial centre—it was in a country town, a district mainly agricultural. When, many years later, the man who grew out of the boy entered politics and fought elections in the industrial North (in Nottinghamshire, Lancashire, York-shire), he got the impression very distinctly that the generation of the early eighteen-eighties was on the whole much more politically minded than the generation of thirty or forty years later. Labour Party meetings in the second and third decades of the twentieth century were attended very largely by the elderly —the survivors of that earlier and more political time. The younger generation were not, in any considerable number, keen on politics. They were much keener on football, football betting, movies, and social entertainment generally. In the early eighties politics was the main entertainment—politics and theology. One of the distinctions between that time and this is that there were fierce debates on points of religious dogma and doctrine which seem in this generation to have died out all but completely. The boy, as an adolescent, found himself caught up in these theological debates, which contributed to the heresies already described.

Much as the boy disliked the tiresome Victorian conventionalism, he wondered sometimes what it was that made so many of the people about him (not all) decent and good folk, as for the most part were the servants, both men and women. What was it in that age, marked by so much that was detestable, which so often produced a standard of conduct so much better than one had any right to expect? The boy could recall cases of maidservants, scandalously paid and treated, who were 'good' in every sense of the term, moral, devoted to sometimes unworthy employers, supporting their own parents out of miserable wages, determined to do right. What accounted for such behaviour by people who came from country slums, from surrounding poverty, often marked by drunkenness and debauchery?

Contrasting statistics do not always tell the whole truth. Wages of a pound a month for a maidservant seem, now, to spell sheer servitude and exploitation. Yet servitude and exploitation do not truly describe the life of servants in the not very wealthy household in which the boy had grown up. On days of high ceremonial entertainment the children—commonly to their delight—were banished to the kitchen. The chatter of the servant-girls revealed pretty clearly their general attitude to the 'servitude' they were supposed to suffer. Obviously they did not regard it as such; often there was affection on both sides. (A passage in one of the letters from the father which has survived the blitz reads: 'I much fear that poor old D., the gardener, is dying of cancer. I could say of him, as King Hal said of Falstaff: "I could better spare a better man." ')

The child, when grown up, was to meet several of the old servants, now become themselves mothers or fathers, heads of households. Usually there was a shift upward in the social scale, the girls no longer going into service but becoming typists, secretaries. In this matter of the treatment of servants, also, 'revolutionary' France did less well than 'conservative' England.

French servants, he was to find when he came to live in Paris, were prepared to accept material conditions no English servant would have tolerated for a week.

The boy's own family presented curious contrasts. In addition to the brothers and sister of whom some account has been given, there was a stepbrother. (The mother of the family had been a very young widow, barely out of her teens, with one child, when she married again.) This half-brother in every point of character differed noticeably from all the others in the family. While still quite young, he engaged in a company-promoting scheme which netted him a profit of something in the order of ten thousand pounds. Though he never his life through was able to repeat any performance on that scale, he contrived to live as though some such sum was his yearly income. He was a quick-witted, engaging scallywag, living from hand to mouth, in great ostentation; 'borrowing' from other members of the family who would never dream of such extravagance. That he thus lived, always on the edge of bankruptcy, did not disturb him in the least. In his old age he calmly announced that he proposed to live entirely on the allowance which his brothers, clubbing together, would provide him. They duly provided the pension.

For the past thirty or forty years it has been fashionable to deride the 'naïve optimism' of the Victorians in assuming the inevitability of progress; and even more fashionable to pour scorn upon their hypocrisy, their refusal to face the ugly facts of life.

A comparison suggests itself. A characteristic of the post-Victorian generation has been the influence in social thinking of the Marxists or near-Marxists who promised Utopia as the outcome of the course which began in Russia in October 1917. The thing became a doctrine, a religion. Some of these intellectuals—notably Shaw—maintained the promises or expectations long after the kind of life lived in the Russian Utopia—the omnipresent police, the slave-labour camps and the rest of it—became undeniable.

Is there nothing of naïveté or credulity in such ready acceptance of a doctrine which made such dazzling promises and produced such satanic results? And as to sham and hypocrisy, Communist propaganda, not merely in Russia and the odd dozen satellite states, in China and India, but in the West, in France and Italy, still buttresses its appeal by such words as democracy, freedom, justice, peace, equality, culture, leisure, welfare, things which are to be found, the peoples of the world are told, only in Russian-dominated societies. One may question whether in naïve credulity, sham and hypocrisy, Victorian society had anything to equal this particular exhibition. And the new ' realism ' has captured half the population of the world and constitutes a threat to the other half, which nothing in the philosophy of (say) Mill, or Lecky, or Henry Huxley, or Herbert Spencer, or any other of the great English Victorians ever did.

Of course, ever since the world began the older generation has nearly always looked upon the younger as ' going to the dogs.' Because this is true, we commonly dismiss the criticisms of the oldsters as just nostalgia of the ' good old times ' order.

But unhappily the event has all too often proved that the oldsters were right. Civilizations have rattled down into chaos and barbarism because each new generation proved a little less able than its predecessor to meet the increasing difficulty of maintaining civilization. How often has it occurred ? Arnold Toynbee suggests twenty times or thereabouts. And that does not tell the whole story. It hardy suffices for men to maintain a civilization. Some of the most stable, like that of ancient Egypt, were systems of organized slavery, subjugation not merely to earthly priests and kings but to the tyrants of the spirit world.

Oldsters hear a good deal from the youngsters these days about the prudery of the Victorian Age ; how its puritanism condemned men and women alike to the neurosis arising from repressions and complexes, and paralysed their self-expression.

One or two facts bearing on that emerge from the story just told. France had no puritan revolution in the English sense ; no ' Nonconformist conscience.' Yet in the result youth in France had less freedom than in England, the position of the woman in a legal sense at least was much inferior. The absence of Puritan standards—hypocritical as they may have been—condemned the jeune fille to an almost purdah existence. She could not mix as freely with young men as English girls could, even in Victorian England. And as to French boys—incidents recounted in the foregoing story indicate the respective degrees of freedom

accorded to male youth in France and in England. Even in
Victorian days the greater freedom of the Anglo-Saxon and
'Puritan' girl—and boy—compared with that permitted in Latin
countries, was a commonplace observation.

And now—somewhat questionably perhaps—Anglo-Saxon
freedom has been pushed further still. From all accounts—
Kinsey's and others—chastity comes rather far down in the scale
of values current among the girls and boys of the modern high
school, or co-educational school. Virginity at marriage seems to
be as much the exception as the rule.

This latitude has been permitted or advocated on the ground
that an early indulgence of the sexual instinct would prove a
preventive or cure of complexes and neuroses which make life
difficult. But all the statistical evidence is to the effect that
neuroses are commoner in this generation than they have probably ever been before, with youth itself displaying a greater
restlessness, and a never-ending search for excitement and
distraction. The youngsters seem to have fewer resources within
themselves, and are more dependent upon external distraction in
the shape of the motor-car, the movie, the radio, television. The
sex instinct is exploited commercially in novels, plays, movies,
newspapers, magazines as never before. Indeed, no previous
generation possessed those particular instruments of exploitation.
There are novels to-day in which hardly a page is free of
physiological minutiæ of sex; while whole pages in some novels
are devoted to anatomical details of seduction and perversity. The
ability to be thus medical and detailed is usually taken as proof of
genius; and anyone who doubts whether it is genius is put down
as hypocritical or reactionary. It is well to be able to look at sex
'frankly and fearlessly,' but as one writer puts it (for the reaction
against this water-closet literature is beginning to set in), 'We're
not looking at sex frankly. We're staring at it until we become
cock-eyed. There is so much written on it,' he continues, 'that
a lot of young people are going to get the idea that married
couples never got out of bed. They do. They have to put out the
ashes. They have to go to work and forget about sex in large
stretches. . . . The white-hot spotlight we've turned on sex has
probably illuminated a lot of dark corners. But do we have to
leave it burning twenty-four hours a day?'[1] It is time we started

[1] Robert Thomas Allen in *National Home Weekly*.

being frank and fearless about a few other things besides sex, including the way in which sex is exploited.

If the matter concerned merely sexual morality it might not have very much importance. But the justification of the New Sexual Morality is—perhaps inevitably—associated with the glorification of 'pure instinct' as the guide of life. Instinct, however, covers more than sex : there is the herd instinct which can so easily develop into a fierce and turbulent nationalism, or a revolutionary fanaticism, or into the doctrinaire ferocity of Communism, unless there goes with it a sense of the moral obligation of the individual to subject the first thought to the second; the thought which is based on judgment of experience. If we are to laud instinct in social and political relations and encourage its indiscriminate exploitation and stimulation, we shall without any doubt begin 'instinctively' to use the atom bomb. Instinct is not enough.

CHAPTER II

ESCAPE: AMERICAN FARM HAND, COWBOY, SETTLER

WHAT happens to a teenager when he abandons the sheltered white-collar existence of student and journalist in Europe, and becomes a migrant manual worker on the frontier, the somewhat untamed frontier?

The answer to that question has some bearing on one of the problems now confronting the Western World, and particularly the British Commonwealth. For the British Dominions to-day constitute the real New World of unfilled spaces, which the United States did when the story here told was enacted. What this particular youngster did was nothing unusual in the nineteenth century. It is not often done to-day; there are so many obstacles to the doing of it; and the fact may prevent the British Commonwealth—so much greater in area and resources than the United States—doing what the United States has done: turn a nation of the thirty millions of Lincoln's day into the nation of a hundred and fifty millions of Truman's in the space of a single lifetime. Without that achievement, which has made the United States the main buttress of the Western World, the East would now already dominate the West; and Western civilization might have received its death-blow; of which more presently.

Within a few weeks of my father's consent (and financial assistance) I was on my way to New York in the Cunarder *Etruria*.

The things which stand out in my memory about that journey —as indeed about the whole American adventure—are naturally the things which no longer belong to the world of to-day; the multitude of sailing-ships in the Liverpool docks and under sail in the Irish Sea and at the Western Approaches; the fact that the *Etruria* herself carried sails in her lockers, in case of emergency. But particularly do I recall one feature which people of this generation seem to find it difficult to believe. Having decided to go to America, perhaps live there, I needed no passport, no visa, no landing permit; no place on an immigration quota, no permission to convert sterling into dollars. I did not possess a passport and it occurred to no one concerned to inquire about one. Beyond a few perfunctory questions by the Customs people on arrival in New York there was no inquiry, check, control of any kind. I walked ashore as one might walk ashore crossing to the Isle of Wight. There seems to be a feeling in this generation that if the freedom of movement which existed then were permitted now, society would fall to pieces, or blow up in disorder. But when that freedom of movement did exist society did not go to pieces or blow up. It was in many respects a great deal more stable and a great deal freer than is the society of to-day.

I recall only one question at the Customs. As I bent down to undo my baggage the Customs officer made a motion indicating that that was not necessary. But he asked quietly:

'What's that in your hip-pocket?'

'A six-shooter,' I replied.

'Keep it there,' he said and indicated he was not particularly interested. It was a cheap Belgian contraption for which I had paid, I think, half a crown, or some such sum. It was a great nuisance, and when some months later I lost it, I did not replace it and never carried a firearm during the whole time out West (save once when bringing cattle from Mexico, when the boss insisted we be armed, he supplying the arms). The fact that I could never 'reach for my gun' because I had not got one may have saved my life on more than one occasion.

Which hints at the answer to the question at the head of this chapter.

The previous chapter opened with a scene in a Lincolnshire garden which revealed a not very well-adjusted adolescent—a precocious, priggish, self-centred young journalist, superficially cocksure yet inwardly terrified at the problems he saw in the society around him; and wanting to escape the responsibility of any part in the decisions concerning them, decisions which might prove to be wrong.

Some two years later, in the Tejon Pass in California at a point where it debouches into the San Joaquin Valley, the same youngster sat eating his midday meal in the shade of a rock, in the company of the foreman of the ranch where for a year or

D

more he had been working. They had just brought a small band of cattle from Mexico and the two, with their Mexican helpers, had been some weeks on the trip, never during that time having slept in a bed or under a roof. From the point where they sat they could see over much of the southern end of the valley, and as they drank their coffee the same thought occurred to both; somewhere hereabouts would be a good place to build a home. At present there was not one house as far as the eye could reach, no smoke, no cattle or sheep, nothing to indicate that man was in the least concerned with it. Yet, as Covert, the foreman, said:

'One day they will get water from these hills; I expect there's artesian water at this end of the valley; there's quite a good little stream running down through Tejon Pass; and over yonder at the turn of the circle I'll bet there are other streams. There's good firewood only a few miles up the canyon.'

We decided to have a look-see as we went over the plains. We saw, as we came down into the valley, that a large field of grain had the previous year been planted for barley hay, and that the crop had been a fair one. (That summer or the next I was to work in a haying camp on that very spot.) At one point we found a Basque sheep-herder, his dog and his small flock. There were a few settlers lower down whose shanties could not be seen from where we had been looking. Some of the cabins were empty— 'filing-claim cabins.' But on some of the quarter-sections, settlers were at work, dry-farming patches of Egyptian corn (millet), on which flocks of turkeys seemed to be doing well. One settler had a milch cow.

The day was sunny without being hot. This was what I had come to the West for: to make a home, make it mainly with my own hands; by the honest sweat of my brow; to see civilization grow up around me in these waste places; to belong to a community of which I was one of the pioneers; a society which could start with a clean slate, free of all the privileges and oppressions of the old stale world of Europe.

I had a few dollars saved; and I knew that I could add to them by work on farm or ranch which now I had learned how to do. The economics of a homestead of my own seemed so simple as I worked them out in my mind while riding along with the herd. Somewhere hereabouts I would find a quarter-section that had not been filed on; so that I would get a hundred and sixty acres of good land 'for nothing.' I would build me a little house that would be my *pied-à-terre* while I did occasional work at the Tejon or other ranches, at harvest or rodeo. With Egyptian corn for chickens I would have eggs and poultry for myself and trade eggs and poultry with one of the travelling Chinese pedlars for groceries, which would be mainly just flour, baking-powder, sugar, tea. Indeed, on my own bit of land I could live for nothing or for a dollar or so a week; while I could earn in the harvest-field forty, fifty, sixty dollars a month: all to be added to my store of capital for the purchase of a gang plough, or what not. Such were the calculations—so fascinating, so exciting. And so fallacious. But at nineteen one saw so little of the fallacy.

What had happened in two years or so was that the intro-spective and somewhat morbid youngster coming from the sheltered life of a Victorian middle-class home, and who had written his father from Geneva of his hopelessness about the evils of the world and his desire to get away to a simpler type of life, had largely shed all these imaginings and had become a man of action, mixing freely with men of action. He had become in a sense a man of too much action, desiring to do too many things at once: to find gold 'in them thar hills,' to carve a home out of the desert, to find new plants that would grow in it. . . . For five or six years, my first great interest was to become part of this new western life and to be successful in it.

How had I got thus far towards the ideal which the above indicates, and what followed? What actually happened to the ideal? How far was it realized?

To answer those questions we must go back a little.

Of the fifty pounds my father had given me to start my new life nearly forty remained on my arrival in New York. For in those days it was possible to cross the Atlantic—being fed and lodged meanwhile—for less than three pounds. A cabin fare, and even in some cases a first-class one, ran to barely more than ten.

About the only thing in those days more expensive than at present was cabs. At the dock I was imprudent enough to take a 'hack' (taxi-driving is still 'hacking' in most American cities) without bargaining as to the price. It cost me almost half as much to get myself and baggage a few hundred yards from the ship to the hotel as it did to get them across the Atlantic. I never again in those first years in America took a hack.

The very evening of my arrival I found myself in the family circle of Robert Ingersoll, the notorious anti-Bible orator. I cannot recall how I got there. Nearly all my life I've hated meeting strangers in that way—intruding into domestic privacy with no particular and specific purpose. I doubt if I had a letter of introduction, so that my enthusiasm must have overborne my shyness. Yet meet Ingersoll I did, and passed an evening, the memory of which has lasted sixty years.

I had gone to his house in the clothes in which I had come from the ship, to find a family party all in evening dress. It made no difference to the cordiality with which Ingersoll greeted his young English admirer, introducing him to those present and during part of the evening showing him round the somewhat gorgeous house. I was admiring a huge vase of true Ali Baba dimensions. and he remarked, 'On festival occasions we fill it with whisky and everybody can come and help themselves.' Whether this was a joke or he actually did fill a vase as tall as a man with whisky I could not decide.

I recall one detail of the talk which had nothing to do with his anti-religion. Ingersoll was a lawyer and, à propos of my voyage across the Atlantic, mentioned that there had come into his office that day a man who wanted advice as to patenting a method of what he called 'jet propulsion.' The inventor declared that with a jet of water little thicker than a lead-pencil he could drive a ship across the Atlantic at greater speed than anything now obtained with screws or paddles. This, believe it or not, was sixty years ago.

Ingersoll, who had a real gift of effective purple passages in oratory, has often been compared to William Jennings Bryan (whose 'Cross of Gold' oration at the Democratic Party Convention of 1896 may have won him the nomination). The comparison is unfair to Ingersoll. Of Bryan it used to be recorded that he could keep a rural crowd standing three or four hours in the rain, and keep them entranced; but that if you asked any of the crowd afterwards what he had been talking about they had not the foggiest idea. But you knew very well what Ingersoll had been talking about if you heard him. He must have been a terror with juries, and with witnesses.

Once, during a lecture, he had disparaged the idea of a possible special providence. A listener submitted 'personal proof of its operation,' in the fact that once, when due to take passage on a ship, he had been 'providentially' prevented by a train accident. The ship went down with a hundred souls. 'I want,' replied Ingersoll, 'the opinion of the hundred on that point.' In that connection he told this story:

A pious Jew, going into a restaurant for lunch, found nothing that he fancied on the menu except some ham. For a moment his appetite got the better of his principles, as it does with all of us at times, and he had some ham. It had been a fine June day when he entered the restaurant; but when he came out the sky was overcast and he was met by a violent clap of thunder and lightning. Turning to a friend who was with him, he said, 'Did you ever hear such a fuss over a little bit of ham?'

Bryan could hardly have told such a story to illustrate his point.

My ultimate objective, like that of the forty-niners, was the West Coast. The cheapest route, I found, was by the Southern Pacific which would carry me via New Orleans. This suited me as I had a vague notion that I might find work on one of the isolated plantations which I thought were still a feature of the romantic South. I soon found, however, that the curse left by slavery and the race issue did not fall merely upon the negroes. White workers were, as a rule, not engaged, because putting them side by side with negroes led to 'complications.' Thus, much of the incompetence of work in the South: the negro worker must not be educated because he must be kept in his place; the white who had some education fought shy of anything like manual labour because it was a thing associated with negroes. Add to this, malaria (the rôle of the *Anopheles* mosquito had not yet been discovered), hookworm, and other troubles of a sub-tropical climate, and it was not surprising that you got incompetence all around. I had found my way somehow to a third-rate hotel in New Orleans, occupied mainly by a fifth-rate theatrical troupe performing at some vaudeville theatre in the city, and occupied also by multitudes upon multitudes of bed-bugs. (On one occasion in the South, when I was shown into a room in the best hotel in the place, I promptly fell through the floor, having put my foot on a rotten plank.) It was during this trip that I got my first

observation of the American negro at close quarters; and I wrote
my sister:

> I could never live in this southern country. To witness every
> day and all day the hourly humiliation of a whole people; to see
> them moved by fear of some act of violence from the whites
> among whom they are compelled to live . . . all this would get so
> much on my nerves that I should end by going off my head or
> pretending that I had negro blood so as to live amongst them
> and organize some sort of revolt. I'm almost disposed to try to do
> it. A man might do worse things with his life.

Later on I came to see more of the Southern white's view; to
believe that had Lincoln lived he would have managed to avoid
the worst features of Reconstruction, by insisting that the South
be left to itself to handle the question along gradualist lines. In
Jamaica, which I have visited and where the coloured population
is numerically preponderant, there has never been a lynching
(something which, when I first knew the Southern States, happened at least every week). Jamaica possesses to-day an all but
entirely coloured government, a result achieved without violence,
revolt, or civil war (save for the Eyre incident, which was not
typical).

On this first visit to the South, the war (there is only one war
for the Southerner even to-day) was barely a quarter of a century
old; that is to say, was distant by only half the time which has
elapsed since my visit. Most of the grown negroes were ex-slaves;
most of the grown whites ex-Confederate officers. ('You can't
spit out of the window,' remarked a Northern fellow traveller,
'without hitting at least a colonel.') 'Colonel' was a courtesy
title you gave to every adult white on first meeting him; and
were seldom corrected. (One innocent Englishman hearing a
Southerner addressed as 'Colonel' asked of which regiment, and
got the reply: 'Regiment? Why, no regiment at all. Just a
natural born colonel!')

Once convinced that hereabouts no white man could get
dependable work, I decided to move on and took an 'emigrant's'
ticket to Los Angeles, a town which (since the moving-picture
industry had not even begun) was small beer as compared with
San Francisco, which all Californians then called 'the City.'

The emigrant cars out of New Orleans in the early nineties
must have been badly constructed by present-day standards. As

soon as we reached the plains the dust entered in clouds, settling on everything and adding to the misery of the heat. There was no dining-car. The train stopped at designated stations while the passengers got out and in twenty minutes or so swallowed a meal—on the whole a sensible arrangement. Each evening a train official came into the coach, and seating himself at a small table assigned the berths to such as wanted them. It was, if I recall, the second day out that I had got into conversation with a young Frenchwoman going, she informed me, to join her husband, and obviously pleased to find someone who spoke French since she had not much English. When the berths were being allocated and the official said casually, ' You and the lady together? You want one berth for the two?' I am afraid the lady nodded.

Now I might be contemptuous of Victorian standards in general but I found then, as on certain other occasions, that the impulse to conform with some of those standards was stronger than any contrary impulse. I was not so much shocked at the suggestion as horribly embarrassed. I felt I was falling short of what the occasion demanded of a man of the world of seventeen. But I made it plain that we had to have separate berths. The lady never spoke one word to me again the rest of the journey.

It was just after this little episode that a lanky six-footer who might have stepped out of the pages of Bret Harte (of whom I was an enchanted reader) came and sat beside me.

' Limey?' he asked. I did not then know the word and looked my ignorance. He went on :

' From the old country? England?'

' Yes, England.'

' What you going to do?'

As I liked the look of this stranger I told him pretty fully what my plans were. It ended by his explaining that he had just taken on a contract for clearing a quarter-section (160 acres) of desert land and levelling it for irrigated vines and alfalfa. He would try me as one of his hands if I cared to take it on : no wages for two weeks and after that a dollar a day and my grub.

Six pounds a month *and* my keep seemed to me pretty hand-some. I saw no reason why I should not save most of the six pounds which at the end of five or six months would about double my capital. I explained, however, that I had a ticket through to Los Angeles. Would I not be sacrificing that? He explained that even if the railroad people would not reimburse it I could sell it to 'scalpers'—agents in half-used tickets, a trade contrary to the railroad rules but at which the railroad people winked. (The trade has since disappeared.) But he asked:

'You got blankets?' A little mystified I said I had not blankets. I was to learn that blankets to the migrant worker were what a horse is to the cowboy of the plains; as much a necessity as food itself.

Two days later we got off at a station which consisted of a small wooden hut and a man with a flag. Waiting for us was a 'buckboard' to which two mules were hitched. We drove over 'roads' made by the fact that others had driven that way before us. After a few miles we reached a store; I bought blankets and a few other necessaries and we then started on the twenty-mile drive to Covert's camp. Here an artesian well had been sunk giving a fair head of water, sufficient, it was hoped, to irrigate a good part of the quarter-section. But first of all it had to be cleared of the sage brush; and contour banks thrown up, by means of which the whole of the area to go down to alfalfa could be flooded piecemeal.

'I'll set you to planting the rooted vine cuttings in some of the cleared lots: you dig a hole, stick in a plant, fill the hole up. You can do it. But watch those fellows with the teams on the scrapers. I shall need an extra hand there in a few days.'

So long as the planting lasted I was under the orders of a German whose blonde wife cooked for him and two or three of the hands in the shack which they occupied. Both were typical Bavarian countryfolk. And the man knew his job. The evenings were passed cracking peach and apricot stones with nut-crackers, taking out the kernels, and planting them in a forcing bed. This secured young apricot and peach plants more quickly than could be done by unaided nature. Whether afterwards these young trees were used simply as stock for grafting I did not stay long enough to find out.

It was not yet the really hot season, so I stood the digging and planting in the warm sand well enough. The nights were surprisingly cold for a reputedly hot climate. I found that my blankets were quite insufficient in the bunkhouse which I shared with several 'Portagees,' and dropped into the habit of sleeping in most of my clothes, following in this the example of the more seasoned Portuguese. Later, when I observed in some of my companions the results of not taking off your clothes at night I dropped the habit, got more blankets, and later, even on the trail, slept in night-clothes—to the immense astonishment of my Mexican colleagues, one of whom said, ' You are the second Englishman I've known take his clothes off to go to sleep. Can't an Englishman go to sleep except in a certain kind of dress?' The Mexican's preparation for the night was usually to throw his boots off. That, too, has its convenient side. Once in northern Mexico I had occasion to pass the night in a Mexican's adobe house (one room). The whole family, men, women, children, all slept in a row on the one floor, with no slightest impropriety.

It did not take long for me to secure promotion from vine-planting to working one of the scrapers for making the contoured banks in the irrigated fields. The scrapers were of two kinds : the 'Fresno' and the 'Buck.'[1] The 'Fresno' resembled an enormously enlarged old-fashioned coal-scuttle on runners with a long handle at the back. It was hauled by two (in heavy ground, four) mules and could scoop up half a ton or so of soil, which could be dumped at the desired spot by a sudden jerk on the long handle. The contrivance was an extremely simple and effective instrument in that country without rocks or tree stumps. Not only could irrigation banks be put up rapidly, but ditches dug just as easily. I soon caught on to the job, thanks in part to the fact that at the beginning the mules knew more about it than I did ; and I let them have their heads. At a later stage I was given a buck scraper to operate. This was simply a long straight board shod with iron which the mules dragged forward. Behind was attached a board some four or five feet long upon which the driver took his stand. By varying the point at which he stood he could control the depth of scrape and quantity of top soil taken off. The load was dumped by stepping off the trailing board in such a way as to distribute the load evenly. The buckboard did the better job in constructing the contour banks of an irrigated field, because the slopes of the banks were more gradual, presenting a better angle for the mowers or reapers later on, and making a bank much less liable to damage and breaking. The Fresno scraper did a much quicker job, but tended

[1] Bulldozers now do all this kind of work.

to dig holes and to make the banks too straight up and down.
Again, this may sound technical. In fact it was all extremely
simple; and ' nothin' to it' as a job to learn. Only once did I have
a bad accident, and that at a later stage in my ranching career
when I was my own boss. It was due to the team and not myself.
I was using a buck scraper on land I was levelling for irrigation,
and towards the end of the day, tired and thirsty, I left the
team of two horses for a moment to go and get a drink. Before
I could return they had bolted with the scraper (though I thought
they were tired out); gone bang through a barbed wire fence, and
disappeared in the gathering dark over the plain. It was not until
daybreak next morning that I could find them. I was by
myself. They had somehow managed to shake off the scraper
but one of the horses had severed the tendon of his near hind
hock, and though I managed to get the vet. to him he had to
be shot. It was a bitter loss at the time (for the team was my
own), swallowing up a considerable part of my slender capital.

I must have stayed in this first job some three or four months
because I recall counting up my resources and finding that what
was left of the fifty pounds with which I started from England
and what I had managed to put by in the three or four months
work on this job gave me over two hundred dollars. Not once in
those months had I left the ranch (or wanted to) and, as the thirty
dollars a month included board and lodging, it was all saving.
I was beginning to feel a capitalist.

I got on well enough with my fellow workmen: Mexican,
Portuguese, German, and American. I got on particularly well
with the foreman, who often came over to the steps of the bunkhouse after supper and had a chat about things European. The
company was ' typically American' in that it was made up of
all nationalities, colours, races. The ' Mexicans' were obviously
predominantly Indian and though often as black as a negro did
not suffer the colour bar to anything like the same degree. They
generally held in great contempt the tribal Indians from the
reservations whom we occasionally saw.

I did not seem to feel in the least, during those first months,
the lack of intellectual interest. The foreman was intelligent
and knowledgeable though I don't suppose he had ever read a
book in his life. I had the sense (wanting to know this new
Western country) to encourage him to talk to me rather than

making any attempt to talk much to him. Indeed, the effect of this first essay in the new life of manual labour was anæsthetic. Under the influence of open air and physical fatigue I flourished physically; slept as I have never slept since; dead to the world until the Chinese cook awakened the hands with his gong at daybreak. I read occasionally—but not much or often—the newspapers that came to the ranch.

In later years I was to take part in discussions concerning the deadening and brutalizing effect of repetition-work; of putting the same kind of bolt into the same kind of hole all day long. But there is another side to that, or many women and some men would not turn to such 'repetition-jobs' as knitting (not, perhaps, completely repetitive in detail). It is quite obvious that women find in the repetition of knitting a sedative effect. I certainly found this about some types of repetition-work on the farm. Occasionally I was put on to plough with a gang plough (one with several shares, sometimes as many as eight or ten, drawn in those days not by tractors but a team of six or eight mules or horses). The job was to walk all day long behind the plough watching the waves of freshly turned earth fall into place. The effect was hypnotic and soothing. A year or two later, when my attempts to become myself a ranch-owner had resulted in problems of debt and crop failures, it was an immense relief to leave town and its creditors and law cases behind and in the morning air to hitch up a team and have nothing more to do or think about than to watch the earth fall in waves along the furrows.

I don't think it stimulated thought; rather did it send the mind to sleep. My brother Harry has saved a few letters which I wrote him from Geneva and later from the days on the plains (when he himself was surgeon to a lumber company in the then wilds of Newfoundland). The difference between the Geneva letters and the early American ones is striking. Looking at them with the detachment of age, the letters from the plains make me wince: the obvious effort to be 'literary,' to say something worth while, makes this elderly man wish he'd never written them. Some of the Geneva letters on the other hand make good reading to-day though they discuss little more than the unrest and pains of a not very well adjusted adolescence.

At the end of three months or so Covert, the foreman, came to me and asked if I would like a new job.

'The superintendent of the San Luis ranch to the north-west here has been taken to the hospital and there's trouble with the greasers. I've been asked to take over things for a bit and if you care to come along, I can give you a job—thirty-five dollars a month all found. There'll be some handling of cattle. The place is so overstocked the cattle are treading on each other's feet. I'll have to send some into the coast range or perhaps into the Tejon country.'

'But I don't know if I'm a good enough rider for cattle work,' I insisted. 'I've never learned to ride cowboy fashion.'

'You don't learn to ride cowboy fashion. You get into the saddle and stay there. The horse does the riding; not you. It does not need rodeo tricks to ride along with the herd. If we go to Tejon I'll go myself and would like to have you along so as to have another white man with me.'

It ended by my agreeing to go. We took train to Bakersfield at the southern end of the San Joaquin Valley and drove thence about forty miles north.

This part of the South-West where I first worked was in a transitional stage of development, turning from a cattle country into one of small settler farmers, many of them on government land which they had not yet 'proved up.' The transition did not in my time involve bloody frays between settler and cattle baron. Some of the cattle barons were indeed making a virtue of necessity. The Kern County Land Company for instance was taking vast tracts, building irrigation canals and then selling the land in small plots of twenty or forty acres for fruit-farming; on the whole doing a good job. They advertised their land in England and attracted a number of English settlers, so that quite an English colony was formed in the Bakersfield section of the San Joaquin Valley. I did not myself become one of their customers but came to know a number of the English folk who did. I was to arrive at my own attempt at ranching by another road.

The ranch where I had my first taste of cow-punching was supposed to be part of the holdings of Miller and Lux, the legendary San Francisco butchers whose property was—so the legend ran—such that they could drive a herd of cattle from the Mexican border to San Francisco and camp on their own land every night.

This job with Covert was my first experience of a proper cattle ranch—if indeed it was a proper one as Covert had said. That year promised to be dry, and though the ranch was at the foothills of the coast range, feed was likely to be short. One of the first things Covert did was to put down two or three thousand acres to barley which he intended to harvest, not for its grain at all but for ' hay.' When the grain was in the milk the whole thing would be mowed (as one would mow a field of fescue at home), stacked, and used for fodder when the green pastures failed. The straw in such a climate was of course very short but that made it the more digestible for the stock. I wondered why barley of all grains was chosen in that climate, for the beards, with the intense heat and dryness, became like needles, cruel for the beasts, which often had festering mouths from splinters that had entered the flesh. The ' hay,' moreover, was full of foxtail grass, the spines of which were even more murderous. I had great trouble in keeping the mouths of my two horses clean of this nuisance.

For with my arrival at the San Luis I acquired two horses as my own property, paying ten dollars (then two pounds) apiece, or some such price for them. One was a gentle little mare as tame as a puppy; the other an ill-tempered roan gelding which quite frequently bucked me off. He strayed one night when I was camping in the Tejon Pass and I never heard of him again.

What Covert had said about learning to ride and about the horse doing the riding and not the man, I found to be true. I learned to ride, and learned to stay on, even when on cold mornings (and I was a good deal colder than the horse) the savage little beasts did their best to throw me. But I simply cannot recall the 'learning.' So far as my memory goes I rode from the first—except for the bucking. All these western mustangs had the trick of a little dog-trot which they could keep up all day, the rider simply sitting still in his deep, comfortable, high-pommel saddle, his foot barely touching the stirrup which was almost always sheathed with leather so that the foot never went completely into the stirrup and consequently was never caught in it if the rider was thrown; and never caught under brush. These heavy leather coverings of the stirrups were not purely *panache*; they had their purpose.

I had some bad moments in the first week or so. On one occasion, before I had become fully saddle-broke, I had to go with some others into the foothills to round up some strays. We

were to be away perhaps two or three days, taking a packhorse
with us carrying the grub and blankets. The nights—and early
mornings—were bitterly cold, and after a somewhat restless
night we would wake at dawn, swallow some beans and coffee,
saddle our horses, and ride helter-skelter down hills full of gopher-
holes after some stray or other. The horses, too, were ill-tempered
with the poor feed and the cold, and my roan threatened to prove
unmanageable. On the second morning, as one of the elder men
handed me some coffee, he saw that my hand shook. Instead of
deriding me as he might have done, he said quietly: 'Don't worry,
sonny. We all get that way sometimes. I used to be much worse.
You'll feel all right when you get up on that horse. And if he
does buck you off you won't get hurt; you'll get up again
and he won't buck. Now drink your coffee, and here's some beans.'
(Red beans were the staple food, morning, noon and night.)

I learned to ride well (I could ride the roan when no one else
could), but was no good with the rope.

I can recall after sixty years a multitude of isolated incidents
of that time much more clearly than the precise sequence of
events—whether this trip into Mexico to shift cattle was before
the prospecting expedition with Covert; just when it was that
I filed my homestead claims; when the well was dug; precisely
when it was I became mail-carrier for the new township where
my homestead claim was situated. But after all, the precise sequence does not matter. It is curious that occurrences of no
possible significance or interest persist in memory with most
pellucid clarity. Sometimes they are just words or phrases used
by people. Covert had a phrase: 'It can't be did,' which I find
myself repeating to-day. Incidents in which I showed myself in
a very bad light, revealing cowardice, vanity, injustice, bad
manners, or mere stupidity, remain with me in painful clearness;
as also do cases in which I won praise. I recall that when I was
carrying the mail to Toolwass, I had bought a little two-wheeled
cart, believing I could make better time with it than on horseback. I had it outside the Cosmopolitan Hotel in Bakersfield,
having put (I think) my little roan gelding into shafts. He began
to play tricks and I feared he would bolt, break the shafts; kill
somebody ... He had just baulked right in front of the hotel and I
could not get him started. The barkeep, a lame, ill-natured fellow,
came out and began to make observations to the watching crowd.

'Do you know, fellers,' he said, addressing the crowd, 'what the trouble is? The guy up there trying to drive is afraid of the little two-by-four poodle in the shafts.' It was true. I knew what the little devil was capable of doing and I don't doubt I was as pale as a ghost.

But I also recalled another incident. I had a team of four horses in a Studebaker wagon outside the post-office with a half-load of lumber. One of the lead horses got astride his trace and began to kick and lunge. I managed to grab him, get him back into the traces and jump aboard. But the whole team now was on edge and did a first-class bolt, despite the heavy load. I knew that with so heavy a load they could not go far, so I drove the whole four through the town with buggies and horses tied up to the sidewalk without hitting one of them, and a little way on to the plain. When they began to quiet down I drove them back into town and collected my mail. Blodgett, the president of the local bank, was standing at the sidewalk and came up to me and said: 'Great Britain' (this was already a nickname for me), 'that was a fine job of handling a four-horse team. If you hadn't kept your head people would have been hurt.'

But it is the horrid things I remember best.

I fear to crowd this record with so many trees of that kind that the reader will lose sight of the forest, or the roads which led through it: an interesting road, to new kinds of life, and so, I suppose, to new kinds of character in the man who travelled it.

After a couple of months or so at the San Luis ranch, Covert announced that he was going to pick up a small band of cattle at Fort Tejon in the Tejon Pass; and asked me to come along. We would stay one night in Bakersfield and another perhaps at the Tejon Ranch. It was my first introduction to Bakersfield, which I was to come to know pretty well. It was at that time a town of some 2,000 inhabitants, of whom I should judge about five hundred (I did not count them) were prostitutes, living in a segregated quarter, Chinatown, though there were very few Chinese in it. (The town, of course, served the needs of the male population of nearly a hundred miles in each direction.) The sidewalks were wooden planks and the roads completely unpaved. (Ed Bailey, the livery-stable keeper, would with great public spirit, occasionally throw down manure and waste hay to render the roads of axle-deep sand or mud negotiable.)

Having left our teams at Ed Bailey's livery stable we stayed
at the Cosmopolitan Hotel. Standards may be gathered from
the fact that this, the second-best hotel, was a wooden structure
with quite a number of 'inside' rooms—rooms that is, without
windows at all and without means of ventilation except the
door; and this in a climate where in summer the thermometer
often reached 120° or more; nor was there any sanitation: you
went into the yard outside. But the beds had sheets, and I had
almost forgotten what sheets were like. The meals (usually
'beefsteak Spanish' or chile con carne) were twenty-five cents,
which you paid the barkeep as you came out. If you had
attempted to tip the waiter you would have risked physical
injury.

Bakersfield (to which I made a pious pilgrimage a few years
ago) is now a beautiful little city of 30,000 inhabitants, with
paved roads and public buildings of which any town in the
world could be proud. Many of the houses are air-conditioned;
the streets embowered in palms and foliage; the two chief hotels
boast a bath for every room (the old Cosmopolitan knew no such
thing as a bath): all representing a rise in the standard of comfort
in life which, if it had occurred in Russia, the American reformers would troop to see. Since it occurred in the United States,
they are little interested. Interest indeed is in the reverse of the
medal, for the country around, which has become a vineyard, is
mainly notable as the scene of the troubles of the migrant
worker, the oakie, the victims of *Grapes of Wrath*. In my day
migrant workers were abundant enough (I was one of them),
but they would have been greatly surprised if you had suggested
that they were the victims of any special physical hardship. On
the whole they fared better physically than the settlers and
farmers who toiled so incessantly. The misery and destitution
described in Steinbeck's book have been due largely to the fact
that the migrant workers of to-day consist of whole families,
women and children as well as men. (The Ford car has made that
kind of migration possible, whereas in my day the migrant
workers were men only.)

We stayed at the Tejon Ranch on our way to the Fort, and
this was my first meeting with Pogson, the Englishman who
managed the ranch for Truxton Beale, then the owner. According
to the legend (with possibly small basis in fact), the ranch re-

presented the original Indian reservation of the fifties, which
'General' Beale, the first American owner, had somehow
acquired in his career as Surveyor-General under Lincoln (thus
the 'General'). Lincoln is supposed to have remarked to him:
'Having become monarch of all you ever surveyed you had better
send in your resignation.' More probably the titles thereabouts
were derived from Spanish grants. Spanish Franciscans had come
from the missions into the valley at about the time that the
English-Americans on the Atlantic seaboard of the continent
were fighting their war of independence. Quickly following the
priests and the missions came the 'Californios,' the vaqueros,
with their padres, families, guitars and herds (descendants of the
cattle brought by Coronado into Mexico). And a very pleasant,
if very primitive, life they seemed to have made of it, in widely
separated ranches that were a kind of self-sufficient Spanish
manor with tamed Indians as servants (the Don's private chaplain
doing a little Indian conversion on the side).

There were not perhaps under the Spaniards or Mexicans more
than a thousand ranches scattered between what is now the
Mexican border and San Francisco, which meant that each had
all the range it could possibly need or use, that cattle were so
plentiful that they could be killed simply for their hides and
tallow. These could be exchanged with American ship captains
(coming up from Boston round the Horn to the California coastal
harbours) for cloth, boots, tools, nails, salt, wine; perfumes and
scarves for the women. Something of the remoteness of the
ranches may be gathered from the fact that I have seen a considerable ranch-house built and furnished without a nail in it:
the beams lashed together with strips of raw hide; the springs
of the beds made of raw hide strips; the mattresses sheepskins
piled one on top of the other.

The Tejon Ranch, with its collection of adobe (i.e., sun-dried
brick) buildings, and its ranch store where the Indians as well
as the ranch hands could buy goods of all kinds, suggested
that old patriarchal life. Indeed at that time the relics of the old
Spanish life were plentiful enough everywhere in those parts.
Nearly all the old place names were Spanish; Spanish words
for everyday things were as much in use as English words. The
Indians or half-Indians on the mountain ranches spoke only
Spanish mixed with Indian words. Pogson, the ranch manager,

E

was a bit cynical about it all and implied, as one Englishman to another, that I was a fool to have left the Old Country: the real opportunities were in the big centres of population, not in undeveloped countries like California. But I was unimpressed.

Tejon Fort (which was not a fort, properly speaking, but a barracks) was still almost habitable, and we camped in some of its rooms. (The last time I saw it, it was a roadhouse with big neon signs outside, the locality possessing a brand-new name—that of a Frenchman belonging to the Hudson's Bay Company who was killed by a bear at this spot in 1830 or thereabouts.)[1]

We corralled our cattle, after collecting them, at Fort Tejon, and brought them down easily enough through the pass. (Later I was to see a man killed in that same pass, and also to spend a cold and uneasy night, having somehow got off the road in the dark.) At the entrance to the pass there was then an adobe saloon or roadhouse kept by a man who explained that he had chosen that spot because he hated loneliness, and hardly a day went by without somebody going through the pass and bringing him a new face to rejoice in.

It was during this trip that Covert and I discussed the possibility (as described at the beginning of this chapter) of homesteading on government land somewhere in the Tejon region.

At Bakersfield we were able to have a look at a map of the claims which had been filed. There were plenty of unclaimed sections, but we saw at once that these were in the bad 'alkali and gumbo' areas—stretches of utterly waste lands through which we had passed on our way out and back. There were large areas of still unclaimed land in the neighbourhood of Lake Buena Vista, but I guessed this land was of a similar character. (Later on I filed a 'desert claim' on a half-section—320 acres—of this land in the neighbourhood of Buena Vista. The claim would be made good and title obtained by a certain amount of reclamation. The claims were never made good as I was not at any time in a position to do the reclamation. It was, however, in precisely this

---

[1] I once dug up relics of still earlier explorers, the Russians—two skeletons with pistols and Russian coins. We so easily forget that in our great-grandfathers' time there was a Russian America—an Alaska which, with the Russian genius for territorial expansion, had already at the time of the Holy Alliance its outposts in California.

area that the great oil resources, which a quarter of a century later were to make the prosperity of Kern County, were discovered. But though we found no suitable unclaimed land, we did stumble across a man who had filed a claim he was prepared to sell. His claim was in a good section of the country, just as the foothills rose towards Tejon. He wanted two hundred and fifty dollars—and this would about eat up all my capital right at the start. This did not seem to strike Covert as anything to dismay me: 'You can get all the equipment you'll need, a good Studebaker wagon, lumber, tools, on credit; and you could pay for them by taking a job here in town, clerk in a store or something.' This did not appeal to me at all. It was not what I'd come to the United States to do. But later the proposal was to be renewed by one of the Weil brothers who kept the chief store in Bakersfield; and who did, to my immense surprise, readily accord credit for the things I needed. A couple of years later one of the brothers (and both of them were the type of Jew who represented at that time in the new country the most cultured and civilized element of the community) said to me: 'Look here, why don't you take a job in my store and read law. You'd easily get admitted to the bar in this state, and I'd start you off by letting you handle my own legal business.' But again, that is not what I wanted—to think up legal trickeries to make commercial skulduggery safe, or save some beastly killer from the fate he deserved. I wanted a retreat, a home in the sunlight and air, a good horse for riding over the open country, and nobody to 'fence me in.'

The end of it was that I bought the claim for a couple of hundred dollars or some such sum. In formal legality there was no such thing as 'buying a claim.' But you went to the land office or a sub-office with two documents: renunciation by the existing claimant and the necessary document for the filing of a new claim. The second operation followed within five minutes of the first, so that there was no possibility of anyone but the purchaser making a claim upon the land; which was claim-free from the moment the existing claimant renounced it.

To file a homestead claim upon the public land of the United States it was necessary, of course, to renounce foreign citizenship and 'take out first papers'—sign a declaration of intention to become an American citizen. I renounced allegiance to all foreign

powers, princes, potentates, whatsoever, 'especially to Queen
Victoria.' I cannot recall that the act gave rise to the least qualms.
I was by no means without feeling for the things which Britain
had done and stood for in the world; and the Anglophobia so
current among the people with whom I worked provoked an increasing rage in me. But I felt that one did not cease to belong
to that civilization expressed in the English language—law, literature, folklore, Bible, moral attitudes, customs—by being part of
the United States rather than of Britain. The United States
had in many respects departed less from English ways than had
Canada, where something like the British flag still flew.

So there I was, a true pioneer. I had come into a country so
new that the land had not yet individual owners. I was to become
one of them. My dream of a free, simple, self-sufficient life in
the open, untroubled by the problems of a restless world, had
moved a step nearer to realization. After filing the necessary
papers and making the necessary renunciation of British citizenship I spent the evening designing my estate of the future;
sketching the kind of house I would build; where I would put
the corral, where the barn; where I would plant trees. . . . But
I don't think I had figured out very clearly how I was to make
a living on this hundred and sixty acres of desert land, where
the rainfall was not more than seven or eight inches a year.
And I had not quite taken in the depth of the poverty and hardship of my neighbours who had been for long trying to do the
very thing I was about to attempt.

Here is a picture of my 'ranch.' A hundred and sixty acres
on a flat plain, with no sign of human habitation in any direction
as far as the eye could reach; treeless, featureless, and for nine
months of the year herbless, grassless. No fences anywhere;
nothing to mark off my bit of private property and land from the
limitless miles and miles of land surrounding it. No water—most
vital fact of all—no garden, no shrub, no plant visible to the eye.
In the distant foothills a few trees could be discerned, trees
which marked a ranch-house otherwise invisible. The nearest
town was nearly fifty miles distant, that town consisting of two
or three brick buildings, a number of frame houses, wooden sidewalks and unpaved streets of deep sand.

Anyhow, I had a clean slate on which to draw my picture of
the future, and I drew the picture with a free hand. Yes, true, the

rainfall would make normal farming impossible. But one day there would be irrigation: we settlers would combine to do something with the stream that ran out of the canyon; or I would dig a well; I would add to this hundred and sixty acres with some grain hay and breed a few cattle, raise poultry, and with a few weeks' work earning cash money, make a living. The land would grow millet even without irrigation and the heads of millet could be fed to poultry without any necessary threshing. Turkeys, I argued, would do well, and with my own wagon and team I could earn money outside the farm.

But so far, except to the inner eye of imagination, there was no house, no shelter, not so much as a tent; not a post to which to hitch a horse.

I found it to be true, as Covert had forecast, that the store-keeper in town would let me have necessary equipment, wagon, plough, cook-stove, hardware, on credit. I was to pay when I could, a degree of trustingness that I found amazing. A team I had already.

The first thing was a house, a cabin, a shelter of some kind. While engaged on some hauling job I had heard of an old frame house that had belonged to a settler, recently dead, which could be bought for seventy-five dollars, 'cash money,' if I would haul it away. It was some forty miles from my claim. It could not be moved bodily but it could be knocked to pieces, and moved piecemeal. This is what I decided to do, and persuaded some wandering hobo to lend me a hand. As soon as we had dismembered the old house and got most of it loaded onto my wagon, the hobo insisted that I pay him off, so that by walking some eight or nine miles across the plains he could get a lift into town where he wanted drink and women. He made few bones about it: he meant to get drunk while he could, and spend a night in Chinatown. This left me alone to haul that load some forty miles across the plains just as the rains were setting in. In dry weather it would have been child's play. But the only track lay over soil which in wet weather became 'gumbo'—mud of a thick stickiness such that the wheels of a wagon after a hundred yards through it became one solid mass and the hooves of the team the size of footballs. But there was nothing for it. I had little feed and next to no water. So I started out.

What follows is described in a letter to my brother Harry

who happens to have kept the letter (one of the very few records which I made at the time of these particular experiences). I wrote :

You ask whether I have any ' adventures' out here. Two or three experiences of late would, I suppose, be so described, though in fact I seem to have very few.

I had to haul some timber about forty miles from here, the relics of an old house I had bought for my shanty on this land. I had engaged a hobo to help me and loading the wagon was no sooner finished than he decided to clear out, leaving me alone. I knew that I would have to cross the alkali country, and grub was reduced to biscuit, cheese and a little water. At the end of the first day I had made, I should judge, at most ten miles—if that. Just about nightfall the rain came very heavily—and I then discovered I had lost the track and was wandering in the alkali desert, probably now in circles. Just as it became pitch dark I noticed that we were in the midst of a dangerously boggy bit— too boggy to let the horses and wagon stand. I should probably never get the wagon and horses out in the morning. Somehow I managed to keep them going by getting from the wagon and pulling them forward. I sunk myself at every step up to the knees and the horses were utterly worn out. I felt the evil mercilessness of the desert; I dare not rest, yet I seemed to make no progress. After, I should imagine, some four or five hours of this sort of thing, the ground seemed to harden (I found later that I had got into the bottom of one of the sloughs with which the alkali desert hereabout is intersected). Having reached harder ground I decided to lay to for the night and await dawn. The few biscuits I had were sodden but I swallowed down some of the pulp, had a drink of water and huddled in the seat of the wagon in blankets, waiting for daylight. When it came I recognized where I was and knew that some four or five miles to the north-west I ought to find a way-side pulperia kept by an Italian. I started off on foot keeping in the right general direction so far as the contour of the hills would indicate it, and sure enough struck the track quite near to the Italian's place. He was very decent (I happen to know about three words of Italian and let them off at him). He suggested I bring the horses in for a feed and wait till the evening when the wind, then rising, and a warm day would dry up the alkali muck somewhat and make it easier to get the wagon out. And that was what happened. But there must have been a jinx on that lumber, for before I got it to my land, I had an even worse mishap.

The 'worse mishap' was that having started afresh after a day's rest for the animals and myself at the Italian's, I had hardly travelled a dozen miles before the whole load was tilted off the wagon while going down the slope into one of the sloughs (pronounced 'slew'). This, too, was at nightfall, and it meant wading into two or three feet of water to unhitch the team, and waiting, sodden, through the night until day, when the team managed to haul the nearly empty wagon to the top. Then, wading into the water, I had to collect the lumber piece by piece and load it on to the wagon—by myself of course.

However, the timber did reach my quarter-section finally and the home-building began. Covert came along to help (he had by this time himself taken up a claim about ten miles away) and before long we had a quite tolerable house erected : a living-room large enough to take a cook-stove (moved outside in the hot months) and two small 'bedrooms' at the back put up entirely by Covert and myself from the seventy-five dollars worth of material. I was to live in it, on and off, for five years.[1]

The nearest water had to be hauled from the bottom end of Tejon creek some eight miles away. Eight barrels were loaded into the wagon and this two horses could manage on the slightly rising track towards the creek. When the barrels had been filled with buckets (a very slow business if you were alone) the team could manage the haul back because it was all downhill. Arrived at the 'ranch' (as I was beginning to call it) the full barrel at the

[1] Just fifty-five years after the building of this house on the plains I was to read a news item in the Press to the effect that some hundred immigrants had returned from an attempt to settle in New Zealand because they found the housing shortage as bad in that country as in England, and preferred to suffer the inconvenience at home. The morning that this item appeared I happened to be addressing a London luncheon and could use it as my text, asking the question how New Zealand could ever have become a Dominion such as it is if the early emigrants had been deterred by the Housing shortage, or how indeed there could ever have been a United States or Canada. California happens to have a fine climate, but many emigrants of the nineteenth century went to countries like Canada and built their own houses (first of all of sod). Some of the youngsters present chose to be offended. It was all very well to talk about building your own house in the wilderness, but we lived now in a different age. It would be unfair to carpenters' and builders' unions even to attempt it, especially in countries like New Zealand. I wanted to know whether the union was made for man or man for the union.

end of the wagon was poured into an empty one on the ground. The emptied one was then dumped on the ground and filled from the next full barrel, this in its turn dumped on the ground, and so on. It all meant half a day a week (in hot weather two days a week) just fetching water. Here as elsewhere, throughout so much of this western country, the one supreme preoccupation of life was WATER.

What were the possibilities of a well dug by ourselves—Covert and me? Covert decided that the general lay of the land looked promising. So we started on it, using the odd pieces of boarding left over from the house, for shoring up the top fifteen or twenty feet. This top section was dug about five feet square and from there on we proposed to make the well circular of a diameter just sufficient to allow a man to use a short-handled pick. We were obliged of course to erect a winch for hauling up the dirt —and the man. As the smaller of the two I did a good deal of the underground work, while Covert did the twisting. After a hundred feet it was ticklish business. As the bucket was hauled up, filled with earth or gravel, it would begin to swing, knocking the side of the well which had (below twenty feet) no shoring at all. The striking of the bucket on the side of the well would send down on top of the man working at the bottom a shower of earth and stones with the possibility that there might be a bad cave-in which would bury him. Occasionally, when I was working underground and masses of stone began to fall on me, I would get a bit panicky and shout to be hauled up. Covert would shout that I was a fool; that in the mines he had sunk hundreds of ' shafts ' and he knew the kind that would cave; this wouldn't. But I noticed that the man who happened to be at the top was usually a bit more optimistic on the point than the man who happened to be below.

At a hundred and fifty feet, however, the well was not even damp, and I began to consider other possibilities. A small creek which had water, I should judge, some six or eight months of the year, lay a few miles to the west of the Tejon Creek. A very little damming up would make a sizeable reservoir from which a ditch of a mile or two would bring it on to my quarter-section and provide water sufficient during the rainy season to give from five to ten acres a thorough soaking so that good crops of alfalfa could be counted upon and perhaps a few fruit-trees brought into bearing. (The average rainfall, in that neighbourhood, it will be remembered, was under ten inches.) The creek itself lay within the boundaries of Tejon Ranch but it continued a good way beyond the boundary. I saw the manager of the Tejon (Pogson, whom I had come to know) and pointed out that he could not very well object to my use of the water, after it had left his territory. What he feared, however, obviously, was that use of the water in that way might establish rights to it and so prevent its damming up at a later stage within the boundaries of Tejon. However he was willing to sign an agreement by which I recognized the right of the Tejon Ranch to impound the water at any time they decided so to do. As I guessed they were very unlikely ever to want to do it, since Tejon Creek would serve their purpose so much better than a dam, I signed.

But nothing came of this project. For about that time my parents—somewhat swayed, I fear, by my rosy accounts of prospects—proposed that my elder brother Alec, his wife and young child should buy land in California, profiting, as my father put it flatteringly, by my experience. It so happened that at that moment eighty acres of unimproved but irrigated land was obtainable about thirty miles north of Bakersfield on what seemed to me exceptionally good terms. So they came over and I began the development of this new property, Alec, from the sale of an engineering business he had, providing a little capital. I still visited my homestead claim every week or so (a drive, if you please, of about seventy miles) while Covert also at times gave a look at the homestead. The country there was settling up, despite the absence of water; so much so that a sub-post-office had been established for the neighbourhood, under a supposedly Indian name, Toolwass. ('Whose tool was it,' asked Covert, 'and what was the matter with his tool?') At a meeting of the settlers Covert suggested that I be appointed mail-carrier as I came into the neighbourhood from town anyhow once a week or so. The post-office authorities allowed a small remuneration—four dollars a trip or something of that order. At the meeting held in one of the cabins the proposal that the 'office' should go to me was not popular. The opposition came particularly from a certain 'Texas' (it frequently happened that a man's real name was hardly used or even known; for many I was just 'Britain') and at one point in the discussion Covert, addressing Texas, asked with complete irrelevance, 'Texas, have you ever studied the penalty for cattle-stealing in this state? I nominate Britain.' Britain was elected. I can't recall how long I was thus a servant of the United States Government but it must have been quite some little time. But I probably found the constant riding or driving more than I could manage together with other work.

The day came finally at the end of five years when I could complete my homestead claim, 'prove up' and acquire definite title. I was to do this at the sub-land-office in Bakersfield. When I went into the office of the lawyer who was to accompany me to the land-office and see that all was in order, I found Covert already there. 'Bad, news, Britain. The whole damned country-side is here to contest your claim and ready to lie their heads off.'

And then for two or three days I sat in an upstairs room and heard these settlers give a mass of false or half-true evidence : I had, ran this evidence, seldom been on the claim; I had left it for more than the six months (which was quite untrue) which the law required, and much more to the same effect. But the real basis of the contest was blurted out by one of the old settlers. It seemed that assistants in Bakersfield stores had recently been filing claims, going to their claims at week-ends, putting in just the legal minimum of work and then, when they had completed title, selling the land. This, rightly argued the old settler, was not the purpose of the homestead law and had got to be put a stop to. All this of course was quite irrelevant to the merits of the case under trial and my lawyer put it to the old man :

'Why pick on this claimant? He is a genuine settler, has put a lot of work on the place, dug a deep well, and has even been mail-carrier for the district. He was no week-end faker. Why pick on him?'

'Well,' retorted the witness, 'because he's a damn Britisher and wears those funny breeches!'

(On one or two occasions only I had committed the *gaffe* of wearing riding-breeches and boots which I happened to have brought from England.)

'And,' continued a witness, 'if he ain't a clurk he's just like one,' and went on to imply it would be better to make an example of a Britisher than someone belonging to 'these United

States.' It seemed to be no one's business to stop this sort of thing in a quasi-legal hearing, in a sort of court of law, and murmurs of applause greeted this outburst. Covert became angry and eloquent in my defence but I'm not sure he improved my chances. The official in charge did indeed explain to me that it was not his business to decide the case or rule out any evidence, but to transmit it to Los Angeles at the Land Office proper. How much or how little of the stuff talked was actually transmitted I had no chance of knowing, but I had a very distinct feeling that the case would go against me.

After it was all over Covert and I were having a drink together when some of the 'contestants' came into the saloon. Seeing us, they made a move to go out, but Covert called them back.

'I'm not surprised you want to run away, but you'd better stay and hear my opinion of you. You're a bunch of lying sons of bitches who've done a better man than any of you out of his rights.' And he thereupon began on the personal history of each in language much more lurid than my publisher would permit. Having done which Covert added: 'Anybody want to fight it out with me? I thought not. You can all go to hell.'

A few days afterwards, a somewhat derogatory paragraph concerning myself appeared in a local paper, and Covert 'took action.' He described it thus: 'I called at the office of the paper and found an office-boy in an outer room. I sez: "Is the editor in?" and the boy said he was, pointing to an inner room, so I went in and closed the door." ' That, for Covert, seemed to close the story. 'Well,' I added, 'what then?' Covert replied: 'Why, when my fists got sore, I stomped on him.' And that closed the incident.

I can quite believe it. Once when Covert was at the 'ranch' with me, having our midday meal and talking about Europe and its politics as he loved to do, three hobos suddenly appeared on the porch of the cabin. They looked pretty tough hombres, and one, after a moment, said truculently, 'Guess we'll take dinner with you.' Covert took stock of the three and in a flat voice remarked, 'Guess you won't.' The spokesman of the hobos, a bit more truculent: 'Oh, yeah? Well, there are three of us.' Covert did not get up out of his chair but somehow a gun was in his hand. 'There are six of us here. Now git. Take a flapjack apiece and keep going along that road. Step lively.' After watching a moment to see that the three kept going along the road, Covert went on, 'But about that fellow Herbert Spencer you were talking of.'

Perhaps I had owed my life to Covert at about the time of our early acquaintance when he was foreman on the first ranch where we worked. Among the hands on the ranch was a man of thirty or thereabouts from southern Europe, Pedro, who referred mysteriously at times to having 'royal blood in his veins.' He talked familiarly of Paris, Vienna, Madrid, Lisbon. In bunkhouse discussions he was regarded as an authority on the world outside the ranch—on what was happening in Europe, and why; what was going to happen; where you got the best food, the best drink. As he was the only one of the company, until I joined it, who had been in Europe, his authority on these matters had no challenge.

My coming to the ranch was, therefore, an annoyance to him. I knew some of the countries and capitals of which he spoke. More than once, in the presence of the others, I put him right as to facts and (very foolishly) showed he sometimes talked nonsense.

Covert, who had sometimes been present at these bunkhouse talks, rode up to me one day on the range, and said in the most off-hand, matter-of-fact way, 'Suppose you know Pedro means to kill you?'

Astonished, I asked why. I had done him no harm. What possible reason had Pedro to risk getting hanged killing *me*?

'He won't get hanged,' said Covert. 'Or, thinks he won't, which is the same thing as far as you're concerned.'

I must have looked my incredulity, for Covert said:

'You went to college, didn't you?'

About this I was very noncommittal. Anyhow, insisted Covert, I had read lots of books. How many? I didn't know—some hundreds, perhaps thousands.

'Well,' said Covert, 'I've never read a book in my life, but I know things which all your books don't seem to have taught you. Can't you see that Pedro is plumb loco, that he'll finish up in the loony-house or on the gallows? All this talk of his about having royal blood means he's lunatic vain. And you ask me what you've done to him. What you've done is to make him look a fool or a liar, and he's hating you for that worse than if you'd stolen his horse or killed his mother. However, it's your business, not mine.'

A week or so later, on a Sunday evening, some of the boys came in from visiting a near-by ranch where the whisky was pretty good. In playful mood they began firing at targets; making an old rooster jump; scaring the Chinese cook. Pedro, who was amongst them, 'dared' me to hold up a book I was reading and let him put a bullet through it. While the argument was going on, Covert suddenly appeared in a near-by doorway and shouted to the boys to stop that shindy and get out of there, as they were scaring women visitors in the house.

After supper that night Covert said, with a grin, as he passed me on his way out, 'A dozen honest witnesses would have testified it was an accident.'

The next week Pedro was—somehow—shifted to another ranch. Abour a year later Pedro killed two men, and the verdict was 'insane.'

This was only the first of many occasions on which Covert, despite, or because of, his 'illiteracy,' was to see at a glance truths which, it would seem, my 'education' failed to enable me to see. And I was soon to learn that his capacity to get at the heart of truth could be applied to abstract matters like politics and morals, as well as to practical things.

Once, when the 'sins of Britain' were being related by one of the hands Covert said: 'So you think Britain should be punished for what she's done—buying those scalps and burning the White House.' The cowboy agreed.

'Wal,' said the foreman, turning and pointing to me, 'there *is* Great Britain. There he, she, it, sits. Multiply him, and his brothers and sisters and his daddy and his aunts, a few million times and you've got Great Britain, the only Great Britain that now exists. Britain, we're going to try you for buying American scalps and burning down the White House. Stand up and tell us what you've got to say for yourself. I expect you've got the scalps in your saddle blankets, and if we find 'em, we're going to hang you to the cottonwood outside.'

On another occasion a small-town politician visiting the ranch had been holding forth on foreign affairs, expanding at length on what he called 'the British peril.' Covert asked: 'You are quite sure Britain is going to do all these things to us in the next ten years?'

Yes, the ardently patriotic politician was quite sure.

'Wal,' said Covert quietly, 'since you know so exactly what a country on the other side of the world is going to do ten years hence, you can certainly tell us what our own country is going to do next month in the election. Will you take a bet on who is going to be elected?' The patriot was a good deal less sure about this and would not bet.

'All right,' said Covert, 'tell us how our own *State* is going to go?'

No, the oracle did not know that either.

'All right,' went on Covert, 'will you tell us how the county is going, and whether your friend Jake Haggin is going to be elected sheriff?'

The oracle was not really certain about that either.

'So,' concluded Covert, 'you can't tell us what your own country is going to do about electing a President next month; you can't tell us what your own State is going to do; you can't tell us what your own county is going to do; you can't tell us what is going to happen to your own intimate friend in politics a month from now. But you can tell us exactly what a country on the other side of the world where you have never been is going to do ten years hence. Pat, you don't know a thing about it! For that matter, nobody does.'

Pat went on to attack free trade. America ought to put a stiff tariff on Mexican cattle, Canadian lumber and wheat. Such foreign goods were ruining the prosperity of America, which had grown great on protection, would grow greater; was destined to spread, to take in Canada and Mexico.

'And so,' added Covert, 'you would end by being a free trader, abolishing all tariffs between us and Canada and Mexico, letting in all those foreign goods without any tariff at all?'

Pat's reply was confused.

The free-silver agitation was just then getting into its stride. 'I want the free coinage of iron,' Covert declared, 'for then we'd all be millionaires with our old cook-stoves.' Even if he *had* got the illustration from someone else, what enabled him to put his finger on the danger point, the inflationary element in this proposal?

When I got to know Covert better, and we had had long talks about the books I had read and he had not, I tried to get him to explain how he managed to be so right, as he usually was, without books at all. He tried to explain.

Once in Alaska he had been obliged to spend a whole arctic winter—a night lasting the best part of six months—in a log cabin, and had been compelled to listen all that time to other men talking. Having good nerves, he had managed to think about their talk, and drew conclusions which, though not given in quite these words, amounted in fact to this:

'As I listened to the men in the cabin during that winter, it became plain to me that when people got to talking and discussing, they soon stop wanting to know what the truth is. Instead of that, they want, above all, to prove that their argument is right and the other fellow's wrong; that their idea, their theory, their party, their nation, their religion, is perfect and all others mistaken. We would get to discussing the best way back to the "outside" when the ice broke. A man would talk himself into standing by one particular plan, and the more you showed it was impossible, the more he would stick by it, until finally you saw that he would far rather lose his life by going his way than save it by going any other.

'I determined to drill myself into wanting, first of all, to know the real truth about anything. Then I came to see that if an idea is false, you could usually find proof of that by some fact beneath your nose if only you would look for it. See if what you do not know for certain agrees with that you *do* know for certain. And in trying to check up in this way I soon saw, by observing the other men, that it was far better to think straight about a few things than to think crookedly about many.'

At the end of a month or some such time after the hearing in Bakersfield, the decision came back from Los Angeles. My homestead claim was disallowed; I had lost my case, and the fruits of most of five years' work, the toil of the lumber-hauling over the desert; of the building of the house; and the danger of the

deep well-digging. It all went up in smoke. This was the end of
a dream.

Both my lawyer and Covert wanted me to appeal against the
Land Court decision and fight it out with the s.o.b.'s as Covert
put it. But as I took stock of things I realized that my attitude
towards 'the simple life in the wide open spaces' was not quite
what it had been when I had looked at the prospect from a distance of Geneva and Lincolnshire. After seven years on the
plains, several of them spent in running on my own, with its
story of drought, short crops, low prices, accidents, loss of stock,
I realized that ranching, or farming, was *not* a 'simple life.' It
had problems and anxieties of its own : frustration, loneliness,
fatigue; usually the deadening pall of debt. This meant that the
'independence' I had looked forward to was a myth. No man in
debt is independent. And among my neighbours on the plains
were very many who, having farmed all their lives and lived
those lives in penury and hardship, were still in debt; their
struggle against debt was superimposed on their heartbreaking
struggle against nature.

But what next? Return home and admit failure as soon as
this?

As so often in life decisions are made for one by circumstance.
I happened to have had a couple of fugitive articles accepted by
a San Francisco magazine; and another by a local paper in
Bakersfield. The editor of the *San Francisco Chronicle* seems to
have seen one of them, and had written me that if I ever came
to San Francisco he would be glad to have a chat with me.

That settled it. I decided to chance my luck in 'the City.'

But before telling of my adventures there—and in the city I
had adventures more significant in a sense than any I had had
on the plains—there are a few aspects of life on the frontier,
when it was a frontier, that are worth recording.

In the five years during which I was proving up on my homestead claim not all the time was spent on my land. Like my neighbours I had to go off and earn money on the side. This I did
mainly by haulage work, with my team and wagon (occasionally
hiring a couple of horses to add to my own two). The haulage
was mainly of ore from the gold mines in the mountains, work
which had the advantage that I went up with a light load—
groceries and such like—and that the heavy loads were downhill.

The uphill journey was safe but hard on the teams, the down-hill dangerous for wagon and man. The roads were crude, roughly hewn tracks full of washouts in the wet weather, and at moments everything depended on the brakes of a heavily laden, rather cheaply constructed wagon. On one occasion, when I was working at the top of the Tejon Pass with a ranch outfit, a heavily loaded wagon did get away from its brakes, ran on to its team and threw the driver off his seat, breaking both his legs. He was brought into the camp and, there being no one else available, I was given the job, then and there, of getting on a horse and riding about sixty miles into Bakersfield to fetch a doctor.

This, of course, was before the days of automobiles, and on a distance of that kind you cannot make on horseback more than at the very best six miles an hour. With a team of fast-trotting mules hitched to a buggy, one could perhaps have improved on this a bit and made with great luck an average of eight or even ten miles an hour. When I was asked to ride into town I had just come off a day's work and felt already dead-beat. However, the foreman put me on to a roan mustang and I started out across the plains to travel the night through. It was a dark night and at that time between the Tejon Pass and Bakersfield there was not a fence or a stake to mark the way. I began to fall fast asleep in the saddle and, as the horse saw little reason to stick to the road, I would wake with a jerk to find him wandering over the plain. In the pitch dark it was extremely difficult to know what to do. The best thing might have been to wait for daylight, but I was terribly afraid of falling asleep and of the horse getting away. However, somehow I did reach town to find that the two doctors of the town were in the midst of a bitter quarrel about some professional point and both at first refused to go out. After much persuasion one did finally consent to under-take the job. The people at the camp had brought the injured man down to the foothills so as to meet the doctor half-way, but the man was destined to die under the doctor's hands shortly after he was reached.

As already indicated, I seemed to learn such necessary things as driving and riding, harnessing a team to a wagon, the driving of a mowing-machine or a hay-rake—to all this I tumbled pretty easily and quickly. The thing which got me down was the sheer physical fatigue of pitching barley ' hay ' in a climate where the

F

thermometer would run to 120° or 130° in the shade. Yet I recall that the foreman at one camp did on one occasion treat me as an old hand. A couple of greenhorns one day came along and asked for a job, which they were given, and then, with innocence asked the foreman where they were to sleep. I happened to be standing near-by when he was engaging the men, and at this request he beckoned me to come over and said something like this: ' I want you to have a look at these guys. There are a hundred thousand acres in this ranch and they have just asked me where they are going to sleep.' We all of course slept on the ground. There was no reason why not, for at that season you could be quite sure that not a drop of rain would fall from the sky, and you could make yourself quite comfortable with your blankets on a pile of hay. Later on, it happened to me that I did not sleep inside a house for three and four months at a time, and I could say at the end of about five years that for five years I had not slept between sheets. On some ranches there were bunkhouses, but they did not provide such luxuries as sheets.

Wages on the ranch at that time were not even remotely on the scale of wages of to-day. An expert cow-puncher thought himself well paid at thirty or forty dollars a month with his keep, and even in the hayfield our wages at most did not run to more than two dollars a day. But I seem to have put by some money. Even before the homesteading days, I was in possession of a horse and saddle—a wicked horse and a beautiful saddle— a fact which gave me a wide range in the choice of jobs. At most of the ranches a man with a horse (which he had not too obviously stolen) would be quite welcome and would always be given a meal and feed for his horse. [1]

It is strange how most of the details of those toilsome journeys —entirely by myself—seem to have faded from memory. Yet one I do recall. I found myself at nightfall with a four-horse team and an ore-laden wagon at the very top, not of the highest peak in the range, but of one that gave me a view over range after range of hill and mountain. In the daytime the foothills were

[1] In the year 1943 or thereabouts, a member of the staff of one of the big movie studios was showing me over the place, and in course of conversation, asked 'Do you know these parts at all?' I thought a moment and said: 'Unless my geography is at fault, I once drove a band of cattle over the spot where we now stand.' My guide looked at me with an expression which I felt meant: 'If you want some superb lying, go to a bloody Englishman.'

bare and brown. But that night a brilliant moon had lent the whole scene a new glamour, and one looked across an almost fairy world; and after feeding the horses I spread what remained of the hay over the ore, so that I could lay my blankets on the top of the load (instead of underneath the wagon) in order to watch the worlds of moon and earth merge the one into the other.

And then there was the prospecting. Covert had been in on the gold rushes to Alaska and had spent a winter there—prisoner with two or three others in a snowbound cabin in the mountains. The gamble of the thing was in his blood and he insisted the chances were good that we might hit some good placer—pockets of alluvial gold in the beds of dried-out or actual streams. On our horses and with a burro (a patient ass carrying food, shovels, picks, pans for panning) we skirted the Mojave Desert and later parts of Death Valley. Though we found some colour—at times encouraging as when we washed out in our pans nuggets the size of small peas—we never struck it rich. A detail of one of these expeditions is recounted in a letter to my brother Harry which he kept. Harry had asked again whether I had had 'adventures,' and again I replied in effect, surprisingly few, adding, however:

I have recently come back from a prospecting expedition in the mountains two hundred miles from nowhere with one companion. During it we took refuge one rainy night in a cave and when I picked up my ground sheet in the morning there was a very hefty rattlesnake underneath, while my companion found three. In a crevice near where we were sleeping there must have been half a hundred. We tumbled into a sheep-shearing camp on that expedition and found the greasers and Indians among the toughest my companion—an Alaskan miner—had ever seen, he told me. We had to sleep there but one kept watch (with a revolver) while the other slept.

I recall that one of the Indians—or half-breeds—at that camp recounted how he had been put on trial for rape of a white girl. We asked him how he got off and the Indian repeated for us his speech to the jury. It ran, as I recall it, something like this:

You jury white men. White man rape 'em (only he did not use the word 'rape') Indian girl. What happen white man? Nothing happen. Indian rape 'em white girl. What happen now?

I don't suppose it was as simple as that, but despite the Indian

massacres Indians were never treated as 'coloured.' Had it been
a negro on trial he would of course have been lynched, even
though his victim—or companion—had been a prostitute. But
Indians were not in the same category, and a national character
like Will Rogers was quite proud of his Indian ancestry. (When
his fellow Americans boasted that their ancestors came over in
the *Mayflower*, Rogers was apt to retort: 'My ancestors met
the boat!')

At that time in the neighbourhood of Bakersfield there was
something in the nature of an English colony. The Kern County
Land Company had started cutting up its big holdings into small
twenty- and forty-acre farms for fruit-farming and had initiated
a big selling campaign in England. Quite a number of English
folk came out, as the result of the rosy-coloured advertising, to
take up fruit-farming under this scheme. There was a settlement
called Rosedale a few miles out of Bakersfield which was almost
entirely made up of English, and a queer mixture they were. The
black sheep of the family shipped abroad to get him as far away
from home as possible; the retired army man who had a notion
to take up farming and had possibly commuted a large part of his
pension in order to buy land under these schemes; even a couple
of English maiden ladies who had been persuaded that by some
magic they could make a success of fruit-farming; ex-Indian
civil servants; tea-planters who had lost their health in malarial
countries—this strange mixture constituted a colony. I got to
know a good many of them. Usually they were charming, entertaining, honest, honourable, incompetent, feckless failures;
but almost always in a crisis showing guts. I recall an ex-Indian
officer, a general, who had brought his elderly wife and a family
of daughters out to begin fruit-farming on the edge of the desert,
where there was a trickle of irrigation water. In India, of course,
they had lived a princely life with unnumbered servants. In
Kern County Lady X was the cook for the whole family in a
wooden shack which, for six months in the year, was an oven.
The girls washed the clothes and worked in the orchard, milked
the cows, cleaned out the manure, ran into debt, saw the work of
years brought to naught by pests or failure of water, the crops
valueless from decline of prices, faced illness, hardship beyond
words—and yet, whenever I passed their way, it meant a
delightful and civilized evening with laughter and allusive talk of

books and London and India. The colony even had organized
amateur theatricals, and I rode forty miles to take part in them.
But I was never a part of the colony itself, because later, when I
finally became a farmer of sorts on my own, it was in an entirely
different part of the country.

A few among those with whom I came in contact became
special friends: Donald Grant and his sister; General Mason
and his family; the Richardsons; the Georges, the Summer-
hayeses. Among those of whom I have special memories is
Wallace the mining assayer, who became interested in some of my
mining finds; his wife and their child (whose tragic end I recall).
Wallace I have remembered with affection and regard my life
through—I beg to assure him if ever these lines should reach his
eyes.

This reference recalls one feature of frontier life little realized
perhaps by those who have not lived it. 'Neighbours' in those
days might be people who lived eighty or a hundred miles away.
In a city apartment the people who live in the floor below may
be strangers during half a lifetime. (I lived thirty years in the
Temple and never once spoke a word to a man who lived the
same length of time in the flat underneath mine.) But in sparsely
populated countries the family living a hundred miles
away, a couple of days' journey by mule or ox-cart, may be close
friends.

During a pious pilgrimage half a century after the time of
which I am now writing, I tried to discover remnants of the
English colony; but nothing remained. This did not mean that
most of the English had returned home, but simply that they
or the succeeding generation had been absorbed into the general
community. It is one of the fallacies of easy generalizations
about the British that they always remain stiff-neckedly English
in a foreign environment; a community apart. This is usually
complete nonsense, at least as far as the United States is concerned. Of all the elements composing the American community
the English are the most easily absorbed. The Irish retain their
national separateness for generation after generation; so much so
that you may talk with a New York policeman with a rich
Tipperary brogue, still calling himself Irish, although he has
never seen Ireland, his father had never seen Ireland, and the
brogue and the Irishry have descended undiminished sometimes

through three or four generations. Other elements, the Italian, the Polish, the Russian, are of course set apart for a time from the American community, even if only by speech and name. Thus it happens that in a city like Chicago or San Francisco, if you want to organize an international demonstration, it is easy enough to find distinct groups of Irish, Italians, Czechs, Poles, Germans, Scandinavians, Russians. But you cannot find the English: they have become so completely American that their national identity has been lost. And the proof is this: for generations in American politics there has been an Irish vote, an Italian vote, a German vote, and, latterly, a Jewish vote. But there has never been an English vote though the English immigration has been greater than any of the others.

One old English settler I did find on one of my subsequent journeys into the part of the country which I knew best. I remember that he was a youngster who had just married in England and had left his wife at home while he made preparations for her to come out and join him on the fruit farm. In the old days, just after he built his little three-room cottage, I had come by his place when he was entertaining a few neighbours at a house-warming. The cottage had been built largely with his own hands. He was going to make it comfortable for the wife and have wall-paper, the kind of wall-paper that she liked—probably the only house with wall-paper within a radius of ten or twenty miles. But as the house was just a frame house of timber, a sort of cheesecloth had to be tacked to the boarding inside as a base for the wall-paper. He explained to the guests of that afternoon in 1894 or thereabouts that if they were to come the *next* Sunday he would have the wall-paper on the walls. When forty years later I called, the first thing I noticed was that the wall-paper had not yet been pasted up on to its base of cheesecloth. The wife had come out, children had been born, they had raised a family, and the wife had died. But in all the struggles that that meant, they had not found time yet in the forty years to stick up the wall-paper. And that I thought told a whole lot about the nature of the pioneering that these people had been through.

In the letter to my brother, in which I recounted the bad experience in the hauling of the timber for my house, I added:

But after I did get the stuff here and had had a good meal or two, and a rest, and began my planning, all those miseries were forgotten. Something like sea-sickness. Six days of a seven-day cruise you pray to die. The last day you spend in an exciting flirtation with an extremely pretty American girl, and afterwards say, 'What a jolly week that was!' Young, we find the past pleasant, are pessimists as to the future; and both young and old we are apt to find the present worst of all. . . . I don't take quinine and I don't now get malaria. (That's to answer a question of three months back. You also asked about diet. Here it is : coffee, oatmeal, beans, bacon, ship's biscuit; breadmaking is a failure : only useful for puttying the cracks in the floor.)

I suppose the sea-sickness analogy was prompted by an incident of my Atlantic passage in the *Etruria*, which, however, I have forgotten. But the analogy has to be turned the other way about to apply to my seven years on the plains. They began with great hope and ended with the sickness of frustration and failure, and what I regarded as an act of injustice. So there is not likely to be much rose-tinted nostalgia. But neither do I recall it as a time of unhappiness on the whole. And one feature above all stands out : the actual physical hardship—the poor food, the sleeping for weeks in the open, the toil and fatigue and sometimes danger— mattered very little. They did not make unhappiness. This came from the anxieties and uncertainties, the fear of debt, the presence of creditors whenever I should go to town (I would sometimes wait outside town until it was dark in order that I should not meet them). It was these things of the spirit that mattered. Beside them the hardships of the flesh hardly counted.

CHAPTER III

AMERICAN REPORTER

So I left the 'simple life of manual toil in the open spaces' to return to newspaper work.

But I did not approach it in quite the mood of my teens in England and Geneva. I was now a little less concerned to spearhead vast intellectual revolutions, and a little more concerned, first of all, to earn my own living and stand on my own feet (something which farming on the plains had not enabled me to do). Certain illusions about the simple life on the frontier farm had been dispelled, replaced perhaps by a somewhat better equipment in the understanding of human nature and the kind of problem it presented to the reformer.

It was an exciting time, that first few weeks in a large city after more than five years in a frontier country where, almost for months on end, I did not see a dozen faces. To sit in the entrance to the hotel and watch the coming and going was itself absorbing entertainment. I remember also very vividly my first night at the theatre—probably the first time I had been to a theatre for over six years. Perhaps the actors were not of the best, but I recall very clearly reflecting, as the play proceeded, that the theatre had somehow created its own convention—just as the Chinese have created a different one—of how men and women behave and what life is. For never, on land or sea, I reflected, have men and women walked, talked, behaved as did these people on the stage. I looked around the audience for some sign on their part of the surprise and puzzlement which I myself was feeling. But there was no sign that they regarded the play as unusual, unreal, artificial, built on a convention. Very soon, however, this sense of strange artificiality passed, and the next visit to the theatre did not produce it; nor have I had it since. It was as though I had acquired immunity to the shock of theatrical unreality.

The San Francisco I then saw was, of course, the pre-earthquake city. One reflection kept recurring : Of all this modern metropolis, with its cable cars and theatres and city throngs, not one stone had stood upon another fifty years earlier. The marks of its mining camp origin—with the extravagance, dissipation, violence and general rowdiness—were still strong upon it. One night, just off Market Street, I wandered into what I assumed to be a normal theatre. As I entered, there assaulted me from the stage words that one occasionally saw written in public conveniences but did not often hear. This was in public, in an open theatre on a main San Francisco thoroughfare. The 'show' exceeded in general dirtiness anything likely to be found in Port Said. The audience, I noted, were all men. Interlarded between the grossest obscenities were passages of intolerably saccharine sentiment about sweet old mothers, and dear old homes, dear little children going to heaven, culminating in an elaborate display of the American flag and raucous singing of patriotic songs by 'strip-teasers' who a moment previously had been enacting unrestrained sexual pantomime. But the story of 'old' San Francisco (it was, of course, a very new San Francisco) has often been told, and need not here be repeated. What struck me about the character of the show just described was its contrast with the puritanism of many of the women in the farming area. (One neighbour of mine on the plains—wife of an early pioneer —found it profoundly shocking that Queen Victoria should have appeared at some formal function in a décolleté dress.)

At the public library I was able to piece together something the history of the city's Press, a history as colourful as most other things about pre-earthquake San Francisco. The story has recently been told by John Bruce in his *Gaudy Century*.[1]

San Francisco had a paper in 1847 ; it had two in 1848, nine in 1849, and the editors fought each other with their fists over minor differences of opinion, and with bowie knives, pistols and shot-guns over more interesting matters. One of them was ' James King of William,' who in 1856 remarked that in the city by the Golden Gate it was then more of a crime to steal a mule than to garrotte a human being. He printed the city's mortality table

[1] Random House, New York.

for 1855 : 487 persons killed, six hung by the sheriff, and forty-six by mobs. Editor King also printed items explaining that one of his rival editors was an ex-convict from Sing Sing who had robbed his mistress in New York. When King's duelling mail piled up, he wrote that he could be found on Market Street, between Fourth and Fifth Streets, every afternoon at 4.30, and that if he was to be shot or cut to pieces, he preferred that it be done in that wide street, where injury to others would be less likely. But it was on Merchant Street that the ex-convict-editor shot and killed James King of William.

Duels were dear to San Francisco's heart in those lusty days, as one reviewer of Bruce's book remarks—a review to which I owe some of these particulars. The famous Terry-Broderick duel of 1859 (Broderick was United States Senator and Terry a justice of the State Supreme Court) was fought in the presence of sixty-seven witnesses, three of them reporters for the *San Francisco Call*, which was, remarks the reviewer, dirty journalism, considering that the first challenges to the duel had been published in the rival *Bulletin*. At about the same time one of the city's papers regularly published a directory, with addresses, of the city's leading brothels.

Mr. Bruce loves best the gaudy history of the *Chronicle*, founded, on a capital of twenty dollars, in 1865, as a four-page daily tabloid 'throwaway,' placed free in the city's cafés, theatres and saloons. With the genius of the DeYoung brothers behind it, and a staff which at one time or another included Mark Twain and Bret Harte, it was soon the liveliest, fightingest paper in town. Life for the DeYoungs was just one libel suit after another, punctuated by occasional shootings. Charles DeYoung, in fact, was shot and killed in his office by the son of an ex-minister, exposed by DeYoung as an adulterer, whom DeYoung had almost killed with his own derringer. The ex-minister recovered, and was later elected mayor. (Some ten years after my first encounter with San Francisco I was to meet in Paris the DeYoung who at that time owned the *Chronicle* and to attempt to sell him the moribund English daily paper in Paris with which I had become concerned.)

It was during my first week or two in San Francisco, and before I secured a newspaper job, that I went through an adventure which gave me a momentary insight into the San

Francisco underworld, its relation to the police (a quite harmonious relationship, be it said) and the relation of both to the local politics of that period.

The hotel at which I stayed on arriving in San Francisco was a very second-class sort of place, much used by farmers from the country, a fact indicated by a notice which hung from the gas brackets (for the rooms, by the way, were lit by gas): 'Don't blow out the gas. Turn it off.' It was while seated in the lobby of this hotel, watching with much fascination the movement of people in and out, that a well-dressed stranger—perhaps I had been too long on the plains to realize that he was a bit over-dressed—got into conversation with me. What was I doing in San Francisco? Where had I come from? What had I been doing? I had no particular reticence in telling him something of my experiences during the preceding five years, and he in ex-change told me a good deal of himself. He was a mining engineer, just returned from the Kootenay country of Southern British Columbia, where he had been installing some mining machinery. In the course of conversation he asked me whether, on the dry land of the San Joaquin Valley, I had ever tried, or others had ever tried, the growing of henequen, the cactus plant which grows in dry soils and produces a valuable fibre. He explained that heretofore the plant was not of much value because no means of mechanical decortication—pithing out the fibre—had been satisfactory, and hand decortication was altogether too expensive. I found the idea interesting because at the time I still had a desert claim on a half-section of dry land which would lapse if I did not do some work on it shortly. And I thought I saw an opportunity of possibly trying some experi-ments or getting some of my ranch friends in the Valley to try them and take up my claim.

'Well, if you're interested,' said my new-found friend, Mr. Knowlton, 'I can show you some henequen plants quite near here, and you will see for yourself how valuable the plant might be if the mechanical decortication turns out to be feasible, which I think, as an engineer, that it will.'

I said that I was very interested. Knowlton explained that the plants he had in mind were in Oakland Park, which we could reach in about half an hour or a little more by taking the street car to the ferry and ferrying across. As it was a fine morning, I readily accepted his invitation to go along with him and have a look-see.

Mr. Knowlton was a pleasant, talkative sort of fellow, and after landing from the ferry, we walked for five or ten minutes or a little more, till we found ourselves in a park-like area where, sure enough, were a dozen or two henequen plants of considerable size. Knowlton broke off one of the fleshy leaves, ripped it open with his penknife, pulled out the interior, and hung it upon the limb of a tree to dry in the sun.

He said : 'You will see the kind of fibre that it produces as soon as the pulp dries out a little.'

We sat down on a stone, and Knowlton almost absent-mindedly pulled out a pack of cards and said, 'I don't suppose you are a card-player or want to play cards here, but I always carry a pack of patience cards around with me,' and he put the pack back in his pocket. 'We ought to give that stuff about fifteen minutes really to dry out,' he went on, pulling out his watch, which I noticed was a good-looking gold one.

'By the way,' Knowlton remarked, showing me his watch, 'how much do you suppose this watch cost me?'

I said, 'Why, I have no idea. It seems to be a gold watch. A hundred dollars?'

'No,' he said, 'it cost me just two dollars.'

'Then,' I said, 'it isn't gold.'

'Yes, it is,' he said.

I asked how he had managed to get it for two dollars.

'Have you ever noticed the big jewellery store in Market Street, where the storekeeper has an auction every morning? His method is to write the word "watch" on a card, shuffle the pack, and then have the assistant walk round the crowd and anyone can buy a card for two dollars, and the man who draws the card with the word "watch" written on it gets the watch. The store happens to be on the way to my office and I would stop every morning for several days to see this operation, until I thought I saw that the card drawn was marked in this way.' Knowlton drew his pack of cards out of his pocket, marked one on the edge, held the pack out to me, and said, ' See if you can spot that mark, because it was just such a mark that enabled a confederate to draw the card so that the jeweller did not have to deliver the watch at all. So the next day I pushed forward, offered my two dollars, drew the marked card, won the watch, making sure that it really was a gold watch. That's how I got it for two dollars. See if you can draw that card again after I have shuffled the pack.' And he proceeded once more to shuffle the pack.

But at that moment a voice behind us said with some annoyance, 'What are you people doing here? Don't you know that this is private property and that a man doesn't like to have strangers playing cards in his garden?'

Knowlton immediately began making apologies. He thought this was part of Oakland Park and we weren't playing cards, he was merely explaining to his English friend here how he had managed to secure a gold watch for two dollars.

The visitor, or the owner of the garden, immediately became interested and asked Knowlton to show again how the thing was done. Knowlton held out the pack and I drew once more the marked card.

'That,' said the third man, 'was a fluke. I am prepared to bet a goodish sum that you could not do that a second time if I held the cards.'

Knowlton replied, 'You can certainly hold the cards and my friend, I think, will be prepared to bet anything reasonable that he can draw the card.' Turning to me, he asked, 'Do you feel inclined to flutter fifty or a hundred dollars?'

I explained that I was not a betting man. Knowlton in a friendly half-whisper exclaimed, 'Oh, shucks, you can pay your expenses in town if you are a bit smart. Take his fifty dollars if he is such a boob.'

It was true that I don't bet, but there was something of a challenge in Knowlton's remark—and something perhaps in the idea that I could win part of my expenses in San Francisco as easily as this from a very cocky and not very polite stranger. So I fished out three twenty-dollar pieces which I happened to have in my waistcoat pocket. (At that time California was full of gold pieces worth twenty dollars. These very big plaques were rarely found east of the Rockies.) Knowlton handed over the pack to the third man. I looked for the mark, drew the card, and it was *not* the card with the word 'watch' written on it.

It came on me suddenly that I had been robbed by a pair of confidence men, like any innocent rube. The sense of anger,

shame, what you will, made me quite inarticulate, and in the
midst of my silence, Knowlton suddenly seized me by the arm,
dragged me a few feet away, and said, 'What the hell happened
to you? Did you get rattled? Why couldn't you see the proper
card? Let's go back and see if he'll double the bet. You mustn't
let him walk away with your money in that fashion.'

In a sort of daze of anger and disappointment I went back
with Knowlton to the visitor, puzzling in my mind how I could
get that money back and could get even. I had no more money
on me. I explained this to Knowlton, who said, 'That doesn't
matter. I would stake you if I happened to have the money with
me. Let's tell this fellow that we will come back to-morrow if we
may, and go on with the game.' Without waiting for a reply,
he turned to the third man and said : ' My friend here would like
to go on with this little game if you are willing.'

To which the third man replied, 'Oh, I am willing all right.
I just want to prove that he can't draw the right card if I hold
them, and that when he drew the right card in the first case,
it was just luck. I will back my luck against his.'

Knowlton, who seemed to take command, said, 'Well, may we
come back to your garden to-morrow morning, since my friend
hasn't got a stake with him just at the moment, and he will be
ready to back his luck against yours.'

'Right you are,' said the third man, and we strolled towards
the road along which ran the trolley to the ferry (deciding not to
walk) chatting of this and that on the way—at least they were
chatting. I was silent, my mind full of half-formed plans of what
I would do on the morrow, because I felt that it suited my book to
see if I couldn't recover the money of which I had been robbed.

Knowlton kept up a pleasant talk the whole way to San
Francisco and left me at the hotel.

At the hotel I formed a plan. It was still the early afternoon,
and I knew that if I went out of the hotel, Knowlton would
probably follow me. What I did, therefore, was to change from
my townee clothes into the more or less traditional cowboy outfit, high-heeled boots, cotton jeans, scarf covering a collar, and so
forth. And so disguised, I slipped out of the back door of the
hotel, and in a street or two distant inquired of the policeman
on his beat where the police station was. There I was directed
to a room in which two men sat behind desks. I began to explain

to the official who seemed to be the one in charge what had happened to me. I had not got very far before he interrupted my story with the simple statement : ' You have been done by a con. man. Now, what was it—three-card-trick-vanishing-pea-trick-poker-trick . . .?' all in one gabble reciting the various dodges to which the confidence men resort. I explained that I did not know what he was talking about, but what actually happened was this, and I insisted on telling briefly the experience of the morning. The man sitting at the second desk suddenly broke in with, ' Oh, oh-o-o-h, that must be Bill Farley ! Yes, certainly, it's Bill Farley.' The first man said somewhat brusquely, ' Well, Bill Farley or not, it isn't our affair. He was operating in Oakland, and you must go to the Oakland police, it's nothing to do with us.' I was thus summarily dismissed.

But I was not in the mood to give up and decided to take the ferry again, keeping a sharp look-out for Mr. Knowlton, and so to the Oakland police. In Oakland the police were a bit more forthcoming, listened patiently, and the official I saw said : ' Well, I'd like to lay Mr. Bill Farley by the heels, so I'll tell you what to do. You come over in the morning, go to this ' private garden,' start playing your game. I will have a couple of our men there and we will pick these two up.'

Part of my trouble at the moment was ready cash. But I knew from my friends who used tobacco on the plains that there was a brand of tobacco which enclosed in the packages some sort of coupon which looked at a distance precisely like a ten or twenty-dollar bill. I asked one of the clerks in the hotel whether he by chance kept any of these coupons, as I was collecting some. It so happened that he did, and he gave me a fistful. These I put in my wallet.

The next morning promptly after breakfast Mr. Knowlton appeared, as cheerful and talkative as ever, and as we walked to the ferry, he said : ' Now we must be sure that you get your money back this time, and perhaps a bit more, so that you can have a little amusement in San Francisco. By the way, you have got money in right denominations, haven't you, because it won't do to start him off with a big bet. You want to get his blood up a little by starting low, you understand, and increasing.'

I pulled out my wallet and flicked the bills so that he could see that I had a wallet full. This seemed to set his mind at ease.

We reached our 'private garden' of the day before, and there, hanging on the limb, was the henequen. We sat down, Knowlton talking entertainingly about his experiences in British Columbia, the chances he had missed with valuable mines. . . .

But the third man did not turn up, and I saw nothing of anyone who might be from the police department of Oakland. We waited fifteen minutes, twenty minutes, half an hour, a bit more, and finally Knowlton himself said, 'Wal, our friend seems to have forgotten his appointment with us.' I agreed, and with a sense of defeat suggested that there was nothing to do but to go back to the city. As we waited for the trolley, I looked around carefully for any who might be police, but saw none. Just as we were getting on to the trolley, however, some man did appear from somewhere—I had not seen him before—and gave me just the slightest wink. Immediately, my spirits rose.

The trolley took, I suppose, about ten minutes from the park where we had been to the ferry. In the first five minutes I was trying to decide in the midst of Knowlton's chatter what my course should be. I had no absolute evidence, of course, that Knowlton was indeed a con. man, but still I felt—neck or nothing.

After about five minutes, I stopped Knowlton's chatter and said, 'One moment before we get off. You must think me very green indeed if you suppose that I haven't seen through all this; and that you and the man who didn't turn up this morning are a couple of con. men who have swindled me out of sixty dollars.'

Knowlton looked genuinely astonished and said: 'I find this very surprising indeed, but not in the way you seem to think. I took you for one of these honest Englishmen looking round San Francisco, and what I find is clearly a blackmailer. Now you may think that you know your way about in this country. But I want to remind you of one thing. Our police and courts are pretty tolerant, perhaps at times too tolerant. But there is one crime about which they have no tolerance at all, and are absolutely ferocious, and that is the crime of blackmail. I haven't made up my mind yet quite what I shall do. But I just want to warn you that I happen to be a man of some repute in San Francisco, a mining engineer in good standing, and one whose word the police would accept, and I am disposed to lay now a charge against you of attempted blackmail.'

He spoke with such conviction and such calmness and quietness that I was plunged immediately into a most awful panic. Suppose I had made a mistake? After all, what evidence had I got?

Knowlton went on talking. He delivered a sermon on the pathetic spectacle of a young man of promise started on the road to crime. He painted a graphic picture of what it would end in. If the underworld did not bump me off (that was not the expression which he used, because it had not yet arisen, but some nineteenth-century equivalent), then the police would.

The trolley, however, was about to stop, and I knew that I must make my decision immediately if any decision was to be made at all. So I said to Knowlton: 'I can't continue this debate any longer except to say that there is actually in the car at this moment a detective with a warrant for your arrest. He will arrest you the moment I rise and give the signal. I don't want that. I want my money back. Hand over the sixty dollars and, as far as I am concerned, the thing is finished.'

Knowlton smiled and said with great calmness and confidence, 'Get up, bring along your policeman.' Whereupon I made a move to get to my feet.

Suddenly Knowlton's voice changed completely from the cultivated engineer's to the accents of an underworld character, as he said with a sort of snarl, 'Blast you, I will give you your money back.'

I said: 'Then hand it over.'

'What—here before the car, everybody? I haven't got it, I swear I haven't got it!'

'You have a watch and chain. Hand those over as security.'

With a sort of whine, he said, 'You can't do that now.'

Again I made a move to rise, and then, in a sort of scramble, as he felt the car slacking up, he lugged out the watch and chain (there were some nuggets, I remember, hanging to the chain) and handed them over to me, in haste and, I noted, in some terror.

The trolley stopped and we both got down. A moment later the man who had given me the sign got down too. Knowlton turned round and had a look at him, and his face broke into a grin as he burst out, 'Why, if it isn't my ol' friend, O'Rourke.' The two shook hands cordially, and Knowlton clapped Mr. O'Rourke on the back, delighted to meet his old friend. O'Rourke said to Knowlton: 'Bill, this won't do. You are sailing too close to the

G

wind. The Chief doesn't want you around here and my orders are to pick you up if your English friend gives the word.'

'English friend!' Knowlton turned to me. 'Who the hell are you anyhow?'

'I am what I have told you, an unlucky Britisher out of a job.'

'Out of a job? I'll give you a job. I'll put you in the way of big money.' All this, if you please, in the presence of the officer. Knowlton went on to sketch the fortunes that awaited me if I would join his push. The officer, however, gave me a sign. I went over to him and he said, 'Don't go to the city with that man. Let him go first. You had better come to the office with me here in Oakland and see the Chief.'

I went back to where Knowlton was standing waiting for the ferry and said, 'If you will come to my hotel to-morrow morning with sixty dollars, you can redeem your watch.'

Knowlton in effect said he wanted to do so, the watch was part of his stock in trade.

The police office was not very far from the ferry station, so I walked over with the officer towards it. I asked him whether he thought that Knowlton would come to redeem his watch and reimburse me the money he had taken. The officer thought so. As gently as I could, I asked whether I would owe the police department in Oakland anything to reimburse them for their expenses, and the officer, without much ado, said yes, he thought so, and that twenty dollars for him and thirty dollars for the Chief would be about the proper thing. We got to the office, I saw the Chief, explained what had happened, and that, since the second man had not turned up, nothing seemed to be gained by the idea of their picking up the pair, that it looked as though I should get the money back, and therefore, as far as I was concerned, the matter had best be dropped. The Chief concurred. To him as to his subordinate, I put the gentle question as to whether I owed him anything, and in a loud voice, for the benefit of some subordinate in the other room, he said, 'NO, NO, YOU DON'T OWE US ANYTHING, WE DON'T CHARGE ANYTHING IN THESE CASES,' but in a very low voice, he said quietly, 'Would thirty dollars be all right?' I indicated that it would.

Next morning Mr. Knowlton, as cheerful as ever, appeared, but he said he had not got sixty dollars, and when I announced that I should have to add at least another fifty for expenses incurred in the Oakland police office, he was extremely indignant at the rapacity and avarice of mankind. He just hadn't the money. But after a good deal of insistence on my part and a blunt refusal to hand over his stock in trade in the shape of the watch until he coughed up, he begged me to go across with him to some bar where perhaps a friend of his would lend him the necessary sum.

The bar proved to be a quite gorgeous affair, and there was a low-voiced confabulation between Knowlton and the barkeep. After a time the barkeep came out and said, 'I would like to oblige my friend, Mr. Knowlton, but I really don't see that he owes you, as you say, a hundred dollars. I could advance him perhaps seventy.'

By this time I was getting a little tired of the whole affair and accepted the seventy as a compromise. The watch and chain and nuggets were duly returned to Mr. Knowlton. The next day I once more took the ferry for Oakland, found the two officers with whom I had dealt before, and after passing the time of day, I paid my debts in that quarter.

Three or four days later, as I came out of the hotel, who was standing at the entrance but my friend, Mr. Knowlton. He immediately grabbed me by the arm and said, 'Look here, did you pay those fellows in Oakland anything?'

I replied, 'Yes, I let them have between them fifty dollars.'

Knowlton's anger knew no bounds. He shook his fists at the heavens and said, 'The sons of guns' (perhaps 'guns' was not the word he used) 'they swore to me that you had not paid them a cent and stuck *me* for fifty dollars.'

That was the end of my adventure. But I was to encounter Knowlton more than once during my work later on as a reporter, assigned to the local police courts. His contacts with the police were still on a friendly basis. He renewed his offer of partnership, suggesting I come into a new development of his business, which was now, I gathered vaguely, some form of counterfeiting. I had casually made the suggestion that there was a good deal to be done in counterfeiting silver coins if only the counterfeiter would have the sense to make his coins of real silver. This puzzled him. How could one make anything at it if one used real silver? I explained that the intrinsic value of the silver in a silver dollar was not a dollar, that you could buy the unminted silver even then for about fifty cents and make a turnover of a hundred per cent more or less, with the coins. If properly done, they would be beyond detection, and in any case, not counterfeit coins in the usual sense of the term. Knowlton regarded this as a stroke of genius and seems to have conferred with some of his friends, because a week or two later he renewed his suggestion and insisted that really I should come in on a business basis. But the proposition did not quite appeal to me.

It not unnaturally occurred to me that the adventure with Mr. Knowlton and his friends in the police force could be made the basis of a story or two that should interest one or other of the San Francisco dailies. I saw the city editor of the *Chronicle*, but he saw nothing in the story. It was either too commonplace or would show the police in a light which would set them against the paper, putting it at a disadvantage in securing stories in the future. But though the editor had no use for the story I have just told, he offered to take me on for a time on a lineage basis. I made the rounds of the police stations, the courts and the city hall, at first with the older hands so that I might learn the ropes. But not much of what I turned in was printed. It was, explained the City Editor, too 'sociological.' A criminal's background and environment was less important than the fact that his counsel had punched the prosecuting attorney on the nose, a fact of the day's proceedings that rated a headline, and which probably I overlooked, in my absorption in the psychology of the accused.

Meantime I was writing a good deal about the real life of the frontier farmer of that day, and of his problems, matters of which the city-dweller seemed for the most part supremely ignorant, and of which my own personal experience had given me some first-hand knowledge. Some of this writing was published in the more obscure of the Western magazines and was reprinted in my *Patriotism Under Three Flags: A Plea for Rationalism in Politics*, to appear a few years later.

These articles revealed the handicaps under which the farmer worked at that time. His position then did not even remotely resemble what it has since become over much of the United States. It was a time of exceedingly low prices for everything that the farmer had to sell and of rapidly rising prices for everything he had to buy, from textiles and reapers to railroad freights and

banking accommodation. These conditions which operated so
harshly against the farmers—the most impoverished of all the
elements in the American population at that time—were
worsened, indeed very largely explained, by the increasing Pro-
tectionism, which could do nothing effective to help the farmer.
There were then no imports of the things he produced, primary
products and food stuffs. Yet the farmers were nearly all Pro-
tectionists, warmly supporting the system which operated so
greatly to their disadvantage. I had found it fascinating to explore
the explanation of this phenomenon as I listened to the arguments
that went on in the ranch bunkhouse, round the camp fire, or
between my fellow homesteaders.

To-day the farmers' lobby is perhaps the strongest in Washington, but at the end of the nineteenth century, when these notes
were written, farmers were both unorganised and politically
immature, and, like most immature folk, subject to easily excited
mass emotions. The commonest emotion was that of a crude
xenophobia, mainly Anglophobia, exploited now by a Hearst,
now by a Bryan, and all the time by Congressional demagogues.
Rational calculation of the farmers' own interest seemed to be
about the last thing that entered into their collective political
decisions. Again and again, one was presented with the spectacle
of this section of the voters sacrificing material interest and
economic advantage to the indulgence of collective emotions, the
nature and origin of which they refused to examine.

This was of course a view running directly counter to the
political philosophies of economic determinism which were to
become so popular during the next half-century. But events, including the coming of Communism, have confirmed the view
which then began to form in my mind as the result of those
early contacts with the American workers and farmers.

Communism is professedly unsentimental, scientific, materialistic. In fact, the masses whose support makes possible
the power of Communist governments are moved and kept in line
by a passion of fanaticism which renders them quite obviously
at times incapable of anything resembling scientific impartiality
or even sane judgment of objective fact.

It is true that at certain points highly rational calculations
of interest did enter into this strange situation of the farmer.
The big industrialists who maintained costly lobbies in Wash-

ington to secure the tariffs which hit the farmer so hard were actuated by a very conscious and acute sense of interest. But the success of this pressure group depended upon rousing emotions which caused the farmer to forget *his* interest.

The process by which emotion could be so aroused as to cause a whole population to forget the facts and their own interest was illustrated during the Venezuelan crisis. Britain happened to be at that time by far the best foreign market for the products of the American farmer and still a source of cheap capital. Economic interest dictated good relations with her. Yet these farmers found great relish in any excuse for quarrel with her, as their reaction to Cleveland's ultimatum to Great Britain demonstrated.

For generations a British frontier three thousand miles long—quite unfortified—had run side by side with that of the United States and had never constituted a threat. But the possibility that Britain, as the result of a long-standing dispute with Venezuela, might extend by so much as a dozen miles a colonial frontier in a South American jungle thousands of miles distant, was suddenly made to seem a deadly threat to the very existence of the United States. Theodore Roosevelt declared it so to be and prayed that 'this time we should have our war.' Mr. Hearst daily demanded it with screaming headlines and was obviously dismayed when Britain—rather than allow hysteria of this sort to set the world ablaze—backed down.

I found it a frightening phenomenon; frightening, because obviously the merits of the dispute about the frontier in the South American swamp had very little to do with it all. Obscure forces of restlessness, vague discontents, seeking a scapegoat, national pride and boastfulness wanting to justify itself, were looking for an outlet. Britain, for the reasons just indicated, happened to be handy, and was served up as the scapegoat by the Yellow Press with Mr. Hearst at the head. When Britain, by reason of her complete submission, could no longer serve, Hearst was soon able, in a matter of a month or two, to find another scapegoat in Spain; and this time got his war. (For years he boasted that he made the war with Spain.)

It was not the Anglophobia as such which at that time I found terrifying. I did not believe that we should come to war with

Britain. But I did believe that politics—in Europe as in America —everywhere tended to be dominated by a temper of irrationalism which would render impossible the efficient and peaceful management of a society becoming every day more intricate and vulnerable. This impression was soon to be strengthened when, as will shortly appear in this chronicle, I was to run into the same kind of irrationalism in the France of the Dreyfus affair and the Britain of the Boer War.

In dealing with the Anglophobia of that time I tried a little irony. One of my articles attempts to list the reasons which, in view of so much Press opinion, justified a declaration of war on Britain. They were: (1) she is a great advocate of the pestilential doctrine of Free Trade; (2) of gold coinage; (3) of a stable and non-elective Civil Service, a subtle device of tyranny; (4) for the advocacy of these heresies she corrupts our free electorate by the lavish expenditure of 'British Gold'; (5) she has more Foreign Trade than we have, and it must be taken from her by stripping her of her Colonies; (6) she is a pirate and land-grabber; (7) her papers speak disrespectfully of the American accent; (8) British tourists are insolent, and wear absurd clothes; (9) she gives rise to Anglomaniacs in America, who turn up their trousers, wear knickers and pyjamas, part their hair in the middle, take 'barths,' and are an offence generally to good Americans; (10) she owns too many American securities, which it is time she sacrificed as legitimate spoils of war; (11) she corrupts our Ambassadors by turning them into 'contemptible flunkeys' and Anglomaniacs (*vide* Bayard); (12) she still insolently repudiates ('she does everything insolently, and I am quoting the *Call* here') the doctrines of 1776, 'she has never acknowledged the principles of freedom of government, government of the people by the people for the people.' She is ruled at home for the benefit of the land barons, and her Colonies are oppressed to pay tribute. She is a standing 'defiance to human freedom'; (13) she favoured the Confederacy (Northern opinion); (14) she did not recognize the Confederacy when she might (Southern opinion); (15) she hates America, and is determined to see her humiliated; (16) we must vindicate the Monroe Doctrine.

'This last cause,' I go on to say, 'for the moment outweighs all others.' I had, I averred, only the foggiest notion of what the

Monroe Doctrine was supposed to be, 'notwithstanding my patient attention to much fiery oratory, learned discourses, and newspaper wisdom.'

'And though I would not for worlds speak disrespectfully of the Monroe Doctrine or the Equator,' I added, 'I have a notion that most Americans are in my case. Some irreverent scoffer in an after-dinner speech the other night was guilty of this ribald jest: Says Jones, "What is this I hear, Smith, about your not believing in the Monroe Doctrine?" Smith retorts, "It's a wicked lie. I never said I did not believe in it. I do believe in it. I would lay down my life for it. What I did say was that I do not know what it means."

'That, to be frank, is my position. I believe in the Monroe Doctrine of course, because I try to be a truly patriotic American. I would lay down my life for it. We all would. The newspaper editors especially are pining to disembowel the Britisher in the name of the Monroe Doctrine. But I must say I wish I knew what it meant.'

I went on to suggest that farmers could not afford that kind of political drug-taking. One article concludes:

> I know of few things more pathetic than the spectacle of a man burdened with toil, with debt, poorly fed, poorly clad, his wife aweary with the monotony of petty drudgery, his children anæmic, enthralled by a political oratory which ignores his debts, ignores his poverty, his toil, and is concerned only to inflame his hatred of a people seven thousand miles away, to tickle a bootless vainglory about the wide 'per-r-airies, stretching from the rock-bound coast o' Maine to the sunny shores of the golden Pacific.' Ordinarily I resent—as a farmer myself—the ill-concealed contempt of the town American for the 'hayseed,' the facile caricatures of 'Judge' and 'Puck.' But when I witness the spectacle I have just described, upon my soul I think he deserves everything in that way he gets.

Although since that was written the economic situation of the farmer has been revolutionised, the psycho-political, or psycho-economic phenomenon which the above illustrates—a situation, that is, in which the most obvious interest of a people is obscured by the emotions of an irrelevant and irrational nationalism—was to mark politics and help to wreck the peace of the world during the next forty years.

After a month or two on the San Francisco *Chronicle* I received by round-about means the offer of a reportorial job on the St. Louis *Globe-Democrat*, which I accepted. I did not do very well at it, though it was an interesting and informing experience. The relations between the underworld in all its phases, the police and the reporters, were even closer than in San Francisco, and at times exceedingly diverting. 'Bohemianism' was the note in the reporters' room. I had been on the *Globe-Democrat* only a few days when one of the reporters informed me that he was coming home with me to my room because he had nowhere else to go: his landlady had turned him out and he had only fifty cents in the world till next pay day. I found this sort of thing in the end a nuisance. Hearing from a miner friend who had done pretty well in California, but was now in Chicago and anxious to see me, I accepted his invitation to stay with him. After a few weeks of fugitive work on Chicago papers I formed a sudden resolution to return home, and did so.

Looking back, I find that I have lived altogether about twenty years in America distributed over the sixty which have elapsed since I emigrated to that country as a boy of seventeen.

About a quarter of a century after my life as farm hand, cowboy, miner, I was to find myself a journalist, member of the staff first of the *New Republic*, then of the *Nation*, and a lecturer in American Universities. My American experience includes therefore contact with two orders or classes of society, and two generations; indeed, three generations: I have taught in the twentieth century the grandson of a man I knew in California in the nineteenth.

Even in my reportorial days I ventured on certain generalizations which I embodied in notes made at the time. Among them are these:

'American government, especially in the cities, is as corrupt as any in the world. Rome under Caligula knew nothing worse. But American society, as apart from government, is healthy, vital, expanding. Schools and universities, welfare institutions of all kinds, multiply without ceasing. Wages, the standard of living, steadily rise. There must be therefore, within this society, some element of vigour and vitality which overbears and nullifies the badness and corruption of government. A society so alive, so vital, so healthy, can afford bad government as a healthy man can stand a good deal of dissipation and a few operations now and again.'

That conclusion, drawn more than half a century since, was, I think, sound. It is very important for us who are developing in Britain a type of society which differs profoundly from that under which the United States grew up, to try to understand what that element of vitality may be, and not allow it to be wholly eliminated as the result of the experiments we are now making.

And there is something else. If the United States could 'afford' corrupt government at the turn of the century, she can afford it less now. Her responsibilities are greater, and government plays necessarily a larger part in daily life than it did then. Nor can she afford her xenophobia and Anglophobia.

The distortion of history by national bias is of course common to every nation. I had had a proof of this in going from the kind of history taught in elementary school in Britain to the kind of history taught in French *lycées*. In reading the two accounts of a given event, it was difficult at times to realize that it was the same. But the distortion of history which, for purposes of nationalist morale or what not, the American farmers and workmen I knew had been taught, was more than usually mischievous ; not merely because it made for 'bad feeling' between the two countries—that of itself has no particular importance—but because it stood in the way of understanding their own society and civilization ; and furnished no preparation for the policy they were later compelled to adopt. The fact that history encouraged so grossly primitive a chauvinist anti-Europeanism, which meant mainly Anglophobia, not only presented very great difficulties to Wilson, as already noted, but to Franklin Roosevelt. Arthur M. Schlesinger, in his *Paths to the Present* (New York, Macmillan, 1949) notes that 'History as conventionally written stresses national differences . . . glossing over the fundamental interdependence of peoples . . . nourishes mutual distrust and contributes dangerously to national vainglory. In the case of the United States, for example, Great Britain is impressed upon the young as a selfish ruler of colonies, an enemy in two wars and a diplomatic antagonist on numerous occasions. Germany hardly figures at all in American histories until under Kaiser Wilhelm II, and again under Adolf Hitler, she emerges as a monster of ruthlessness. The existence of three thousand miles of unfortified boundary with Canada receives the barest mention. . . .'

My own experience confirms this. Educated Americans have in the past been complacent about the misreading of history, and have often accused me of exaggerating the extent of Anglophobia. Yet it has been a powerful factor in American politics for two centuries. There exist 'professional' Anglophobes: the main theme, for instance, of the McCormick press, with the Chicago *Tribune* at the head, as also with the Pattersons and Hearsts, has been that the one enemy that the United States had to fear was Britain. (The one enemy in fact which has always been associated with the United States in its deepest crises has been Britain.) When, as related above, I found myself at times a visiting professor in American universities, I would be met with puzzled stares of incredulity when pointing out the fact that without the British Empire there could obviously have been no United States; that it was made possible by English resistance to Spain in the sixteenth and seventeenth centuries; to France in the eighteenth; to Russia and her Holy Alliance in the nineteenth; and that if there had been no British Empire in 1940—no Gibraltar, no Malta, no troops in Egypt, no defence of India against Japan —then Hitler and Hirohito would have won the Second World War. All this would come as a shocking surprise where it did not infuriate an inherited Anglophobia.

I have sometimes asked my students: How do you explain the difference between the civilization north of the Mexican border and that to the south. South are—or were until very recently— feudal conditions in which the peon lived at a coolie standard of life, periodically robbed of such poor possessions as he had— to say nothing of his life in so many cases—by a succession of revolutions, by local bandits, by the Mexican equivalent of what in China would be called war lords. The United States, with all its shortcomings, is relatively free from all this. What accounts for the difference? I would seldom get any intelligible reply, and it seldom occurred to the student that history was a study that might have furnished some answer. In an age when security of western civilization against the latest thrust from the East depends upon avoiding the cleavage between American and British policy which it is so clearly the Russian purpose to produce, a better understanding of our common history would seem to be called for.

CHAPTER IV

RETURN: PARIS JOURNALIST,
NEWSPAPER 'OWNER'

WITHIN a fortnight of landing in England from my seven years in the United States (mainly on the western plains) I had secured a newspaper job in Paris—in reply to an advertisement.

This was a sufficiently quick change of environment. If some years of cow-punching and ranching could be considered a rest from intellectual effort then I could be said to have brought a fresh, or refreshed, mind to the interpretation of the dramas that were about to unfold before me: the Spanish-American War, the Dreyfus Affair, the Boer War, the drift to the First World War, and the parts played by such actors as Joseph Chamberlain, Northcliffe, Jaurès, Zola, Clemenceau, Ramsay MacDonald, Balfour, Grey, Esher, Lloyd George, Briand, Herriot, Wilson, with all of whom I was to come into contact.

The job I secured was as sub-editor and general factotum of the *Daily Messenger*, successor to *Galignani's Messenger*, a daily newspaper published in English ever since the royalist restoration in 1814. (It had continued to appear even during the Hundred Days which preceded Waterloo.) It was therefore getting on for a hundred years old when I joined it in 1898. Its contributors in the past had included Byron, Thackeray and other giants of the nineteenth century, as well as a variegated assortment of black-guards living by their wits in Paris. When I joined the paper it was published in an old, dingy, seventeenth-century house in the Rue Croix des Petits Champs just opposite the Hotel de l'Univers et du Portugal. The composition and editorial rooms (i.e., one editorial room) were on the third floor and the flatbed printing machines in the cellar. The compositors were made up of English printers who for some reason or other (which it was not always discreet to investigate too closely) had wandered to Paris years before and stayed there, and who generally, after half a lifetime in France, hardly spoke a word of French. There were several

Frenchmen in the composing room, who by some quirk of circumstance spoke fluent and perfect Cockney English. Bateau,
the foreman, looked like a Frenchman out of some comic cartoon :
rotund with moustache and imperial, and of military bearing.
He spoke French sonorously and could (and at Chapel festivities
did) recite Racine and Victor Hugo like a member of the Theâtre
Français ; and, as you handed him some copy, was apt to remark,
'Cor blimey, I wish those blasted correspondents wouldn't send
in such bloody dirty copy. What in 'ell do you suppose we are to
do with scratchin's like this?' These—Bateau, and his colleagues Servat, Bordini—were the true bi-linguals. Where, how,
they came by their languages I never enquired.

Methods in the composing room were astonishing : stickfuls of
the old worn type would be tied together on the stone with bits
of string, wetted with a sponge and the proof taken by smacking
the galley so made up with a brush.

My salary at the start was two hundred and fifty francs a
month, (i.e., £10 gold) out of which I paid fifty a month for a
room at the Univers across the street; gave the garçon five francs
a month for bringing me a jug of water for the flat tin bath I
kept under the bed; and dined for 1 franc 15 centimes at the
prix fixe restaurant next door. The one franc fifteen included, if
you please, soup, hors d'œuvre, meat, vegetables, sweet, wine;
and a napkin as large as a table cloth. It was evident, therefore,
that I could live on the two fifty a month. When after a month
or so my salary was raised to three hundred a month—a gold
ten franc piece every day of the year practically, I knew that I
had attained opulence. Compared with the nagging anxiety of the
ranch, with its drought, crop failures, diseases among the stock,
unpaid bills at the store, the humiliation of debt, mortgages . . .
this job in the dingy street of Paris was peace, security, and
prosperity. Here was the real simple life, not in the nerve-trying
hazards of agriculture in the 'wide open spaces.' The preoccupations and scruples which had so racked me a few years
previously in Geneva, the fact that I might not be able to find the
solution to the world's ills, that the world about me was still the
victim of preposterous fallacies and cock-eyed sociology, no longer
kept me awake at night. The financial problems of the simple life
in the open spaces had brought home to me the feeling that a
man's first duty to society was to support himself ; to be beholden

to none. Having realized that I could do the job at the *Messenger*
on my head, to say nothing of being able to introduce a few
obviously necessary reforms, I was in fact happier than I had
been for a long time.

And things began to happen. Warden, the editor, was offered
the Paris correspondentship of the old London *Standard*, as
substitute or assistant to Farman (whose sons some years later
were with the Wrights to be pioneers of the aeroplane). Automatically I fell into Warden's job, or jobs. He had been giving
the *Eclair* items of news, secured by telephone from London from
the early editions of the dailies there. I developed this and turned
the daily *Eclair* column into a sort of review of the English Press;
and was paid separately for it. As the Dreyfus affair was getting
into its stride I asked American newspapers whether they would
like letters and cables on it at my discretion. They would. Very
quickly I found myself earning not far off two thousand francs
(at the then rate of exchange eighty pounds) a month. After the
penury and struggle of farming this seemed fabulous, fantastic.
(The last time I was in Paris a quite modest dinner for myself
and friend at a decent restaurant cost me a little over two
thousand francs.)

For about four years I edited the *Messenger,* wrote a daily
piece for the *Eclair*, did correspondence for a small group of
American papers, of which the old *Philadelphia Record* was the
chief. During that time the *Messenger* linked up more closely
with the *Eclair*, moving from the old building in the Rue Croix
des Petits Champs to take quarters in the *Eclair* building which
was modern, with electric light (in the old house we had had gas);
and good mechanical equipment. The move made my work for
the *Eclair* easier, and caused me to expand my contributions to
that paper.

Which brings me to a point I would like to make clear. I do not
want to create the impression that because I wrote daily for a
French newspaper I was therefore a master of literary French.
I was not. After a period at a French *lycée,* a year or so attending
classes at the University of Geneva, and having been a voracious
reader of French literature all my life, I have necessarily a pretty
good working knowledge of the language. But I found that
writing French correctly took time, attention and energy which
could better be devoted to the political and social subject matter

with which I was dealing. I came therefore to an arrangement
with a junior member of the *Eclair* staff. I would dictate my stuff
to him (in French) and woe betide him if the past participles did
not agree. At one stage, indeed, I came to a trading agreement
with an elder member of the staff who, in addition to being on
the staff of the *Eclair*, held a position at the French War Office—
that of translator of letters in English sent by Englishmen or
Americans offering inventions to the French government. The
official's English was a good deal worse than my French. So after
he had taken my article at my dictation he would fish out of his
brief case the day's War Office letters in English and I would
dictate to him the French translation. All this work, be it remembered, was during the most hectic period of the Dreyfus
affair, of which more presently. No man, certainly not this man
in his twenties, could keep out of partisanship in such an affair.
My work at the *Eclair* kept me up very late : I usually did not get
to bed until six in the morning, sometimes not until seven. I was
thus able to grab all the Paris morning papers and read them in
bed. Sometimes I did not get to sleep until nine or ten in the
morning : sometimes the noises of the city were too much for me.
(I had a little apartment at one time in the Palais Royal where
at eight o'clock or thereabouts housewives would hang rugs and
carpets on to the balconies outside their windows and beat them
with an instrument that made a noise like a cannon. It was so
maddening that I would go out at times on to my own balcony,
and imagine myself the possessor of a rifle, shooting these noisy
creatures as I once shot deer in California.)

Occasionally I would give it up as a bad job and take the
train to Meulan-Hadricourt where I kept a little half-deck sailing
boat, and take her out and sail along the beautiful reach of the
Seine Valley that stretches between Triel and Mantes. But the
ripple of the water as I sat at the tiller would naturally produce
after a night without any sleep at all an intense drowsiness. On
one occasion I went fast asleep holding the tiller and sailed bang
into the tow rope of one of those enormously long strings of
magnificent barges which ply between Rouen and Paris. It nearly
meant shipwreck. Only the loud profanity of the bargees
awakening me in time prevented it.

I spent much time on that boat (for which I had paid three
hundred francs). I had it fitted with a tent (the boom serving as

the ridge pole) that made it quite habitable with bedding that
packed away under the half-deck. Many happy—and solitary—
hours were spent therein. The gardes champêtres could never
take me seriously when, in reply to questions as to what I was
doing tied up at night in some quiet corner of the river, I said
I preferred at times sleeping on my boat to sleeping at an inn.
(This was before the days when boy-scouting and various forms
of tourism had familiarized even the urbanized French with the
attractions of camping.) On one occasion I was actually arrested
as engaged in some nefarious nocturnal activity; poaching, fishing out of season or something. But the Justice of the Peace,
sympathetic to the idea of le sport, then coming from England,
understood; and ended by asking me to lunch at his villa which
he had named—the name appearing on the garden gate—
' Drinking-Sport Villa.' But to the country folk, this sleeping on
boats by people who had the means to sleep in a house, was
merely a sign of being a little 'touched.' One evening an old
fisherman whose job was to net the friture de Seine that the
riverside restaurants advertise, rowed by with his fat wife in the
stern. I heard him say, jerking his head in my direction, 'Tu vois
ca? Ca couche dedans.'

The Eclair people were of course violently and bitterly anti-
Dreyfus and pro-army. I was as decidedly pro-Dreyfus, or pro-
revision and anti-army. And my contacts with the Eclair only
made me more so. It is almost impossible in this generation to
make clear how the case of an Alsatian Jew, falsely accused of
treason, should absorb for several years the attention of every
country in the civilized world—and should have dominated
French politics, overthrowing governments, provoking riots,
assassinations, suicides, for at least ten years. Kennedy Jones
once told me a story of how when he was editing the Evening
News Alfred Harmsworth said to him : ' Jones, you're making
too much of this Dreyfus Affair.' K.J. replied : 'Alfred, did you
ever hear of the crucifixion of Jesus Christ ? ' Alfred said he had.
' Well,' retorted Jones, 'this is the biggest newspaper story since
that.'

For the mass of newspaper readers the story was just a daily
whodunit. Spies, stolen documents, foreign agents, suicides in jail,
mysterious disappearances, veiled women, midnight visits, the
whole bag of tricks. But encountering the temper which I found

among the *Eclair* staff I realised that here were passions and
irrationalisms which reminded me somehow of the emotions I
had encountered in the United States at the time of the
Venezuelan crisis with its nationalism, chauvinism, Anglophobia.
The relation between the two phenomena—and certain other
manifestations of collective passion—was later to form the text
of a book on political irrationalism, of which more presently.

The anti-Dreyfus forces quickly built up their own mythology.
There was a 'syndicate of Treason' operating behind the scenes
to destroy the authority of the army. At the head of it, of course,
was Britain. One eminent general, testifying at Rennes, declared
that to his 'certain knowledge' twenty million francs had
'crossed the frontier' for the purpose of subsidising the campaign
of treachery in France. (He seemed to think that money had to
be smuggled in bags like narcotics.) The money came from
England. It was one of the curiosities of the Dreyfus Affair that
for the anti-Dreyfus forces England was more criminal than
Germany, on whose behalf the treason was supposed to have been
committed. For demagogues like Lucien Millevoie (of the *Patrie*),
Déroulède (of the delightful soldiers' songs), Edouard Drumont of
the *Libre Parole* (the Streicher of French anti-Semitism) England
was the real enemy. This was partly accounted for by the fact
that the French nationalist was still smarting from the humiliation
of Fashoda—one more retreat by France. But it was explained
far more by the older fact that Britain had been—within the time
of men still living—the centre of that resistance to the effort
which, had it succeeded, would have made France the master of
Europe, to the advantage, in the French view, of European unity
and Western Civilization. These attitudes are more permanent
and deep-rooted than we sometimes assume. 'What,' asked a
member of the Chamber of Deputies at the time of the Fashoda
crisis, ' is this England that has proved so great a nuisance to us?
It is merely a French colony that has turned out badly.'
(' Qu'est-ce que c'est cette Angleterre qui nous embête tellement?
Ce n'est q'une colonie francaise qui a mal tournée.') The outcome
of the Conquest was merely one manifestation of the malevolent
forces within the English which corrupted and transformed the
civilizing influence of France.

Again and again as I listened to the nationalist and militarist
fustian of the Chamber, or read the leaders in the nationalist

H

Press, it seemed just a French echo of what I had heard in the
United States; with the same fallacies, the same refusal to recognize fact, the same defiance of the evident, and incidentally
the same Anglophobia. But the phenomenon could not be
explained by the universality of Anglophobia, however much that
may be a fact, because, though nationalists bring Britain into
it, their real target is the liberal element in France itself; and the
Jews. Their anti-Semitism is not explained by ignorance of the
facts, for the chief facts by which they ought to correct their
conclusions are the Jews themselves with whom they come into
daily contact. Those facts, seen every day, are precisely the facts
the nationalists ignore.

A propos of French Anglophobia we are apt to forget how
narrow is the gap sometimes which separates us from ancient
history.

As a child wandering along a road in Lincolnshire I got into
conversation with an old man breaking stones—as one used to
see them before the coming of the asphalt and concrete road.
He began to talk about *his* childhood; what he could remember.
' And then,' he added, ' I 'listed and went to foreign parts. I
fought with the Duke at Quarter Brass.' When I got home I
asked my father what the old man meant and then learned it
meant he had fought at Waterloo. Quarter Brass for Quatre Bras
was the 1815 equivalent of ' Wipers ' for Ypres in 1915.

My father of course could have talked with many who fought
at Waterloo, or Trafalgar.

Towards the close of the *affaire* a newspaper colleague in Paris
brought me the manuscript of a history of it which he had
written and asked me to read it and give my opinion. It
was a well-documented record, giving almost day to day the
incredible developments—the upsetting of governments, the lies
into which statesmen were led, the forgeries, the murders, the
suicides. Having read most of the manuscript, I said: ' This
is a very careful account. You have given nearly all the facts
except *the* fact; the fact that this case, which began simply as the
alleged wrong judgment of court martial, has dominated the
whole political scene in France for at least ten years, and held the
attention of mankind for something like half that time. Judicial
errors are so common that nearly all judicial systems have made
provision for them in appeal courts. Errors of that kind are part

of the imperfection of men. Why then did the request for a revision precipitate so many overwhelming passions? You have neither explained that nor brought out the fact of the feeling and the passion.'

This reached such a point that whether a candidate for, say, the directorship of the Opera had been Dreyfusard or Anti-Dreyfusard might determine his appointment. I once asked an old doctor friend in the provinces why he had not been made chief surgeon in a hospital. 'Because,' came the reply, 'j'étais Dreyfusard.' On more than one occasion during the course of the affair, publication of both the *Messenger* and the *Eclair* was delayed because of fights in the composing room. Two compositors would get to discussing their 'takes' and end by going for each other with their loaded composing 'sticks.' On one occasion I helped to carry out the casualties to the ambulance. Another incident I recall occurred when I happened to close an article that I had written on the morrow of the rejection by the *Cour de Cassation* of one of the appeals for revision with the words : '*C'est fini.*' That evening, as Bateau the foreman came into my room to get copy to begin the night's work, he stood in front of my desk and dramatically said : 'C'est fini, eh? Eh bien. Moi, je vous dis que ça commence.' And he pulled out of his pocket Zola's historic letter which had appeared that day in *l'Aurore*, 'J'accuse'. Of course, he was right. The most dramatic phase of the case began when Zola entered the *affaire* and, with the simple power of his pen, raised the whole issue afresh.

Trivia of the case stick in one's memory. In the trial of Zola the court had made the ruling that there must be no raising of 'la chose jugée,' of matters already adjudicated. When Labori, Zola's counsel, was near to his peroration in his address to the jury, he made a brief reference to 'la chose jugée', and made a long pause. Everyone wondered what was coming next. (At that time, despite general secularization, some of the French Courts had still a crucifix hanging over the Judge's seat. There was one in this Court.) In a very silent Court, Labori, raising his voice and pointing with his hand to the crucifix, said :

'Violà la chose jugée . . . I don't know whether you gentlemen of the jury want to play the rôle of Pontius Pilate much as it was played in that case, in that chose jugée . . .' It made a very fine forensic effect.

After the court I happened to be making some notes, sitting at a café table with one of the American correspondents sitting opposite to me. Labori had, of course, used the French form of Pontius Pilate, 'Ponce Pilate.' My American colleague across the table, when he came to the name Ponce Pilate in the news agency flimsy from which he was reading, threw down his pen in vexation and said : 'I thought I knew every personality in the Dreyfus Affair from Paty du Clam to Colonel Piquart. But who the hell is Ponce Pilate?'

At the end of a year or two the *Messenger's* affairs reached a crisis, not in my department of the editorial, but in the management. The paper was still being composed with movable type— now worn down to illegibility—and printed without stereo-typing on a flatbed machine. A complete set of new type would cost a fairly heavy sum and the cost of composition would remain high at a time when the advertising revenue was falling off. (The general appearance of the paper with the old type would have put off any advertiser.) The paper was owned by the proprietors of a London woman's weekly publication, and managed by their nominee in Paris who, whatever his qualities otherwise might have been, knew very little indeed of the mechanics of newspaper production. An agency of the Linotype Company had just been established in Paris and was finding it hard going to sell machines to a conservative-minded trade. The obvious step for the *Messenger* was to install linotypes (which did not involve capital expenditure since they were paid for on the hire system) so that even on flatbed machines the type would be new every day; improving the general appearance of the paper and so the chance of increased advertising. But the manager for one reason or another boggled; mainly, I think, because he feared to be let in for unknown expenditure. To overcome this I suggested that I myself would compose the paper on contract—for a sum considerably less than that then being expended, and would at the same time guarantee 'new type every day.' In the end this was agreed to. The paper improved enormously in appearance; and I worked the machines two shifts : in the day-time doing composition for the considerable number of printers or publishers in Paris who were producing English material of one kind or another. I also composed for a time a weekly paper run by 'Count' Hamon, the Cairo palmist who so mystified both New

York and London by the supposed accuracy of his diagnoses or horoscopes or whatever the palmists call their output. All this meant an almost twenty-four-hour day attention to mechanical and business details, in addition to editing the *Messenger*, writing its editorial, doing a daily column for the *Eclair*, cables and letters to American papers. . . .

And then, after the crisis on the printing side of the *Messenger*, came one on the financial side. There was a warning that the owners in London were getting tired of making good the losses and were shortly closing down the paper. For long the paper had been living on anticipated revenue. When an advertiser entered into a contract for, say, three months, the paper drew a three months bill upon him for the amount, and discounted this bill with a private banker, a method of financing common enough in France at the time.

Accounts were therefore extremely difficult to disentangle. But I got a strong impression that with improvements and good management the paper which had lasted for nearly a hundred years could last a little longer. I made therefore this proposition to the London proprietors: if they would transfer the whole of the twenty thousand one-pound ordinary shares to me, I would give them half the amount in debentures. The proposition that they should pass over the whole of the shares in the company for no cash at all to a man who had barely a shilling to his name, took their breath away for a moment. But it was not difficult to put to them a strong case for the proposal: they had decided to wind up the company and cut all their losses. I was prepared to offer them ten thousand pounds of debentures, and attempt to carry on the paper. If I failed to make a success they were in no worse position than at that moment since they proposed to wind up the paper. If I succeeded they became possessed of ten thousand pounds—debentures, it is true, but valuable securities if the paper did succeed. The point was not a very difficult one to grasp and they grasped it. (The exchange of shares for debentures was not quite in the simple form described, for that would have been in violation of company law as it then existed; but we were to get round the difficulty.) Before completing the deal I was to have a ninety-day option to purchase, in order to give me time to go more fully into affairs. In those ninety days I should have sole control of the paper and its business.

I well recall my night trip back to Paris having completed this deal in London. Up to the point of dealing with the proprietors it had been a sort of battle of wits which I had found great fun in its way. But now I was saddled with the actual job of finding each week, out of the proceeds of a concern in a great muddle, wages and salaries of thirty or forty people. Their livelihood in a sense depended on the skill with which I could manage this business. Some of them were personal friends. What if, after all, I could not do it and under my management the paper which meant a livelihood for half a hundred people came to an end? As I walked up and down the platform at Calais waiting until the Paris train was ready to start I developed a most appalling funk; and, as a by-product of my gloomy reflections, saw the 'capitalist exploiter' in a new light. If I made a success of this thing, I should perhaps secure a larger income than the men with whom heretofore I had worked as fellow employees. I should be regarded as an exploiter: by some of them with a measure of resentment. The fact that my success would be the means of saving their present means of livelihood would of course be completely overlooked. I had no illusion on that point. When things went wrong on the paper the kicks would be for me; when they went right I should be 'getting rich out of the labour of others.' I knew that I was returning to the fears, anxieties and responsibilities that I had known as a nascent 'land-owner' and farmer in California. In that moment at Calais I looked back with some nostalgia to the time when ten francs a day as editorial cook and bottle-washer had seemed prosperity and security.

And my fears were all too justified. The deeper I went into the financial condition of things at the business office the worse the muddle which was revealed. The discounting based upon the advertisement contracts ran in certain cases beyond three months, and gave rise to all sorts of complications, with which this present record need not be burdened. There were disputes with the London people as to what part of this anticipated revenue belonged properly to them, for moneys advanced, or belonged to the prospective proprietors. It began to look as though I would have to exercise my right under the option not to complete purchase. But as a final card I decided to try to sell the paper.

Alfred Harmsworth (not yet Lord Northcliffe) was a man whose politics I detested and whose influence on the public

through his papers of enormous circulation I believed to be
malign. But after all, the old *Messenger* had no politics; its circulation and success depended upon providing the day's news to
the English-speaking people (American as well as British)
travelling or living on the Continent. It was not and could not be
an influence worth considering in the shaping of national policy,
American or British. The influence I thought so malign could
hardly therefore be exercised through this particular organ. So,
at least, I argued when I went to London to put the matter
before Alfred Harmsworth.

This was my first personal encounter with a man whom I
was to come to know so well and to be closely associated with for
a decade. At this time he was at about the peak of his fortunes,
'the young Napoleon' of Fleet Street. He had come to that
street of adventure without a penny, still in his teens, and already
was the owner of some twoscore publications of every kind and
description. I looked upon him then as a sort of journalistic
Frank Sinatra before whom the male bobby-soxers of the newspaper world worshipped and swooned.

It was with this sort of defiance and prospective dislike—an
attitude somewhat modified however by the hope that he would
buy the paper I was trying to save—that I was shown into his big
room with the thick carpet, the ornate desk at one end, the shaded
lights and all the other stage effects—or what I regarded as
stage effects. I emphasize my somewhat superior attitude because
in the first few minutes of our talk he was to turn the tables on
me. I had written him putting broadly my proposal. I supplemented it with a few comments.

'The paper,' I urged, 'has lived a long time—ever since
Napoleon in fact. It was published during the Hundred Days.'

This appealed to him.

'That's a point in your favour,' he replied, 'because you
can't grow trees; and trees are nice things to have about one.'
And then suddenly : 'What's your circulation ? Your letter does
not state it.'

I told him, and a miserable small figure it must have seemed to
the man who boasted of circulations in the million.

'And your gross advertising revenue I see is . . .' and he gave
the figure from the letter, and went on : 'This is out of all pro-

portion. It is of course a fraud on your advertisers. They are not getting their money's worth and I'm surprised that a man of your scruples should be concerned in that kind of business.'

This was something of a facer to a man who had entered the room in a temper of moral superiority to this newspaper 'pirate.' I stammered some sort of justification.

'You cannot measure the value of an advertisement in a paper like this, which is on the table of every hotel lounge on the Continent, entirely in terms of circulation. And my object in coming to you is to have means to lift the circulation very considerably so as to give the advertisers a better deal. Under your proprietorship the whole situation would alter.'

We discussed the matter amicably enough, and Harmsworth made it plain that he did not mean the accusation of 'fraud on the advertiser' to be taken quite seriously. I had to explain something of the complications in financing; the fact that the title was not, at present at least, vested in me; and that the present manager would do what he could to prevent my selling the paper, fearing his job would not survive change of proprietorship. I recall one casual remark, 'Have you offered these people five thousand pounds spot cash? It's wonderful what a cheque for five thousand pounds flourished under a man's nose will do.' My reply implied that if I had five thousand pounds to flourish around in that way I should not be coming to him. After a time he called in his secretary, Sutton ('Sutkins,' now Sir George Sutton, Bart.), and asked me to go into the whole matter more fully with him.

The upshot of it all was that he turned down the offer. Part of the reason, I felt pretty sure, was that he did not want to enter into any sort of dispute with the then proprietors over title, or be concerned at the very beginning with any internal office intrigue which might make it difficult to give the paper a really new start. And perhaps our talk had given him the idea that instead of re-starting an old paper he would start an entirely new one—a Paris edition of the *Daily Mail,* under my management and direction which, in fact, was shortly to happen.

I notified the proprietors that I should not exercise my option to purchase; that the paper was once more completely under their control, to carry on or not as they saw fit. The paper closed down. Luckily, the personnel were not long out of jobs: I was able, a little later as manager of the *Mail*, to take on some of the staff.

But I could not foresee this of course at the time of the stoppage of the *Messenger*. For some months I lived in a state of deep depression. Once more, as in California, dreams had ended in a rude awakening. Colleagues, members of the staff whom I might have saved from the miseries of lost jobs and unemployment if only (I felt) I had shown more competence and more skill in the management of this affair, had not been saved. True, if I had kept out of it altogether the result for them would have been the same; but my intervention had not helped them.

Yet it was in the midst of these harassments that there appeared (in 1903) my first book proper—*Patriotism Under Three Flags: A Plea for Rationalism in Politics*. It was a first attempt to deal with a phenomenon which was to disturb, perplex, and frighten me during the whole of my life, and to run like a red thread through everything that I was to write during the next half-century.

The phenomenon in question was the tendency of human judgment in social and political matters to be utterly distorted, warped, and twisted, both in its interpretation of objective fact and in its estimate of the means by which a given policy can be carried into effect; distorted by emotional forces within ourselves, forces of whose nature, of whose very presence, indeed, we seemed for the most part to be unaware. Events showed that these emotions could on occasion make us completely blind to what ought to be self-evident, to simple facts of the external world beneath our noses. We are thus capable, ran the theme of this first book, of walking into an abyss while denying its existence. The thing had taken various forms throughout the ages, and men had given it various names: nationalism, herd instinct, patriotism, partisanship, fanaticism, *esprit de corps*. But events which had marked the whole human record indicated its nature better than definitions: events like the wars between little Greek cities, highly civilized though they were, revealing an inability to live in peaceful co-operation; an inability which led finally to the destruction of a civilization which promised as well perhaps as any before or since. The same forces were revealed in the process by which a religion of mercy and compassion came quickly to endow itself with instruments of ferocious repression like the Inquisition; or in the wars of Mohammed, the spread of a

religion by fire and sword; or in the later wars between Catholic
and Protestant which came near to destroying Europe as utterly
as other fanaticisms had destroyed Greece. And now (this being
the aspect with which the book mainly dealt) nationalism seemed
to be developing into a force even more damaging to Western
Civilization than had been the conquests of Mohammed or the
religious wars of the seventeenth century. If the author had had
before him the spectacle of what the forces of irrationalism could
do with seventy million educated Germans under Hitler; or what
the doctrinal fanaticism of the Communist creed could do to the
Russians under Stalin; and could do indeed to the peoples of half
the world, many of whom will shortly possess the means of all but
complete annihilation—if he could have drawn upon these facts,
his indictment of irrationalism and the plea for some sense of the
moral obligation to discipline our more destructive instincts
would have very greatly gained in force.

As it was, I dealt with those manifestations of irrationalism
which the previous ten years had brought to the surface. The
opening paragraphs of the book read:

> Few generalisations would seem at first sight to have less justifi-
> cation than these: That the motives underlying national
> behaviour in such events as Cleveland's Venezuelan message, the
> Hispano-American War, the Dreyfus Affair and the South African
> War were essentially the same . . . in that passions were excited
> most in defence of a policy which affected welfare or interest
> little or not at all; or affected it adversely.
>
> Adverse judgments of national conduct in those events
> generally assume cupidity and avarice as the impelling motive,
> the subordination of moral considerations to material gain. Such
> judgment is unjust. . . . It is neither to cupidity, nor even justifiable
> self-interest, that political appeals have in the great crises of the
> last few years been addressed.

The implication throughout is that the nations have been led
astray by the demagogic exploitation of the subjective irrational
forces within ourselves, an exploitation not necessarily conscious,
since the exploiter himself, journalist or politician, is usually
subject to the same compulsions. The author specifies:

> The interest or well-being of the American could in no way be

advanced by the interference of his government in the dispute
between England and Venezuela which he so passionately demanded; as little could that of the Frenchman by the condemnation of Dreyfus which for over two years Frenchmen
regarded as of such importance as to outweigh all other political
considerations whatsoever; nor could the passionate Mafficker of
London gain aught by the conquest of the Dutch republics he was
willing to make such sacrifices to secure.

The book was in fact a blunt challenge to materialistic and
economic determinism, the germs of which had for long been
present in much current interpretation of events and was to
gain immense popularity in the next few decades. The challenge
was based on the quite simple proposition (to be greatly elaborated
in subsequent books) that men are not guided by facts but by
their opinions about the facts, opinions which may or may not
be correct; and usually are not, precisely because of these dis-
torting forces.

This is a much more familiar thesis now than it was at the time
Three Flags was published. It is to-day implicit in many of the
conclusions drawn by—among many others—John Dewey,
Graham Wallas, W. Trotter, Reinhold Niebuhr.

'The only way in which society can be made safe from dis-
ruption or decay,' writes Trotter in his *Instincts of the Herd*, ' is
by the intervention of the conscious and instructed intellect as a
factor among the forces ruling its development . . . there is no
remedy for man's ills outside his own efforts.' To which Reinhold
Niebuhr (*Moral Man and Immoral Society*) adds : 'It is fair,
therefore, to assume that growing rationality determines the
degree of vividness with which we appreciate . . . the extent to
which we become conscious of the real character of our own
motives and impulses, the ability to harmonise conflicting
impulses in our own life and in society, and the capacity to
choose adequate means for approved ends. In each a development of reason may increase the moral capacity.'

I have gone at a little length into the underlying theme of this
book, because it is a theme which has run through almost every
book I have written, and because something like ninety per cent
of the early criticism directed at my work was on the ground
that it 'ignores human nature' or 'assumes that men are always
guided by reason.' Which, of course, turns things upside down.

A further reason for raising the matter at some length is that my ten years' association with Northcliffe, still to come, had an ulterior motive : to discover whether it was possible to make of the popular Press more a means of developing greater rationalism in politics and less an instrument for exploiting irrationalism. Indeed, much of the analysis which that first book attempted was centred upon the Press. For, obviously, the particular disorders of the public mind with which it dealt were closely related— either as cause or effect, or as both—to the way in which a paper of large circulation by pandering to public passions inflamed them : what the Hearst Press had done in America about the Spanish War, Harmsworth had done in Britain in the case of the Boer War ; and seemed in danger of doing in respect of Germany.

Yet, if any progress at all was to be made against the prevailing disorders of the public mind, that mind had to be reached largely through the Press. How could this be done ? How could sense and rationalism be made as attractive as the Hearsts and Harmsworths seemed to make nonsense and irrationalism ? This was—is—the fundamental 'Problem of the Press.'

In seeking some solution of that problem it did not help very much merely to abuse the Press lords—which the highbrows and intelligentsia did so plentifully. If the 'big' public, as distinct from the small minority, simply would not read the better type of newspaper, it became an impossibility to reach that public through that kind of paper. This was the dilemma. The first step was to understand what it was in the popular papers which caused readers to gobble them up by the million. Unless we understood that, we were not understanding one aspect of the facts upon which society is based—the way men think, the things they find interesting and the things they don't; their scale of values, and how such scales become established in human communities. Without knowing this, we know almost nothing about human society—and were certainly not equipped to deal with its errors and evils. Certain definite questions nagged at me. How far was a newspaper proprietor at the mercy of that Gresham's law of the Press by which an editor who does not exploit sensationalism will lose his circulation to a rival that does ? I once put the question to a Fleet Street editor who was playing up a particularly nauseous fable : 'Do you really believe this tripe ?' and he replied : 'Of course I don't. But it's a good circulation-getter. And if I refuse to handle it, Jones across the street will, and run away with my circulation. I intend to run away with his before he can run away with mine.'

How far was it possible to make the life-and-death things—war and peace, the evils of poverty, the preservation of our freedoms—more interesting to the millions whose pennies made the fortunes of the newspaper lords, than the sort of things the lords purveyed—trivialities, gambling, football, divorce, sex, *et alia*? How far could the desire to know the facts, the truth, prevail over the partisanship of the party sheet or the nauseating triviality of the tabloid?

All this was running very much in my mind when, some months after the closing down of the *Messenger*, I received a wire from Alfred Harmsworth, asking whether I could come and see him in London. I could. What happened afterwards belongs to the next chapter.

CHAPTER V

A DECADE WITH NORTHCLIFFE

THE climate of this second interview with Northcliffe was very different from that of the first when I had attempted to sell him the old *Daily Messenger*. Coming to the point briefly and sharply, he said: 'I would not buy your paper but I'm prepared to buy you. I have decided to produce, or reproduce, the *Daily Mail* in Paris; and I think you are the man who can do it for me. Will you take it on? You will be independent of the London organization and will have a completely free hand from the very start; engaging your own staff with no interference from me or the people at this end at all. You will be head of the whole Continental organization. You can make three major mistakes and I shall not hold it against you. After that we'll see. Will fifty thousand pounds be enough to start on, with a further fifty thousand in reserve if needs be?'

All this was rather breath-taking. I stammered something to the effect that my political views were not his. 'In fact,' I remarked as gently as I could, 'I regard you as the most mischievous man in England.'

'What's that got to do with it? I am not asking you to write the leaders of the *Mail* or become responsible for its politics. I'm asking you to undertake a job of administration by which this paper' (taking up the day's *Mail*) 'will appear every morning in Paris and reach the chief Continental centres a day before the other London papers. As a matter of fact, most of the chief Conservative newspapers in England seem to be run on the business and administration side by extreme Scotch Radicals.'

I still objected: 'My bent is more towards political discussion and the kind of newspaper work connected with it than towards administration.'

'Yes, so several people I've spoken to about you warned me. They say you are a bit of a crank, too literary and viewy to

make a good business man. I don't agree. You quickly get to
understand details and appreciate their importance. You understand people, which is the main thing in administration. If you
want a thing well done you must get other people to do it. You
can't possibly do it yourself in a big business. Choose the right
people and treat them so as to get the most out of them. By the
way, where are you staying? The hotel round the corner here?
A filthy hole. You must come and stay at my house in Berkeley
Square. Always stay there when you are in London. Just telephone my people you're coming.'

(I never did arrange things in that way. Whatever the luxury
or friendliness, I find it difficult to be really at ease in other
people's houses. But I was to be a frequent visitor at Sutton Place,
Northcliffe's big country house near Guildford; and sometimes at
his house near Broadstairs on the North Cliff, whence came his
title. Sutton Place was to be the scene of extremely interesting
week-end parties with J. L. Garvin, Maxse, John Buchan, Philip
Kerr. Seton Thompson, Kennedy Jones, Hamilton Fyfe, on one
occasion Lord Roberts, as fellow guests.)

Well, here was an opportunity to learn at first hand something of the secret which had enabled this man to reach the
mind of the British public more successfully than any other of his
generation. Perhaps that secret could be used on behalf of the
right ideas as well as on behalf of the wrong. The means which
Northcliffe had applied to one end I would, if possible, learn to
adapt to a very different end.

It is altogether unlikely, of course, that I should have refused
Harmsworth's offer even if there had been no ulterior motive
connected with the problem of the public mind and the Press,
which had been so absorbing me. Here was a career, a settled
income, association with people who were interesting, however
much I might detest their politics—interesting in part, perhaps,
because I did detest their politics. But also, very much in the
background of my mind, was that other consideration.

It was no easy job that I had taken on—not made easier by
the fact that Harmsworth insisted at times on my interpreting
quite literally his statement that things would be left to me
entirely. I would write asking him: 'Are you prepared to take
on a twenty-year lease for a printing and editorial building
and spend five thousand pounds altering it?' And he would

reply: 'I thought the arrangement between us was that you should decide these things and take the consequences. If you make a mistake in a decision of that character it will be a very black mark against you. Decide it.'

Such experience as I had had on the mechanical side of the old *Daily Messenger* hardly served me here. The *Messenger* was a four-page paper printed on a flatbed machine straight from the linotype. The *Mail* was an eight-page paper with a prospective circulation that would put flatbed printing out of the question, and would demand the use of a stereotyping plant and rotary machines. And the Chief was in a hurry. (He usually was.) My relations with the *Eclair* came in handy. I was able to arrange for the use of their stereotyping and rotary plant; and to take over the old composing and editorial offices vacated by the *Messenger* a year or so previously (and even find a flat for myself at the top of the building, so as to be on the spot day and night until such time as we had a permanent building of our own). I was able, furthermore, to put my hand on a nucleus composing staff with at its head Gunsberg, the exceedingly able Czech who remained with the paper until the coming of the First World War when his Austrian nationality involved his intern-ment (and, alas, death). Pfister, originally on the *Messenger* as advertising manager, I took over in the same capacity, and a marvellous job he made of it. And so on down the line. One of the biggest difficulties of course was with the French Post Office. It was necessary to install a private wire from London running right into the office for the transmission of all late news; and the delays were maddening. (*The Times* had had a private wire from Paris to London but it was now a question of getting one from London to Paris.) Nevertheless, within little more than a month I had managed to produce the first trial—rehearsal—number. And here Lady Luck stepped in to help in making my position secure with the Chief. He had had vaguely in his mind, I think, the conventional method of starting a daily paper, some-thing like the process he had employed with the London *Mail* at its inception: the business of securing new machines, new build-ings . . . a matter of six months at the least. It so happened that the Chief had come to Paris on some jaunt or other the very evening of our trial run, without knowing that it was taking place, and I knowing nothing of his arrival. After the excitement of that night I did not feel much like sleep, and taking half a dozen copies of the new paper walked along to the business uptown office I had taken in the Place de la Madeleine to have a talk to the people there, and deal with the morning mail. While I was dictating to my secretary—about ten-thirty—in walks the Chief to pass the time of day and ask me to lunch. We talked and I said nothing about our having had a trial run. He asked questions:

'Any new trouble with the Post Office? Shall I try to have the Postmaster-General to dinner so that you can have a talk with him? We could arrange it this week-end if you can get over?'

I did not say anything but bent over and pulled from the bottom drawer of my desk one of the trial copies we had run off the night before, and holding it out, said: 'Would you like to see this morning's *Daily Mail*?' (This was about eleven in the morning and the Chief knew that no London paper could reach Paris until about six that evening.) He did not tumble to it at first —but when he did, and when he realized that the job about which he had been worrying more than I realized perhaps, was (as he thought) in fact accomplished, he burst out: 'This is magnificent, magnificent. You've done a splendid job, splendid,' or words to that effect. At that moment I could have had pretty well anything in his gift.

Alas, I knew that he was misjudging me. I was neither as good a businessman nor as good an administrator as he seemed to suppose. I hated the details of business, though I think I saw the vital importance of details, which the Chief also appreciated and so many intellectuals did not. I realize—too well for peace of mind—that it is no good writing the best of letters on the most important of subjects if your secretary renders it all useless by misdirecting it, or the office-boy by dropping it on the way to the post. I had to preach everlastingly that though the paper could get on for months without me—and later on, frequently did— catastrophes would occur if certain things entrusted to office-boys were left undone. And I funked—and too often evaded—the horrid task of dismissal. I would be ill for days at the prospect of having to get rid of some man whom I probably liked. This indeed I found was common among employers. (When, at a later date, I was to hear Marxists of all tints painting employers as quite indifferent to dismissals, if not indeed as sadistic monsters

I

who took pleasure in the business of sacking, I knew that they just did not know what they were talking about; and it made me a little doubtful of certain of their other conclusions.)

My life-long friend Evelyn Wrench—at that time a member of Harmsworth's team, editor of the *Overseas Mail*, who later founded the Overseas Club, the English Speaking Union, and was to become chief proprietor of the *Spectator*—would occasionally come over to Paris to replace me when I went off on a holiday. In his memoirs he has sketched the kind of thing this job involved. As his sketch is likely to be more detached than mine I reproduce it:

Angell introduced me to the heads of departments and told them that in his absence I was to be treated just as he was. 'He is as nice as he could be,' I wrote home the following week. 'He leaves on Friday for his holiday, and each day he has been putting me more and more in control so that actually his going away will not make much difference. I know you would smile if you could see me surrounded by some of the members of the staff, gesticulating wildly. The staff is very cosmopolitan; French for the most part, twenty to thirty British, two Swiss, a Bohemian, a German, a Swede and an American.' A good kindergarten for a citizen of the world.

The Paris DAILY MAIL was the London DAILY MAIL in miniature. The organization was sufficiently small to enable me to become familiar with all sides of newspaper production: the machine room, the composing room, the art department, the advertising department, the managerial side, the circulation department, the travel bureau, the telephone room to London, the reporters' room, and, of course, the editorial department. . . .

I loved my work, and for eight weeks I usually put in ten hours a day at the office. During my stay I only had one day off. Ours was a seven-day paper, Sunday or week-day made no difference. My only time off was in the evenings and sometimes on Sunday afternoons. I had my report and London work also to keep going, so I brought my secretary over from Carmelite House and I gave her all my correspondence in England dealing with London matters, and I had a French secretary for Paris and Continental DAILY MAIL letters.

The work was extraordinarily varied and my mail bag came

from every part of Europe. I got the *Reisefieber* (travel fever) again. Hitherto, the names of the letter-headings had been associated in my mind with holiday tours, now they became as much part of the daily round as Glasgow, Leeds, Cardiff and Manchester. Our prosperity was intimately bound up with the tourist trade and hotel business. The local Syndicat d'Initiative, Kur Verwaltung, or hotel magnate wrote indignantly about some indiscretion on the part of our editorial staff. Perhaps that morning our news columns would have reported a local tornado or hail-storm, the absence of foreigners, continuous bad weather or an outbreak of spotted fever. Paradis-les-Bains was up in arms. Our advertising manager, an extremely efficient Swiss, M. Pfister, would come into my room with a look of dismay on his face. From M. Pfister's standpoint, '*Messieurs les clients n'ont jamais tort.*' We must support Paradis-les-Bains, where the sun always shone; why should those unimaginative editorial people always be looking for skeletons in the cupboard? Only last week he has received a 10,000 franc contract from the district. We really must be careful not to hurt local susceptibilities. That evening there would be interviews and discussions between the editorial and the advertising departments. The editor was up in arms. What did the advertising department think the paper was? A rag just to boost our advertisers? As far as he was concerned, the whole advertising staff might go to — or Paradis-les-Bains! And thus I was initiated into the eternal conflict which takes place in most newspaper offices between the editorial and business sides.

M. Pfister, whose name was pronounced by the French staff as if it were spelt Pfist-a-i-r-r, with great emphasis on the last syllable, was a glutton for work. He knew every hotelier, casino manager and restaurant proprietor in Europe. With many of them he was on Christian-name terms. He knew their wives and families. If there was any trouble in Monte Carlo or Madrid, he would run down there and smooth things out.

Another evening there would be rumours of trouble in the machine room, as the French or English Trades Union was threatening to come out on strike. There were hurried conferences with the 'Father of the Chapel.' Or perhaps there would be dissatisfaction among the 'readers.' I was always very sorry for the whole class of proof-readers. They were usually well-educated men on whom devolved the thankless task of reading everything, down to the classified advertisements, before it was passed for the press, to detect errors. They spent their lives in a world of roaring printing-presses, glaring arc-lamps and a smell

of printer's ink. I hope there is a law of compensation in the
next world, and that they will pass their days by gurgling streams
meandering through buttercup meadows, with larks singing in
blue skies above their tired heads, as recompense.

Or perhaps there were more intimate internal problems.
Rumours reached me that young Tom Smith was, during office
hours, carrying on with Madame Lebrun, and if her husband got
to know about it there would be trouble : ' You know what these
jealous French husbands are.' I would have to act the part of the
' heavy ' employer. I cautioned him that, if he must play Romeo,
he would be well advised to seek his Juliet outside the office staff.
No personal entanglements in business had always been my motto.
I became much attached to the French staff. They were so human.
They were so much more get-at-able than the English people.
Madame X would tell me her problems. Her son and heir was
making a fool of himself over a woman twice his age. No doubt
the sex problem was just as much to the fore in England, but
somehow it seemed to be more talked about in France.

As *Directeur-général du* DAILY MAIL, many doors were open
to me : and I soon found that the position of journalist carried
more weight than in England.

Much of the task which was mine for ten years would have
only a technical interest for journalists and newspaper managers,
and has no proper place here. There were the usual troubles—a
couple of lightning strikes, a couple of libel cases; and some near
shaves.

One of our minor troubles was that London was continually
wishing on us bright young journalists who, they thought, would
be improved by a course in Paris, but whose French was a little
elementary, producing incidents like that in which a young
reporter, learning that a British industrial magnate or ' captain of
industry' had just arrived in Paris turns in a story about him.
The visitor is described as that eminent ' chevalier d'industrie.'
This to a Frenchman means crook but seemed to the youngster
pretty good French for captain of industry. If this particular
captain of industry had a grudge against the Chief I might have
been in for a bad time. But the thing blew over. The Chief's
interest in aviation, and the prizes which he offered (ten thousand
pounds for the first flight from London to Manchester) brought
me into contact with the early aviators : with Blériot, Paulhan,

Wilbur Wright, Santos-Dumont, and others. I happened to witness the first real aeroplane flight in history.

For weeks Wilbur Wright had been at Le Mans trying out his machine, saying that he 'might' have a trial flight the next day, with the result that newspaper-men and Ministry of War Officials would gather for the show, and then Wilbur would decide that something was wrong and would not go up. The French became very sceptical. The Wright brothers had said very little about what they had done at Kittyhawk at a time when European aviators were timing their flights in seconds and half-seconds. One French newspaper-man put it to me: 'These Americans are bluffing. They tell us next to nothing concerning their alleged flights in America. Do you ask me to believe that an American has actually flown and then said nothing about it? That would be a miracle greater than flight.'

On one particular Saturday afternoon a few score had gathered at Le Mans as usual, since Wright had said he would fly that afternoon (as he had said several times before). The few who had come down to see the flight were quite sceptical. Wright had a French mechanic who apparently had very little English and Wright had learned a few words of French. As he got into the machine he had instructed the mechanic that he would say, 'One, two, three,' and at the word 'three' the weight of the pylon which launched the plane was to be released. The French engineers and newspaper-men gathered round as Wright got into the plane and began to mock and imitate Wright's French, so that, when he said, 'Oon,' a score or two of voices around echoed, 'Oon.' When he said, 'Deurs,' those around said, 'Deurs' in a sort of chant. Wright then said, 'Troise,' and those around, still mocking, said 'Tro——' The mocking suddenly ceased because Wright was in the air. And he stayed in the air more minutes than any human being had ever stayed before in a heavier-than-air flying machine. On his return the sceptical and mocking Frenchmen were of course just as demonstrative in the other sense. 'We,' said one Frenchman, 'are mere children beside this American. He has conquered the air; we only played with it.'

In the winter Northcliffe would often stop on his way to the Riviera and occasionally ask me to go with him. On one occasion we went on a long motor tour exploring northern Italy and staying at all sorts of out-of-the-way places. (I recall the way in which the lame chauffeur, Pine, would let loose a vivid flow of Cockney profanity at French and Italian drivers of wagons, sometimes ox-wagons, when they refused to let him pass.)

I often wondered why Alfred, coming on to the Continent for a holiday on the Riviera, would want to take a business associate with him. One would suppose he would have wanted above all to get away from business and all that reminded him of it on these holidays. But that wasn't his way. He didn't seem to mind having as a holiday companion someone whose association must have reminded him all the time of his work. The truth, of course, was that Alfred did not dissociate business and pleasure. Business in fact was his pleasure. One day he turned casually to Lady Northcliffe and asked, 'What were we dining about that night with the X's?' For Alfred most lunches and dinners were 'about' something or other. (Breakfast he usually had in bed, so as not to 'waste energy' in dressing. After morning coffee and an hour's reading of the papers—his own and his rivals'—he would call in his secretary and dictate instructions.)

Northcliffe frequently turned up unexpectedly in Paris, and sometimes he found it convenient to hold meetings of the Carmelite House (as it then was) G.H.Q. away from London. The commanders, he said, could meet in Paris in an atmosphere of greater detachment and more away from detailed interruptions than was possible in London. Alfred liked me to sit in at these discussions so that I could see the wheels going round, and the Paris office became frequently a meeting-place for Kennedy Jones, Sir George Sutton, Lord Rothermere, Thomas Marlowe (Editor of the London *Daily Mail*), Andrew Caird, Wareham Smith (Advertising Manager of the *Daily Mail*), Arthur Mee, Editor of the *Children's Newspaper, Children's Encyclopædia*, etc., Evelyn Wrench; and sometimes gatherings of the members on the writing side, Hamilton Fyfe, Webley, Ward Price, Charlie Hands, and, when Alfred took over *The Times*, a good many *Times* men as well. I saw a good deal of Moberly Bell who was the *Times'* manager at the time Northcliffe took it over, and something of Sisley Huddleston.

The autobiography of Evelyn Wrench, from which the sketch of daily life in the Paris *Mail* has been taken, contains some illuminating flashes into Northcliffe's strange personal character; flashes which reveal the uglier as well as the better side. My own record, however, is not concerned with Northcliffe as a person but as a force in the life of his generation, a force exercised through his papers, and through his genius for reaching the popular mind.

Of course this capacity of his to know what the public wanted was the source of his power: it explained first of all the immense circulation of his papers, and that explained their immense advertising revenue, which explained his great wealth, which again, was a contributing factor to his power. Sometimes newspaper men have said to me: 'I too understand the taste of the public but I'm not the owner of fifty newspapers. It is his command of capital that does the trick.' But they forget that when he started Alfred Harmsworth had no capital at all—'not a bean' as he said to me once. And they forget that great capitalists— Liberals, notably,—have spent literally millions in trying to establish more 'serious' daily papers than the Harmsworth brand, and have lost their money to no purpose. Their great capital was no avail against the particular genius of Harmsworth for understanding the mind of those for whom he produced his papers.

This does not mean that he was merely a pander. He knew for instance that every man (and woman) was prurient and liked pornography; but he knew also that most of them (in England at least) had their puritan side, and had a certain idealism about the proper relation of the sexes. He never attempted to outdo the more lurid of the Sunday papers; never attempted to produce a paper which depended in any large degree upon pornography; he knew that such an interpretation of human nature would have been altogether too narrow.

From first to last my own main concern was to understand what it was in the Chief's mentality which gave him such success in that field. To understand that, would be to understand the 'million-mind' itself, in so far as such a thing exists. I knew, after the writing of *Patriotism Under Three Flags*, that, if we were to wrestle with the weaknesses which so often make human society so sorry an affair, we should have to acquire something of the knowledge Northcliffe possessed so abundantly.

His lessons on the scale of values were at times surprising. The private wire between the London and the Paris office which made it possible to produce the Paris *Daily Mail* was a very costly affair, and it was my business to keep down the quantity of material transmitted by wire and to cut down things that could be transmitted by train or post. I remember once our London man (Mildred—'Miss Mildred,' as I think Alfred christened him) had sent a story over the wire as to the correct way to blow your nose. I sent a note to Mildred saying that instructions as to how to blow your nose need not be sent over the wire at the cost of a halfpenny a word. Alfred happened to see this letter. When I saw him a few days later in Paris he recalled the matter and said, to my surprise, 'You were quite wrong to pull up Mildred about sending the nose-blowing story over the wire. It is quite important. Don't you know that the three things which are always news are health things, sex things, and money things. Health and sex and money always; and quickly. Some other paper might have picked it up and you would not have been able to use it.'

Alfred once put the reason for his success thus :

'When I came into the field our papers were produced for a public of about half a million—the public of clubs, the small political world. Who was serving the remaining thirty-nine million or so out of the forty? Heretofore it had been assumed that anything was good enough for them. I determined to put as much care and genius in making things plain to the mill-girl (or her employer, often just as ignorant) as a *Times'* leader writer takes in making things plain to the clubman.'

To give the common man—or woman—the mental food suited to his, or her, circumstances, likes, dislikes, preferences was, he often explained, no easy matter.

Although Northcliffe liked to tell the story of the man who, meeting him for the first time, remarked : 'You don't strike me at all as the kind of man who would read the *Daily Mail*.' Alfred *was* that kind of man. Apart from this he took immense pains to see that the type of reader represented by the docker's wife or the mill-girl, or chorus-girl or fashionable lady was treated seriously. Every once in a while he would have his cook prepare dishes—cakes, puddings, what-not—from the recipes published by one of his women's papers, and woe betide the editor if they did not turn out well. He would want to know whether the editor occasionally tried out the recipes in the same way, and if not, why not. One interview with the editor of a girls' paper was reported to me. 'Have you observed,' said the Chief, 'that in your serial now running in ——, the Earl starts his career at twenty-eight and goes to the altar with the mill-girl at twenty-five?' The editor was a bit casual.

'Does it really matter?'

Whereupon the Chief put some questions :

'What were you earning in Fleet Street before you joined our organisation?'

'Four pounds a week.'

'What are you earning now?'

'Twelve hundred a year.'

'Why do you suppose I have multiplied your salary five times over?'

The interviewee was a little confused in replying.

'I pay you this salary,' went on the Chief, 'in order that you should take as much pains and care in the material you turn out for the readers of this girls' paper as the leader-writer of the *Times* does in addressing *his* readers. And your casualness shows you are not carrying out your side of the contract.' Northcliffe thereupon proceeded to flay the victim alive.

Another interview was related to me. Northcliffe had to deal with the editor of a 'comic.' The 'comic' was on Northcliffe's desk as the editor came in. 'Smith, sit down. Why don't you put paunches on those policemen? The public expect comic police-men to be fat. And the persecuted husband must always be thin. That fellow does not look henpecked, he looks as if she fed him too well. Be careful, or we shall get too refined.' The rebuke in such cases might be either with a laugh or with the Napoleonic scowl, so schoolboyishly Napoleonic that (almost) the visitor would laugh.

George Langelaan, who was with me for some years on the Paris *Mail* as my personal secretary, and afterwards became Northcliffe's secretary, and who, like nearly all my secretaries, both men and women, has remained a lifelong friend, has a num-ber of anecdotes to illustrate this schoolboy trait in Northcliffe.

Once, when both of them were staying at the Trianon Palace Hotel at Versailles, Langelaan mentioned that a curious little Chinese puzzle he had, made of six pieces of wood, had been undone and left on the mantelpiece of his room. Northcliffe saw the chance for fun, 'Call the *maître d'hôtel*.' Northcliffe looked sternly at him, 'I take a little wooden ornament with me, a puzzle, wherever I go. Someone of your staff has undone it. Here it is, have it put together again.' The *maître d'hôtel* carried out the undone puzzle on the palm of his hand. From time to time Northcliffe had reports brought to him by the valet as to how things were going. Apparently the puzzle worked its way upwards from the staff to the manager's office, everyone trying to put it together in order not to offend 'milord.' There was even a night session. Next morning Northcliffe sent for the *maître d'hôtel* again. What about the puzzle? The *maître d'hôtel* looked very red and worried and tired. He conveyed the management's regrets, and would Milord allow the management to replace the puzzle, which no one had been able to put together. 'Where do you come from?' asked Northcliffe. 'From the Schwarzwald.' 'Well, I guess a hundred pounds might help you start opening your own small café.' This was when that sum represented real money. 'Sit down there, and if you can put the puzzle together you get the hundred pounds. I give you half an hour while I get ready to go out.' The *maître d'hôtel* worked away at the puzzle, hindered more than ever by excitement. Northcliffe came into the room again when time was up. 'Well?' Then the German's temper came out. He banged the puzzle pieces down on the table. 'I could not do it if I tried for six months!' and rushed from the room. 'That will give them a lesson not to meddle,' said Northcliffe.

Langelaan relates that once, when driving from Sutton Place to Carmelite House, Northcliffe saw a bargee woman tramping beside a barge horse. She was wearing a strange bonnet. 'Look, Langelaan, that's the same bonnet you see in Leach's illustrations to Dickens's works.' He knocked on the front of the car and got the faithful Pine (described in his will as 'my chauffeur and friend') to stop. 'Get out and ask her where she got her bonnet.' 'In a minute,' relates Langelaan, 'I was running beside a surprised barge-woman with one eye on her horse and the other suspiciously on me, who wanted to know where to buy a bonnet. She gave an address in Hoxton. When I climbed back into the car, Northcliffe immediately dictated a letter to one of his editors, and next day a bright paragraph appeared on barge-women's bonnets, an unchanged fashion since the days of Dickens.'

Northcliffe was on the whole generous to his staff; and if he felt that a sacking was called for, he generally made an attempt to find another place for the victim. His reputation for ruthlessness in this regard was probably worse than his actual conduct. He took sudden and impulsive likings for people, and just as violent prejudices at times against others. He had also at times a very rough side to his tongue, but though I was with him for ten years and gave him, I should think, plenty of occasions to show what he could do in that regard, he never once showed brutality of any kind.

I once asked him why. It was on an occasion when, in my presence, he had given an Alsatian we were employing a dose of Billingsgate and tongue-lashing of which I had never heard the equal. When the victim had departed I asked the Chief why he never talked to *me* in that way. 'Because,' he replied, 'that is not the way to handle you. You are sensitive and thin-skinned. If I were to talk to you like that, you would walk out on me; and I have work for you to do. That lout we've just dismissed has a skin as thick as a rhino; and the only way to get something into his head is with a coke-hammer.' The Chief was not right. That was *not* the way to handle the Alsatian either, as afterwards I learned. But it was the Chief's mood that day to lash out, and having relieved his feelings on someone else he could talk sense to me. He once spoke to me about these fits of irritation and regretted them very much. 'A man as powerful as I am ought not to let his temper get away with him.'

But that was when he had the Napoleonic mood. He was subject to unconscious, or half-conscious, poses, almost bordering on the make-believe. One day during a long motor drive, more or less to keep talk going, I summarized what I had so often suggested: 'It must rejoice you that you have found your true *métier*—to give the big public the reading matter you know it wants.'

'That's not my *métier* at all,' he replied. 'My real job is statesmanship, and one day I'm going to prove it.' After a fashion, of course, he did. He got rid of one Prime Minister and put in another. But the total record does not add up to statesmanship.

It is worth while looking at that record, for Northcliffe stood as an immensely powerful force in the shaping of the mores and values of his time.

The England of the eighteen-eighties, into which he came as a journalist of sixteen, was the England of William Morris, Darwin, Huxley, Tyndall, Newman, Carlyle, Herbert Spencer, Bradlaugh, Gladstone, Dilke, Parnell and all that they stood for in social and moral and intellectual ferment; it was the England of Fabianism, Positivism, Æstheticism, the beginnings of political Labour and Feminism, of a definite Republicanism, of the struggles around Irish Home Rule. Men were beginning to find out the industrial revolution; to discover that steam and electricity had not really liberated England, but rather had filled it with slums and a new and perhaps worse oppression and poverty, and were looking for salvation to new social and moral ideas. A few young men were dreaming dreams of the new world that they would cause to be born.

To all this young Alfred, who was one day to play so big a rôle in the politics of his generation, seems to have been completely indifferent. There is not a trace of his having been even distantly interested, or that any of these causes, or the special journalism associated with them—which would have been a heady wine to another type—had the slightest attraction for him. Yet journalism —which means necessarily dealing with public affairs—was to be the passion of his life and the source of his wealth and power.

We get the key to Northcliffe's incredible success, to the real character of his influence and the nature of the problem which the Northcliffe influence in British politics represents, in the fact that the journalist who was to have more weight in politics than any journalist his country had known laid out his campaign for the capture of the nation's mind by disregarding political ideas and movements altogether, and by turning to the journalism which concerned itself with sport, the bicycle, photography, amusement, boys' interests. Not only was this the type of news-paper work in which he mainly engaged as a free lance in the years from sixteen to twenty-three, but the same method of approach is reflected when he came in his later years to establish papers of his own. For him 'public affairs' were not politics and affairs of State, but, for the women especially, the fashions, 'Society,' what people were wearing; for the men, sport, the 'human element' in the police cases, personalia in politics. Study of the inattentions and the trivialities of the human mind became with Northcliffe a profound science.

The millions bought his papers because of their way of reporting a boxing match, of distributing pictures to reading matter in a certain proportion and in a certain way, presenting the fashions as they had not been presented before in the daily Press. And having obtained power by exploiting that order of motive in the public, he used the power for purposes to which the motive had no relation. It was because of such things as his sports or his fashion page that Northcliffe became an enormous force in deciding the issues of Free Trade and Protection, peace and war.

That is the paradox of the Northcliffe power. To make a man ruler of the Queen's Navee because he polished up the handles of the big front door so carefulee, is consistency itself compared to the reasons which at times made Northcliffe the arbiter of peace and war; now and again the most powerful man in Europe. As this is true in large degree of the Northcliffes and Beaverbrooks in Britain, it is true of the Pattersons, Hearsts, McCormicks in America.

I have known the editor of a popular daily admonish one of his contributors in this wise:

'NO PROBLEMS! Nearly all facts are interesting—until they constitute a problem. Do not puzzle or worry your reader with things he finds difficult to understand.' In other words, facts in any form save that which might lead the reader to think about them, to reflect how one fact affects another, and the resultant combination affects life. That, presumably, sets up a process in the mind of the reader which he finds either tiring or disturbing.

I am dealing here, of course, with the popular Press as it existed in the first decade of the century. Of recent years the 'serious' type of newspaper has usually a much larger circulation than it had at the time of which I write; it occupies relatively perhaps a more important place. But the rules which Northcliffe laid down would still seem to dominate the popular papers of the middle century. (That is the view of the Royal Commission which reported in 1949—of which further mention will be made presently.) In a recent account of the success of the *Cleveland*

(U.S.A.) *Press*, the editor points out that the newspaper of to-day has to be more 'dynamic' (sensational?) than ever, since it has to 'compete with radio, the news magazines, television, automobiles and a thousand other things for people's time and attention.' The editor goes on : 'The *Press* is not all I want it to be, but at least it's a paper you pick up on the front porch wondering what the hell it's up to now. . . . Most national and world news is still written in abstract terms of issues, not people, and I have no patience with abstractions.' 'The *Press*,' adds the account, 'is no place for a reader to keep up with the world outside Ohio.' Yet Ohio, to the point of life and death of its industrial and very bombable cities, may have to be concerned with what goes on outside Ohio. And what applies to Cleveland applied of course with greater force to a Chicago dominated by a Bertie McCormick's *Tribune*.

It is noteworthy that one of the characteristics most commonly observed by those who came in contact with Lord Northcliffe was his dislike of an argument, of the discussion of an abstract idea. Quick, alert, with a wide knowledge of curious facts, extremely sensitive to what people were feeling, he had not the patience to follow even the simplest discussion of an issue like Free Trade and Protection, Feminism, a currency problem. Concerning these 'theories and abstractions,' as he would have called them, he admitted he had no fixed principles or ideas. And the conduct of his papers about those things revealed it.

I recall that at a luncheon one day at the Webbs', at which Wells was present (it was a sort of reconciliation feast after Wells's ill-natured lampooning of the Webbs in one of his novels), we all discussed why it was so extremely difficult and expensive to make a success of a 'serious' paper like the *Manchester Guardian*, which dealt with the important things, and was animated by social theories of one kind or another; and what could be done to build up a Press which should not be trivial, sensational, tendentious, and mendacious. Reasons of detail for the difficulties of the 'serious' paper were given. But I insisted that the real cause lay in the mentality of the men who started and directed the serious paper. They did not possess that 'common mind to an uncommon degree' which A. G. Gardiner attributed to Northcliffe, and which enabled Northcliffe to reach the common man and become what Gardiner described as 'the most powerful single individual in England.' The serious Liberals had a scale of values—giving importance to ideas, to certain social theories. It was not the scale of the million-a-day public which sought primarily entertainment, entertainment usually in sensationalism and trivialities; and to have its prejudices confirmed and animosities encouraged. Unless something of this scale of values was innate in an editor or director who desired to be read by millions, he would be certain to fail.

Yet Northcliffe himself could on occasion see how unbalanced was the presentation of the day's news in the popular Press. At a luncheon given to him in New York (reported in the *New York Times* of 6 November 1908) he remarked that 'the world, as seen through the newspaper, is a rather strange place. When I come here, as I am happy to say that I do very often, I read the pages of cablegrams, and especially Sunday cablegrams, from London, and I see that England is chiefly peopled by suffragettes, impecunious aristocrats, and four or five amazing society ladies, "Fashionable Beauties," whose names and antics are recorded, and whose photographs, taken over twenty-five years ago, do steady service very regularly. I wonder if it ever occurred to the gentlemen who send these Sunday cables that there must be some other people over there to conduct the gigantic export trade of Great Britain, to manage her cotton mills, to maintain her mercantile fleet carrying seven-tenths of the world's goods, her shipping-yards, and a navy that has been heard of at times?' But at home in London, 'I see what an amazing fellow Uncle Sam is. Apparently nature here is engaged in nothing but tornadoes. Financiers are always in panics; the politicians are all engaged in grafting from each other; there is only one law; and that the unwritten one. But when I come here all the Americans I meet are of an extremely normal type, and I find a steady growth and prosperity unexampled in my personal observation.'

It was on this occasion that the chairman received a characteristic telegram from Mark Twain:

I am sorry indeed that I cannot be at the Pilgrims' dinner to Lord Northcliffe, whom I hold in high esteem and friendly regard. I ask him to forget for a moment that he is a legislator and join me in a health to the sacred memory of that great Englishman who on this day 303 years ago tried to blow up a Parliament which was meditating a limitation of copyright, but was defeated by the mistaken interference of a Providence more interested in spectacular mercy than in plain, square justice.

I think Northcliffe was helped in the understanding of the multitude by a schoolboy element in his character. I suppose ninety per cent of the male public remain largely boys their lives through—witness again their immense interest in sport. For most of them an election is just a glorified football match. Which side is going to win? And as to war, before 1914 vast numbers quite nakedly welcomed it as immense fun, a glorious adventurous episode in their dull lives.

He realized the need for everlasting repetition in order to get a single fact home to the public, summarizing his principle with this aphorism : ' Most people have never heard of Pears' Soap ' —Pears' Soap being at that time the most advertised thing in England. I recall also that when we were discussing, I think it was in Paris, one of the stunts that the *Daily Mail* was running (it happened to be Standard Bread, the stone-ground grey bread that some people considered the secret of health), Andrew Caird, or someone present, remarked, ' You know, Chief, I think our people are deadly sick of this Standard Bread stunt. We have been running the damned thing for nearly two months now.' Alfred flushed a little in irritation and, asking for a secretary, dictated a message for Sutton : ' I want an article in every issue of every one of my papers about Standard Bread for one year.' And then turning to Caird (or whoever it was), said : ' At the end of the year, Caird, somebody may have heard something about Standard Bread.'

In later years, engaged in a propaganda slightly different from that for Standard Bread, I was to find the same difficulty in getting my colleagues in that campaign to believe that this everlasting repetition of a point is in fact necessary.

In view of the foregoing it will be understood why I found it difficult to get Northcliffe to generalize, because though he was guided by certain principles he was not always conscious of them. He had no sense of talking down to the public but assumed, for the most part rightly, that what would interest him would interest them (which of course confirmed Gardiner's aphorism that he had 'the common mind to an uncommon degree'). Nor could he for a long time understand why I should regard him as on the whole a mischievous force in public affairs. (I never made the slightest attempt to disguise that opinion.)

If he had had to summarize his position I think he would have put it (it was implicit in much of his talk) in some such way as this :

'I did not make this public mind that you talk about. It was there when I came into Fleet Street. I have understood it better than my competitors, that's all. You, as a democrat, believing in popular wisdom [I did not; he was here merely repeating a common confusion about 'popular wisdom'] ought to rejoice that I have given these millions what they like and what they approve. If your view about politics can be put in such a way that they will interest my readers and not put them off, rest assured that my columns are open to you.'

This was before the appearance of my book, *The Great Illusion*, which had some measure of success in appealing to the public mind. As soon as I had demonstrated that a large public could be interested in the aspect of politics with which that book dealt, he was as good as his word and the editorial page of the *Mail* did become at a later stage in our relations fully open to me, though the ideas expressed and the politics defended were often in flat contradiction to the paper's editorial line. Those who so readily condemn Northcliffe and his methods might make a comparison beween, say, the *Herald* or *Reynolds* of to-day and the *Mail* of yesterday. Would either of those Labour papers print repeatedly long articles giving the Conservative point of view, strongly critical of the paper's? Yet the *Mail* did an equivalent thing in my day when it would print sometimes two-column articles on its editorial page in general condemnation of its nationalism, militarism, and xenophobia. Furthermore, I sounded Northcliffe as to whether he would print articles from members of the Labour Party, as for instance, from Ramsay MacDonald; and I am pretty sure he would have done it if MacDonald had been ready to co-operate—of which a word presently.

In the years that followed my first contact with Northcliffe I was to write a great deal about 'the problem of the Press,' in-

K

cluding a book entitled *The Press and the Organization of Society*, first published in 1922 and republished in 1933.[1] I was also to be concerned with an experiment in the co-operative ownership of the *Daily Herald* by the Trade Unions, the story of which is told later in these pages. They also deal with some conclusions of the Royal Commission of 1949 on the Press—conclusions which, on the whole, are confirmatory of those drawn in my 1922 book.

Northcliffe's most notable contact with the public life of his country occurred after I had ceased to see much of him (though he discussed it with me when he was High Commissioner in America). I cannot end this sketch without a word or two concerning it.

The details of the Asquith-George-Northcliffe episode of 1916 are still matters of controversy, but the broad outlines are plain enough. In 1915 Northcliffe—whose sincere conviction that he was pursuing a policy essential to the success of British arms need not be doubted for a moment—began a campaign of violent criticism of the British Cabinet as it then existed. All were included—Balfour and Grey were attacked as bitterly as Asquith and Haldane—except one : Mr. Lloyd George. Partisans of Asquith represent Lloyd George as having gone behind the backs of his colleagues to come to a bargain with this outside critic : 'Support me against the others and I will support your policies.'

Well, there is more than one way of describing such a situation. What we know is what happened : That Asquith and Grey went, that their going was largely the result of the fierce campaign Northcliffe waged against them; that Lloyd George, whose claims were warmly supported by the Northcliffe Press, came into power as Prime Minister, that he and Northcliffe became extremely intimate, and that Northcliffe came to occupy various offices—among them Director of Enemy Propaganda (of all things), and head of the British War Mission in America. Titles were distributed among Northcliffe's newspaper staff like pies at a picnic—knighthoods to correspondents, baronetcies to business managers, Orders of the British Empire to head clerks.

Such was the relation between the two up to the Armistice.

[1] By Heffers, Cambridge.

And then Northcliffe made it plain that just as he had decreed who should govern—and consequently what policy should be followed—during the war, so he intended to dominate the conditions of peace. Already he had made himself virtual arbiter of what policies the nation should be allowed even to consider. When Lord Lansdowne and others presumed to suggest for the nation's consideration the policy of an earlier and negotiated peace, he had decided that the British people—or as many of them as his papers reached—should not be allowed to know that responsible people were making such a suggestion.

The first tussle with Mr. Lloyd George came at the 1918 election. Northcliffe had demanded among other things that the Germans should be made to pay 'the whole cost of the war.' Now Lloyd George knew perfectly well, as his memorandum showed, that the Germans could not be made to pay the whole cost of the war, and that it would be disastrous to try to make them. It was evident that in going to the people for a 'mandate' in 1918, he wanted to be free of any such undertaking. The Northcliffe Press was immediately on his trail and there began one of the campaigns that it knew how to organize. Day after day the Northcliffe papers shouted a slogan: HE HAS NOT SAID IT. The public began to demand that he 'say it.' Well, at the end Lloyd George was obliged to say it. And the saying of it bedevilled his subsequent policy and was one of the factors in bringing about that economic and political chaos in Central Europe which helped to produce the Second World War.

Once the election was over a subtle change in the attitude of the public set in. It had had its fill of crises and politics and sensations and national disasters. After five years of war strain it wanted to amuse itself . . . and Northcliffe discovered that in this new mood of the public his rampagings against Lloyd George fell flat. If the Prime Minister would indulge in an occasional diatribe against the Germans the public were content to leave him alone. Mr. Lloyd George soon realized this and said in effect to Lord Northcliffe, 'Do your damnedest!' (Had he taken that line earlier in respect of the Reparations problem, the total results for Europe would have been better.) There came an occasion when, in a speech in the House of Commons, Lloyd George declared that his erstwhile colleague and confederate 'had no more judgment or reliability than a grasshopper.' And the House roared its approval. He had defied his Jove and no thunderbolts fell. Nothing happened. For the time being George was master of the situation and Northcliffe found that he was now powerless. And when Lord Northcliffe left on his much-heralded world tour, some of his newspaper colleagues were unkind enough to suggest that it was to nurse his discomfiture at having been worsted in this duel with the politician who owed his accession to high office in no small part to the journalist.

In other circumstances, when the public is not in a state of emotional fatigue, but ready to react once more to the stimulus of mass suggestion, power might once more rest with the newspaper proprietor.

But never again was this particular newspaper king to exercise such power as he did during the First World War. Always cursed with a certain instability of health—which some of his friends thought hypochondriacal—on the eve of sixty Northcliffe's condition became extremely disturbing. His own insistent suggestion, in the pride of his youth, that a man is never at his best after forty, had its effect perhaps on his own self-confidence at sixty.

And defects of temper and disposition, the patience and self-control which the management of an unstable health demand, had not perhaps been improved by thirty years of autocracy; by never having cultivated the discipline which comes of being obliged to consider any view opposed to his own.

There will not perhaps be another Northcliffe in England just because there are certain to be many minor Northcliffes. And it is better so.

What moral judgment shall we pass on him, if judgment we must pass at all?

Let us keep two things clear. To give the public what it wants may be at times—not always of course by any means, but at times—extremely bad for it. When it happens to have acquired certain prejudices that may create a good deal of havoc in the world, it does the world an ill-service to feed that prejudice, persuade its victims that it is a virtue. Yet so to be deceived is precisely what the public likes; to undeceive it is something it will resent. But the belief (which happens to be that of the present writer) that to pander to public weaknesses is in some circumstances a very mischievous occupation, is in no way inconsistent with the belief that immense industry, great genius, singleness of purpose, can all be devoted to that mischievous end. Nor is it inconsistent with the belief that knowledge of what the public wants can be used to better ends.

To the end of worsening at certain crises the character of the English mind, making it more trivial, less balanced, sometimes more cruel and vindictive, Lord Northcliffe contributed as no man before him. One may detest (as I do) the task which on occasions he accomplished, and admire (as I do) the real genius he brought to it.

One need not too much blame the man. He was the embodiment of certain social forces. Little given to introspection, Northcliffe doubtless followed such garish light as he happened to see.

If blame there be, it is with the public.

Part II

THE LIFE JOB

CHAPTER I

WATCHING THE FATAL DRIFT

THE work of starting the Paris *Mail* had entirely absorbed me during the years 1904-5 and most of 1906. One practical problem followed upon another too quickly for me to give much attention to the international scene. By the end of 1906, however, I had a little time to look around—and the Anglo-German situation seemed suddenly to take on a frightening form. It revealed a monstrous growth of precisely the kind of irrationalism with which I had dealt in *Patriotism Under Three Flags* and described in the last chapter but one.

One felt in one's bones that things were blowing up for war, and my increasing contact with people around Northcliffe did nothing to lessen the feeling. Northcliffe indeed was looked upon by the Liberals of that day as the head and centre of the prevailing emotionalism. But being close to the Carmelite House crowd, I knew that the trouble went very much deeper than the sensation-mongering of a group of papers, mischievous as that was.

It may sound harsh, coming from one then regarded so generally as a pacifist, but the thing which disturbed me most was not merely the prospect of war itself. Nations had until then recovered with surprising rapidity from the devastations of war, and Europe might recover from the one which threatened if only intelligence were applied. But there was the rub. An almost child-ishly melodramatic view of the situation stood in the way of any detached consideration of the real problem. This was so to use the power of the British Empire as to accord to France and Russia security against Germany, and Germany security against the other two; and to win ultimately the support of the United States to that policy. The issue was not conceived in these terms at all. The popular theory was to the effect that Germany, from motives of pure greed and malice, was concocting a plot to invade England, turn it into a German province, enslave its

135

people, take its trade and carry off its women. A number of books and numberless articles were written on that theme; there was a play about it, *An Englishman's Home.* This invasion out of the blue, by Germany, was to take place at a moment when she was confronted with the prospect of a two-front war by Russia and France, and when consequently every consideration of military—and every other—interest would prompt Germany to keep Britain out of it, neutral; at least until Russia and France had been disposed of. True, the Germans might have been as blind as the British, and probably were; and German policy dangerously aggressive. But in that case the obviously wise course for us in Britain was to raise persistently and without ceasing the underlying issues as Germans saw them, including the issue of Russia's potential power, and show that we were prepared to discuss those issues rationally. The general public never got within a thousand miles of that kind of discussion during the first few years of the century. We had instead long disquisitions on the evil nature of the 'German race' (Tacitus being much quoted in that context), when clearly no such thing as the German 'race' existed; and when, if ethnic factors went for anything, we should have done better to recall the fact that nearly every homely word we use—man and God, flesh and blood, mother and father, son and daughter—began as a German word, and that to the older Germanies we owed much of our religious Reformation, to say nothing of our Royal House. We made much of the 'innate dislike' existing between the two peoples as though it was sound policy to go to war like two dogs that fought because they did not like each other's smell. Specific differences, like those arising out of the Moroccan dispute, the Baghdad Railroad, had been settled. There was no definable demand which we were asking and Germany was refusing; or which she was asking and we were refusing. There was the naval rivalry. But that, like most else, was a symptom of the mutual fears. Germany's fear of Russia we simply ignored and insisted that the whole situation arose out of Germany's wickedness. That, and that alone, made war 'inevitable.'

Of course, the foregoing refers, not to the few writers who here and there did in some measure raise the basic questions, but to the great mass of the public to which the Northcliffe Press appealed and out of which it lived.

Northcliffe, with his genius for catching the mood of the moment, saw no reason to check the impulsive and rising pugnacity of the public. He had indeed little consciousness that his own papers had contributed to it. 'But it is what the public *feel*,' he would urge, 'and surely a paper must reflect public feeling?'

True, later on, he was to open his columns very freely to my own views; (my articles often running to two full columns on the leader page) but this was after I had proved by a best-seller that the public could be made interested in a rational analysis of the situation, could be given, and come to like to be given, some notion of what this coming war would be about; what the issues were. But the relatively few articles I could do were a drop in the bucket of countervailing views.

Of course it is easy to be wise after the event. It is also wise, as I happened to have remarked in another context. One can see now with a clarity not permitted to any of us perhaps—at least not to this writer—before 1914 what our fears really were. Yet in retrospect it seems pretty simple : If Germany conquered France and Russia she would have such preponderance of power over us that we should be unable to defend even our most elementary rights. In any dispute with her we should just have to accept her verdict, the verdict, that is, of the rival litigant. This was a position which no free people should be asked to accept. So far so good. What solution did we propose? That Germany should accept that position by being rendered so powerless that she would have to accept the verdict not merely of Britain, but of France, who had been our enemy as well as hers for centuries; and of Russia just emerging from semi- or less than semi-barbarism.

It was a Balance of Power war. And Balance of Power had a bad smell with nearly all Liberals—including this one, although later on he came to see that power politics were the politics of not being overpowered. The evil of that policy lay not in the power but in the fact that power was premised as the instrument of rival litigants instead of being pooled in order to become the support and guarantee of Law, at first, doubtless, a very rudimentary law, the basis of which we had to find, to agree upon.

But this is to get ahead of our story. The first job was, if possible, to get the public started on a discussion of the more tangible issues in a mood of rationalism. What was the coming war about? What was our final purpose? How would victory ensure it? If only the conversation could become thus rational in temper, even over one or two points, something like understanding of the general situation might be achieved.

I tried to discuss the thing in realist terms with Northcliffe, and with the people he would sometimes gather for week-ends at Sutton Place, or at long luncheons at the Savoy. This gave me fairly full opportunity of judging the prevailing state of mind on the Conservative side of politics and journalism. From these meetings I carried away one outstanding, unforgettable impression. Here were a group of men—editors, 'publicists,' journalists, commentators on public affairs, publishers, budding politicians and diplomats, parliamentarians, soldiers, who all their adult lives had made some study of foreign policy. They were writing about it constantly, were in the habit of discussing it with the foreign ministers of Europe, with the great political figures of their time. I was the most obscure among them all, present, perhaps, only because I held an outpost of the Northcliffe Empire in Paris and Northcliffe seemed to feel that I had a point of view which it would do his staff and his friends good to hear. I was quickly to find that these men, many of whom had great influence in politics and journalism, and public life generally, all accepted as truths so self-evident as not to be worth discussion certain 'axiomatic premises' which were, I soon became convinced, either dangerous half-truths or complete and utter fallacies. The half-truths formed the basis of their underlying philosophy, which was in the main crudely fatalistic. Man could do nothing to prevent war because war was part of his nature; he was not merely swayed by subconscious or unconscious forces within himself, which is true, but the completely helpless puppet of those forces, which is not true. The fallacy led to strange conclusions: human nature being unruly, undisciplined, prompting men to act on the first thought, rather than the second, *therefore* it was foolish to strive for discipline, to urge reason; to try to bring the first thought as far as possible under the control of the second.

It is important to note the underlying determinist or fatalist philosophy of the time because it explains so much of the failure to face objective fact, or to believe that anything effective could be done about it. In our generation of A-bombs and H-bombs, this fatalism, expressed in the view that you must accept war as inevitable because you cannot change human nature, is less fashionable. We realise now that we may not be able to change human nature; but we realise also that unless we can change human behaviour we are without any sort of doubt due either for simple extinction, or for life under ruthless dictatorship. And it would be a world dictatorship if nations can never be reasonable.

This philosophical aspect of the matter was a bit too elusive and abstract for useful discussion at those Sutton Place week-ends and the Savoy luncheons, so I would try to bring the question of the Anglo-German conflict down to some concrete issue between us: What were the Germans asking that we could not give? Since a war against Britain would also mean war with Russia and France, involving that nightmare of German strategists, two fronts, it was not something that Germany would undertake with a light heart. What were the motives which made her willing to take those enormous risks?

Maxse of the *National Review* happened to be included in one of the Sutton Place week-end parties. Taking me up, he said at last something like this:

'Germany will fight because she must expand. Every year an extra million babies are crying out for more room. . . . She needs the wheat of Canada, the wool of Australia, wherewith to feed and clothe her people. This is not mere envious greed. It is stern and vital necessity for her. But these resources belong to us, are needed for our posterity, and we, as their trustees, must hold them. It is an ultimate struggle for bread. It may not be a Sunday School view of the situation, but it is the true view.' [1]

Whereupon another of the company present quoted Jackie Fisher (Admiral Lord Fisher) who a little earlier, commenting on the German Navy Law of 1908, had said: 'That we have eventually to fight Germany is just as sure as anything can be, solely because she cannot expand commercially without it.'

The company at dinner immediately welcomed Maxse's contribution to the discussion as a realistic, rational and completely adequate explanation of German policy. Northcliffe himself supplemented Maxse's statement: 'Germany intends to secure a

[1] Something to this effect later appeared in a *National Review* article.

war indemnity of something in the region of two thousand million sterling, which would give such capital equipment as to make her industrially the master of the world.'

I remember thinking : 'These people, whose policy so far has been a matter of intuition, impulse, now feel that they can explain it rationally. They can give whys and wherefores, not merely assert : and it has exhilarated them enormously.'

Yet here was obvious nonsense being asserted as obvious truth. If the war was for Germany a struggle for bread, wherewith to feed increasing population, what was to happen after she had lost the war and we had won it ? After the war German women would still continue to have children. Were we going to use our victory to deny them means of life ? Could we ? The problem would remain as insistent as ever ; and war, though we won it, would not solve it. In fact, however, Germans were at the very moment of these discussions buying the food of the British Dominions on the same terms as the British. Germany did not need to conquer Australia in order to get its wool any more than we needed to conquer the Southern States of America in order to get their cotton. As to our paying a 'vast indemnity,' we could do it only by still further expanding our foreign trade, and re-taining our industrial power which would be a curious way for Germany to expand her trade, the markets of German factories. Conversely, if we won and exacted a great German indemnity, it would mean the expansion of German foreign trade, the growth of German industrial power, which means potential military power, making of a Germany with an expanding population (nearly twice that of France) situated in the heart of Europe a tough customer to ' hold down,' however many Dreadnoughts Jackie Fisher might persuade the country to build for him.

But all attempts to put the discussion on this basis were un-availing, brushed aside by such aphorisms as 'Nations are not guided by logic-chopping.' The argument seemed to be that, faced with the responsibility of our country's future, the welfare of its people, its defence against alien domination, we were justified in throwing aside all foresight and insight, the facing of hard fact and of truth, because 'men are by nature un-reasonable,' that is to say, congenitally incapable of understanding fact and truth.

If I had foretold that Britain would be completely victorious in two great wars in the course of a quarter of a century; and that following these two stupendous victories she would be bank-rupt, dependent upon the economic assistance of the United States; the actual food of her people so limited that the 'roast beef of Old England' became reduced to an ounce or two per week for each person; that her Empire would be in process of dis-solution; even her fleets placed under the command of American admirals, her position as a world power quite secondary to that of the United States,—if anything like what has actually happened had been forecast, it would have been regarded as just lunatic raving. Yet somehow the feeling arose in me that we were on the edge of a catastrophe of that order. I do not wish to suggest for a moment that the vague fears which followed that talk at dinner prompted a clear and precise vision of what was actually to follow in the next twenty-five years. Indeed the picture I drew fell far short of the appalling subsequent event. But the fears I felt were deep and real and *The Great Illusion* was born of them. The thing which frightened me then—as it frightens me now —was the ease with which men can be made blind to objective fact, a gulf or brick wall to which they may be driving their society. This fact-blindness was not confined to the Northcliffe circle of Conservatives. One found it also at that time in some degree (and in only slightly different form) in radical and Socialist circles—especially in Germany—and was to find it in still greater degree in the post-war period. The Socialists managed to express what was essentially the Maxse theme in the double talk of the Marxian philosophy expounded sometimes in huge volumes of erudite verbiage. 'This hideous war of 1914–18,' wrote Bernard Shaw in *The Intelligent Woman's Guide to Socialism and Capitalism*, 'was at bottom a fight between the Capitalists of England, France and Italy on the one side and those of Germany on the other for command of the African markets.' While a Shavian disciple (H. V. Rutherford, M.A., M.B., Cantab., in *War or Peace?*) tells us that 'Capitalism stands Sphinx-like with-out a wrinkle of humanity or morality on its ugly face as the motive power behind the other causes of war . . . no capitalism, no more war. The problem of all problems resolves itself there-fore into a change from Capitalism to Socialism.'

To-day most of the Left has abandoned this position. But for a whole generation it was accepted as unquestionably true by most radical intellectuals both East and West.

My feeling, then, in the first decade of the century, was that if the economic fallacies, whether Rightist or Leftist, could be clarified, the exposure might lead to a more rational approach to the subject as a whole.

But how reach the public at all? As to newspapers, I was painfully aware of the dilemma as Northcliffe had stated it: a newspaper proprietor or editor cannot move ahead of the mood and temper of the public. If he does not reflect existing standards or prejudices, competitors will, and steal his circulation, and in the end the more rational will be put out of business by the less rational (illustrating that social Gresham's Law to which reference has already been made). This seemed to put the popular writer in a cleft stick: if he runs counter to prevailing prejudices, tastes, standards of what is important and interesting, he loses his readers. If he panders to those standards he helps bring about the very condition of which he becomes the victim.

Of course the alternatives are not necessarily as rigid as all that. An editor might underestimate the capacity of the public to take a little common sense in its daily newspaper diet. There could be no absolutes in these matters: here, as elsewhere, 'the essence of truth is degree.' And what might apply to newspapers might not apply equally to books, pamphleteering. Would it be possible to do with a book, say, what a newspaper editor might not feel justified in trying to do with his shareholders' property?

So, despite the complete failure from a publishing point of view of *Patriotism Under Three Flags*, I decided to have another trial with a book.

CHAPTER II

THE STORY OF A PAMPHLET

I CALL this the story of a pamphlet because, although it concerns a book of considerable length, the book started as a short monograph dealing with a particular political crisis of its time : the drift of the Western world to war. The pamphlet gradually developed, by a series of enlarged editions, into a discussion of the whole problem of war, its economic, political and psychological causes.

In one sense it is a typical literary success story—that of a book rejected at first somewhat contemptuously by the publishers to whom it was submitted, and then becoming a best seller. They rejected it mainly on the ground that it discussed a subject, 'peace,' which, then at least, bored and irritated the public, so that a book dealing with it was for that reason deemed unsaleable. This verdict prompted the author to publish an abbreviated version of his manuscript as a pamphlet, at his own expense. For a time it was completely neglected by the professional reviewers to whom it was sent, a fact which seemed to confirm the opinion of the publishers. Yet this book, rejected at first alike by publisher and reviewer, was ultimately—and in a relatively short time—translated into more than twenty languages and went through many editions, with sales running into millions. It provoked world-wide discussion of problems still before us ; led to the beginnings of a ' movement ' which spread rapidly throughout several countries : and prompted the establishment of institutions and foundations designed to bring the theme of the book before the public.

If success is to be measured by such things, the book was an unusual success.

But if success is to be measured by the degree to which it achieved its underlying purpose of so modifying current political thought as to check the drift to war—then it must be accounted a failure. Two World Wars followed its publication, the second at least due to the general disregard of the truths it tried to express. It is that failure to have any visible influence on the course of events, more perhaps than the pamphlet's success as a publishing venture, which has lessons for this generation. For if the peoples of the world ignore, or fail to understand, the causes which produced the two wars of our generation, they will almost certainly drift into a third. To disregard experience is to risk repeating it.

It is true that the failures here described were no greater than those of the Western statesmen and diplomats in two wars. They saw the wars coming and—presumably—did their best to stave them off, but could not. Wilson, with all his immense authority as the head of the most powerful state in the world at that time, a personal power, that is, greater than that of any other man living, was utterly defeated, broken by his own people in his attempt to initiate a foreign policy which would have contributed to the prevention of the Second World War. Churchill, in the years between the two World Wars, was quite unable to make his influence or his oratory effective in persuading his country to follow a policy which might have prevented the coming of what he himself has called The Unnecessary War. Franklin Roosevelt, with all the authority of the United States behind him, failed to make that authority a means of checking a Stalinist-Russian expansion which may still plunge the world into a third war. Furthermore, the efforts of the statesmen were in the years between the wars aided by great private, but worldwide organizations of propaganda like the League of Nations Union in Britain, the Carnegie Foundation and similar organizations in the United States. All these efforts, private and governmental alike, failed. The Second War came; the third threatens and has already in the form of the cold war involved diversion of mountainous resources all over the world from the needs of peace to warlike preparations.

Churchill is right in his insistence that the Second War need not have come. Its coming was due to the time lag of ideas; a time lag common to all nations but most strikingly shown by America. If (to cite again an example already given) American public opinion had been ready to adopt in 1920 the degree of internationalism it did adopt in 1945 (and in still more decisive form in 1950), the Second War, it is safe to say, would not have occurred. This is true even if we regard the new policy as having failed : for the 1920 situation was less difficult. In 1950 the principle of giving economic and military aid to help Western Europe defend itself is accepted on the whole by the American public. Wilson in 1920 could not secure a promise to defend France if again attacked by Germany, and instead of Marshall Aid, America passed Johnson and Neutrality Acts ; Britain had the years of appeasement, her own form of neutrality and isolationism.

Obviously public education in the essentials of peace failed. Why? The facts related in this chapter and the next may help in finding a partial answer to that question.

What advocacy and persuasion in the matter of international policy, even when carried on during all the interwar years by a score of distinguished writers and a hundred organizations, could not do, the actual coming of the Second World War, and the obvious jeopardy in which the West has been placed seem now at last to be bringing about.

The phenomenon is often invoked as an argument against any discussion of the war problem : 'Men are so made that they will be convinced only by experience, facts, events ; mere argument leaves them unmoved. What's the good of talking?' With all its air of 'realism' and 'facing the facts of human nature,' such a conclusion does not face the facts of human nature at all. For it is part of human nature to discuss human problems, to have theories concerning them. The morning paper demonstrates that much. The question is not whether we shall discuss public policy—we do it in any case endlessly, noisily, raucously, passionately. The question is whether we are to carry on the discussion with some regard to evidence, some sense of responsibility to truth and sound judgment ; or with disregard of those things in favour of indulgence in atavistic emotion.

There have been hours, of course, this last forty years when this present writer has been attracted by the foolish cynicism 'What's the good?'; when he has been inclined to echo what Clemenceau is supposed to have said upon his death-bed : '*Les imbéciles ont raison.*' More than once the feeling came upon me during the writing of *The Great Illusion* that I myself was an imbecile to suppose that the flood of human imbecility could ever

L

be stemmed by efforts of reason. But when I stopped writing the book I made the discovery that it was more uncomfortable to stand aside, inert and inactive, while monstrous follies were being proclaimed, than to obey the impulse to say something, do something.

So I kept on writing. The manuscript finished, I submitted it to one publisher after another. All of those whom I approached shied violently. In one or two cases, I would, when in London, call on the publisher who had received the manuscript and discuss it with him. The interview would run something like this:

Publisher: 'This is a book about peace, is it not?'

N.A.: 'In a way, yes.'

Publisher: 'I understand you are a journalist, Manager of the *Mail* in Paris?'

N.A. 'Yes.'

Publisher: 'Then you, of all people, ought to know that the public do not and cannot be persuaded to read books about "peace."'

N.A.: 'But this is about peace with a difference.'

Publisher: 'What difference?'

N.A.: 'Well, for one thing I do not oppose the maintenance of our armament, particularly the naval armament, and I don't think mere arms reduction the road to peace.'

Publisher: 'Then what is the book about? What is its purpose?'

N.A.: 'It is to prepare the way for an understanding with Germany: to try to find out what motives are pushing her to aggression, what she wants, what she is driving at; to clear our minds as to what we want and are driving at and see if the two cannot be reconciled. At present both sides are moved by ideas of irreconcilable conflicts of interest which make even discussion useless if not impossible.'

Publisher: 'But what we want is just to be left alone, not to be attacked. You cannot argue very much about that with Germany: and the only argument that will be effective is to be so strong that she won't attack us.'

N.A.: 'But that is precisely what the Germans say—they believe that Russia will one day attack them, or Austria: that France, being allied with Russia will enter, and we shall support

France; and that to prevent this they must greatly increase their strength.'

Publisher : 'Well, of course, I cannot enter into all that, but it strikes me, if you will allow me to say so, as highly speculative, theoretical, unpractical—and dangerous. This war is coming and we must face it and be prepared, and the only effect—if any— of books like the one you propose is to weaken our will to be prepared and to face facts. There always have been wars : always will be. They are inherent in human nature ; and you cannot change human nature. I'm sorry, but we cannot publish this kind of book, especially not just now. Perhaps one of the Quaker publishers might do it.'

This from the more tolerant of the publishing world. One or two more intimate friends, especially those in Carmelite House with whom I discussed the book, were even blunter : 'Avoid that stuff or you will be classed with cranks and faddists, with devotees of Higher Thought who go about in sandals and long beards, live on nuts.'

It may be a little difficult for those of this generation to get the full flavour of that advice and to realise how well founded— in one sense—it was. An advocate of peace did indeed run that risk, and publishers, alas, shared largely the prevailing temper.

The end of it was that I decided to try no more publishers and to have the book—in an abbreviated form—printed at my own expense and publish it through Simpkin Marshall, the book distributors. I kept the statement of the case down to twenty-eight thousand words, called it *Europe's Optical Illusion*, signing it 'Norman Angell' (my baptismal name being Ralph Norman Angell Lane as already explained) in order to keep this bit of pamphleteering distinct from my work as managing director of the Paris *Mail* and subsidiary publications.

The book was sent to about a hundred papers for review, and I waited. I waited a long time. Beyond the formal two- or three-line notices of its appearance, for many weeks not one single notice concerning it appeared.

This was worse than the fate of *Three Flags*. So that was that.

After this interlude of what Northcliffe would have called

'butterfly-chasing,' I tried to prepare my mind henceforth to concentrate purely on the *Mail* work, to throw in my lot with the Northcliffe organization, make biggish money, buy a bigger and better sailing boat, and have as jolly a time as possible until Europe blew itself to pieces.

As a last gesture, however, I sent copies to between two and three hundred selected public men, concerned with politics, in Britain, France, and Germany. (As the book was obviously going to be all 'remainders,' I might as well scatter it pretty freely and widely.) At first, nothing happened. But after about three months a few things did begin to happen. Lunching with some newspaper colleagues—foreign correspondents for the most part —one of them remarked casually to another (neither knowing anything of my concern in the matter) 'Have you seen a book called *Europe's Optical Illusion*? At a diplomatic dinner the other night several people talked about it and said it was bound to be something very important. I've never heard of it.' Neither, apparently, had the reviewers. So I wrote a line to Massingham, (whom I knew slightly) then editing the *Nation*, begging him to glance at the book, which I suggested he would agree was either great nonsense or very important. If he thought it nonsense, say so; if important, say so.

The result was a two-page review of the book, done, I believe, by H. N. Brailsford. This I sent to a score or so of journalists. In a few months reviews came in scores and hundreds, not only from Britain, the United States, and France; but Germany also. Within eighteen months of the first appearance of the book it had been translated into French, German, Italian, Spanish, Dutch, Norwegian, Danish, Swedish, Russian, Polish, Finnish, Roumanian, Bulgarian, Czech, Arabic, Turkish, Japanese, some Indian languages, and published in those tongues.

One account tells the story in these terms:

Early in 1909 there fluttered quietly into the book world a small pamphlet of about 100 pages. It was published by an obscure publishing house, it bore a name which was practically unknown, it dealt with one of the most hackneyed subjects in the world, it appeared at the thickest of the book season, and was immediately followed by a General Election. Anyone knowing anything of the conditions of the sale of books would have said that this little pamphlet had not five minutes to live, and that there was no miracle which could save it from being still-born. Well, in three months it was being printed by tens of thousands, its subject-matter was flooding the English and American Press in columns, Cabinet Ministers referred to the author, the German Ambassador in London made it the text of a diplomatic announcement, and the King was presenting copies of it to his Ministers. . . . The reason? Simply . . . that the author, Mr. Angell, in a hundred and odd pages, had riddled the accepted axioms of modern statecraft. This was a large thing to do, by an unknown man, in 100 pages; none the less, it was done. Mr. Angell has compelled, on the part of all honest thinkers, a new mode of thinking on the whole question of war.[1]

The book was to go through many editions, one as late as 1933. It appeared in abbreviated form in the Penguin series in 1938, nearly thirty years after its first appearance, and sold about a quarter of a million copies in that series.

In his *History of the Reign of King George the Fifth* D. C. Somervell notes that 'the man in the street had been much impressed by Norman Angell's *The Great Illusion* . . . the most widely read and persuasive of all the handbooks on pacifism. Even King Edward VII read it, and he seldom read anything that was neither official nor amusing.' This historian adds, however, 'Seldom was a book more discussed and less understood,' and he goes on to refer to a strange misrepresentation of a nature I shall indicate presently, and which constitutes I think the strangest—and perhaps the most illuminating—part of the story.

I have suggested above that in drawing any lesson from this experience one should distinguish sharply between the publishing success and the political failure. If *The Great Illusion* had not reached the public at all, had been without any considerable sale, that is, its story would have little interest for those concerned to reach the mind of the public with reasoned argument. It could be dismissed on the simple ground that its message, good or bad, never had a chance to be heard, and would furnish no basis for judging how far its method was sound. But the book provoked discussion all over Europe and America. H. N. Brailsford wrote that he doubted 'whether any man since the days of Paine and Cobbett had written a pamphlet comparable in force and inspiration to theirs, until Angell riveted the attention of a con-

---

[1] Tighe Hopkins, *Daily Chronicle*, 11 Feb. 1910.

tinent on his *Great Illusion* . . . compelling it to listen to an unanswerable calculation. . . . One held one's breath while he did it.' Yet its argument failed to influence policies to any visible extent. It failed, moreover, in another sense : the case it tried to present not only came to be distorted in the public discussion; some of its basic ideas were turned completely upside down, and it was interpreted as advocating policies which were the exact contrary of what it did advocate. This indicates some fundamental defect of presentation in a book that was highly, at times extravagantly, praised for its clarity and lucidity.

As already related, I was drawn into this work because convinced, convinced to the point of chronic sleeplessness, that we—Britain, Europe, perhaps a large part of the world—were headed for war, and that we could avoid that outcome only by negotiations which could not succeed unless we took stock afresh of the ideas which accounted for the drift. In that mood and with that motive the book was written. With this result : that perhaps seventy or eighty per cent of those who have heard about the book (but have not read it) believe it to have been an essay attempting to show that war had become 'impossible,' that the bankers would stop it, or that the money would run out. Of the references to it which I still receive I suppose half describe the book in those terms. Typical of the references to it still appearing is that which occurs in a review of a work on foreign investment in the November, 1950, issue of a serious monthly publication. [1] 'In the year 1908,' begins the reviewer, 'there appeared in England a book which was read extensively, not only in English-speaking countries but all over the civilized world. The name of the book was *The Great Illusion* and . . . the widely accepted thesis of this book was that the outbreak of any major war was impossible in those days because of the complex and interrelated situation in international finance, industry and commerce which made its participants in all civilized nations realize the futility and disastrous consequences of war. This theory, widely accepted, was utterly annihilated by the outbreak of the First World War.' The reviewer goes on to discuss—and dismiss—'Norman Angell's exploded theory.'

Among a mass of other cuttings my eye catches this one—a letter to the *Newcastle Journal* of 12 February, 1947 :

[1] *Cresset*, Minneapolis.

Sir Norman Angell, the author of *The Great Illusion*, so much discussed, welcomed so gladly, sold so well, proving beyond all possible doubt whatever before 1914 that the bankers would never permit war to come because it would be so expensive, such a waste of wealth, should now write another ' *Great Illusion*.' This should, of course, be dedicated to all the electors who voted for a Labour Government!

In forty years literally thousands of such references have reached me via clipping agencies, British and foreign, or through other channels. Another recent one consists of a report of a warning to his students by an American university president against 'the attractive fallacies of Norman Angell who believed that there could be no more war.'

Consider the letter quoted above. A newspaper reader, writing nearly forty years after the appearance of the book under discussion and registering the impression of his time concerning its message, is witness to the fact that the message has been completely reversed; that the net result of forty years of wide sale and much debate has been to re-enforce the very opinion which it was the purpose of the book to destroy. Here, surely, is a strange outcome with some sort of moral.

For the simple fact is that there is nothing whatever in the book—not one word—about war having become 'impossible'; or that the money would run out; nor about war coming to an end because the bankers would stop it. No one who had read the book could possibly believe that that was its meaning. Among the hundreds of reviews of the book at the time not one suggests this nonsense. Indeed the internal evidence of the case should have destroyed the legend from the first. If the author really believed war to be impossible why should he have disturbed himself—abandoned the career in which he was having considerable material success and engaged in an ungrateful and thankless agitation—to prevent something which he believed could never happen? Yet, though no reviewer so far as I know has ever written that the book said it; though no one who read the book could believe the author said it, that legend is the most indestructible of all the impressions left by the book among those who really matter, that is to say, the anonymous masses who accept or reject policies, who make and unmake governments; and who seldom read books.

Once started, the legend proved indestructible. Several years before the first war I find myself writing in the *Daily Mail* (e.g., 15 Sept. 1911) to the effect that, far from regarding war as 'impossible,' I felt it to be in the then prevailing ignorance of certain facts extremely likely. Typical of the kind of protest I was constantly making was a letter to the (London) *Saturday Review* (8 March 1913):

> You are good enough to say that I am 'one of the very few advocates of peace at any price who is not altogether an ass.' And yet you also state that I have been on a mission 'to persuade the German people that war in the twentieth century is impossible.' If I had ever tried to teach anybody such sorry rubbish I should be altogether an unmitigated ass. I have never, of course, nor, so far as I am aware, has anyone ever said that war was impossible. Personally, not only do I regard war as possible, but extremely likely.

I suppose from first to last I have made some hundreds of such denials—with no visible effect whatever.

It would be easy, of course, for an author who has seen 'the truth he uttered twisted to make a trap for fools' to ascribe it all to the stupidity of the indifferent masses who just wanted to save themselves the trouble of readjusting themselves to a change of idea and so resorted to 'protective misrepresentation.' (If we can satisfy ourselves that the new idea is ridiculous we need not worry to consider it.) All that may be true. But to present certain political truths in such a way as to break through the confusions of the mass mind was precisely the job I had undertaken. That hurdle should have been cleared from the start. It was not. What explains the failure?

If that question is to be answered, if this experience is to throw any light on the way in which modification of political ideas may be brought about (which is our major problem to-day) then the story must not be limited to the failures. The successes, too, can teach us something.

Side by side with the growth of this myth among the non-book-reading public, there was very great interest shown by those who did occasionally read books. That interest gave rise to the 'movement' described in the next chapter, and, as soon as the results of the war began to be manifest, to a wide recognition of the fact that the book was being vindicated by events.

In 1920 the *Daily News* (Feb. 25), taking stock of the post-war situation, notes that 'after five and a half years in the wilderness, Mr. Norman Angell has come back. . . . His book provoked one of the great controversies of this generation. To-day, whether he likes it or not, he is a prophet whose prophecies have come true. . . . It is hardly possible to open a current newspaper without the eye lighting on some fresh vindication of the once despised and rejected doctrine of Norman Angellism.' A. G. Gardiner, who had edited the *Daily News,* wrote : 'It is more than a book. It is part of the vast episode through which this generation has lived, and all that has happened since it first appeared has served to confirm its thesis and to make it one of the great documents of history.'

It was in that year (1920) that I wrote *The Fruits of Victory* : *A Sequel to 'The Great Illusion.'* On its appearance Keynes wrote me that he thought it '*extremely good* and have read it with the greatest satisfaction and agreement. I am so glad that after a long period of pamphleteering you've taken up your pen again to do something of really permanent importance. What incompetent devils reviewers are ! Those I have seen do the most grossly inadequate justice to "The Fruits." But I expect the public will be more discriminating. I've really nothing to criticize in the book, but I want to tell you how immensely I like it,' and he goes on to indicate passages which appealed to him more particularly. Some years later, when I began to wage war on the appeasement policies of the British Government, he wrote, in the *Nation,* in similar warm terms supporting my position. Before the war (when I first met him at Cambridge) I think he had, like more orthodox economists, been sceptical of my forecast in *The Great Illusion* that on the morrow of a general European war it would prove in practice quite impossible for the victor to collect an indemnity commensurate with the war's costs. But the two decades following the war were to see a great change in the general attitude of economists towards my general position. Thus Professor Lionel Robbins (Professor of Economics in the University of London) writing some years later in his book *Economic Planning and International Order,* notes that 'my various works, though not primarily addressed to professional economists, mark an epoch in the discussion of these problems,' and he mentions *This Have and Have Not Business* as ' an admirable statement of his fundamental position.'

In circles less academic, but closer perhaps to the workaday world of finance and politics, acknowledgement went even further and sometimes came earlier. Speaking at the Sorbonne a few months before the outbreak of the first war—on 27 March 1914, to be precise—Lord Esher, the Chairman of the Committee on Imperial Defence, told his French audience that he had had 'an opportunity of listening to very confidential enquiries into, and discussions of, the economic effects upon our trade, commerce and finance on the outbreak of a European war in which we ourselves might be engaged. This enquiry extended over many months, and many of the wealthiest and most influential men of business from the cities of the United Kingdom were called to give evidence before those whose duty it was to conclude and report.' He added :

> I am sure that very few, if any, of those eminent witnesses had read his book, but by some mysterious process the virus of Norman Angell was working in their minds, for one after the other, these magnates of commerce and of finance, corroborated by their fears and anticipations the doctrine of *The Great Illusion.*

One may say then that the book did have some success in modifying the ideas of what is normally the very small minority that interests itself in the more fundamental political questions, perhaps increased somewhat the size of that minority. But the main unpolitical mass, with little interest in, or capacity to deal with, fundamental political questions, still remained overwhelmingly subject to the confusions, fallacies, illusions which the book discussed. The difference between the two groups is not one of 'education' in the ordinary sense, for the 'educated' are often socially and politically as uncomprehending as the 'uneducated,' sometimes more so, as the 'educated' Germans under Hitler and the erudite Marxists who established the Russian State (and their counterparts in the Communist parties of the West) so abundantly indicate.

Glancing through reports of lectures, recalling the replies I have given to questions at those lectures, re-reading letters from critics, or the protests which I have at times made to people like the University President who spoke to his students of the 'Angell fallacy that there could be no more war,' I have been struck by the extent to which the debate as a whole bears on the one overwhelming problem now facing us in this mid-twentieth century—the rallying of sufficient good judgment about international relations to make the potential power of the Western World an instrument of peace instead of war. For that reason, and also because it indicates the kind of discussion which has been the main occupation of my life, I have thrown many of the points of the discussion together to make a composite picture. Here it is:

ANGELL: I want to know what led you to suppose that any man—outside a lunatic asylum—who had taken stock for ten minutes of the living world about him, would put down in black and white that 'war was impossible'; or that, if he thought this, he would go about trying to prevent something which he believed could not happen.

CRITIC: But look here. I understand your thesis to have been that war did not pay; that victory itself would be economically ruinous. If no enemy could gain any advantage by victory, would indeed be all but ruined by it, why should he engage in so profitless an enterprise? Surely your conclusion must have been that he would not attack and that the days of war were ended.

ANGELL: That was not at all my conclusion, as I have so emphatically, repetitively insisted in almost everything I have written. Is it your experience that men are only guided by valid judgments? Facts determine human conduct only when men see them as facts.

CRITIC: So you believed that if you could persuade men that war did not pay, they would cease to go to war? You must assign to the economic motive a much larger place than I do.

ANGELL: On the contrary, I assign a small place to economic motive as such. But while I do not believe that men make war for 'profit,' in the stockbroker sense, I am quite convinced that men cannot make peace unless the economic illusions I discussed are dispelled. An economic issue which involves the means of life for millions ceases to be an economic problem and becomes a profoundly moral one, one of national right. The almost universal view in the first decade of the century was that a country in Germany's position had to 'expand' in order to secure the means of life for her own people. You could no more get agreement between two parties holding such convictions than between two cannibals one of whom should say to the other, 'It is evident that I must eat you or you must eat me. Let's come to a friendly agreement about it.' So long as they hold that opinion they won't come to a friendly agreement. They will fight. I tried to make it my business in that first decade of the century to show the two contestants that their fight was unnecessary and irrelevant : that there was plenty of food for both if only one would stand on the shoulders of the other to get the fat coconuts out of reach of either acting alone. Until this truth had been brought home all attempts at peace-making would fail. They did fail. The underlying assumptions so affected international relations as to make rational discussion of the issues impossible. All this, by the way, is quotation from my books.

CRITIC : A pretty parable, but not relevant to our situation.

ANGELL : You were drawn into a conflict which arose out of the failure of other nations to live together peacefully because of the confusions, particularly the economic confusions, I made an attempt to unravel.

CRITIC : But it is not relevant to-day.

ANGELL : Circumspice. At this moment, in the year 1951, the whole of the western world is, we all agree, in mortal jeopardy of the loss of its hardly-won freedom, because the other half of the world has fallen for a grave economic fallacy which it has converted into a new religion. Its devotees are dying in Korea and elsewhere with all the fanatic heroism of the soldiers of Mohammed engaged in a Holy War. This peril, the prospect of the horrors that Koestler and Orwell have painted for us, is the direct outcome of the appeal of an economic fallacy.

CRITIC : Russia's position is due to the second war, which came because the European allies made a bad peace. Versailles made worse the anomaly that Britain, with a population of fifty million, owned something like a quarter of the earth, while Germany, with eighty millions, was left without so much as a single colony. Don't you think that the resources of the world should be more equitably divided?

ANGELL : It seems to me that for someone who began by repudiating the idea that economics entered into the causes of war, you are attributing a good deal to economics. But they are the economics of Alice in Wonderland. I don't agree with the Lindbergh interpretation, that the war came because Britain owned too much of the earth and Germany too little, because the very words he uses are meaningless. Britain does not 'own' her empire at all, did not even when the British Raj remained in India.

CRITIC: Are you seriously suggesting that, when a nation annexes territory, it does not by that fact add to its wealth? You might as well suggest that when my rich aunt dies and leaves me her Long Island estate I shall not be better off.

ANGELL: When a nation annexes a province—as when Germany annexed Alsace and when France annexed it back—there is a change of government, which may be good, bad or indifferent. But there is no transfer of property from one group of owners to another: the houses, gardens, fields, furniture remain in the same hands after annexation as before. The Lindbergh thesis reveals a crude confusion between 'owning' and 'governing.' Britain governed India, but did not own it.

CRITIC: But surely out of her government of India, with its four hundred million population, there were enormous advantages for the traders, the investors, the financiers?

ANGELL: Well, just consider certain quite verifiable facts. During the whole of the nineteenth century British trade and investment in the Americas, North and South, which she did not 'own' in your sense, were very much greater than in India, which she did 'own.' When Britain 'lost' the American colonies in the eighteenth century, her trade and investments in them did not cease but became much greater.

CRITIC: In sum, you think the Empire has been a dead loss, an evil burden? Well, the remedy is easy. Get rid of what remains of it.

ANGELL: Empire is not necessarily and always an evil burden. It is one of the tragic confusions which bedevil this subject that Liberals and Progressives seem to have been so hypnotized by the picture of the Empire as an instrument of capitalist oppression and exploitation, which, speaking with any accuracy, it was not, that we have failed to grasp the reason of Empire and the kind of alternative we should attempt to find for it. Empire in the nineteenth century was often a means of ensuring a necessary international government over large areas where such government did not exist. Government of India by Great Britain was not necessary to British trade, as was proved by the fact that for a hundred and fifty years before the conquest of the country British trade flourished, and the old East India Company repeatedly instructed its servants to avoid political involvement. The British Government took over only when disorder, chaos, became rampant and it looked as though the Balance of Power would be upset if France were to fill the vacuum, seize the resources of India and make them an element in the world struggle then going on. If Britain had been defeated in India she would probably have been defeated in Canada and in the Ohio valley; a French Empire would have extended from the St. Lawrence to the Mississippi, and the United States as we now know it could not have existed. It is true that in the eighteenth-century scramble for power, trade and monopoly privilege played its part. But when that struggle ended in the expulsion of France and Spain from territory which is now the United States, and gave us as result the emergence of a single nation of a hundred and fifty million people as distinct from a number of separate independencies on the pattern of Latin America, it meant a great deal more for Western civilization than the mere enrichment of a number of capitalists. And in any case, the eighteenth-century type of Empire was not that of the British Commonwealth of the nineteenth century. If such a Commonwealth had not existed in 1940, after the fall of France, if there had been no British Gibraltar, no Malta, no troops in Egypt to meet Rommel; no defence of the Suez Canal, then Hitler would have won the Second World War. The British Empire had defects as great in their way as the defects of the Roman Empire. But when this latter went to pieces it was not followed by something better, but by the Dark Ages. It is quite possible for something similar to follow the break-up of the British Empire unless we have the wisdom to create an alternative instrument of order and government which will do the job better.

And so the debate went on about that pamphlet—for forty years. I found I had to fight on several fronts. At first against the more reactionary of the nationalistic Conservatives who refused to see any problem except the wickedness of Germans.

'The cause of war is Germans,' wrote Lord Cromer. But I was quickly to find that even more mischievous in the long run to the creation of a peaceable world were those who insisted that the cause of war is Capitalism, and that the sole remedy lies in world Socialism. A third front was that of the Pacifists—those who believed that armaments and power were in themselves the cause of war, and that government without power would bring us peace.

The Conservative attitude was deeply fatalistic. Indeed, for most of that generation war was like the weather and the earthquake: it came or it did not, quite irrespective of the wills of men. It was in vain that one argued that though men did not make the weather, they did make war.

The more sophisticated, like the Bellocs, Chestertons, Yeats-Browns, fortified this attitude by insistence that I was in fact preaching Pacifism in the modern sense of non-resistance. They refused to differentiate between internationalism and non-resister Pacifism of the Quaker kind. Belloc insisted that the issue was that presented in his couplet:

> Pale Ebenezer thought it wrong to fight,
> But Roaring Bill (who killed him) thought it right.

Whatever else that couplet may have been, it was no reply to any argument of mine, which, throughout, has been that we shall be in danger from the roaring Bills until we organize collectively to restrain them; restrain them mainly by standing for the defence of their victims. From the very first I accepted the fact that society—and this included the society of nations—must defend its members from violence; that they cannot defend themselves individually; and that the only effective defence is collective defence.

It is perhaps impossible to bring home to one age or generation the intellectual and moral odour and feel of a previous one. At the turn of the century, it was not merely the implication of crankery which made it difficult for any man to state a case for the avoidance of war. There was an implication of a want of manliness, virility, in such an attitude. You were necessarily a physical coward. And indeed the disciples of Hilaire Belloc, G. K. Chesterton, and men of that school assumed that the theme of *The Great Illusion* was a plea for running away from duty and honour because it paid so to do.

Nearly all of this now has, of course, disappeared. We no longer take the view of Theodore Roosevelt that men will degenerate if the habit of war ceases. We realize that war is in itself no more to be desired than such pestilences as cholera, the plague, leprosy, which will often bring out nobility and courage in those who fight those evils. And although the public mind may be as confused as ever about the method of cure, it has at least accepted the view that cure is to be sought. For the alternative now is vast collective suicide. This is a new fact, and one the public can at last understand.

During the three years following the first publication of *The Great Illusion* I still lived in Paris. As the foreign editions appeared the debate extended to many foreign countries and I personally was brought into it in three of them—the United States, France and Germany—in the shape mainly of lectures in the universities of those countries. In Britain it meant much newspaper discussion, a good many articles for the *Daily Mail* itself. There was heavy work, of course, in connection with the foreign editions—decision as to which publisher in which country would prove most suitable; the checking of translations, and many other details of that character. In passing, it is interesting to note that I carried on a free and unhampered correspondence with a Moscow publisher concerning Russian and Polish editions; and much correspondence with Jacques Novikov about the translation of his books into English. All this, of course, was under the Czarist tyranny.

As can be well imagined, it was not easy to give a whole mind to the management of the *Mail* while the very different work above described was going on. I would appear at meetings in England which meant often night journeys from London after a lecture at, say, the Institute of Bankers, to keep next morning an appointment in my Paris office with an important advertiser or wholesale newsagent or to meet the compositors in order to deal with a threatened strike.

By 1912 I had ceased to draw any salary from the *Mail* and

had made arrangements for giving up my position on the paper. Northcliffe was extremely decent about the whole thing. Only once, I think (when I had gone off to the United States on what I wrote him was 'a week-end visit') did he mildly protest that, 'After all, you know, you *are* supposed to be running the Paris *Mail*.'

Although I was not conscious at the time of allowing the work on the *Mail* to suffer, I must have had subconsciously a troubled conscience about it and perhaps was affected by the strain. For long afterwards—twenty years or so—I went through a period of bad nightmares, the theme of which was laborious and unsuccessful efforts to reach the *Mail* office in order to clear up some trouble that had arisen there. These nightmares, repeated at intervals during a year, set me wondering. Were they a roundabout way of expressing a feeling unavowed to myself that I had been a romantic fool to suppose that one man could do anything effective to stem the flood of war-making forces? Quite a number of people, some of them extremely realistic and worldly wise, had said in public that this book would in fact have the effect of stemming those forces. For my own part, I was too busy in the day-to-day tasks that came up to know whether I believed it or not. Certainly I believed there was a chance, or I should not have given up the management of the *Mail*, which had not merely material attractions—Northcliffe had made the job an extremely comfortable one for me—but had the immense psychological advantage of being a task at which one could show results; at which one could be demonstrably successful.

Were those curious nightmares some evidence of an unconscious, unavowed conviction that, given the course taken by events despite all the agitation in which I helped, I should have stuck to the newspaper business and its advantages, and never have attempted to challenge public folly?

In any case, in 1912 I decided definitely that agitation for preventing the war then looming could not be combined with management of the *Mail*. I gave up my directorship (though I believe I was nominally a director till 1914), gave up my Paris flat and moved to London.

The debate had become a 'movement' with which the next chapter deals.

M

CHAPTER III

A MOVEMENT TO HALT THE DRIFT

As the close of the last chapter indicates, it was a bit of a wrench to make a clean cut with the journalistic and business activities which had been my life in Paris for more than fifteen years. In that time I had known most of the English and American correspondents then stationed in Paris and had come to know a good many of the figures in French literature and politics. Happily the shift to London did not mean any break in friendship with Northcliffe, as part of the story which follows will show. One link with the Paris life remained. When I announced to the middle-aged peasant woman who had been my housekeeper for some years that I was giving up my flat in Paris to live in London, she rather took me aback by remarking, '*Très bien, Monsieur. Quand est-ce que nous partons?*' I went on to explain that in order to do housekeeping in London, she would have to know English, and she didn't. Oh, that was nothing. She would soon learn English. She would go to—what do they call it?—l'école Berlitz. My assurances that she would be lonely and unhappy in a foreign city went for nothing. So this peasant woman of fifty actually did toddle off every afternoon to the Berlitz school and did, with peasant obstinacy, learn sufficient English to get by and do shopping in what she called Rue Fetter Lane, when I shifted my household gear to 4 Kings Bench Walk, in the Temple.

It was in these chambers that I was to live for thirty years. The house of which my flat constituted the top floor—with Harold Nicolson underneath—survived the blitz, but only just; what my housekeeper called an 'ascendiary' bomb finding its way into the kitchen and being extinguished by a friend of Nicolson's, since I was away that night.

The move did not come suddenly. For a year or more I had been discussing it with Esher and Harold Wright, Joseph and Arnold Rowntree, J. A. Hobson and one or two others whom I had come to know. Probably I should have made this move in any case, but it was the insistence of Esher and the steps he took in creating the Garton Foundation which decided me to make the break when I did.

Esher seems to have been one of those to whom I had sent a copy of *Europe's Optical Illusion* when it looked as though that book was to be all remainders, so might as well be given away somewhat haphazardly. In any case, before any notices by reviewers had appeared, he wrote me through the publishers, saying in effect that he did not know who I was ('I have not been fortunate enough to read other work of yours'), but that the book could be as significant as Mahan's *Sea Power*—something indeed in politics comparable to *The Origin of Species* in biology. In short, the terms were most extravagant (and as noted in a previous chapter were embodied later on in a lecture which Esher gave at the Sorbonne). He would be delighted if we could meet. I replied from Paris that my work lay there and described what it was. The upshot of the correspondence was that we did, after a month or two, meet in London. By that time reviews had appeared, the ideas were beginning to be generally discussed—and Esher was more interested than ever.

When I first met him, I did not quite appreciate what his rôle was in English political life and had hesitations. I knew that one of his main interests was military. He was chairman, at the time, of the Committee of Imperial Defence and I distrusted the military mind when it came to political and social questions. What I did not then realize was that he was more than merely a confidant of the King; that he had made it his business to understand the mind and qualities of the party leaders, financiers, writers, journalists, of his generation; and, standing outside their party differences, to set up contacts between them, and between them and the King. The failure on my part fully to realize how all this, coupled with his very genuine intellectual interest in the ideas I had expressed, might have made him an incomparable instrument in promoting my purpose, was at a later stage to lead me into a major error.

It was, I think, over a luncheon at the Savoy, that we first discussed some organisation which he would help to create. It was indispensable, he insisted, that I give up my work in Paris and come to London. I objected that I had opportunities in Paris, liked Northcliffe, and had certain obligations to him. 'You don't understand the significance of your own work and what it might accomplish,' Esher said. 'I sent your book to all sorts of people with whom I come into contact, including Edward Grey and Arthur Balfour, and have spoken to them about it. They agree that you have thrown new light on this subject and have suggested a new approach to a terribly difficult problem. It might do much to prevent a catastrophe. In view of that, how can you possibly bury yourself in Paris making more money for Northcliffe? There are fifty people who can manage the Paris *Daily Mail*. At present there is only one who can explain and expand the message of *The Great Illusion* as you can. Here is what I suggest.' And then Esher outlined his plan. He would persuade one of his wealthy friends to provide funds for the establishment of a 'Foundation' to promote discussion of my ideas. Esher's son Maurice, who was an able, hard-working fellow, might be secretary.

Very shortly after this talk Esher notified me that Sir Richard Garton, a wealthy industrialist friend of his, was prepared to provide a considerable sum to finance an organisation of the kind we had discussed; and that Arthur Balfour was ready to be one of the trustees. Would I come and talk things over? The four of us met and thus was born the Garton Foundation, in the form of a non-profit-earning company, the Articles of Association of which state that 'The objects for which the Company is established are: To promote and develop the science of International Polity and economics as indicated in the published writings of Mr. Norman Angell.' Maurice Brett became secretary, John Hilton, who in later years became a Cambridge don, and still later a famous broadcaster, was Brett's assistant. I had general direction of the Foundation's activities. I had no salary, but the Foundation paid my secretarial and office costs.

Thus, within three years of the publication of *The Great Illusion*, and while yet occupied with the day-to-day work of the Paris *Mail*, the ideas I had put forward had already grown into a 'movement,' generously and unexpectedly supported. I knew that time was short, but if things continued to move at this pace, it might still be possible to bring about a change in public opinion which might stave off that coming war and by so doing prevent it altogether, and put the world on the road to peace.

Among the documents which I overhauled so many years after they were written, were piles of rough manuscript notes made by myself at odd moments (sometimes in the middle of sleepless nights), trying to formulate something which could serve as a guidance for the movement which sprang up in the first decade of the century. What, very simply and clearly stated, were the truths we desired to bring home to the public? In what order of importance? A combination of one or two of these 'guidances' enumerating the points which were to be emphasized gives this result :

(1) It is not necessary for a nation to have or retain within its political control the sources of food or raw material; nor would war necessarily give it that control. Such control is necessary only for purposes of war. Get rid of war and the necessity disappears. (Why do you want the coaling station? So that we can go to war. Why do you want to go to war? So that we can have the coaling station.)

(2) No war can be *economically* advantageous; the inescapable economic chaos resulting from war makes economic benefit from victory impossible. There is no sort of realisation of this truth by the public.

(3) The notion that after a great war the victor will be able to make the vanquished pay its costs is complete fallacy. This, too, is demonstrable in terms of the economic structure of the modern world, its banking, credit and monetary systems, all extremely vulnerable.

(4) War is not the outcome of fate, or nature, or the 'inevitable' processes of history. It is not made by nature but by men; it represents the failure of human wisdom.

(5) That wisdom need not fail. We may not be able to change human nature but we can certainly change human behaviour, or we should still be fighting duels, torturing witnesses in our courts of law, burning nonconformists at the stake.

(6) Non-resistance is no remedy. Where men, or nations, are not defended against the violence of the criminal or the merely fanatical by the collective power of their society, each will try to be stronger than the other, each claiming the right of defence by preponderance of power, thus denying to the other the right of defence he claims for himself. Each tries to be his own judge in his own dispute. Yet if either yielded to the force of the other,

force would settle the dispute. If reason, impartial judgment, is to prevail, the victim of lawless violence must be defended by society. The evil we fight is not power, but failure to put power in the right hands—in that of the law. Arm the law, not the litigants.

(7) We must therefore make it clear that our first objective is defence rather than peace, in the sense that we try to lay the foundations of the only method by which we may secure peaceful defence; by which power may be used to deter aggression and violence.

(8) The first efforts should be directed not at the creation of ambitious world constitutions but at bringing about a wider public understanding of the issues involved. To translate our general principles into actual policy we should, first of all, drag into open discussion the differences with Germany. We do not in fact at present know what they are. Having started with a nucleus agreement between the English-speaking nations, bring in France, Russia and Germany and attempt to set up a new Concert of Europe rather than persist in the attempts to prolong an unstable Balance of Power. This 'Concert' must be built up piecemeal, until the power behind the nations which are like-minded in their conceptions of the good life is sufficiently great to deter the aggression of those set upon imposing by force their own views of their own rights.

All such notes were tentative. The over-ruling need was to secure a more rational temper in dealing with the international situation as it was then developing.

What was accomplished in a little over a year after the establishment of the Garton Foundation may be gathered from an article which appeared in *The New Statesman* of 11 October 1913 (Bernard Shaw and Sidney Webb were then on its board) headed 'The New Pacifism.' I never learned who wrote the article. It is in part as follows:

The publication of the first number of *War and Peace*, 'A Norman Angell Monthly,' is a notable event in one of the most important movements of our time. It is only four years since Mr. Angell's pamphlet, *Europe's Optical Illusion*, was published, a work as unimposing in form as it was daring in expression. For a time nothing was heard of it in public, but many of us will

remember the curious way in which reports of its contents and
of the effect it was having upon eminent people filtered through
from all kinds of odd quarters. The whispers grew gradually in
strength until they had swelled into something like a roar; *The
Great Illusion* was issued, and 'Norman Angellism' suddenly
became one of the principal topics of discussion amongst politicians and journalists all over Europe. Naturally at first it was
the apparently extravagant and paradoxical elements in the new
Pacifist gospel that were fastened upon most. Here was a man—a
man with a pseudonym coming out of nowhere—who was convincing crowned heads and ministers that the whole theory of
the commercial basis of war was wrong, that no modern war
could make a profit for the victors. . . . People who had been
brought up in the acceptance of the idea that a war between
nations was analogous to the struggle of two errand boys for an
apple, and that victory inevitably meant economic gain, were
amazed into curiosity. Men who had never examined a Pacifist
argument before read Mr. Angell's book . . . and now, after only
four years, organisations responding to his stimulus are springing
up all over the country. At the head of them all in wealth, in
significance, in potential influence, is the Garton Foundation for
Encouraging the Study of International Polity, with Mr. Balfour
and Lord Esher on its directing board.

The article goes on to note that 'the theory and practice of the
new Pacifism are sharply distinguished from those of the old.
. . . The Angell school holds that, as practical methods of promoting the cause of peace and ultimate disarmament, the mere
preaching of abstruse doctrines about violence, the tinkering
slowly, and even stealthily, with international law, the struggling
to get Germany to cut a Dreadnought off her estimates if Britain
will do the same, are weak in conception and ineffective in
operation.' And adds:

Mr. Angell's way is to face the facts of contemporary opinion,
to discover the misapprehensions cherished by the common mind,
and to dispel these misapprehensions by clear statement and
logical argument. Underlying the struggles and jealousies of the
diplomats he finds widely prevalent errors and loosenesses of mind
which must be removed or corrected before any stable international polity is possible. . . . In his task of educating public
opinion along his own particular lines Mr. Angell will receive
invaluable assistance from the new paper. We share his view that
the journal would be improved if his name were not spread over

it quite so much. But this is a minor defect and otherwise the new paper is admirable.

I was not responsible either for starting or managing it. It was edited by William Searle (who remains to-day after nearly forty years a close and valued personal friend). In the first number of the paper he printed a letter from me in which, while wishing ' all the good luck which this enterprise of yours and the others deserves,' I expressed doubts as to the wisdom of calling it a ' Norman Angell ' monthly. While making no formal objection, I begged him to make it plain that he was presenting an idea, and not a person.

In his leading article Searle gives the reasons for associating the paper with my name. ' It is,' he writes, ' the best way we know to indicate the nature of our objects and methods, and their differentiation from those of the Older Pacifism. For, however little we may desire to disparage previous Pacifist effort, it is obvious that only a real difference can justify the separate expression which this journal hopes to embody.'

' That difference,' he goes on, ' does not reside in the fact that we value the economic as opposed to the moral plea.' When ' economics ' involve the livelihood of millions they quickly become moral questions. The article continues :

> That failure of understanding which gives us war is not a mere perverse brutality in one special field of human intercourse, to be cured by an improvement of intentions and a finer sensitiveness. It is the natural outcome of certain misconceptions which can only be corrected by those intellectual processes that have marked all advance in understanding. The Europe of the Religious Wars and the Inquisition; the world of the Crusades and Heretic-burning, of asceticism and serfdom, of chivalry and *jus primæ noctis*; the vindication of honour by the duel and the justice of the ordeal; the obtaining of evidence by torture; religion by physical compulsion, was not a badly-meaning, but a badly-thinking world, and the men who destroyed it—the Bacons, the Montaignes, the Luthers, the Voltaires and the Rousseaux—were perhaps in intention inferior to those who made it. We emerged from it by correcting a defect in understanding; we shall emerge from the world of political warfare or armed peace in the same way. . . .
>
> We must bring before the mind of the European public the significance of a few, simple, ascertainable, tangible facts in such fashion that they will frame unconsciously a working

hypothesis of international society, which will lead to deductions sufficiently correct and sufficiently widespread to do for the political groups what has already been done for the religious groups.

Among the contributors, one or two of whom appear as critics of the movement, were Bertrand Russell; Arnold Bennett; H. N. Brailsford; J. Ramsay MacDonald, M.P.; Admiral Sir Cyprian Bridge; Prof. E. G. Browne; Viscount Bryce; Charles Roden Buxton; Prof. Edwin Cannan : Lord Sydenham of Combe; Lord Courtenay of Penwith; G. Lowes Dickinson; Miss M. E. Durham; Viscount Esher; Roger Fry; Frederic Harrison; John Hilton; F. W. Hirst; J. A. Hobson; Jerome K. Jerome; Sir Harry Johnston; Vernon Lee; Lord Loreburn; L. G. Chiozza Money, M.P.; E. D. Morel; Alfred Noyes; Arthur Ponsonby, M.P.; Sir Henry Primrose; 'Rifleman'; J. M. Robertson, M.P.; Philip Snowden, M.P.; Mrs. Swanwick; G. M. Trevelyan; Sir Charles Waldstein; Harold Wright. Willy Pogany usually did the cartoons, and C. E. Fayle ('Macflecknoe') contributed witty and amusing verse.

The names of the contributors indicate an outstanding feature of the movement : it included many from every side of politics, and nearly every group in the social and economic struggles of the time : bankers and businessmen, Socialists and Labour politicians; Quakers, Big Navy people, and some 'absolute' pacifists. ('Pacifist' previous to 1914 did not necessarily connote non-resister.)

Huth Jackson, then the governor of the Bank of England, was for a time Treasurer of a fund subscribed to promote the work; Henry Bell, the General Manager of Lloyds Bank, was a frequent figure at our Conferences both in England and abroad. Charles Wright of Lloyds (Insurance) was an active supporter. Academic personalities figured, sometimes prominently in one way or another; Lowes Dickinson of Cambridge was a constant contributor to *War and Peace*; and the Universities had societies devoted to these discussions. I recall vividly some of the early discussions in Keynes' rooms; and that Keynes more than once went out of his way to encourage and approve. Esher himself lectured on this new effort at both Cambridge and the Sorbonne.

At the same time that undergraduates were discussing them the ideas were the subject of much Hyde Park oratory. (Wilk

Haycock, of Manchester and later M.P. for Salcoats, was one of the open-air stars and a loyal personal friend.)

While the Garton Foundation with Lord Esher and Arthur Balfour as its Trustees played a big part, the Independent Labour Party at the instigation of Keir Hardie discussed taking a hand. Keir Hardie had suggested that the I.L.P. might produce a penny version of *The Great Illusion*, an idea also supported by Bruce Glazier of the *New Leader*. I recall a luncheon in the House of Commons with Keir Hardie the 'cap-wearing revolutionary.' Whatever may have been the case at an early stage of his parliamentary career, he showed sense and judgment at the time I met him. He put the point that though he wanted the I.L.P. to do a penny edition of the book, he felt it might depart too much from the policy I was following of keeping the movement distinct from all parties. 'You will be well advised,' he added, 'not to associate it too much with men like me.'

For a variety of reasons the idea of the penny edition was not carried out.

There were, I suppose, a hundred organizations in Britain of one kind or another connected with this movement—War and Peace societies, International Polity Clubs, Norman Angell Leagues, an organization known as 'R.U.I.R.' (the Right Understanding of International Relations) under the chairmanship of Miss Talmadge which was active and did good work. The most vigorous provincial organizations were in Manchester, Leeds, Glasgow—my old friend and colleague Leonard Behrens being responsible for the Manchester organization and Sir Donald Stevenson, then Lord Provost of Glasgow, for the one in that city.

The real 'punch' of the movement, its most powerful impetus perhaps, especially at the beginning, was given by the younger men—men then unknown but so many of whom were to become distinguished. After a debate at the Cambridge Union in the early part of 1912 Harold Wright (who had been President of the Union) and some of his friends formed the Cambridge War and Peace Society and brought into it a good many undergraduates. I had at that time a little sailing yacht on the Seine and I thought it a good idea to have seven or eight of the men most active at Cambridge join me for a week's sailing. The little party, in addition to Harold Wright, included Hubert Henderson, now Sir Hubert Henderson, Warden of All Souls; Dennis

Robertson, of Trinity; Geoffrey Toulmin, the industrialist, Willie Searle, and two or three others. For the best part of a week we sailed, swam and, when wet, 'argified' in the tiny cabin, planned how the war we all knew might come might be prevented.

The flat at 4 King's Bench Walk, was destined to be the scene of all the more confidential confabulations of the Movement, the place of meeting for the G.H.Q., composed generally of Ernest Fayle,[1] my secretary; Harold Wright; John Hilton; Bernard Langdon-Davies; Mrs. Manus; Willie Searle; sometimes Philip Baker (now the Rt. Hon. Philip Noel-Baker, who has held high cabinet office in the Labour Government and was for so long the valiant aide of Robert Cecil in the fight for the League); Leonard Behrens of Manchester; and Maurice Brett, Esher's son. Here, over tea, we would discuss the broad lines of policy. The policy was carried out administratively by the Garton Foundation, whose trustees, as already noted, were Garton, Esher and Balfour. It was usually my business to obtain the acquiescence of Esher and Balfour in the decisions at which we arrived.

After the war the same rooms were to be the scene of conferences between those interested in the peace. Ramsay MacDonald was a frequent visitor, as were Charles Trevelyan, E. D. Morel, with occasionally Maynard Keynes, Hamilton Fyfe, George Lansbury. The occasional foreign visitors included Walter Rathenau, who, on the occasion of his visit, lay on the sofa, discussing the German problems until three in the morning, not very long before he was assassinated.

The British end of the movement was only a part of it and after the outbreak of the first war became the minor part. *The Great Illusion* had appeared in the United States by 1910, and by 1912 the Carnegie Endowment had asked me to talk at several universities, which I did, to be followed a year or so later by Bernard Langdon-Davies. Nicholas Murray Butler, then the head of the Carnegie Endowment, was keenly interested, as was Andrew Carnegie, with whom I spent a whole day talking about the effort he was making. The Endowment arranged for a widespread

[1] Author of several books, including *The New Patriotism*; a memoir of Harold Wright; a history of shipping and insurance during the First World War.

advertisement campaign in Germany of the German translation of *The Great Illusion*, and I followed this up with a lecture tour of the universities of Jena, Göttingen, Hanover, Heidelberg, Würtzburg, Leipzig, Frankfurt, and Berlin, where Student Corps (egged on by some of the professors) turned out to wreck the meetings—which they did, with chairs flying, benches torn up, the fight being, however, not as between audience and platform, but between one section of the audience and another.

I carried away from this German visit the strong impression that, if we could have had five years in which to work among young Germans, we could have diluted Prussianism sufficiently to have rendered it much less dangerous, helping to prepare Germany for that 'Western' rôle which she must somehow be brought to play if Western Civilization is to defend itself against the pressure from the East.

A useful link at that time between Germany and the West in this connection proved to be the second generation of German-Americans—Americans whose parentage was German, often the liberal German of the 1848 revolution. These young German-Americans, who before 1914 went in considerable numbers to German universities, had already begun to form student clubs where they could discuss international affairs with their German fellow students. I discussed the possibilities of this move a good deal with George Nasmyth, the brilliant young American scientist who made so good a start in the German universities along this line. Nasmyth, however, died of typhoid at Geneva shortly after the war.

Three conferences stand out in my memory: the one held at Le Touquet in France in 1913; that held at Old Jordans in 1914; and that at Cornell University a year later. Those attending Le Touquet included a considerable number of French people—authors, journalists, lawyers, politicians. At Old Jordans more than half of the members of the conference—which lasted a week—were American or German, coming for the most part from the universities.

A full report of the 'International Polity Summer School,' the conference held at Old Jordans, still exists, a book running into four hundred pages. It might constitute a useful historical document if historians were interested in the way in which the young men of that generation thought and felt. In reading through this report after an interval of more than thirty years, I am struck by the high intellectual standard which marks all the discussions—a standard which is the more notable when compared with that which characterizes some of the youth conferences after the Second World War, especially when these are dominated, as they often are, by the Communist element, shouting slogans about Anglo-American capitalist imperialism. In the report, running to four hundred pages, of the mainly student gatherings at Old Jordans in 1914, one may hunt in vain for anything approaching the intolerance, fanaticism, vindictiveness, that seem to have marked a great number of the Communist-dominated gatherings this last twenty-five years.

When a somewhat similar meeting was held at Cornell, the prospectus was headed by this passage from Mill's *Essay On Liberty*:

> In the case of any person whose judgment is really deserving of confidence, how has it become so? Because he has kept his mind open to criticism of his opinions and conduct. . . . No wise man ever acquired his wisdom in any mode but this; nor is it the nature of human intellect to become wise in any other manner. The steady habit of correcting and completing his own opinion by collating it with those of others, so far from causing doubt and hesitation in carrying it into practice, is the only stable foundation for a just reliance on it.

So very many, alas, of the later, interwar generation of youngsters would have regarded such a statement as 'despicable bourgeois deviationism.'

Lewis Gannett, who was present at the conference, writes of it nearly thirty years later, that the book which had prompted the conference ' has entered so much into the texture of ordinary American thinking to-day that it is difficult to recall its tremendous impact three decades ago. Norman Angell was not arguing non-resistance; he was no peace-at-any-price pacifist; he was appealing to self-interest. . . . It was exciting doctrine to a group of college students and graduate students who met at Ithaca. That was where I first met Norman Angell, and that was one of the richest weeks of my life. The frail-looking little man prodded us, contradicted us, provoked us, and stimulated us—and he became a moulding influence in the lives of quite a group.'

In a later chapter appears a note on Esher's personality, not merely because of the rôle he played in the movement here described, but because of his strange rôle generally in the political life of Edwardian England. What was the basis of his interest in this movement and the trouble that he took about it? To suppose, as more than one Leftish friend of mine has suggested, that he espoused this cause with the object of sterilizing it, of seeing that it did no harm to his friends in the armament business, is not to be realist, but blind to the very mixed nature of most human motives, and to some of the commonest elements of that mixture. Assume for a moment that he was just a very cunning fellow and was thinking first and foremost of the interest of his social order. His public profession of belief was to the effect that war would ruin the capitalist system. Why should he not believe this with sincerity, especially in view of the fact that two wars have had precisely the effect in England that he said they would have? The truth is that he was interested in ideas as such, like his fellow trustee, Arthur Balfour. That men can have a feeling for ideas, doctrines, quite apart from material interest, the whole history of philosophy, of doctrinal strife, of the religious wars, shouts at us.

Esher stated his position—and that, he told his audience, of Balfour—in the lecture already mentioned which he delivered at the Sorbonne in Paris a few months before the outbreak of the First War (on 27 March 1914). It was sometimes argued, he pointed out, 'that in the crises of nations it is not the sounder reasoning that decides; it is passions, interests, outside events, and that something vague, undefined, curious almost to mystery, that in bodies of men is called political instinct. But,' he insisted, 'we must not be entrapped by a phrase, and I beg of you to try to define political instinct, if it is possible, and to inquire whether it is not like, let us say, religious instinct, susceptible of cultivation, of modification and of change.'

He went on to say something of my own work and to outline the growth of the movement in Britain, notably in the universities. ' Suppose,' he went on, ' that this thesis of Angell is true and that no material advantage of any kind can be wrested from the vanquished without an equal price to be paid by the victor. Would not this truth, when grasped, completely change in the long run the belief of which I have spoken? The thesis of

Galileo was not more diametrically opposed to certain ideas than that of Norman Angell, yet it had in the end a measure of success.'

Esher normally detested public appearances of this kind, and I have not any doubt whatever that his impelling motives were, first, an intellectual interest in a subject closely related to military science, which he had studied, and, secondly, a desire to give to the defence of order a stable society in Europe, a rational, arguable basis. The lecture in Paris (he spoke in French) was the more significant perhaps in that it was given two years after he had discussed the matter in a public lecture at Cambridge (2 Dec. 1912). In that earlier picture he had emphasized particularly the immensely powerful factor of unreason, irrationalism in human affairs. 'If,' he said, 'George Meredith is justified in saying that when men's brains are insufficient to meet the exigencies of affairs, they fight, you can well understand that, given the casual methods of politicians and the clouded atmosphere of political strife, the failure of reason to withstand the assault of prejudice and passion is not so strange or unaccountable.'

But he agreed that it was preposterous to leave the matter at that, and he spoke of the fashion in which the new movement was discharging the task of strengthening, putting a higher degree of vitality into the rational consideration of the problems of 'War and Peace.' He was not unhopeful of results.

What might be called the 'Esher' technique of government was part of Edwardian England. (Its stabilizing influence has been strikingly described by A. N. Whitehead.) Its results were on the whole as good as those produced by government anywhere in the world. To have applied that method to the movement with which I was concerned would probably have been as good a way as any of ensuring the widest acceptance for the ideas it aimed to promote. Later I was to reject that method in favour of party affiliation (with the Labour Party) and to regret that I had done so—a matter to be discussed later.

Indeed, at the moment when the movement had reached its peak the earth was to be shaken under our feet, compelling a re-examination of all methods, all conclusions, all questions.

In a preceding chapter I have indicated what I regarded as the chief defects of emphasis in the pamphleteering which produced this movement. The same defects marked the movement

itself. Usually—very much against my own wishes and counsels—
the emphasis was on *peace*. It should have been on defence, and
on the truth that competitive armament as we know it in the first
decade of the century could not possibly achieve effective defence;
that for each to be his own defender, rejecting co-operative and
collective defence, was to leave the way open for the aggressor to
pick off his victims one by one. I tried repeatedly to emphasize
the fact that the one way to make force progressively an instrument for its abolition was to use it for the restraint of violence
by defending collectively the victim of lawless violence.

The fact that the Pacifist of the non-resister, early Christian
type, flocked to the movement tended to add to the confusion
which existed in the public mind as to any difference between
Pacifism and Internationalism; and to keep the discussion to
abstract principles and away from the problem of their practical
application. This group, made up largely of Quakers, was in
single-mindedness, disinterestedness, sincerity, the salt of the
earth. My admiration for Quakers has always been such that
looking back I see I was simply incapable, temperamentally, of
refusing to have them associated with us. And I constantly hoped
they would take a position somewhere along these lines : 'While
we as members of the Society of Friends are opposed to military
force in any form, we do recognize a moral difference between
force as used by the policeman acting for the community and the
law, and force as used by the burglar. To those therefore who feel
that armed defence of the nation's interests is morally justified,
we suggest that it is their duty to see the power so employed
approximates to that of the police—the collective power of the
nations as a whole defending the members of the international
community from aggression.'

By allowing peace, as distinct from defence, to be pushed into
the foreground (especially in the organized movement which grew
out of the pamphlet) the effort came to be regarded by very many
as a simple anti-armament, anti-power, anti-war campaign. The
summary of the book's theme as 'War does not pay' was convenient but misleading, for I insisted that war might pay very
handsome dividends in terms of defence, of the right of a nation
to live under its own institutions free from violence.

It is easy to realize now how this faulty distribution of emphasis
arose. The book was written in a generation in which poets and
bishops actually praised war for itself, 'God's red rain' (as one

Bishop put it), a cleanser, a moral stimulant. Nonsense of that kind had to be cleared away. Furthermore, there was no general realization of the extent to which a world war would render so much of Western Society unworkable. What it would really mean had to be brought home.

And of course there was something else : my immense sympathy and fellow feeling with the absolutist, the pacifist of the early Christian type, who said flatly, 'I will have no part nor lot in a thing so dirty and damnable.' My head knew that this simply would not do; that that was not the way to get rid of the evil thing. But my heart yearned to make common cause with him. I never yielded to that yearning, but it was always there.

It would seem that the cloven hoof of a hatred of war as war, would come out more in my conversation than in writing. Bernard Falk in one of his books of character sketches (under the heading, 'Cowboy as Dialectician') wrote :

... each time I bumped into him I had a pretext for discussing his book *The Great Illusion*, the most famous, as it is the most lucid, political pamphlet published this century.

A frail-looking man of small build, who from his lean ascetic features might easily be mistaken for a lawyer or physician, Norman Angell surprises his friends by the extraordinary vehemence which he develops when orally propounding his views. Yet put a pen into his hand and leave him to express his ideas in undisturbed solitude, and nobody could turn a cooler, more detached front to the world ... the main purpose of his writings is to induce men, in their dealings with one another, to substitute reason for passion.

A verdict which I would modify only to the extent of saying that I would put emotion, passion it might be at times, behind the obligations of reason, the obligation to hear the other fellow, to consider his case, to want to know the truth.

When all criticism is spent and all qualifications are made, the fact remains that something or other gave this movement for political rationalism a vitality which enabled it in the course of two or three years, as the facts just related indicate, to spread over a great part of the world. Someone writing of it years later remarked : 'What that movement needed was time, and time was the only thing denied it.' He went on to point out that time was denied it largely by one of those accidents which determine

N

the timing of history. If the fanatic's shot at Sarajevo had been delayed a few years, Western Europe might have acquired a mood which would have enabled it either to avoid the war, or if the war had come, to have made afterwards a peace that would not have led to the Second World War.

I felt deeply that a war delayed might be a war prevented. And this belief was to dictate a course of action much criticized even by many of my friends, and which the next chapter relates.

CHAPTER IV

EFFORT FOR A BREATHING SPACE

A NEUTRALITY LEAGUE

SOME idea of the political unpreparedness of the public for the war which began in August 1914 may be gathered from an incident which sticks very much in my memory. About the middle of July, 1914, Northcliffe had asked me to lunch to discuss some problems of the Paris *Mail*. (I had resigned from the paper a couple of years previously and by 1914 had no place at all in the Northcliffe organization. But the Chief seemed constantly to forget this and would ring me up. . . . 'What are you up to in appointing X to that job in Paris? Don't you know . . ?') After lunch Northcliffe said, 'Come up to my room and I will show you some of the preparations we are making for the war.' I went up. The floor of his room was covered with photos of ambulances, artillery, nurses, Red Cross units. He gave me details of the preparations he was making for the war—in Ulster! For the moment he had forgotten Germany and as a man who had been born in Ireland, he was altogether absorbed with the *Irish* war.

Now, whatever else one may say of Northcliffe, he certainly had an extraordinarily keen sense of what the public were interested in. And just then, in July 1914, they were interested in Ulster; not Germany.

I tell this nearly incredible but true story because it illustrates the suddenness of the final coming of war.

The last days of July were for me taken up with the biggest international conference (to which reference has been made in the last chapter) which our movement had managed to organize. It had brought together a considerable number of American students (some of whom were afterwards to become distinguished in American public and academic life) as well as German and French.

Young Englishmen and young Germans had for over a week been discussing the differences which divided their two

179

countries. The discussions were sometimes heated but always marked by honesty and sincerity.

I came back to King's Bench Walk to find my desk loaded with telegrams and letters : from the various organizations, societies, International Polity Clubs, Study Circles, which had been the outgrowth of the Garton Foundation : Where are you going to stand if war breaks out?

Well, where were we?

Unless one understands something of the state of mind of those who had worked in the movement described in the last chapter, the episode which follows will seem inexplicable.

Here were a group of men, most of whom were by no means pacifist in the present sense of that term ; they believed, that is, in a nation's right to defend itself; believed that power and armaments could, with wisdom, be made the instrument of peaceful defence and of international order, much as the police power of a national state can be made the instrument of peace and law. Our opposition was not to war or force as such, but to a war fought in such conditions that its most probable result would be to render the nation more insecure than ever and prepare the way for still more wars.

It was clear that, as Lloyd George, the war-time Prime Minister was later to aver, the country was 'stumbling and blundering' into the war. In that case I, for one, believed deeply that it might prove the beginning of the end of all free and humane society. This was no sudden conviction, nor one held simply because I never heard it challenged. I had, on the contrary, lived most of my life so far among Conservatives, traditionalists, romanticists, American, French, German, English, who regarded my view as nonsense. And the deeper I became engaged in this discussion, the more did the coming of the war appear to me to be the result of an irrationalism which threatened somehow to engulf the world.

And here war was upon us, at our very door on this beautiful July morning (the 27th) just as we had returned from the Old Jordans conference, so encouraging in all the evidence that it gave of the ferment of new and more hopeful ideas in the minds of the youngsters there gathered; youngsters now to be thrown into the furnace already beginning to blaze. Once war came, reason, reasonableness, the temper by which alone there could be sound judgment of facts and workable solutions, would fly out of the window.

At first there was little passion. This was to be the war which would end war; that would make the world safe for democracy; it would vindicate the rights of small nations; bring to an end the era of armament, conscription and militarism which had lain so heavily upon the peoples of Europe. (Britain was the only state in Europe at that time free of conscription.) It was to make this and other free countries secure from the aggression of less democratic powers and would place defence and the economic life of our nation upon safer and sounder foundations.

I did not believe for one moment that any of these things would be achieved by our victory, unless we could use it with a wisdom which I knew the war itself would do so much to destroy. What was I to do? What was I to urge those who had joined me in a movement described in the last chapter?

Any course taken at that fateful August week-end involved enormous risks. But it seemed to me then, confronted with the need of making a decision within twelve hours, that the least risk lay in delaying the entrance of Britain into the war a few weeks, possibly months. As a neutral, Britain could exercise pressure upon *both* combatants, the Franco-Russian Alliance on the one side and the Austro-German on the other. Each would attempt to meet her views; one in order to prevent her becoming an enemy, the other to persuade her to become an ally. The sort of power which Britain could exercise as a neutral would disappear the moment she entered the war. Her influence should be used, I felt, to bring about a conference of the great European powers; a sort of pre-war armistice to determine the conditions upon which peace could be made; or the conflict deferred.

We are apt at this distance to feel vaguely that we went to war with Germany to repel an attack upon us. The simple fact of course is that, however justified our war, Germany was not then attacking Britain. Germany very much desired British neutrality and would have been willing to pay a very great deal to secure it. What really motivated us was the fact that if she conquered France and over-ran the Continent we might be at her mercy, helpless to resist anything which her half-insane emperor might dictate. Even so, her primary purpose was not directed at France, whom she had defeated and conquered so completely less than half a century previously; a fact which did not result in threat to Britain.

One dominant consideration at that time in my own mind—

as the terms of the Manifestos we then published and which are reproduced below reveal—was the position of Russia in Europe after the promised 'destruction' of Germany.

Looking back, I think the most astonishing thing about the public discussion, such as it was, which preceded the outbreak of war was the all but complete disregard of the position of Russia; and what a Russian victory over Germany, a victory made possible by our power, might involve. I had attempted to call attention to this neglected factor a month or two before the war by articles in the English Press (including articles in the *Daily Mail*, but the subject simply did not 'bite.' Curiously enough, it was the more intelligent military men who saw the importance of the point. One of them, repeating, I think, a common adage amongst them, said : ' It will take us five years to get the Russians into Germany—and fifteen to get them out.' It will take rather more than fifteen.

So I urged upon my friends in the movement that the best chance of averting the disasters that would follow upon war was 'temporary neutrality.'

To this end, at a little before midnight on Thursday, July 28, we formed the Neutrality League. This was the Thursday preceding the August Bank Holiday, and everybody was trooping out of town. So it meant hundreds of telegrams to people in the country and even abroad, in no mood to make the kind of decision which we were asking of them. We had managed to agree on the terms of a Manifesto during the day of Thursday and tried to arrange publication.

This Manifesto dealt mainly—some of the leaflets we published and distributed dealt almost entirely—with the relation of a Russian victory and German defeat to the Balance of Power policy for which Britain was supposed to be standing. The Manifesto pointed out that the complete disarmament of Germany (which we were already beginning to demand) plus a great increase in the power and territory of Russia, would upset the Balance of Power enormously by making Russia the potential master of Europe.

Below are extracts from the Manifesto which was published in a number of papers and circulated by leaflets, some of which were headed, ' Shall We Fight for a Russian Europe?' Dealing with the alleged purposes of our intervention—the Manifesto—the date of which, please remember, is July 1914——states :

It is urged that we must ensure the Victory of France and Russia in order to maintain the Balance of Power.

If we are successful in securing the victory of Russia in this war, we shall upset that balance enormously by making her the dominant military power of Europe, possibly the dictator both in this Continent and in Asia. Her own population numbers 170 millions, while she is the head and leader of populations numbering at least 200 millions, partly Asiatic and Mohammedan. All her history shows her to be impregnable by invasion. She has not the modern commercial and industrial life which is paralysed by war, and she is likely to feel the strain of war less than more highly developed nations. She is able to put nearly six million men into the field, to draw upon vast resources of human military material, only partly civilized, governed by a military autocracy largely hostile to western ideas of political and religious freedom.

Germany, on the other hand, is a nation of 65 millions, wedged in between hostile States, highly civilized, with a culture that has contributed greatly in the past to western civilization, racially allied to ourselves and with moral ideals largely resembling our own; possessing a commercial and industrial life that is dependent upon an orderly and stable Europe. Our two peoples have maintained unbroken peace since their earliest history. The last war that we fought upon the Continent was for the purpose of checking the growth of Russia. We are now asked to go to war to promote it.

The Manifesto also dealt with some of the probable economic results. 'A state of war in England,' I wrote, 'would render it impossible for Britain to remain the financial centre of the world. The function which London fulfils would temporarily, and perhaps permanently, be transferred to the other side of the Atlantic.'

Shortly after the declaration of war, I find myself writing in the *Mail*: 'Whatever may be the future place of the Slavs, Teutons, French or English in the world, this war is not going to settle it. . . . We may inflict or bear atrocious suffering, but when it is all over . . . the problem will remain.'

What the British and French publics of 1914 seemed to have

ignored then, and in the year or two which preceded, was that
again and again Germany and Middle Europe had had to face
the full shock of invasions from the East; that, though Britain
had been disturbed by the Bear that Walks like a Man, it was
because the Bear threatened British interests, not in the home-
land, but in the Eastern Mediterranean, at the Dardanelles, in
India, thousands of miles away. But for the Germans, Russia was
at their doors. Hardly a fort or castle in Eastern Germany but
bore witness to the attack of Russian armies of the past. France
seemed to have forgotten that Russian troops had been encamped
in Paris less than a century before; and that other Eastern peoples
had been knocking at the doors of the West, as in recent times
historically at the doors of Vienna; that five hundred years after
Charles Martel had thrown back the Eastern flood, it returned,
more powerful, more menacing than ever, in the armies of
Genghis Khan, 'Emperor of Mankind' (a title he came un-
comfortably near to justifying). I tried repeatedly to remind the
public at home that Germany was in 1914 part of the West; and
that in breaking up the West we should create a vacuum of
power into which the Russian masses, and even more remotely
the dead weight of the Asiatic masses, might move.

The event, of course, has added some enlightening notes to
those far-off warnings—or speculations if that is the better word.

A few papers published the Manifesto in whole or in part in
their editorial columns; but it became necessary to insert it in
some as an advertisement; some papers even refused to insert it
as an advertisement. Half a million leaflets were printed and
distributed by some two hundred voluntary workers in London
and the provinces. There were meetings in Trafalgar Square.
Three hundred sandwich men patrolled most the main streets
of London. Members of the House of Commons were personally
interviewed.[1] And so on.

[1] One little incident of that time sticks in my memory. One of the Ellis
sisters (which one I do not remember), having learned that banks might
close as the result of war hourly expected, determined, it would seem, to
make sure of her contribution and, instead of sending a cheque, had gone
to the bank and obtained five hundred sovereigns in a bag. This she brought
to my chambers at 4 King's Bench Walk in the Temple and, in the presence
of the dozen or so workers collected in my office, poured the five hundred
sovereigns on the table. Harold Wright, who was present, remarked;
'Take a good look, everybody. You will never see this sight again.' He
proved a pretty good prophet.

The list of names of those who gave financial and other support to this effort is a long one and includes men now eminent in the Labour Party, three publishers, two eminent physicians, several University professors, peers, bankers, journalists, newspaper owners, lawyers, bishops. As they might be embarrassed by this reminder of their association with a 'subversive' effort of that kind, their names are withheld. Two exceptions may perhaps be permitted.

C. P. Scott, the famous owner-editor of the *Manchester Guardian*, was among those supporting the Neutrality League. In a letter from him, dated 5 August 1914, he writes : 'I enclose a cheque for ten pounds towards your campaign fund. With all your promptitude you were too late, as we all were. It is a monstrous thing that the country should find itself at war to all intents and purposes without being consulted.'

And Arnold Bennett wrote : 'The telegram which you sent to me on the 1st, although it was re-telegraphed to a fresh address, only reached me to-day, as I have been away yachting and unable to make the ports I intended. I am in entire agreement with your arguments, but in my opinion it is impossible, and even wrong, to try to govern a country on a plane of commonsense which is too high above its own general plane of commonsense.'

It was, I think, Edward Grey who said, after the declaration of war, ' We should have had to fight in any case but the issue of Belgium, the fact that we were under obligation to defend her against the violation of her independence, made us a united nation. It gave the war a moral purpose.'

As a description of the state of British feeling that was, of course, correct. But the statement can serve to hide certain facts which we have not faced, and must face if we are ever to achieve a warless world.

When Grey said that we should have to fight in any case, he had in view the fact that a German victory in Europe, making Germany master of the whole continent, would place *our* independence in mortal jeopardy. For that supreme reason we would never acquiesce in German victory even if the moral quality of the German state had been a good deal better than it was; any more than we would acquiesce in the victory of Napoleonic France, though the Napoleonic political philosophy included liberal and progressive elements not present in the Prussian.

What we did not see, however, in 1914 was the sense in which we sacrificed Belgium to the needs of maintaining what we thought would prove to be the Balance of Power. When the German government just before the war asked Grey: 'If we respect Belgian neutrality and do *not* cross her frontiers with our armies, will you keep out of the war?' Grey could give no undertaking. 'Which means,' in effect retorted the German militarists, 'that in terms of military advantage it does not matter whether we respect Belgian neutrality or not. We shall face British hostility in any case. If therefore there is a military advantage in going through Belgium we should go.' Had Britain been able to say, 'Respect the Treaty and we will not join the war against you,' it would have been to the military advantage of Germany to respect the Treaty. Our power would have been a true 'sanction,' operating as power within the state does, to ensure a peaceful defence of the putative victim of violence. The aggressor does not aggress because he fears the penalty. If he gets the punishment anyhow the punishment loses its deterrent effect. Belgium had to be sacrificed to the maintenance of the Balance of Power. We did not secure that Balance. It was a vain sacrifice.

Other purposes were sacrificed vainly. We said this was a war for democratic freedoms and we accepted as allies in that purpose Czarist Russia, a Japan already planning the conquest of China, an Italy shortly to become Fascist. As part of a democratic Europe we set up or gave a new form to Estonia, Latvia, Lithuania, Poland, Czechoslovakia, Yugoslavia, Hungary, Roumania, Bulgaria. The fate of those states to-day is a measure of our success in making the world safe for democracy. The truth is, of course, that the alliance of Russia was accepted not because we believed she would strengthen the democratic forces of the world but because we had to find a counter-balance to the power of Germany.

There was nothing consciously hypocritical or new in this. It is a commonplace of history that the ally of to-day—welcomed as a fighter for right—becomes the enemy of to-morrow; and the enemy of to-day the ally of to-morrow. It happens because there is still no general undertaking of the means by which in the international field we may use power to restrain lawless violence.

In the *Nation* of 8 August 1914 I wrote:

> All other speculations as to the causes of this catastrophe, or
> lessons to be drawn from it, must take into account this central
> and pivotal fact : that the people of Europe have not yet learned
> so to organize their society as to make their conduct obey their
> intention. We are all of one mind to do one thing, and we all do
> the exact reverse. . . .
>
> This essential helplessness of men, their failure to have formed
> a society which can carry out their intention, goes a great deal
> deeper than mere political or diplomatic machinery. One must
> look for the prime cause . . . in the defects of an education which
> makes it impossible for the mass to judge facts save in their most
> superficial aspect . . . to keep two correlated facts in view at the
> same time. In all this business, the average man has overlooked
> so capital a fact as the predominating part to be played by the
> Russian autocracy manipulating 150,000,000 of peasants, at the
> real head, it may be, of 200,000,000 in control of a country im-
> pregnable by its bulk, much more resistant to the paralysis of war
> than more developed nations, largely hostile to Western con-
> ceptions of political and religious freedom. This fact is obscured,
> because another fact, the alleged menace of Germany, has taken
> hold of the public mind. . . . One such fact at a time : in the
> Crimean War we saw Russian barbarism but not Turkish; in 1914
> we can see German barbarism but not Russian.

The stand I had taken in the Neutrality League, a stand which
seemed to put me 'in opposition to the war,' brought me immediately great praise from the absolutist anti-war groups; praise
for consistency, 'integrity,' adherence to ideals. Not then, but
somewhat later, I was to question seriously whether I was not
being praised for the wrong thing. It should have been my job to
fight for the triumph of the ideas which might, if they prevailed,
bring the international anarchy to an end. And that would
depend upon those ideas making headway among the conservative as well as among the radical and revolutionary elements.

Among those who particularly praised my stand at the time
of the outbreak of the first war was Bertrand Russell. He called
at my chambers a few days after the dissolution of the Neutrality
League to say : 'I thought you were one of those who were for
peace in peace time and for war in war time. I see I was mistaken.
I believe that if you were to give a lead to the young men, you

would produce a great anti-war movement. There are thousands now, owing to your stand at the outbreak of the war, who would follow any lead you would care to give.'

But a mere ' anti-war,' non-resister negativism did not appeal to me. Nothing is easier than to excite in youngsters a deep, sincere and passionate hatred of the cruelties and idiocies of war. But this emotion does not solve the problem of war : does not enable us to see the forces and motives (good and bad) which lead to it ; nor to frame the policies which will help us avoid it.

If, having blundered into war, we were not to blunder into a bad peace, provoking further blundering wars, then the civilians, who would have the final responsibility for the kind of peace that would be made, would have to bestir themselves. The men who were to die could bring us victory ; they could not bring us peace. Peace would depend upon the use which the civilian made of the soldier's victory. The recognition of that fact explains the steps taken by some of us and described in the next chapter.

CHAPTER V

FOR A WORKABLE PEACE

At midnight following the day of the declaration of war—which of course put a sudden end to the Neutrality League—I was lying in my room at the Temple half-dead with fatigue, the whole place in a disorder of papers, proofs, packages of leaflets, placards; another room was piled high with plates and dishes, remnants of meals which had been prepared for the workers who had filled the place day and night for three days; suggesting somehow the strewn battlefield of our dead effort. Just then the earth seemed slipping from under one's feet.

Had I been in the habit of seeking such escape (or had a digestion sufficient to stand it) I would have drunk myself into insensibility.

At this moment there came a knock at the door, and I went to answer it, supposing it to be one of the people who had been working at our last and forlorn attempt to delay the war. But there stood Ramsay MacDonald. I asked him in.

MacDonald was then chairman of the rapidly growing Labour Party, which had been largely his creation and which nearly twenty years later (his more severe critics would say) he was to do his best to destroy. ('He guided the Labour Party from the cradle to the grave', ran the adage.) As he came into my room he threw himself down on the sofa, and with his face in his two hands, said,

'I have just resigned from the chairmanship of the Labour Party. Why? A man who has opposed our entrance into the war cannot lead a party that is going to support it. I am waiting until this fever has died down and our fellows, particularly those in the I.L.P., will come back. What are *you* going to do?'

I had known MacDonald for two or three years; had met his wife and children. He used to come occasionally to Paris to meet French politicians or Labour Leaders—Jaurès, Longuet, Jouhaux among others—and I would arrange luncheons, and act as interpreter. In the next year or so I was to see a great deal of him, sometimes almost daily and in the next twenty years to be a member of the rank and file of the party which he led. In the split of 1931, although I did not follow him, I understood his difficulty better, I think, than most of the party. Yet I never managed to get very near to him; never managed to break through a hard shell which seemed to encase him. Many of those who knew him told me they had just the same difficulty. It forbade the easy intimacy which, on the whole, marked my relations with so many of his colleagues; of which more presently.

I was greatly surprised at this midnight visit; wondered why he had come; and did not yet know what I *was* going to do.

I was too done in (hardly having been to bed for three days) to discuss the merits of this or that course. MacDonald suggested that those of us who realized the dangers the country would run into at the eventual peace-making should meet and discuss the matter. He went on to remind me that John Burns, Charles Trevelyan and John Morley were resigning from the government and that important political developments might result. I was too tired, too dismayed, too much knocked about by the events of the last day or two, to take in much of it. What was borne in upon me at the moment was that the hopes of twenty years and the severe labour of nearly ten had gone up in smoke; I knew the feeling of a man who, having spent half his life building a house, was now watching it blazing before his eyes.

So after a desultory talk we left it that we should meet again in a few weeks' time.

In a day or two I began to feel the need of physical action and it crossed my mind that I might join one of the Quaker Ambulances that were now forming and get work at the front in that way. As my old doctor friend, Archibald Warden of Paris days, was spending the summer holiday with his children at Sangatte near Calais, I managed to run over and discuss possibilities. The end of it was that I did later join his ambulance at Dunkirk and became for a time one of his stretcher bearers.

I was to have gone as Warden's hospital orderly but simply could not conquer the technique of attendance at operations, the names of instruments and other details. I volunteered to be stretcher bearer. I saw some little of the front, but still more of the dressing-stations and hospitals. Perhaps the feature which stands out most vividly in my mind is that of the railway shed at Dunkirk where the wounded, after first treatment at the advanced dressing-station, were dumped. The scenes were diversified : a woman nurse giving preliminary treatment, in the full public eye, to bad venereal cases, without so much as a screen to shield the very naked men ; in another corner a Belgian priest giving the last sacraments to a dying soldier ; in the midst of so doing he catches sight of an English Duchess whom he had met 'doing the front', he interrupts or hastens the final consolation to greet the Duchess across the line of cots. 'Bon jour, Mme la Duchesse. Vous allez bien, ' ; and then resumes the interrupted conversation with the Almighty.

I was not long in the ambulance. The number of typhoid cases was appalling ; yet the officers in command treated it as a normal and inevitable part of war and the commanding officer whom I interviewed declined to be disturbed. 'It was inseparable from active service.' (The interview, I recall, was made in company with Irene Noel who afterwards married Philip Baker, then with a Quaker Ambulance with which indeed he remained during most of the war. During my own brief interlude at the front I saw some little of Baker who had been my supporter in a Cambridge Union debate on armaments.) I disliked the official fatalism which insisted that nothing could be done about either the typhoid or delayed treatment of the wounded ; decided to approach the authorities in Paris, but after an utterly fruitless chase of officials there, I had to give it up.

The experience both at the front and in trying to deal with the bureaucratic incompetence of war time, had the effect of convincing me that my job was elsewhere. That job was to do what one could to see that this did not happen again and that out of the mess came some sort of workable peace.

So I returned to London. Within a few days of my return, there took place at my Chambers in the Temple a meeting of Ramsay MacDonald, Charles Trevelyan, Arthur Ponsonby, Philip Snowden and E. D. Morel. Out of that meeting grew the Union of Democratic Control. Those just named formed the original Executive Committee and E. D. Morel (who a year or two later was to beat Winston Churchill in an election fight in Dundee) was secretary. J. A. Mason joined us a little later.

A publication of the Union thus describes its purpose :

This country is at war, and has for the moment one over-whelming preoccupation : to render safe our national inheritance. The Union of Democratic Control has been founded for the purpose of trying to secure for ourselves and the generations that succeed us a new course of policy which will prevent a similar peril ever again befalling our Empire. Many men and women have already joined us holding varying shades of opinion as to the origins of the war. Some think it was inevitable, some that it could and should have been avoided. But we believe that all are in general agreement about two things : First, it is imperative that the war, once begun, should be prosecuted to a victory for our country. Secondly, it is equally imperative, while we carry on the war, to prepare for peace. Hard thinking, free discussion, the open exchange of opinion and information are the duty of all citizens to-day, if we are to have any hope that this war will not be what most wars of the past have been—merely the prelude to other wars.

The Union, which was formed long before the League of Nations constitution had been drafted, or even discussed, forecast as the appropriate governing principle of British foreign policy the following :

The Foreign Policy of Great Britain shall not be aimed at creating Alliances for the purpose of maintaining the ' Balance of Power '; but shall be directed to the establishment of a Concert of the Powers and the setting up of an International Council whose deliberations and decisions shall be public, part of the labour of such Council to be the creation of definite Treaties of Arbitration and the establishment of Courts for their in-terpretation and enforcement.

This reflected an attempt to placate the ' no power ' element in the organization, but was sound as far as it went. The ground was so shifting in Europe that the balance of to-day was bound to be the imbalance of to-morrow, the ally of yesterday the enemy of to-day; and the perpetual search for a balance inevitably made the ends of power subject to the means; as when (in the manner described in the previous chapter) the war to make the world safe for democracy accepted as part of the means a great increase in the power of Russia—which would not be likely to render democracy more secure. It will be noted that the outline of the

U.D.C. policy as quoted above embodies the principle that was enunciated later by President Wilson: an unstable Balance of Power should be transformed into a Community of Power; instead of the great nations seeking to balance each other they should combine to defend the victim of violence.

It may be noted also that of the six founding members of the U.D.C. one was to become Prime Minister of Great Britain; another her Chancellor of the Exchequer; another President of the Board of Education; another Undersecretary of State for Foreign Affairs, and another (Morel) was, as I have said, to defeat Winston Churchill in a Parliamentary Election.

It was Morel, the tall, handsome agitator, to whom some millions of natives in the Congo owed cessation of atrocities which might have continued much longer but for his heroic efforts; who, as its secretary, really made the Union of Democratic Control. It quickly obtained a very large membership; and published a monthly organ entitled *Foreign Affairs*, which ran for many years and which, for a time, I edited.

Immediately on joining the U.D.C. I offered to resign from the Garton Foundation. But the Trustees did not act on the suggestion then, thinking, I imagine, that I should get tired of my connection with politicians. It was a full year later (11 October 1915) that I received a letter signed by both Garton and Esher. It ran:

> Your original work in connection with the Foundation has been of such value and interest and the spirit of inquiry in which you at one time were willing to approach the political, social and economic questions with which the Foundation deals, was so broad and unprejudiced that we urged you strongly to abandon your identification with which we thought that you had somewhat hastily connected yourself, rather than abandon the agreeable relations that had hitherto existed between yourself and the Foundation.
>
> This you have, for reasons no doubt conscientiously overpowering to you, been unable to do; and you have been forced, by convictions which we respect but do not share, to carry on a propaganda in the United States upon lines that made cooperation between you and the Foundation difficult and undesirable.

And so, after pointing out that ever since the outbreak of war I had ceased to have any business or close relations with the

o

Foundation, they desired, in severing connection, to record that they would 'always remember with interest and with admiration your intellectual achievements and friendly personality.'

The Garton Foundation carried on for a year or two, mainly as a means of facilitating researches by John Hilton into problems of war financing, unemployment after the war and other phases of war and post-war problems which did not impinge too closely on the more controversial aspects. Hilton was to have a quite remarkable career following his association with me and his subsequent work with the Garton Foundation. Although not a university graduate, he secured a chair of statistical studies at Cambridge which later he was to combine with work at the B.B.C. which made him one of the most popular broadcasters in England.[1]

After about 1915 I saw little of Esher and nothing of Garton or Balfour. Esher's attitude underwent a change as the war progressed—a change, so far as I was concerned, towards a sort of casual bitterness and hostility. He became contemptuous of the efforts of Wilson to secure some sort of post-war international organization and occasionally sent me messages by Hilton which seemed to hint that he looked upon my own line as having degenerated into the naïve sentimentality of conventional Pacifism. Partly this change in him was due to the growing brutality of the German war leaders, partly to the feeling that in dropping the non-party character of my work and becoming associated with Labour Party leaders, I had in a sense let down Garton, Balfour and himself; that if I had intended to work through party politics I ought not to have accepted the help of organisations like the Foundation.

All this, of course, failed to take into account the vast changes in the whole international problem wrought by the war itself. But I saw the point of view of Esher, and Balfour—and some years later came to ask myself whether there was not a good deal more in their doubts of a party approach than I was disposed to believe at the time.

Many of my friends warned me against the step of becoming associated with party politicians like MacDonald and Snowden. Northcliffe telephoned and lectured me at length. 'My dear boy,

[1] Edna Nixon's *Life of John Hilton* deals at some length with Hilton's connection with the Foundation, and my own work.

he said earnestly, 'you are making the greatest mistake of your career. Here you are, having created a movement peculiarly your own; you have the ear of the public in a way no other pacifist has ever had before—and you go and mix it all with a lot of doubtful politicians, some of whom I'm shortly going to flay alive in my papers. Why on earth do you have to go and do so silly a thing?' It was all said in sorrow rather than anger and a year or so later when we both happened to be in the United States he insisted that I go and stay with him at a house he had taken at Pelham Manor. But I discounted Northcliffe's advice: I knew that that was just the way he would react.

Among the letters warning me against what the writers regarded as a mistake I find two from a very curious source. One is from Erskine Childers, author of the spy story *The Riddle of the Sands*; ardent admirer of and worker in the British Navy, and organizer of rebellion in Ireland. The other letter is from his wife. The fantastic tragedy of Childers's life was that he finally suffered death by execution, not at the hands of the British, but at the hands of the very Irish government he had helped to form, in the sense that it had arisen as the outcome of the movement of rebellion he had joined.[1]

Mrs. Childers (a charming Boston woman, at that time virtually a cripple, but accustomed to going with her husband on yachting cruises which more than once they asked me to join) writes (20 Jan. 1915) that because 'my husband and I think of ourselves as two of your good friends and your best well-wishers,' she will 'take the courage to say things you will have heard before and may not like.' She goes on:

I have been longing to see you and talk with you about the Union for Democratic Control. Forgive me if I tell you how sorry I was when I saw your name with those of MacDonald and Trevelyan, not because of anything against them, for they are good men, but because I felt you were becoming a politician and in so doing were cutting off a great part of your powers. They both are men who arouse antagonisms and by injudicious public utterances at the beginning of the war impaired the usefulness

[1] His execution was an incident in the conflicts which arose between the Republicans and the Free Staters, a civil war marked by assassination and counter-assassination. What was peculiar in the case of Erskine Childers was that he had fought for Britain in two wars—the Boer War and the First World War.

of what might have been of immense value if said later after the war is over. This of course was their own look-out. But I was sad when I heard you were working with them, for I think you had everything before you and this war proves all you have taught.

In reply I wrote to Childers to say that I was not in the least angry and suggested an evening to talk it over. Theirs was typical of the attitude of a good many friends, notably, as already mentioned, of Esher. How far they were right and I was wrong, is discussed in a subsequent chapter, because it bears on the means of reaching the public mind and of preserving among the public the temper of rational discussion. Some of the Olympians of that time failed to preserve such a temper. Although the letters I received from people I knew were usually decent and arguable, I received a number that were not. Among them was one from Wells (whom I knew slightly and was to see more of later and be associated with in his efforts to secure a commonly recognized code of human rights). Part of his letter was later embodied in a fierce personal attack upon me in the Press. It was a little before this that he made a similar Press attack upon the intellectual qualities of Shaw, rating them very low indeed. In a letter addressed to the members of the Executive Committee of the U.D.C. as a whole he thought it well to make a reference to the obscurity of MacDonald's birth. I appear to have replied to Wells in the Press, because among letters of that time I find one from Lady Courtney in which she writes: 'I read your answer to H. G. Wells to my husband and we both thought it admirable. His attack on you would have been quite incomprehensible if one did not know . . .' and here there follows a verdict a bit too severe for quotation. 'Yet,' she goes on, 'he is a brilliant writer, has the popular ear and is right about peace (in the main)—and other questions we care about—and we cannot afford to lose any effective help there, though *I* should have as little personal relations with him as possible, so much do I dislike his moral tone. . . . I think the time will come when you and your friends and others from other sides of the Peace camp must commune together and take counsel. I should be very happy if in the autumn our house could be of any use.'

Against E. D. Morel the Chesterton-Belloc group carried on a malicious vendetta accusing him of being 'a paid agent of Prussia.' Morel discussed the question of a suit for libel, but the general impression seemed to be that in the then state of public opinion a jury would accord him a farthing's damages and that the case would cost him two or three thousand pounds. The general temper of the public might be illustrated by an incident related to me by a friend who had attended a public meeting in the North, convened by a group of organizations, including Trade Union branches. A resolution concerning the war and the kind of peace which ought to be established was presented and passed with only a very few dissentient votes. Immediately after the chairman had announced the result, one of the public got up and asked the chairman whether he was aware that the resolution the meeting had just passed was word for word one of the resolutions of the Union for Democratic Control. A gasp of surprise went up on the part of everybody, and the chairman quite calmly thereupon accepted a motion to rescind and condemn the resolution, a condemnation which was immediately passed by an overwhelming majority.

An attempt to hold a meeting of the U.D.C. which I was to address in Cambridge degenerated into a rag of serious proportions, and was indeed marked by the death of one undergraduate, despite the intervention of the Senior Proctor who came to the meeting in an attempt to restore peace. A sack of flour which undergraduates had managed to lodge on a beam above the platform, and the contents of which were intended for me, found a target in the Proctor. One of the undergraduates engaged in the operations got on to the roof of the building, lost his foothold, fell, and later died from his injuries. The meeting was abandoned. But the undergraduates were out for my blood and the police, after a struggle of about a couple of hours, managed to get me to a fire station where we barricaded ourselves. Meantime a contingent of undergraduates had gone to the house of the don where I was staying and managed to push down about fifty yards of garden wall.

Among the notes of that time I find the letter of a correspondent in the *Daily Mail*, typical of the prevailing anti-Germanism, congratulating the authorities of a seaside town for having placed over their band-stand the notice: 'All music by German composers has been withdrawn.' The letter goes on to ask 'When are we going to see similar placards outside the Albert Hall, the Queen's Hall, Covent Garden Theatre, or wherever music is being performed throughout Great Britain?' The demand became general. 'Boche Music Must Go' shouted the *Mail* editorials. Such music, said the paper, is 'wily Pro-Germanism,' a subtle form of German propaganda. 'Wherever they have penetrated during the War,' wrote a contributor, 'one of their first cards has been to organize concerts.' Sir Henry Wood was castigated by a correspondent because he conducted a concert which included Wagner. Mr. Diaghilev joined in. 'German music is suffocating miasma,' Brahms a 'putrefying corpse,' 'Beethoven a mummy,' and, 'as for Schumann, I see in him nothing but a homesick dog howling at the moon.' And then, to vary things, a Christian clergyman is violently fulminating against 'the insult to his parish' which he believed the sheltering of some starving Austrian children by householders in the neighbourhood, constituted.

It was some time before this that I was solemnly expelled from a well-known West End club[1] as any card-sharper might have been. But I shed no tears. I had joined the club at the insistence, I think, of Evelyn Wrench, who thought I ought to have, apart from my chambers in the Temple, a place where I could entertain people—British and foreign—concerned with my work. But so little of a club man am I that although I was elected, paid the stiff entrance fee and for a year or two the yearly dues, I never once set foot inside the place (even to sign the register): so it could hardly have been on personal grounds that the committee decided to expel me. I insisted that the committee cite some specific reason for their action and, after some longish delay, they solemnly replied that their action had been due to the attitude which I had taken upon the question of the Freedom of the Seas, and to the fact that my writings were 'hostile to British interests and repugnant to the feelings of the members of the Club.'

Yet contrasting kindnesses were without number. At about this time I had a communication from the Rowntrees which, like so many of my contacts with them, touched me very deeply. Their solicitor, Richard Cross, who met a tragic death by drowning a year or two later, came to me one day and said in effect: 'The Rowntrees realize that you must have expended much of your

---

[1] I refrain from mentioning the name in order not to associate the members of this generation with the silliness of a previous generation for which they are not responsible.

income and resources on the work you have been carrying on these last few years and are wondering if it has not depleted those resources a bit too much for your comfort. If it has, they would regard it as a great privilege to make a contribution to the cause of peace by providing you with an income during the next few years.' Fortunately I was not in such a position that that became necessary, and what with occasional lecture tours in America and royalties, I have always managed to rub along without help of this kind. But it struck me then that this gesture was characteristic.

The incident recalls my friendship with Joseph Rowntree, who was responsible for all the big modern development of the great York business. I often stayed with him in York and got to know his family pretty well. It was Joseph's habit on Saturdays, even when he was eighty-five years of age, to take the train to Scarborough and walk along the cliffs, preferably in company of a visitor, which I happened to be on several occasions. He would take with him four, possibly six, biscuits, three for himself, three for the visitor. That was the luncheon. His people were of the type that kept to the old Quaker simplicity. I recall that on one of these visits his wife apologized for the fact that new potatoes were being served in the early spring. They were not, as I might suppose, bought in the luxury markets. They were grown in their own garden and they felt therefore entitled to have them at this unusual season.

When the United States came into the war, public opinion there showed as much violent-mindedness as had been revealed in Britain. One was reminded once more of Samuel Johnson's aphorism : ' In war-time people want to hear only two things : good of themselves and evil of the enemy. And after war, I know not which is to be feared the more, garrets full of scribblers who have learned to lie, or streets full of soldiers who have learned to rob.' A Columbia professor proposed a bill making it a penal offence to teach the German language to an American citizen; such teaching should only be by special licence granted after careful investigation as to whether the student is one hundred per cent, chemically pure, American. . . . Did the director of the

Boston Symphony Orchestra refuse to play 'The Star Spangled Banner'? Are there GERMANS in the orchestra? The headlines screamed at one. Indeed the mob mind in the United States often outdid that of Britain in violence and silliness. The violence was often excused on the ground that at least when the peace came the country would be forewarned against the renewal of 'German wiles,' would realize the necessity of taking its part in preventing the recurrence of any mischief Germany might initiate in the future. But in fact that was not all what happened. The passion wore itself out and the reaction contributed to three natural—and disastrous—results. For many Americans Germany as the main culprit was soon replaced by Britain, who had, in the popular view, managed to hoodwink the American people by her astute propaganda; this in its turn led to a reversion to isolationism, rapid and intense; and when the really barbarous Germany of Hitler developed, its danger was underestimated and met with appeasement. I recall after an American lecture about 1924 remarking to Walter Lippmann, 'The majority of this people believe that in entering the war they were made victims of a vast hoax,' and his reply: 'If you don't know that about American public opinion at this time you don't know anything.'

The recollection of this sort of silliness brings home to-day a fact which has not perhaps been sufficiently recognized or analysed. Public feeling against the Germans in the first war was much more passionate and its manifestations much more idiotic, than in the second war. Yet the Germany of 1914 was—as the previous chapter has insisted—a much more civilized Germany (with an astonishingly free Press, a powerful Socialist party, no Nuremberg Laws, no concentration camps, no political prisoners, no Gestapo) than the Hitlerite Germany we were to appease for so long before finally fighting her. The second war was relatively free, both in Britain and the United States, from the crude hysteria which marked the first.

The very people who during the first war showed this passion against a relatively civilized Germany were to treat as warmongers those of us who insisted that the 'new' Germany had become a danger to Western Civilization. Very soon I was to be made extremely familiar with this ugly side of the public mind.

CHAPTER VI

PRIVATE MISSIONS TO AMERICA: THE WILSON CONTACTS

By the spring of 1915 it did not require much prescience to realize that the length and outcome of the war, the possibility of a workable peace, would depend very largely on the policy of the United States. Early in the year, I had received an invitation from the Carnegie Endowment to become 'Director of Studies' at a Summer School of International Relations to be held at Cornell University during that summer; and decided to accept the invitation.

I was still at that time keeping some, but a rapidly diminishing, contact with the Garton Foundation. In a letter to Esher dated 5 May 1915, I wrote, letting him know that I proposed going to America for a time, adding, 'There is not much that I could do at present at the Foundation here, and such activity as we have agreed upon is being well prosecuted by Hilton and Fayle. I think the slight rearrangement of personnel recently will be all to the good. Heretofore a payment has been made to me which I have in turn expended on help for work in connection with the Foundation; but now the cost for Foundation work is directly defrayed by the Foundation and no payments are made through me or to me at all. I am quite sure this is a more suitable arrangement. The work now being done by the Foundation will prove useful as the war draws to a conclusion and the more permanent problems arising out of it are puzzling the minds of the public.'

After receiving this, Esher wrote, asking me to go and see him for a talk before I left. Unfortunately, I was compelled suddenly to leave at an earlier date than I had intended and got his letter only on my arrival in New York. I do not think that I ever saw Esher again.

James Bryce, who had been British Ambassador in Washington and who was more sympathetic to my attitude in the war than

he thought it wise perhaps to admit in public, gave me a number
of letters of introduction to politicians and others in the United
States. They were to prove useful.

There was no difficulty, on that occasion, about passport, or
in securing a berth on the old *City of Paris*. We sailed from
Liverpool a week after the sinking of the *Lusitania* and were to
steam through much of its wreckage, including life boats with
dead bodies sprawled over the thwarts. Evidently the captain had
received orders on no account to stop, for we ploughed at full
speed through it all, without stopping to recover the bodies or
to see if by chance there was life in some of them; which con-
ceivably there might have been.

The Summer School or Conference at Cornell followed the
lines which we had followed at the Old Jordans conference of
the previous year and which have already been described.

Prominent among the students were Manley Hudson, subsequently of the Harvard Law School and member of the World
Court at the Hague : Lewis Gannett, whose description thirty
years afterwards has already been quoted; Hu Shi who was
later to become Chinese Ambassador to the United States and
whose command of English was already amazing, and with
whom I have maintained a friendly contact ever since. The run-
of-the-mill American students who attended were less interested
in ideas as such than students in Europe would have been;
demanded cut and dried solutions, a world constitution, (' Why
not a United States of the World?') all set out in written documents so that the whole thing could be dismissed by signing on
the dotted line. I had very great difficulty in persuading them
that if they went into that sort of project without any examination
of their own real feelings, about, say, their nation's right to live
under institutions which differed from those of the rest of the
world, and about such things as Asiatic immigration, they would
be the very first to repudiate the grandiose constitutions they
proposed so casually. The enthusiastic, flamboyant welcome given
two years later to Wilson's suggested League of Nations, to be
followed by its still more violent rejection (together with rejection
of Wilson himself) in the election of 1920 was, alas, tragically to
illustrate the point and to vindicate my misgivings.

As soon as my job with the Cornell Summer School was
finished, I received a cordial invitation from the editor of the

New Republic to take part in their editorial discussions. It ended in my becoming for about a year virtually a member of the staff.

The paper was then financed largely by the Straights—Willard Straight and his wife Dorothy Whitney Straight—with, I think, Tom Lamont having some interest. The staff at that time included Herbert Croly, the editor, Walter Lippmann, Alvin Johnson, Felix Frankfurter, Francis Hackett, Philip Littell, Charles Merz, while occasional contributors included William Hard, Randolph Bourne, John Dewey, H. N. Brailsford, Graham Wallas, and Harold Laski. There were weekly staff luncheons at which usually some outside visitor was entertained and questioned. Northcliffe, when he was High Commissioner in the United States, was one such visitor, Lord Eustace Percy another. Now and again some members of the staff would spend a week-end at the Straights' house on Long Island hammering out issues of foreign policy.

Francis Hackett, that rare bird, an entirely sane and realistic Irish nationalist, and Philip Littell, who wrote so charmingly of ' Books and Things,' both men enchanting in their separate ways, became rather especial friends of mine. Francis Hackett, after I had left the paper to return to England, wrote an entertaining (and all too flattering) character-sketch of me. With Charles Merz I was to renew contact in the days of the second war, by which time he had become editor of the *New York Times*.

It is no reflection upon the present *New Republic* to say that the paper of 1951 does not occupy quite the special position that did the paper of 1916–17. At that earlier date it was in a sense a mouthpiece of the White House. Some of the staff—notably Croly and Lippmann—were in fairly constant contact with Wilson. Independently of the *New Republic* I had contacts of my own with Wilson, mainly through Colonel House, whom I saw from time to time. The number of memoranda with which I supplied Wilson must have been from first to last considerable. It was all done very informally—and quite privately. I was careful to have no contacts at all with the British Embassy (where indeed I would probably have been received at that time with icy coldness) in order that anything I wrote or discussed with the White House people should have no official colour and should be regarded for what it was—simply the contribution of a private and unofficial Englishman who happened to have written books on international affairs. So private and personal were these relations that when, after a year or so in England, I returned to the United States, after the country's entrance into the war, I was one day put under virtual arrest as a seditious person by some newly established Security Office in New York.

Two plain-clothes security police having called at the little apartment I then had on 116th Street just by Columbia University, I was told that I must accompany them to the headquarters of their superior officer. He proved to be a very brash, cocksure young officer, suggesting a loutish undergraduate in a brand new uniform. 'What was I doing in the United States? Where was I born? What were my origins?'

Most of the questions he asked could have been found by reference to 'Who's Who,' but there was some impulse which prevented my suggesting that. And when he asked me what references I could give in the United States as to my bona fides, it was on the tip of my tongue to say, 'Well, you might ask the President.' But I knew that that would not do, nor indeed even to suggest that they go to Colonel House, because, although there was nothing ' illicit' in those contacts, they were not through the Embassy. (There was not as yet any Un-American Activities Committee, but equivalents were just coming into being and the administration's enemies might exploit any injudicious statements of an Englishman, especially one commonly regarded as a pacifist.) So I contented myself with giving the names of my publishers and a few editors. Assuming from this that I had some acquaintance with the newspaper and book world, the young man began to question me as to the ideas, characters, habits, and associations of people whose names he had on a list before him. They included such subversive characters as the editors of the *New Republic*, Norman Hapgood, Walter Lippmann, Felix Frankfurter. The inquisitor was persistent. What was my opinion of them? What were their opinions? I think he enjoyed it but I declined to discuss these personalities, suggesting at this point that there were plenty of sources open to the officer other than my own opinions expressed in such circumstances.

I never heard any more of this incident, and it is just possible that some superior officer may have rapped him over the knuckles. Unlike Bertrand Russell, who was very proud of his prison experience, this was the only occasion in which I found myself marched through the streets between two plain-clothes policemen.

The incident was to leave a very unpleasant taste in my mouth for some time. Was the security work of the United States usually entrusted to young cubs of this character? And were the liberties of United States citizens to be placed in such hands? (My own worst experience was to be at the hands of British official-dom, as recorded in the next chapter.)

It seems to have puzzled friends and critics alike that, having stood for at least temporary neutrality for Great Britain in August, 1914, I should by 1915 be arguing that neutrality for the United States was, in the world conditions which by that time had developed, a policy disastrous alike for the interests of America and future peace. There was of course no contradiction. The conclusion that in our little world of to-day, with its annihilation of distance, neutrality is a completely unworkable principle of international policy, follows ineluctably from the central theme of everything I had been writing, that theme being the interdependence of modern nations, not alone in economics but in defence. If you are dependent on the power and wealth of another for your own security and welfare you cannot afford to see that other destroyed; you cannot be 'neutral' to aggression upon him, an argument which seems so self-evident to-day, but was denied in 1914 as far-fetched nonsense. The neutrality proposal was an attempt to get breathing space, taking a calculated risk.

In an editorial article of the *New Republic* of 20 May 1916, I pointed out that the attempt of the American government to maintain the legalistic fiction of neutrality paralysed that government in the defence of its most vital interests. If America had really desired to treat both combatants alike, she would have denied munitions to Britain as in fact they were denied to Germany by Britain's command of the sea. Neutrality so interpreted, I went on to point out, implied that America would sell munitions to Germany if she could come and fetch them. So long as the United States maintained that position, the Germans would say, 'If we could have commanded the sea we could have transferred the economic alliance of America from our enemies to ourselves. . . . The vast national resources of America would act, not as a silent pressure on the side of the good behaviour of nations and the respect of treaty right, but on the side of naval rivalry irrespective of right or treaty obligation of the general interest of nations.

At one stage of my communications with Wilson I had suggested that the American public was in grave danger of slipping away from any real understanding of his underlying policy; that they had not yet grasped the principles which seemed so familiar to him. The President seems to have resented the suggestion. He overrated, I think, his command of the American public mind. It is true that among intellectuals and newspaper men of the better sort, the *New Republic* crowd, and men like Norman Hapgood, his cause was understood, warmly approved. But this understanding did not reach to the ninety-eight per cent that was to matter so much when the time for ratification of Wilson's work in Paris arrived. Curiously enough, Northcliffe, who had always understood the fact that the public only very slowly grasped a new idea, seemed to think that the President had complete command of the electorate. One day, talking things over with Northcliffe in his offices on Fifth Avenue, I expressed my own doubts as to whether the American public, once Wilson had left for Paris, would continue to follow him. Northcliffe did not agree. Taking my arm, he walked to the window of his office and said, ' Look down that street. Do you see any single soul not wearing a straw hat? Do you see any man wearing a straw hat that differs from all the other straw hats? That is how Americans wear things on their heads or inside their heads. This people is an imitative people; a follow-the-leader, follow-the-fashion people. They move in masses. And now that they are in this war they will move in a mass behind the Commander-in-Chief.' I was doubtful, and events, alas, were to confirm my doubts. In this connection I had an article in one of the monthlies which, if my memory serves, was headed : ' Why the President May Fail.' He might fail, I suggested, because in truth the American public did not as yet understand what he was driving at, a view which quite a few of the more far-sighted commentators were beginning to express. ' How,' asked the *New York Times* editorially, ' can Mr. Wilson at Paris, or even at Washington, know what the American people think about these momentous questions when as yet they do not themselves know what they think about them?' And it went on to suggest that the President might find the Senate rejecting conclusions reached by him in Paris.

When Wilson began to outline his project of a League he had overwhelming but impulsive support from the American public. The League to Enforce Peace was supported by nearly all the leaders of the Republican party, and by practically all the governors of the states. I was present when Taft made this statement: 'If ever it should happen that the Republican Party should repudiate the League of Nations I shall resign from that party immediately giving to my resignation all possible publicity.' Wilson was deceived by all this; he believed that his battle was won so far as public opinion was concerned. And others believed it, too. Why Wilson was deceived—or deceived himself—is described in a sketch of Wilson and his work (written at the time of his death) which appears at the end of this chapter.

By way of familiarizing the public with the underlying principles of the kind of League for which we hoped Wilson would stand, I was active during the summer and autumn of 1918 with 'The League of Free Nations Association,'[1] which was the forerunner of the Foreign Policy Association. For some six months about fifty of us met once a week.

I drew up the 'Statement of Principles' in which I suggested that the purposes of the League of Nations were to achieve for all people, great and small, (1) security: the due protection of national existence; and (2) equality of economic opportunity. These purposes supported by considerations accepted by the Association, as follows:

Both these purposes demand for their accomplishment profound changes in the spirit and principles of the older international

[1] Lewis Gannett writes in the *Book of the Month Club Bulletin*, Feb. 1943: 'Angell was in 1918 one of the inspirers of the League of Free Nations Association, out of which grew both President Taft's League to enforce Peace, and the Foreign Policy Association. He was one of the earliest advocates of the League of Nations, and one of its severest critics. He always preached co-operation with Soviet Russia, and always rejected the basic tenet of the Marxists, that industrial capitalism makes war inevitable.'

statecraft. The underlying assumption heretofore has been that a nation's security and prosperity rest chiefly upon its own strength and resources. Such an assumption has been used to justify statesmen in attempting, on the ground of the supreme need for national security, to increase their own nation's power and resources by insistence upon strategic frontiers, territory with raw material, outlets to the sea, even though that course does violence to the security and prosperity of others. Under any system in which adequate defence rests upon individual preponderance of power, the security of one must involve the insecurity of another, inevitably giving rise to covert or overt competitions for power and territory dangerous to peace and destructive to justice.

The fundamental principle underlying the League of Nations is that the security and rights of each member shall rest upon the strength of the whole League, pledged to uphold by their combined power international arrangements ensuring fair treatment for all.

During the four years of the war and the two years or so following, I published, either in the United States or Great Britain, six books elaborating the above theme but relating it very closely to the future position of the United States in international affairs. The books in the order of their appearance were: *The Dangers of Half-Preparedness*: *A Plea for a Declaration of American Policy*; *The World's Highway*: *Notes on America's Relation to Sea Power and Non-Military Sanctions*; *The Political Conditions of Allied Success*: *A Plea for a Defensive Union of the Democracies*; *The British Revolution and the American Democracy*: *An Interpretation of British Labour Programmes*; *War Aims*: *A Plea for a Parliament of the Allies*; and *The Peace Treaties and the Economic Chaos* which dealt with the economic disasters that would almost certainly follow from some features of the Peace Treaties (as they did follow).

The first of the above-mentioned books was the expansion of an address delivered in Washington on 28 February 1916, in which I tried to show that if we do not know for what a foreign nation's power stands we are obliged to meet it with equivalent or greater force, so that there is likely to grow up a situation in which two nations, or groups, in competition, can only be secure if each is stronger than the other, an attempt to base policy upon a physical impossibility. The Allies did for the moment know the immediate purpose of their own power: the defeat of

Germany. But unless the Allies were agreed upon their purposes when they came to make peace the alliance would probably go to pieces. (As it did.) It was not, I explained, 'an argument that the advocate of preparedness is asking too much, but that he is asking too little; not that we do not need armament, but that we need something else as well; it is an argument not against preparedness, but against preparedness by dangerous half-measures,' and that discussion could not be left till the end of the war: 'Human nature being combative, coercive, guided largely by impulse and passion and very little by reason and reflection, to expect wisdom at such time is to ask intellectual and moral miracles of men.'

I recall that the highest praise for this published address (it was pretty well received) came from Walter Lippmann in a long review in the *New Republic*.

The signing of the Armistice found me in America but I left almost immediately for Paris travelling to Bordeaux in a rat-infested ship with Henry Scattergood, a member of one of those Philadelphia Quaker families with a record that goes back to William Penn's time. He was going over for some Quaker Service work and displayed in it the dedication and abnegation which is so commonplace with Quakers and should reduce us ordinary mortals to silence and humility in their presence. With him was Rufus Jones, 'the Quaker Saint'—a title I am sure he disliked, for his saintliness had nothing of the de-humanized quality we commonly associate with saints. Both were an honour to the Society of Friends—but then most of its members are. I have enjoyed Scattergood's friendship half my life and nothing was too much trouble for him if he felt it could help me.

The little group aboard also included William Allen White, the country editor who made of his small town newspaper a national organ. In his autobiography he has recounted something of our common experience. Here are some extracts:

Bill and I shared our cabin with Norman Angell, who was also a table-mate, and I came to admire and trust him and have held him in affectionate esteem through all these years. . . . As we

P

dropped south toward Bordeaux, our landing place, the weather
moderated and we walked the deck a good deal, treading on
shell-pink clouds of iridescent dreams about world peace. There
was rumour and gossip about the League of Nations which Wilson
was determined to establish, and Angell had a lot of ideas about
the League—better ones, I discovered later, than Wilson had.
But we talked at the table and on deck in our chairs and afoot,
about the League and Europe and the peace, and it was a highly
profitable journey. I disembarked with much more baggage in
mind and heart than I had in the hold. It was my introduction
to international politics. . . .

White goes on to relate how we also shared quarters in Paris
—the 'we' including his son Bill who was to be among the first
of the plucky band of American journalists to tell the truth about
Russian Communism (and to get plentifully kicked by American
Leftists for his pains); and who was later in life to acquire a great
reputation as an author of political reporting books, and of good
screen writing for Hollywood.

My knowledge of Paris enabled me to find for our little gang
somewhat better quarters than those we were assigned, and
White relates how ' we left the *Normandie* and tucked in for
nearly five months at the Vouillemont. There lived Ray Stannard
Baker, who was the President's mouthpiece to the Press, and Ida
Tarbell, who was writing something about the peace for the
American Magazine. Dorothy Canfield used to come occasionally.
Half a dozen men who were more or less attached to the
American delegation to the conference lived there; Quakers who
were doing reconstruction work in terms of many millions of
dollars in devastated France; and, for a time, Oswald Garrison
Villard, and one or two correspondents from the London papers.'

Despite my fairly frequent indirect contacts with Wilson—
through memoranda and lengthy talks with those who saw him
personally—on only one occasion did I see him face to face and
talk with him freely and privately. The impression I carried away
was mainly one of remoteness from the mind of the mass for
whom he felt himself to be speaking. On the occasion of his
death I attempted an appraisal of his place in history. While my
general conclusion was that ' one day his monument would cover
the earth,' I also added that ' on the human side, he failed. The
intellectual character of some of his contributions in the shape

of his pronouncements was often miles above the common standard of his time. But though he talked so often about the common people and the plain man, he had no quick and intuitive understanding of the underlying forces of public opinion.' It was not merely that he kept putting his foot into it by such things as 'Too proud to fight,' truths which, by their expression, lent themselves to distortion by his enemies. He adopted at times an attitude of aloof and schoolmasterish autocracy which to the average Congressman or Senator was maddening. At the beginning of the war he seemed to have recognized the danger that Americans would ' lose our heads along with the rest.' He remarked to Frank Cobb of the New York *World*, ' Once lead this people into war and they will forget there ever was such a thing as tolerance.' But he took no steps, or quite inadequate steps, to forestall this. And House himself was sometimes a bad adviser, a man not of Wilson's intellectual standards. I repeatedly wondered why Wilson should surround himself with intellectual inferiors—until I recalled that that was a habit with people who possessed great power and underwent its peculiar influences upon themselves.

I made some private notes at the time *re* Wilson. They were : (1) He is taking no adequate steps to keep his own people informed of his purposes or even relatively sane; yet if sanity goes everything goes and he will be defeated in his aims. (2) He refused a bi-partisan delegation, in part because he was a bad hand at conferring and co-operating with others. (3) Showed a lack of flexibility about the League. (4) He was not strong and forceful and insistent just where he should have been—about the guarantees to France, as urged by Clemenceau when the Treaty embodying them came before the Senate.

There came a moment in his career when he was literally unteachable, although, alas, as we know from Keynes' testimony, he could be bamboozled. The Government of America during the years of war was of course a dictatorship, as all governments in time of war tend to become. But it was a dictatorship without human contact. ' Seeing people exhausts me,' he once remarked to a friend. He missed altogether the importance of the jingo wave which swept up a month or two after the entrance of America into the war and which he did nothing to check. He allowed the precious Mr. Burleson to put many of the real friends of a ' fourteen-point peace ' in jail. Even his Victorian Liberalism should have taught him better than this. He would do all the speaking, he implied on one occasion. The result of that policy was that he spoke in effect to people whose emotions and violent-mindedness had rendered them deaf to everything but war-time pugnacity and national partisanship.

One need not search for very complicated reasons for his failure in Paris. He was coming to the Old World to bring it a new standard, to induce it to break down the old tradition of retaliatory nationalism and punitive settlement. But he came at a moment when all that was articulate in the American people was clamouring for, first and foremost, a punitive and vindictive peace—and for very little else.

In the sketch (*Foreign Affairs*, London, March 1924) from which some of the foregoing observations are taken, I note that there is a curious tendency among some European historians to burke this fact of American emotionalism and hysterical national-ism, 'The American jingoes became momentarily all-powerful after the Armistice, and Theodore Roosevelt a figure im-measurably more popular for a time than Wilson. Such a post-war feeling was bound to manifest itself in some degree in any case, but it was greatly worsened by the fact that those whose public function it would normally have been to expose day by day, week in, week out, the folly of jingoism, were silenced by the machinery which Wilson sanctioned. Journalists were denied "mailing privileges" for their papers, men like Debs were sent to prison, professors were retired, and congregations indicted their Christian shepherds under clauses of the Espionage Act. The story of what happened under that Act, the heresy huntings, harryings, the smellings out of "treason," the railroading of men to jail for speaking disrespectfully of the Constitution, or failing to stand up when a barrel organ played the "Stars and Stripes" —all this to-day would read like a bad joke. Americans would not believe it to be true. But it was true, and it is in the heart of Wilson's failure. It is because it was true that he had not the driving force behind him to make his dreams a more immediate reality.'

The above was written, be it noted, in 1924, by which time, presumably, the witch-hunting epidemic, the smelling-out of political heretics, had for the time being burned itself out. But the anti-German debauch of the year or two following the First World

War was a mere vicar's tea party when we compare it to the temper which followed the Second War, during Truman's second term. The fury was only partly anti-Communist. It was directed also against Europeans in general. But the brunt of it was directed against the American administration itself, particularly against Truman and the State Department. Henry Adams tells us in the story of his education that the State Department has always been the target of popular dislike if not hatred, since it is for the average American a constant reminder of a world which he would prefer did not exist, or which at least would leave him in peace. A typical newspaper 'letter from Washington' (in the *New Yorker* of 27 Jan. 1951) notes that the Administration policy has been under an attack 'whose fury and bitterness it would be impossible to exaggerate,' and goes on to say that 'what is extraordinary about the attack is less its fury and bitterness than the fact that most of the time it has found no defence in any Congressional quarter. Not a single member in either house has seen fit to put in a kind word for what are after all the official policies of the United States government.'

What must be the effect of this upon the soldier in Korea who is called upon to give perhaps his life, or to suffer the loss of frostbitten feet and hands, for a policy which is bitterly condemned by the popular papers he reads and all but unanimously condemned by his representatives in Congress? One commentator remarks that if we are to judge the army by Congress the 'soldiers of democracy' fighting in Korea do not know why they are there, are not sure whether they should be there at all; do not know what they are fighting for. Is it thus that we are to give to our peoples of the West a faith fit to meet the fanaticism of the Communist world?

I put the question because it is an ultimate one for the democracies of this generation, and because certain personal experiences of my own may throw some light on the way in which governments handle or mishandle this problem. One such experience is outlined in the chapter which follows.

CHAPTER VII

WHY DO GOVERNMENTS BEHAVE LIKE THIS?

WESTERN governments are beginning, but hardly more than beginning, to recognize the importance of explaining their policies to their own people and to foreign countries. The peoples of the West must understand, and thus acquire some faith in their own political principles as a counter-balance to the power of the fanatical convictions of Communist peoples. To which end the United States government has made a beginning with such efforts as 'The Voice of America.' One modern political writer goes so far as to put the alternative in a book's title *Persuade or Perish*.

It cannot be said, however, that Western governments have been notably successful in this field. Occasionally they make howling mistakes which may be worth noting as indicating the tendencies about which we should be vigilant. The story which follows, a personal experience of my own, may have some relevance in this context.

In both the First and the Second World Wars, Britain's victory, like that of her Continental allies, depended upon securing the co-operation, support and ultimate alliance of the United States. By 1916 the British (i.e., the Allied) military position had already become exceedingly precarious; without American help defeat was certain. But the speed and degree of American intervention was highly uncertain. Public opinion in America was deeply divided, hesitant. Isolationism was deep-seated, the German and the Irish vote (the latter influenced by the Easter rebellion) were factors which politicians did not care to disregard.

At that juncture an Englishman, familiar with the American scene, having gone to America, and having a certain public there[1] for his books, urges in many lectures and articles, in terms most likely to appeal to an American public, co-operation of the United States with Britain and her European allies. His suggestions and ideas reach the White House. Not wishing, however,

---

[1] One of his books outlining the British case in the Second World War and addressed to the American public sold about 300,000 copies.

to evade conscription and thinking he might come within its scope, he returns to England in 1916. He finds that he is not liable and on volunteering for army service, is rejected. Feeling that his most useful work is in America, he applies for a passport.

Whereupon the authorities make it clear (1) that he will not be permitted to return to America; (2) he will not be permitted to contribute to the American Press; (3) any private communications to American public men or journalists will be suppressed by the postal censor.

The bare facts would seem to suggest that the government had some unrevealed knowledge of sinister communication with the enemy or that the man against whom these measures were taken was moved by some subtle design inimical to British interests. There were no such communications or design. Nor indeed were they ever alleged, though the matter was thrashed out in Parliament and was the subject of much correspondence with officials.

The story is best told in extracts from certain records and documents of the time. Thus the *New Republic* of 1 Sept. 1916, notes that, 'According to newspaper reports the British government has refused to issue passports to Bertrand Russell and Norman Angell,' and goes on to suggest that 'the object of the refusal must be that of preventing Messrs. Russell and Angell from fulfilling engagements in this country to lecture' because it was feared 'they might talk about the war to Americans in unorthodox language.' In that case, continues the article, 'the American friends of Great Britain can but regard such behaviour with profound discomfiture, chagrin and grief. . . . In Mr. Angell's case the refusal to allow him to keep speaking engagements is, if true, of a peculiar stupidity. During his last trip to the United States Mr. Angell did more than all the other Englishmen who have come over since August 1914 to make the idea of unneutrality in relation to the war persuasive to American public opinion.'

In the next issue of the paper there appeared a longer editorial which I hesitate to quote and do so only because it is necessary to the telling of this particular story and because it illustrates the hazards in the development of ideas in international politics. The article appeared on 16 September 1916 (at which time I may remind the reader I was in England), is headed 'What Norman Angell Did,' and is in part as follows:

Mr. Wilson's speech of acceptance contained one sentence which overshadows anything that has been said or will be said during the campaign. In the years to come that sentence will surely gather a significance which has been ignored in the heat and haste and distraction of the moment. The statement that ' no nation can any longer remain neutral as against any wilful disturbance of the peace of the world ' is a doctrine the importance of which it is hardly possible to exaggerate. The fact that it is uttered now by the President of the most powerful neutral, by the President of a nation which has practised and preached international laissez-faire, is a reversal of such importance and with such endless consequences that it would absorb our attention if we had a just perspective on our own future. . . . The principle that neutrality is obsolete is the basis of organized peace in the world.

The foregoing paragraph refers to a development of Wilsonian —and ultimately American—policy which is too often forgotten. At the outbreak of the war, President Wilson in very solemn and urgent terms impressed upon the American public the duty of neutrality. Americans were, he insisted, to be neutral not merely in word and deed, but in thought. The pronouncement referred to did constitute therefore, as the commentator indicates, a complete reversal of policy not merely with reference to the War then in progress, but to the future. For a President to declare formally that in the world which the war was bringing into being, the United States would never again be able long to remain neutral in any major international conflict was something in the nature of a revolution in policy. The article in the *New Republic* goes on :

The particular words used by Mr. Wilson are worth noting. He speaks of neutrality as no longer possible. This attack on neutrality originated with a man who should have the credit for it. It originated with Mr. Norman Angell, and the words used by the president are Mr. Angell's own words.

Mr. Angell spent last winter in the United States lecturing and writing. In the weeks preceding the last crisis with Germany over the *Sussex*, he formulated the doctrine that neutrality was obsolete. It emerged after hours of discussion on the basis of memoranda which were many times recast. The results reached the President, not only directly but through his confidential advisers, and there can be no doubt that the most important sentence in Mr. Wilson's speech was written by Mr. Norman Angell. . . .

Most of the semi-official visitors have hurt more than they have helped by their insensibility to America and their moral pretentiousness. But Mr. Angell quickly and effectively did an incalculable amount to convince leaders of American Liberalism of their international responsibilities. He drew us closer to that England with which alone an Anglo-Amercian understanding is possible.

It is pretty shameless to quote an article about one's self in such terms, but it is impossible otherwise to convey the full flavour of this episode, and the warning it may give as to what may happen sometimes to governments when charged with the task of public information.

The more persistent the Foreign Office refusal of a passport became the greater did my own desire to get to America become. I even played with the idea of getting a job as ship steward under an assumed name, in order to do the government one in the eye. My letter file reveals, however, that what I did was to worry my friends in government offices. Thus a letter to Philip Kerr [1] telling him that ' I am still " holding off " several journalistic and parliamentary friends who would like to take up the case of my passport because I am still hoping that the Great Anonymity by which we are ruled will see wisdom in this matter ultimately and let me do about the only useful work I can do.' I went on to point out that ' my inclusion in the Press Censor's Black List worsens a misunderstanding already great enough concerning my opinions and writings, and submission in silence would seriously—and unnecessarily—affect my future work as a journalist and author. I want to assure you that it is not from any desire wantonly to make a fuss ; and I will not let the passport question be raised if I can help it.'

It was while waiting for some action about my passport that I received a letter from Croly, the Editor of the *New Republic*, asking me to cable an article, addressed especially to American pacifists who were opposing the country's entrance into the war. Their attitude, explained Croly, was seriously hampering Wilson.

A day or two later I received from Walter Lippmann this letter :

[1] Afterwards the Marquis of Lothian and Ambassador to the United States.

My Dear Angell:

Before this reaches you you will have had a cable from Croly asking you for an article that we could print immediately. Ever since the Germans proclaimed their new submarine warfare we have had an exceedingly hard time in this country dealing with the pacifists who simply want to avoid trouble, and we feel that an article from you justifying America's entrance into the war on liberal and international grounds would be of immense help to us. You will of course know that with Wilson in office for the next four years there is no danger at all of our taking an imperialist line in the war. We would use it first of all to resist German maritime aggression. Secondly, to start going America's participation in world affairs, and third, to bring in America to stabilize the settlement. To us it looks as if the present opportunity might almost be decisive in the history of the world, because there is a chance by America's entrance into the war to crystallize and make real the whole league of peace propaganda. We all know what we owe to you in convincing us of the justice of this view, and it sometimes makes me boil with anger to think that there are Englishmen who speak bitterly of you when as a matter of fact you have had more influence than any other one Englishman I can think of in preparing the background of ideas which would convince Americans who are now in power of the necessity of their taking an active rôle in the war. That service, though it has been in some measure indirect, has been immense. . . .

I hope you can come over here. You may do more than any other man to cement the liberal alliance between this country, Great Britain and France.

Very warmly yours,
Walter Lippmann.

The article for which Croly and Lippmann had asked was duly filed with the cable company and I assumed had been dispatched, since at this time, though my passport had been refused by the Foreign Office, there had been no reference to an embargo upon contributing to the American Press. But about a fortnight after the receipt of Lippmann's letter, I received a cable from Croly: 'Why no article?'

I managed to get an interview with the Chief Censor, in order to find out why the article had not been sent. In answer to my inquiry he did not say a word, but got up, went into an adjoining room and came back carrying a book which he laid before me. It was the official instructions concerning the censorship of correspondence and articles. He pointed to a paragraph which in

effect said that the censor was under no obligation to explain the
reasons for the suppression of Press matter, or for the refusal to
forward letters. As the censor had not spoken a word, I did not
see much reason to be very voluble. I rose, said simply, 'If that
is the attitude you take there is nothing more to be said,' and
walked out of the room.

The refusal of a passport and the embargo on my journalistic
work seemed equally inexplicable. In a letter to Croly I write
that 'Rather provokingly, I have in my possession a private letter
from Mr. Balfour to a friend of mine who says that from the
point of view of the Foreign Office there is no objection to my
going to America, while I have also another private letter to
myself from a prominent Foreign Office official, who happened
to have heard me speak in America, and who writes that he
thought the matter I was talking exactly the stuff that it was
necessary to say at that time. But of course I cannot use either
of these letters for the purpose of supporting my application for a
passport.' The letter goes on to suggest that, 'added to the normal
prejudice of the bureaucrat against outsiders who discuss foreign
policy, and whom he regards as interfering amateurs, there is the
fact that I am supposed to be rather particularly a friend of
Bertrand Russell, whom the War Office seem to have on the
brain. (Though a friend of Russell's and one who has protested
against his persecution, I do *not* share his pacifist views.)' Which
is a reminder that Bertrand Russell at that time was going
through experiences very similar to mine.

My sense of frustration had evidently made me wonder what
the nature of my future activities would be, for towards the end
of the letter to Croly I write that 'If in the future I work mainly
in England, I shall have to associate mainly with the ultra-
revolutionary parties in order to be able to do anything at all.
And I am not that kind of revolutionist for nuts and would far
rather work constructively in the field of internationalism, if the
authorities would allow. The net result of their shutting up people
like myself and giving a completely free hand to people like Leo
Maxse, Bottomley and Northcliffe, is that these latter have everything their own way and give the tone to public opinion. And an
opinion so dominated, with no restraining 'ballast,' ends by
becoming quite unmanageable. The Government deliver themselves into the hands of these extremists.'

It was, of course, in keeping with the whole comedy that I should receive, a few days after dispatching the letter to Croly, an intimation from the postal censor that it had not been forwarded, since it 'tended to convey an inaccurate account of the censorship in Great Britain.'

But meantime the episode was taking an interesting development. Coming downstairs after my interview with the censor, I ran into a member of Parliament (Pringle) whom I knew. Full of my grievance, I told him the whole story. Now Pringle specialized in questions in Parliament. He asked me to let him have all the documents concerned. A few days later he put a question in the House, and got a reply so evasive that he managed to raise the matter on the adjournment, and a long debate followed. Pringle stated the facts as above related, including the fact that the government had issued instructions that none of my writings, whatever their nature, were to go abroad. Other interesting details emerged in the course of the debate.

The account which follows is extracted from Hansard (Parliamentary Debates, Fifth Series, Vol. XCIII, 9 May 1917).

MR. PRINGLE: The answer to the question which I put was rather strange. It was given by the Leader of the House. He said that the article had been suppressed because it was prejudicial, whatever that may mean and, on being pressed, the House was informed that there were certain statements in it which indicated that America had not preserved neutrality in the former part of the War. Why should it matter that Mr. Norman Angell should state that? If any British Minister said America had really not been neutral during the early part of the War, but had been specially favourable to the Allies, there might have been some reason for banning that exportation, just as we banned the exportation of the celebrated comparison of the Kaiser to Mohammed, which was made by the present Prime Minister.

In order to understand the situation, we should realize what this article was. He sets forth very briefly the reasons for American participation, the reasons which he believes would appeal to pacifists in America, and his first point is that:

> In all but legalist fiction America has been at war with Germany for the last two years, affording assistance to the Allies more real than that afforded by certain of the formal belligerents like Japan. Not only have American brains and hands created

vast quantities of the weapons by which the Allies have been able in critical periods to maintain their resistance, but as the *New Republic* has so often shown, American policy in the matter of the blockade, etc., would have been very different except for the unmistakable decision of the American people that nothing should be done really to embarrass the Allies' cause and so favour one which might menace the national security and the freedom of mankind. This was right, but it was not neutral. The condition after formal declaration of war will differ only in degree, not in kind, except that America's position will be open and honest, instead of evasive and equivocal.

I understand that that is the paragraph to which exception was taken. Can any reasonable man in this Committee say that there was any harm in that paragraph appearing in an American newspaper over the signature of Mr. Norman Angell? Whom was it going to embarrass? Whom was it going to assist? Was it going to do anything to interfere with the cordial relations between America and this country? Allow Germany the comfort of the quotation, whatever comfort she can obtain from it. But that is not all. Mr. Norman Angell delivered in America more than a year ago a series of lectures, in which he advocated this thesis, and, indeed, these lectures have now been published in America; so that what additional trouble could be caused if this particular sentence was published in America in addition to all that Mr. Norman Angell has written and said there already? The article goes on :

Secondly, this fictitious neutrality only served to obscure the general realization of America's responsibility and international obligations by perpetuating the illusory sense of islolation from world politics. Until that is broken down America can play no fitting part in the creation of a Society of Nations. The formal pact of war, by dramatizing what already exists, will compel that interest in America's relations, the absence of which interest has been so great an obstacle to constructive pacifist effort in the past.

Surely a very fair contention !

Thirdly, the same fact of dramatization will have a corresponding effect upon European opinion. America's formal alliance with European powers will bring home what is not yet realised here, namely the decisive value of American resources to the Allied cause, and consequently their prospective value to the collective forces of the Society of Nations. The national organization of those resources under a state of war will make them of still greater value, perhaps indispensable, to the Allied cause in the future. The anti-Americanism of the recent past in Europe will be replaced by the cordial welcome of American aid.

As one reads this article one is almost driven to the conclusion that the Government does not want America to participate in the War. What other reason could there be for suppressing it? It is well, when considering this article, to realize exactly the position which Mr. Norman Angell has made for himself in America. He has been one of the people who have spoken in America during the War. We have sent a great many emissaries to America, some with success and others whose efforts have not been of particular value to anybody but themselves. To indicate exactly what was the position of Mr. Norman Angell, I wish to quote a passage from the *New Republic* of 16 September 1916:

The member quoted from the article of that date cited above. Yet the man who has served his country and America more than all Englishmen since the War began is not to have his writings cabled to America, because he has been a critic of the Government. He has been an independent critic. I am not always in agreement with Mr. Norman Angell, but I think he is one of the few men in recent years who have brought an independent mind to the study of international relations and who has also made a contribution of value to that study. But this is the man whom our present Government prevents from sending anything abroad—the man who of all Englishmen has served his country and ours since the War began, and who drew America ' closer to that England with which alone an Anglo-American understanding is possible.' Is it because Mr. Norman Angell represents that England with which alone an Anglo-American understanding is possible that a gentleman in the Censor's office has decided that nothing which he writes is to go to America? Had the Government really been anxious to do the worst they could, this is precisely the action which they would have taken. . . . I wonder if it is because those responsible really do not want to have America's entrance into the War justified on liberal and internationalist grounds. If that is their object they are likely to succeed by suppressing Mr.

Norman Angell's writings, but that would certainly alter the character of the War from the point of view of very many of us in this country. I think that the House of Commons should insist on an explanation from the Government of this action, and I think they should apologize for this stupidity, and that this ban upon the writings of this distinguished writer should immediately be withdrawn.

MR. HERBERT SAMUEL: Mr. Norman Angell, from whose views as a rule I entirely dissent, or at least in many particulars, as most of us know, is a very distinguished publicist. He was invited by the *New Republic*, which is one of the leading and most influential papers of the United States, to send an article by cable for the purpose of influencing pacifist opinion in America, and to support the entry of America into the War on the side of the Allies. I think no one can deny that pacifist opinion in America during the War has been a very important element in the decision of American policy. It carries, and no doubt properly carries, great weight with the American Government. It is equally obvious that anything that could from any quarter usefully be done to assist to bring pacifist opinion into line when the American Government was about to take this momentous step of entering the War on the side of our Allies and ourselves, ought to be done and would be a useful thing to do.

Who is most likely to be able to influence pacifist opinion in America? Not violent and vehement partisans of war at any time and for any purpose and to be carried to any extreme, but obviously a man who has himself advanced pacifist opinions. Set a pacifist to catch a pacifist. If we wanted by our own methods of propaganda to influence pacifist opinion in America, I should have thought that Mr. Norman Angell, if his views allowed him to do so, would be the very man whose assistance we ought to enlist, and that was the view of the *New Republic*. . . . Now it does appear to me that a very grave error was made in this case. If there were some passages in this article which were judged to be deleterious, with a man so well-known as Mr. Norman Angell, what would have been easier than to ask him to come to the Press Bureau or to the Propaganda Department of the Foreign Office, point out to him the particulars which it was thought would be disadvantageous, and to ask him to modify those particulars, and I have no doubt it would have been quickly done.

But that was not the course adopted, and, for my own part, I feel convinced that far more harm has been done in America by the suppression of this article than would have been done in Germany by its publication. . . .

MR. BONAR LAW: I most certainly say that any Government responsible for the conduct of the War which deliberately allows views of that kind to be circulated abroad would instantly deserve to be asked to resign and give place to others. As regards the article of Mr. Norman Angell, I have looked into it, and I say again that nothing is more difficult than to decide whether or not an article of this kind should be suppressed. Some of those who have spoken, notably the hon. Member for East Mayo (Mr. Dillon) were wrong in saying that this article was stopped because of its effect on the Germans. That is not so. The right hon. Member for Cleveland (Mr. H. Samuel) suggested that we might have asked Mr. Norman Angell to take out the part to which we took exception, and he would at once have done it. I do not think that my right hon. Friend can have read the article. The point to which we object was one of the main arguments on which the article was based. Let me just read to the House one sentence— it is nothing discreditable to Mr. Norman Angell—to show why the Censor stopped this article. It is a sentence which comes last in the article :

> Firstly, in all except legalistic fiction, America has been at war with Germany for the last two years. It has afforded assistance to the Allies more real than that afforded to certain of the formal belligerents like Japan.

That was the kind of statement going to Germany from this country, that American neutrality was a sham, and that she had been at war with Germany all the time. That is the effect of the article. The Censor is responsible, and he may have been right or wrong in dealing with this article. I admit that there is room for difference of opinion, but we are entitled to take into account that the general object of the article was to get the assistance of America. There is reason for difference of opinion, but surely, at the very time when whether or not America was coming in was trembling in the balance, it was at least doubtful whether or not the assertion going from this country that America had been belligerent in all but name from the beginning was not such a statement as might do harm. It is a point which is open to difference of opinion. (*An Hon. Member: 'No!'*) I think so, and I believe hon. Members will think so. I learn now from my right hon. Friend that at the time the article was sent in—and he was informed that it would not be allowed to go through—the request should have been made to make an alteration. I really do not know how these matters are worked, but, on the face of it, I should say that was a request which it was possible might be complied with; and I might make inquiry as to whether or not that is the kind of method which might be adopted in future in dealing with articles.

A week or so after this debate I telephoned John Buchan (at that time head of, or concerned with, the Information Department of the Foreign Office), asking whether he could see me. He immediately agreed to do so. (I already knew Buchan pretty well. The publishing firm of Nelsons, of which he was a director, had produced a cheap but attractive cloth-covered edition of the French translation of *The Great Illusion*, which sold in large quantities; and had done the same with the Spanish edition, ensuring a large sale over the whole of Spanish America. We remained on the friendliest terms until his death in 1940.)

Our interview ran something like this:

ANGELL: When I applied for a passport some months since, the Government in its wisdom decided to refuse it on the general ground that it was not in the public interest that I should go to America. I propose to apply once more for a passport, and if it is again refused, I am afraid that nothing I can do will prevent my friend Pringle from asking another question in the House.

BUCHAN: (With a dry twinkle) My dear Angell, you cannot blackmail us here. Of course you cannot. But I think I can tell you for your information, that since the debate in the House the other night, H.M.G. has seen a great light, and that if you care to apply for your passport, I have reason to believe it will be granted.

I did. It was.

Q

One of the other passengers on the voyage to New York was my old friend and Carmelite House colleague, Hamilton Fyfe, who was later to be my colleague and editorial boss on the *Daily Herald*, and to whose life of Northcliffe reference has already been made. The ship was hung up for a couple of days in Lough Foyle in order to dodge, and allow the Navy to break up, a big concentration of enemy submarines. Among the craft sheltering in the Lough was a full-rigged Scandinavian sailing-ship. The captain decided to risk a sortie and with a favouring but very gentle wind drew away under full sail, and in most ghostly fashion, into the moonlight—the sort of spectacle which a lover of sailing-ships (I happen to be one) may witness but once or twice in a lifetime and will never witness again. For now no truly full-rigged sailing-ship sails anywhere on the oceans of the world. The sail training ships are not full-rigged.

Shortly after my arrival in New York I heard a familiar voice when I answered the phone.

'Your old enemy, my dear boy, the voice you think so evil.'

It was Northcliffe, now High Commissioner to the United States.

'Not an enemy, my dear Chief.'

'Well, why did you not come to me when you had trouble about your passport? However, you must come and stay with me out at Pelham.'

I did so and met some strange animals there collected, and heard some strange stories of the diplomatic triangle Britain-Germany-America. The United States Post Office authorities apparently had been extremely ' co-operative ' with the British Security Service during the period of American ' neutrality.' One story, perhaps apocryphal but accepted by the dinner-table guests as probably true, was to the effect that the German Ambassador's Private Typist passed on all her carbons to the British Embassy; which was counted as one up to the British, until it was found that the carbon copies of the British Embassy were finding their way regularly to the German Embassy.

Part III

LEFT TURN—WITH DOUBTS

CHAPTER I

BY WHICH ROAD?

AN earlier chapter has related how, after the outbreak of the First World War, conceiving the most urgent task to be a workable peace, I turned, as the means readiest to hand, to co-operation with men whose bent was towards an internationalist policy. They happened to be men prominent in the politics of the Left, including at the outset Ramsay MacDonald, Philip Snowden, Charles Trevelyan, Arthur Ponsonby, E. D. Morel, and, a little later, George Lansbury, Gerald Gould, Clifford Allen and a number of trade union leaders. The earlier chapter has also recorded how I was warned by friends of diverse political persuasions—from Northcliffe, the Tory newspaper lord, to Erskine Childers, the rebel in Ireland; from Esher, the confidant of the King to Keir Hardie of the Labour Party Left wing—that that was not the way to approach the problem of a foreign policy calculated to produce peace.

Were these friends right? If so, to what extent and why?

I have already hinted that, looking at the matter with the easy wisdom which comes after—very long after—the event, I feel that the friends who gave me such counsel were on the whole right and I was wrong. But the decision was not simple and cannot necessarily be applied to present situations or as support for the idea that party government can be brought to an end. It is at least possible that the only way in which the public as a whole can control governments at all is by depriving one party of power when that power is abused and supporting the rival party, that party to be restrained in its turn in the same way.

Given the circumstances as they revealed themselves at the beginning of the war in 1914 and still more perhaps at the close of the war and in the decade that followed, and given also my own nature (a man learns it only perhaps as the years go by), this move towards the Left was inevitable.

I had every reason to know that among the Conservative Party were, here and there, men as disinterested, wise and competent politically as any to be found in English politics. In peace time they are able to exercise great influence on the rank and file of their party. But the war mood which manifested itself in 1914 was one of instinctive and atavistic passions, obscuring perception of the plainest fact. This mood seemed to take charge particularly in the Conservative party. Sometimes the leaders themselves were infected. Esher, for instance, at the end of a year or two, became strangely embittered. The long-drawn-out war got on his nerves. Towards the end of 1916 I had written him about an article of his which seemed to accept the principle at least that Britain and France should begin to have some fairly clear ideas of the peace terms they would be prepared to accept; the sort of formulation which American opinion was beginning to demand—'and American opinion,' I had written him, 'is now a thing we have to consider. Perhaps a word from yourself in the right quarter might help things along in this sense.' Esher wrote that 'American opinion cannot be satisfied since we are out to take Alsace-Lorraine, to draw Germany's teeth if we can, and to keep most of her colonies. Therefore, why imagine that you can argue with an idealist like Wilson, who does not see that Germany acted like a burglar and that we mean to punish her accordingly? All the high-falutin' notwithstanding.'

It was indicative of the degeneration of that time, that a man of Esher's intellectual quality and realism should write in these terms. I am sure that his peace-time mind would have recognized immediately that Wilson's early political intervention was the necessary prelude to a military intervention and that Allied victory itself might—would—depend on bringing this about. What happened to Esher seemed to be happening to the rank and file of the Conservative party, and to the government, as an incident like that related in the last chapter reveals. That incident seemed to emphasize the fact that such actions did not reflect considered policy at all; they were merely part of the general attitude of hostility to political heretics.

The Conservatives seemed to give free rein to the emotional pugnacities of an instinctive nationalism. At the tribal stage of development this sort of motive may have had survival value. But in our kind of world I felt it could be suicidal (as Germany was shortly to prove for the second time) and that the growth of the opposing party would help to keep it in check.

The Labour Party was by its doctrine internationalist; much more rationalist in its approach to foreign policy than were rank and file Conservatives, more prepared to make the changes which a truly international order would demand. It seemed to mean business about its internationalism in a way which the Conservatives did not. I could not then foresee that a great part of the Left would before long transfer the blind pugnacity of nationalism to the field of the class war with results quite as dangerous to peace and freedom as the older fanaticisms had been.

I don't think my own individual experience at the hands of the Conservative elements and of the Government during the war—related in the last two chapters—had much to do with my decision, except as pointing up a general attitude that had to be taken into account. (I had taken the first steps towards the Labour Party before the club expulsions, the placing of my writings on the index, and the refusal of passport.) Certainly I never for one moment thought of myself as a martyr, or the victim of any 'plot' of persecution. But I was enraged at the crass stupidity of that kind of thing, and did perhaps associate its stupidity mainly with Conservatism (though later it was to be demonstrated that Socialism could display blindness as great, though to different objects). Anger at Conservative behaviour was provoked much less, I think, by the fact that Conservatism stood mainly for the interests of the privileged classes, than by the fact that it was proving itself quite incapable of doing even that; as events were so soon to demonstrate.

It was a paradox of the situation that the war which the Conservatives did so little to prevent and many of them really welcomed, was destined to destroy the order of society for which they stood, while the Socialists, overwhelmingly anti-war, were to see their cause immediately aided by the war's results. The second war, also fought for freedom, was to see the cause of an Oriental despotism, masquerading in the garments of Leftish revolution, triumph over half the world, and to compel Socialists to associate themselves with anti-Socialist powers in order to preserve the most elementary freedoms.

If, however, the lights went out in 1914, as Grey on that

evening of the third of August saw them going out, it is well for
those of us who now see danger in the Socialist doctrines to
remind ourselves that the lights were not put out by Socialists.
Nor did the Conservative errors end with the war: the maintenance by Britain of the blockade long after the German armies
had surrendered; the maintenance of impossible reparations
claims for nearly fourteen years after the making of the Versailles
Treaty, (a fact which contributed enormously to the financial
disintegration of the European economies); the withdrawal of the
United States into extreme isolation—these measures were
not the work of Socialists; they were the work of Conservative,
'practical' businessmen, quite unable to take in the meaning
of what the best of their own leaders (the Robert Cecils, the
Edens, the Cranbornes, the Macmillans, and, later, Churchill)
were telling them.

I remember Jan Smuts saying to me in 1920 or thereabouts
something to this effect: 'The League ought logically to find its
most ardent defenders among Conservatives. But it won't. They
will of course try to destroy the very instrument which alone,
as things are, might save their kind of world.'

The sort of thing we were up against at that time is illustrated
by an experience with which I was concerned in 1919. A group
of food experts, administrators, officials, lawyers, bankers,
businessmen, disturbed by the condition of things in Europe,
formed themselves into a 'Fight the Famine Council' and
organized a conference in London in order to place the facts
before the public and make recommendations to governments.
The contribution of the Northcliffe Press to this effort was to
burst out into screaming headlines of protest against holding such
a conference at all, since the Germans (particularly, it would
appear, German babies) had merely got what they deserved. This
Press gave the names and addresses of some of the members of
the conferees for the purpose, apparently, of encouraging mobs
to go and break the windows of 'traitors' who could concern
themselves with the fate of 'enemies'—particularly enemy
children. Yet to save the Austrian and German people from
famine was an obvious interest of those classes desiring to prevent
subversive revolutionary movements.[1]

Nevertheless, it was perhaps more by a series of steps, the final

[1] See my *The Peace Treaty and the Economic Chaos*, Swarthmore Press, 1919.

outcome of which I did not clearly foresee when I took each one of them, that I found myself in 1920 a member of the Labour Party; by 1922 nursing the constituency of Rushcliffe in the Labour interest; fighting that constituency in 1924 and losing the election, though much increasing the Labour vote; in 1926 fighting Rossendale in Lancashire, and losing the election; Bradford North in 1929 and winning it. In 1931, though very strongly urged in that constituency to stand again, I resigned; in 1935 (knowing I could not win) I stood for London University (being in the United States at the time).

Once having joined the party, I seem to have travelled pretty rapidly to the Far Left. The years 1917–1927 were, not unnaturally, in view of the Russian events, years in which revolutionism was in the very air. It reached England, as I discovered on my return from the Paris Peace Conference (where I had spent a couple of months with American and English correspondents, as mentioned previously) and from the Berne Second International, which Northcliffe had asked me to report for *The Times*. At Berne I saw a good deal of Ramsay MacDonald and shared a room with William Bullitt, who subsequently became United States Ambassador in Moscow and, later, Paris. Return to England after the absence of a year or two brought home to me the fact that quite a number of small groups in England (including some I.L.P. branches) were advocating Sovietism and armed revolution. I recall a meeting in the Holborn district one night with Ernie Hunter in the chair and Clifford Allen [1] helping the chairman's efforts to prevent there going through a resolution which meant that the Labour movement should aim at the Sovietization of Britain. Saklatvala, the Indian who afterwards became a member of the House of Commons, argued the case for the class war with tense, fierce passion. 'We must fight on the principle that he who is not for us is against us.' He would quite cheerfully have sent eighty or ninety per cent of the British population that were not 'for us' to perish in Arctic Labour Camps if only he could have the power. There were a number of young Irishmen present, extremely contemptuous of the whole business of voting and party procedure. 'Tell us to what stations of the revolutionary army we have to report when the word is given, is all we want to know.' I was at work on the *Herald* at

[1] Afterwards Lord Allen of Hurtwood.

about that time, and under the presidency of George Lansbury
a committee, considerably to the Left of official Labour leaders,
had prepared a programme which was published in the spring
of 1917. (Some eighteen months before the Labour Party had had
its post-war programme approved by the party conference.) The
character of thought on the more extreme Left at that time may
be gathered from the outstanding proposals of the Lansbury-
Herald programme which included expropriation of private land-
owners and capitalists, without compensation; payment of all
men and women willing to work even when their work happens to
be not needed, just as soldiers are paid when they are not fighting;
'Ownership by the State, management by the workers,' to be
applied immediately to Mines, Railways, Shipping, Shipbuilding,
and Engineering, Electric Light and Power, Gas and Water; the
national properties in mines, railways, shipping, land, to be leased
to the Unions 'on conditions which will ensure every member at
present money value a minimum real income of one pound a day.'
Management by the unions reflected the Guild Socialism of
which at that time G. D. H. Cole was the high prophet and to
which I was greatly drawn.

In a book published in the United States in 1919 I attempted
to sketch for the American public the general trend of Labour
politics in Britain.[1] Its tone is for the most part entirely favourable to the Labour Party and even to the Left of the official
leaders of that party. But even in that book I warned that:

> If the Socialism of the future is merely to mean a transfer of
> ownership in land and capital from the individual to the State,
> preserving the type of mind and feeling which we now know in
> Western society, the Socialist organization of nations is likely to
> give us a condition even more susceptible to bitter military con-
> flicts than is the capitalist and individual economy. . . .
> Individualist capitalism and trade is 'naturally' inter-
> nationalist, rather than nationalist. Much of the internationalism
> of Socialist parties in the past has been fortuitous. . . .
> The first fruits of the nationalization of wealth is to diminish,
> not to increase, that economic interdependence of nations which,
> of itself, would constitute, in some measure, a mechanical check
> to war. And if our Socialism after the war is to be of the type
> which the war has produced so far, we shall be confronted in the
> immediate future with a deliberate attempt to break down the

[1] *The British Revolution and the American Democracy*, New York, 1919.

international basis of industry, and to replace it by a nationalist one, giving rise to a competition in self-sufficiency and a scramble for the separate national control of the raw materials of the world in undeveloped territories.

The general forecasts of that 1919 book were not fulfilled in the years immediately following the First World War, but nearly all of them have been in the years following the second war. It is after the second war that the 'revolutions' and the psychological conditions there forecast have come.

Whatever my revolutionary tendencies may have been at that time, they were almost always checked, if not quite cured, by the bearing of the revolutionaries who turned up at some of the meetings which I then attended pretty regularly. These men often revealed in every word and gesture cold and bitter hate of some 'class' they would have found it very difficult to define. It was obvious that some need of their natures prompted them to find an object of hatred and vengeance. The idea that men of that character should by some means or other manage to make themselves masters of Britain, made one's blood run cold. The majority of the Labour Party were not of that character at all. But the tendency in all revolutionary movements is for a small violent minority to take charge and impose their policy.

Among the letters I received from old colleagues in the 'movement' discussing the wisdom or otherwise of turning Left, is one from Dennis Robertson of Trinity, sent in the first instance to Harold Wright. I was in the United States at the time. Robertson asked Wright to send it on to me because, wrote Robertson, 'I do feel that owing probably to absence and overwork and nervous strain, he is in danger of losing the chance of a lifetime of permeating and helping to guide the thought and action of the majority of common-sense people, instead of beating his head against a wall in a way which no doubt, like all such actions, would bear fruit in future generations, but would let the supreme opportunity in the world's history slip by.' The letter contains, apart from its reference to myself, a few forecasts so much confirmed by the event that it seems worth quoting.

After expressing a hope that I would not become the mere mouthpiece of the I.L.P., which would, he says, 'unnecessarily excite prejudice, narrow his public and fetter his activities,' Robertson says he would like to see me 'go on with those new developments he was reaching after that last night at Jordans—the whole idea of partnership, of economic and territorial and moral and emotional division of Labour between nations,—to hammer out its practical applications with regard to colonial policy and mutual international guarantees, of whatever practical question seems uppermost, and to throw the weight of his logic and imagination on the side of the sound core of Liberalism and Labour and perhaps (as I hope) of the new Imperialism of the Round Table school. They will need it, and I believe they will deserve it.'

Another part of the letter makes an interesting forecast which has been all too fully justified by the event :

I thought my phrase 'Angellism has always underestimated the value of the State' would annoy you. I quite agree that the Prussian Moloch-worship is and is likely to remain the greater danger. But I don't think any propaganda is going to be anything but academic which does not recognize that the state or, if you prefer, the organized nation, is a convenient and reasonable association 'for the good life of its members' as Aristotle hath it. Take economics. I don't think myself, making all allowance for Syndicalist experiments and for diffusion of property on the Belloc plan, the rich are going to be made much poorer or the poor much richer without a pretty considerable advance towards collectivism, extending to control of high finance and to matters of foreign trade (this does not mean tariffs) so that Angell's scorn of the picture of nations as 'business units' is likely to become progressively less true.

There is one passage in Robertson's letter which aroused my interest. Expressing the view that non-resistance was at the time he wrote just not a practical question of politics at all, he ventured the guess that it might become so 'at the next threat of explosion,' and asks : 'Have you read . . . a stodgy but thoughtful pamphlet signed Commentitius, wherein the author narrates to a patient Chinese statesman in 2000 A.D. the story of the great war and the great peace, and how its threatened rupture about 1950 was averted by a non-resistance movement led by England, the times being ripe in a way they are not now?'

I have never seen this pamphlet, but it sounds prophetic.

I realized that the war would inevitably have the effect of accelerating a development towards economic collectivism (to which Robertson makes reference). The forces within industrialism would have made some tendency in that direction inevitable in any case. Throughout the four elections in which I took part as candidate I emphasized the point that I was a Socialist because no modern industrialized economy could function at all without large and increasing doses of control by the community. I would illustrate by pointing out that in the days when transport was by horses and wagons along already constructed roads, there was no need for the government to intervene much in the industry: a man bought a wagon and team of horses and went into the business. But when railroads came along they could not exist at all until the government had granted a franchise, given the right to condemn private property where necessary for the right of way, and Parliament had fixed the terms of the franchise: how much should be charged, what regulations for safety should be taken, and a thousand and one conditions laid down. This was interference in private business with a vengeance. And then, of course, railroads were not entirely private business and had to be publicly controlled, though not necessarily owned. But so had banking, which had power by the extent to which it could through its control of credit and the discount rate influence the value of the money in everyone's pocket. (The control exercised in ' capitalist' America over the insurance business is to-day more far-reaching than in 'socialist' Britain.) It was no longer an issue between an all socialist state and a completely non-socialist state. Capitalism was inevitably becoming partly socialist, and a society entirely socialized would be one entirely enslaved. In any case, Britain could not possess a completely managed economy because things indispensable to the daily life of her people— meat of the Argentine, cotton of the United States, food and raw materials of every kind—were under foreign, not British, control.

We could only bargain, not command. Our government might dictate to us what clothes or furniture or food we should buy; but it could not dictate to foreigners how much of our manufactures they should buy, nor the rate at which they would sell their food. Yet unless they did buy those manufactures our people would starve. We had to engage in commercial competition at the national level in order to live at all. A country as self-sufficient as Russia might talk of complete socialism, absolute control throughout. Britain could not. For her it was not a question of absolute socialism versus absolute capitalism, but at what points in what way and within what limits socialism was to be invoked.

The more ardent members of the Labour Party did not like this approach at all. They wanted a clear-cut division between 'socialism' and 'capitalism.' One had to be all black, the other all white. As Dave Kirkwood put it to me, 'Air ye for the Revolution, or air ye against?'

I felt this doctrinaire division between the blacks and the reds, the slipping into 'class war' attitudes, to be infinitely mischievous for two reasons given in the next chapter.

In one respect my anticipations about working with the Labour Party were justified. It was easier to talk internationalism to a Labour Party audience than to a Tory one. I liked the big meetings, especially perhaps when they were a bit hostile. But I felt them to be an exceedingly bad means of helping toward the understanding of a subject. There was always the temptation to rhetoric and invective. An audience a bit bored with the best of arguments woke up if you began along the lines of 'J'accuse,' indicting the enemy for all the crimes of the calendar. This was all the more foolish in my case since usually I had the support of men of all parties. When I fought Nottingham, a sort of manifesto urging my election was signed among others by Arnold Bennett, Canon Barnes, Noel Buxton, Edward Carpenter, Lady Courtney, G. Lowes Dickinson, Hamilton Fyfe, G. P. Gooch, Austin Harrison, J. A. Hobson, Dean Inge, Jerome K. Jerome, J. M. Keynes, Lord Loreburn, H. W. Massingham, Sir George Paish, Cecil Roberts, Arnold S. Rowntree, Bertrand Russell, Sir D. M. Stevenson, Graham Wallas, Lord Weardale. Among those who came and electioneered for me were Sidney Webb, G. B. Shaw, R. H. Tawney.

My election manifesto of 1922 anticipated the 'export or die' slogans of 1945 and 1950. It ran:

> There are living on the soil of these islands twice as many people as that soil of itself can support. About half the population live by exchanging manufactures or services based on coal, for the surplus of food and raw materials produced by foreigners. It is an inevitable, but extremely artificial situation. The amount of foreign trade necessary to maintain a civilized standard of life is only possible so long as there can go on in security a great traffic across frontiers, not unduly impeded by customs dues or protectionist tariffs; so long as each area produces that for which it is best fitted, the people of one state having access to the raw materials of another, across its territory perhaps to the sea; all being able to count in some measure upon fair stability in the value of money, security of commercial contract, and so forth.

The Manifesto goes on to point out that 'this economic internationalism, the survival and development of which alone will enable Britain as we know it to live,' has rested heretofore on utterly unsound political foundations. Unless a sounder foreign policy strengthened those foundations Britain would sooner or later face conditions of ruin which not even 'Socialism' could make tolerable.

Alike at Nottingham, at Rossendale and at Bradford, I announced in effect that I would kiss no babies nor talk class war; indulge neither the bourgeois nor the revolutionary demagogy.

The closing paragraph of the Bradford election address ran:

> In promoting the policies outlined above I shall oppose any tendency to Revolution or violence; or to the nursing of hatreds at home or abroad; and give no doctrinaire allegiance to any 'ism,' being neither hypnotized by names, nor frightened by them, but shall examine, from whatever quarters they may come, the methods most likely to prove practical and to promote the nation's welfare.

In the ten years preceding my election for Bradford North in 1929 I had been seeing a good deal of MacDonald, and of the members of his first government in 1924.

Indeed, as already related, my contacts with MacDonald went back to 1910, while I was still living in Paris, when he would come over for a week-end to meet French Socialists—Jaurès, and

Longuet notably—and I would arrange the meetings—usually luncheons—and act as host and interpreter. The fact that Longuet had married a daughter of Karl Marx gave him a certain place in the history of Socialism, on personal as well as on intellectual grounds. It all helped MacDonald to get an insight into Continental Socialism about which, on sound grounds I think, he had misgivings.

It was also at about that time that I suggested to Northcliffe that it might be a good plan to have a Labour man like J.R.M. write occasionally in the *Mail*, putting the Labour point of view. Northcliffe was disposed to agree and I asked MacDonald whether he would consider such an offer; but he somewhat loftily refused to 'soil his hands' with that sort of contact. He seemed to think the suggestion a dodge of Northcliffe's to dish the *Daily Citizen*, then being started. This was not the case. My own motive was to afford Labour a bourgeois public; Northcliffe's motive was to capture a part of the Labour public.

A year or two after this there followed the close association with MacDonald in the work of the U.D.C. already described. He was at that time in the wilderness and in those two or three years I came as near to intimacy with him as I ever came. But even then there were signs of the qualities which are more generally born of success than of adversity. I found it extremely difficult to break through the hard shell to which I have previously referred.

During his first government in 1924, I heard from him in one way or another pretty frequently. Two long letters—written in his own hand—were in connection with an entirely trivial matter —a letter from E. D. Morel published in the *New Leader*, which I was editing for a few weeks in the absence of Brailsford, the regular editor. J.R.M. quite obviously resented any criticism at all from those he regarded as his friends. 'If,' he writes, 'a well-informed attack upon Liberals and Tories had been conducted in the *New Leader* there would have been far less desire to criticize ourselves. The best form of defence is always attack. It is the sort of half-hearted and detached academic backing that we get which slowly but steadily undermines confidence. I wish our friends who edit newspapers and write for them would quietly sit down and appreciate the enormous change that has taken place in the mind of the country since we came into office. We may be criticized to the heart's content of our critics and we may be told that we are disappointing our friends, but every election, both for Municipal and Parliamentary purposes, shows that the party is stronger than ever it was. That very robust fact is somehow bigger than the sort of things that appear so prominently in our Press.'

In foreign affairs MacDonald was a Victorian Liberal. I doubt if he had worked out in his mind a foreign policy which differed from the somewhat naïve optimism of the old Liberal who was satisfied with political laissez-faire in the international field, sustained by moving rhetoric about the wickedness of armaments, the balance of power, secret diplomacy, and so forth. A number of letters to me from Arthur Ponsonby, MacDonald's Parliamentary Under-Secretary at the Foreign Office, reflect the latter's fear that MacDonald's policy would soon be indistinguishable from that of the more woolly-headed Conservatives. Ponsonby writes me in April, 1924:

> As the P.M. is likely to make a statement on foreign affairs on the adjournment motion on Wednesday, how would it be for a few of you to write him a letter early in the week, putting to him some of the points not so much of eventual policy, but of more immediate importance? Without criticizing the policy he has pursued, attention might be called to omissions and to what is being felt in I.L.P. circles. . . . . The absence hitherto of a syllable of sympathy for Germany and the need of saying something helpful which will prevent or mitigate the swing to the Right. A more distinct pronouncement in general differentiating our attitude towards the whole international situation—League of Nations, international disarmament—from that of the Tories . . . and so forth. . . .

On another occasion Ponsonby writes, asking whether I would go to see him at the House, bringing two or three others—' Gillies, Lowes Dickinson, and perhaps a back bench M.P. or two.' Ponsonby went on to say that he doubted if the P.M. read the Advisory Committee's memoranda we had prepared. 'I do not want him to meet you in order to give you information, but rather for him to hear what the party are saying, thinking and proposing. If we found it useful we might make it periodic. . . . Afternoon at the House of Commons is preferable to morning at the Foreign Office.'

In reply, however, I find that I expressed a good deal of scepticism as to whether suggestions made in this way would be much good. I pointed out that attempts along these lines on more than one occasion had had a tart reception from the P.M.

One incident at that time, very soon after MacDonald took office in 1924, struck me particularly. Edouard Herriot (at the time Prime Minister of France) came to London to discuss with MacDonald Anglo-French relations generally. With a view to some newspaper and book work I was then doing, I had asked Herriot if he could squeeze in a quarter of an hour for a talk. Herriot replied immediately that he would be delighted. (Herriot had been a reader of mine.) Would I come to his hotel? We talked for an hour on the general problem of French security and Britain's hesitations about any sort of definite commitment. We found ourselves in complete agreement. And then the conversation took a more intimate turn. Herriot made a suggestion: ' You know MacDonald. Won't you go and have a talk with him —not as coming from me, of course,—and prepare his mind generally for what I shall have to say to him.' I told Herriot that I did not at all like the job; that J.R.M. was not an easy man to advise, and did not easily take counsel with his friends. But Herriot was insistent. As a result, I telephoned the P.M., who asked me to lunch the next day. I have managed from the jumble of papers left by the blitz to unearth the notes I made at the time. They relate that ' In the hall, I tumbled into Mrs. Swanwick, who apparently had been asked to luncheon by Ishbel, but then, as Ishbel for some reason was not there, the P.M., I gather, had to ask her. Perhaps that altered a little the complexion of what followed.' (Mrs. Swanwick was not only a Pacifist, but an absolutist of the most unbending, uncompromising kind.) The notes continue:

I found the P.M. with Sydney Arnold. The last time I had lunched with the P.M., Sydney Arnold was there too. When we went into the big state dining-room, there was Mac's Dutch housekeeper, whom I had met years ago in Lincoln's Inn Fields, and later in the little house in Howitt Road in Hampstead. There was Arnold, Mrs. Swanwick and myself. Much small talk which I found irritating as I was itching to get on to the subject I had come to discuss with MacDonald.

The P.M. had to tell us of the place where we could hire horses for riding at half a crown an hour. (Did Mac ride?) Then he gave the details of the case which had provoked a Mexican difficulty—the English woman who had lived for thirty years in Mexico, whose land the authorities wanted to confiscate for village allotments, or something. He had the whole story, and told it at great length. The question arose in my mind as to whether Prime Ministers are really busy folk. For otherwise, why in the name of goodness should he have bothered to read through the details of this case?

It was not until we got up from lunch that I found the opportunity for which I had been waiting. The Press, I pointed out, would be very inquisitive about M. Herriot's visit and I was taking him—J.R.M.—at his recent word as to getting the facts from him before writing about them. The French, as the Press had made evident recently, were anxious for some sort of undertaking along the lines of the Treaty of Mutual Assistance. 'Our own party rank and file do not understand the Treaty of Mutual Guarantee; and if you have to make any concessions to Herriot in that direction, it might be well to make them familiar with the reasons.' (I was of course anxious to avoid the appearance of being in any way Herriot's emissary.)

Mac turned on me with some irritation and vehemence and said the whole idea of a Treaty of Mutual Guarantee was exploded. There were no good reasons for it, except militarist reasons. He had definitely rejected it. 'You know,' he said, 'the first result would be the increase of the British army.'

'But the point is,' I said, 'that Herriot will ask for it.'

The notes then relate the conversation as follows:

MacDonald: 'Let him ask. I knocked out Poincaré on that.'

Myself: 'But if he assumes the thing is hopeless, why does he reiterate this claim in almost every statement that he makes?'

MacDonald: 'Because he has not thought it out. It is like these Belgians. They came here with their scheme of economic boycott, and in a couple of hours we had shown them that it was impossible.'

Myself: 'But won't Herriot put the old, old question: "If the Boche attacks once more what will England do?" How do we reply? How do we meet the argument that Germany might be deterred from any future aggression if she knew beforehand that

R

we should support France; and France might be more reasonable.'

MacDonald: 'I shall tell Herriot that if France behaves well there is virtually no chance that the Boche will attack.'

Myself: 'I agree that that may be the probability. But Herriot's parliamentary position is difficult. He can hardly as a report of his mission tell the Chamber: "I have seen Mr. MacDonald with reference to guarantees and he has assured me that if only we behave nicely to the Germans there is no need for guarantees."'

MacDonald: 'It is not my business to help Herriot's political job at home. The thing for us to remember is that if all these guarantees to go to war are given in the end we *shall* go to war.'

'And all that,' say my notes, 'with an air of brushing the thing aside, not facing it as a very difficult, doubtful, open subject, a fact which he would have to meet. And at this point, Mrs. Swanwick joined in with the classical objections to any commitment of any kind. Mac turned to her, evidently pleased at being supported. Yet I could not leave the thing at this. I said: 'I am putting the case as it will be seen by Herriot . . .' And then, with irritation, MacDonald interrupted something to the effect: 'And I am putting the case as it is, as the facts are.' And I thought he added something to the effect that 'That is what I want *you* to do. To put my case, not Herriot's.'

I realized then that MacDonald did not want reasons or counsel, but support, encouragement, agreement. And that came out a little later when, again raising the question of a possible statement for the Press, he said that it was not possible, but started off on what was almost a tirade against Herriot, or the *New Leader*, and said that he would rather give an interview to the *Manchester Guardian*: 'What I want is good hearty support; not this superior attitude of criticism, and qualification.' And he added something to the effect that I seemed to have become hypnotized by Bob Cecil, and his Treaty of Mutual Assistance. It was along the wrong lines—hopeless! And again Mrs. Swanwick concurred. And again MacDonald purred at the undercurrent of adulation in her voice. (She was afterwards on the British delegation to Geneva and was obliged to concur, 'shrieking all the way,' as she told me, in the Geneva Protocol,

every bit as committal and entangling as Cecil's Treaty of Mutual
Assistance. She was to write me a little later a letter of bitter
reproaches for my 'apostasy' from Pacifism—an apostasy of
course imaginary, since I had never been pacifist in her sense
of the term—and describing her despair at the collapse of all for
which she had struggled.

This attitude of MacDonald's dismayed me the more because
I had already acquired a strong conviction that all real prospect
of effective collective defence in Europe depended first of all upon
agreement between France and Britain as the nucleus of the
police power of the League. If, in order to put power behind law
and transform the Balance of Power into Wilson's Community of
Power, we were to wait upon agreement between all the members
of the League, then I thought I knew that collective security
would never become a reality. I did not believe that effective organization of human society was brought about in that way. It
grew from a nucleus of agreement between two or three who
would then attract others to it by offering the new adherents the
privileges and securities the initiators claimed for themselves.

I find notes of an earlier luncheon meeting (4 Feb. 1924) at
which the P.M. discussed the general situation and its relations
to the party Press. The notes are interesting because they reveal
tendencies of MacDonald's mind which were to express themselves in a dramatic *coup de théâtre* politically, seven years later.
The notes again testify to his anger with the *New Leader*. 'What
we want is for the *New Leader* to carry on socialist propaganda,
and I want the I.L.P. to carry on a socialist propaganda, instead
of which everybody wants to be a Cabinet Minister, or if they
do not want to be a Cabinet Minister, they want to make a
Cabinet of their own.'

The Trade Unions at that time were already discussing the
possibilities of the general strike, which was to come later. 'If
the strike comes off,' the P.M. insisted, 'the Labour government
comes down ; or, what would be worse, we should have to install
a national government, a sort of coalition. Already, when Bromley
got his people out, we had immediately to consider measures for
requisitioning lorries for the purpose of getting coal distributed.
Coal was already beginning to fail the factories, electric light
stations, etc. Here, because a little tiny group of Bromley's best-

paid men had to sacrifice a microscopic fraction of their very high wages, the whole of the rest of the workers had to pay levy.' The notes of the talk continue with MacDonald saying:

> It was not the rank and file that are the trouble. The locomotive men did not want to strike—it was Bromley who wanted to get a kick at Thomas. So in this case, dockers do not want to strike. It comes from Bevin. The dockers who are threatening to strike were earning ten to eleven shillings a day. That was not of course enough, but it was ridiculous to pretend that it was starvation wages and that they could not postpone things.
>
> The problem was to show these people that if they did strike, they could not win in the present circumstances. They would not get victory by striking, and they would sacrifice their capacity to put political action into operation. There was every sign that the trade of the country was looking up. At present the employers simply would not grant the extra 2s. Later on, when trade had revived and some small boom was on, they might.

Somehow those notes cast a shadow before the events which were to occur a few years later.

CHAPTER II

WAS THE LEFT TURN RIGHT?

I SUPPOSE my experiences in the House were those of most freshmen members. I wondered the first two days whether the ceremonial and the millinery had much use, but decided when I saw how the sartorial dignity of the Speaker helped in the squelching of disorderly and unruly members, that it had. I was impressed, first by the good nature and secondly by the bad intellectual quality of most of the members on both sides. Six hundred members seemed to me a mob; two hundred would have made a much better consultative assembly. (Walter Lippmann, who was my guest in the House once or twice, was, however, struck with the fact that it was much more a truly consultative assembly than was the House of Representatives in Washington.) In the Committee work upstairs more business was done when members spoke sitting down instead of standing up to speak. (It is astonishing what a difference in the intellectual quality of a debate a little physical detail like that can make.) I very seldom spoke in the chamber and much to my surprise was elected to the Consultative Committee of the Parliamentary Party; and was a member of that committee until after the Great Schism of 1931.

I took my job seriously, but discovered very quickly that if I continued to do so too ponderously I would either go mad or be driven to give it up altogether. But then I had earlier—as far back as my teens, thirty years before in the United States—made the discovery, looking at the matter from the point of view of the ordinary voter, that democracy as we know it involves certain assumptions which are in fact fantastic absurdities; and that one has to accept these absurdities because the only immediately available alternative is something very much more evil. In the United States the farce was illustrated particularly in the long ballot of the great cities, where the overworked factory hand, or haberdasher, or barber, or teamster, or railroad switchman was asked to decide whether X would make a better judge than Y, or B a better accountant or keeper of records than A, and so on down some hundreds of names, never having so much as seen X or Y or B or A, and knowing nothing of their competence, nothing of the qualities their positions would demand. This method, of course, was an inheritance from the village green democracy of the New England township, where the villagers could decide that Jake would make a better sheriff than John because, having known Jake and John all their lives and knowing more or less what the sheriff's job demanded, they could give a competent decision. But the device, when applied to a city like Chicago, became of course a roaring farce or a 'racket' by which a city administration entered into partnership with professional gamblers, crooks, pimps and killers.

Yet I was to ask myself many times in the House of Commons whether the functioning of the Mother of Parliaments, while free from the gross corruptions involved in the long ballot, did not involve absurdities almost as great. A typical order paper is that —taken quite at hazard—of 4 June 1931. It includes these bills :

Nursing Profession (Wages and Hours) Bill; Buildings (Escape from Fire) Bill; Petroleum Bill; Wireless Telegraphy (Bedridden Persons) Bill; Spiritualism and Psychical Research (Exemption) Bill; Protection of Animals Bill; Coal Mines (Minimum Wage) Act; 1912 (Amendment) Bill; Works Councils Bill; Local Authorities (Municipal Savings Banks) Bill; Advertisements Regulation (Amendment) Bill; Mining Subsidence (Compensation) Bill; Solicitors Bill; Employment of Disabled Ex-service Men Bill; Religious Persecutions (Abolition) Bill; Protection of Dogs Bill; Coal Mines (Protection of Animals) Bill; Performing Animals (Regulation) Bill; Hire Purchase Bill; Married Women (Torts) Bill; Juries (Exemption of Firemen) Bill; Industrial and Provident Societies (Amendment) Bill; Retail Meat Dealers' Shops (Sunday Closing) Bill; National House-building Bill; National Industrial Council Bill; Proprietary Medicines Bill; Assurance Companies Bill; Trout (Scotland) Bill; Sunday Observance Act (1780) Amendment (No. 2) Bill; Rights of Railway Passengers Bill; Rent (Reduction and Control) Bill; Adoption of Children (Scotland) Bill; Access to Mountains Bill; Law of Property Act (1925) Amendment Bill; Racecourse Betting Act (1928) Amendment

Bill; Hospitals (Relief from Rating) Bill; Exportation of Horses
Bill; Miners (Pensions) Bill; Criminal Justice (Amendment) Bill;
Sale of Cheese Bill; Third Parties (Rights against Insurers) Bill;
British Museum and National Gallery (Overseas Loans) Bill; Grey
Seals (Protection) Bill; Probation of Offenders (Scotland) Bill.

True, all these bills went through a process of sifting by experts,
of drafting by competent civil servants and of discussion by Committees upstairs. But the final decision had to be given by members who were non-expert, the member from an agricultural
constituency passing upon mining and railroad legislation and
the miners' representative passing on agricultural problems. The
absurd side of it was brought out at division time. When the
division bell rang you jumped up from your tea or dinner, ran for
the division lobby where a party whip stood shamelessly shouting,
'Government in aye lobby,' and as you walked through you
would ask your neighbour, 'What's this about?' And usually he
would not know. This was an exhibition bad enough from the
democratic point of view when your party had a clear and
overwhelming majority in the electorate. As these lines are being
written there does not exist either in Britain, France, or the
United States a government which has any such clear electoral
majority. Most of the democratic governments of the Western
world are minority governments. The majority of the 'People',
however divided otherwise, have declared by their votes that they
do not want the government which now rules them.

This does not condemn democracy as a political principle; for
the fact remains that wherever those absurdities exist the nation
as a whole is better off than where they do not. But the
absurdities do condemn some of the present techniques of democracy, which will fall before the totalitarian challenge unless
we can correct them.

The years of MacDonald's last government were to provide
tragic illustrations of the degree to which the modern democracies
have come into being unequipped with the knowledge or judgment necessary for the decisions they are compelled to make.

The Parliament had no sooner assembled than it became
evident that the mounting unemployment figures would soon
present us with a bankrupt unemployment fund, and that the
economic blizzard already beginning to sweep over the world
would shortly present us with something like national bankruptcy.

However deeply the roots of the trouble may have lain in economic maladjustments of all kinds, the immediate problem was financial: how to provide money for the unemployment fund by any method that would not produce still more unemployment. Monetary cures were very much in the air at the time and some of us, with a view to clarifying our own minds, formed a 'Currency Group' and asked various bigwigs to talk to us and answer questions; usually at a private dinner. On one occasion, not very long after Keynes had published his pamphlet, 'The Economic Consequences of Mr. Churchill,' I presided at a small gathering where Churchill was on one side of me and Keynes on the other. On another occasion we had Montagu Norman as quiz victim. These meetings were not confined to the Labour Party, and, with one or two others, I tried to make them non-partisan and non-doctrinaire. We made a plea for a stocktaking of the situation which should be free of all the old assumptions.

I cannot pretend that these private meetings did much to help the well-meaning but tired and elderly ex-Trade Union officials who made up so much of the membership of the Parliamentary party. The experience of these men, in their struggles with employers, had been that the 'master class' always talked financial difficulties, and if the interests of the workers were to be protected, such talk had to be disregarded.

In the case of the younger men—ardent doctrinaires or intellectuals—everything was answered by 'Socialism.' When we had 'Socialism' no such things as financial crises would or could exist. Yet two facts of the situation stuck out like carbuncles on a man's nose: First, the country must buy most of its food and raw materials abroad and must pay in a money that foreign and non-socialist producers would accept—a fact which seemed to introduce 'finance' somewhat pertinently. Second, the Labour Party held office by virtue of Liberal-Capitalist co-operation.

The moment the Liberals withdrew their support from the Government it would fall.[1] When therefore in reply to such questions as 'How are we to meet the debt of the Insurance Fund (which reached soon after we came to office £115,000,000)? How stop the mounting unemployment figures (soon to reach the 3,000,000 mark)? How stop the drain on the Bank's reserves?'—

[1] The respective numbers of the parties in Parliament were; Socialists 287; Conservatives 260; Liberal and Independent 68.

to these questions one got the answer—from nine out of ten of the Labour Party rank and file—'We must work for complete Socialism.' And then one felt a slight nausea at the evasion and futility of such a reply.

We could certainly have had Socialism by reducing the country to famine. For famine would mean complete control of all food, all resources, and all capitalists; equal shares for everybody, the end of the profit motive, and all the rest of it. But we should not get prosperity and freedom, which is presumably the purpose of Socialism.

There was a dreadful tendency in the day-to-day discussion, in the party Press and on the hustings, to dramatize—melodramatize—the situation by representing it as a conflict between the villain of privilege and capitalism on the one side and the heroic and virtuous 'people', prevented by wealth and power from applying the necessary remedy, on the other. In other words, most of us drifted into using the terms of the class war. We saw the matter as a war which had to be won. This was fundamental falsification. It was not a war that had to be won; it was, as already indicated, a difficult and baffling problem that had to be solved, and could only be solved by co-operation with the 'enemy.' The official policy of the party was to recognize this need for co-operation. But there was growing up a mood, a temper, a mass emotion, in conflict with the Party's more deliberately decided line. 'Gradualness,' for which we were supposed to stand, implies of course an obligation not to bring the existing system to a breakdown, and implies provisional co-operation with those at present in possession. Yet a great many of the members simply had not made up their minds whether their policy was to smash the existing system—or let it go smash—or to co-operate with elements outside the Labour Party in enabling it to carry on. When one pointed out that the signs seemed to indicate we were heading for a smash, the younger or the more doctrinaire members thought it all to the good : out of the ruins we should build the New Jerusalem. Apart from being extremely doubtful, given Britain's day-to-day dependence on a non-Socialist outside world, it did not happen to be the party's proclaimed policy. Gradualness meant avoidance of breakdown. Yet one could not discuss the matter for five minutes in private talk with a group of members without realizing that, with many of them, this elementary and vital point had not been settled in their minds, although most members rejected Marxism as a theory.

It was impossible to put the case for avoiding paralysis or financial dislocation without being charged with undue regard for the interests of the ' master class.'

Though not a diary keeper, I made a habit while in the House of taking notes of my talks with members and with industrialists and businessmen from my constituency whom I would some-times see when they came to London. At the end of six months or so I embodied the results of these talks in a printed memorandum of some twenty thousand words entitled ' Government and Unemployment' and circulated it at first privately. (This was later expanded into a small book in collaboration with Harold Wright entitled *Can Governments Cure Unemployment?*)[1] In this monograph I pointed out that the breakdown in Britain and America synchronized with the demonstration in Moscow that Communism had come to stay. ' If Communism steadily improves in its results while Capitalism steadily gets worse, or if the workers of the West get the impression that such is the case, whether it is so or not, the results are likely to have an importance on the life of the West transcending any other single factor whatsoever.' This was the challenge we had to meet. I went on to discuss proposed remedies, including monetary remedies, leading up to the suggestion that the facts of the situation, political and economic, called not necessarily for coalition but for close co-operation between the then Labour Government, not only with the Liberal and Conservative Opposition, but with the leaders of the business and banking world, and a very clear intimation that the party really did adhere to its policy of gradualness, evolution, and stood resolutely against allowing or encouraging a break-down. In other words, the memorandum was in effect a plea to forestall and render unnecessary by that kind of informal co-operation the coalition government which a year or so later MacDonald formed, to the dismay and very great damage of the party as a whole.

[1] Dent and Sons, London and Toronto.

The history of the crisis of 1931, already told in a round dozen histories, with its monetary implications told at length in such documents as the *Report of the MacMillan Commission*, can hardly be attempted in these pages. It interested me of course because here we had illustrated in tragic form that interdependence of modern nations, the nature of which had been so little understood by the general public (including the public of 'practical businessmen' and stockbrokers) and which had been the burden of so much I had written before the first war. In *The Great Illusion* I had insisted to the point of weariness that if we persisted in forcing or allowing the breakdown of the economic structure of central Europe as the result of our victory, we in Britain would in the final result suffer disastrously ; pointing out that the interdependence of the world had grown so much in degree during the previous generation as to be different in kind from anything known previously; that the world economic organism had acquired sensory nerves through its banking and monetary structure. And here it was all happening before our eyes.

The acute phase of the crisis began, like the Great War, in Austria, with a declaration of insolvency by the Credit-Anstalt, the principal bank of that country, in June 1931. This caused a 'run on Germany,' in other words, a demand by Germany's creditors for the repayment of floating debt and short-term loans. The principal international bankers met and made a 'standstill' agreement by which they agreed to renew their advances to Germany until the end of the following February.

To the difficulties of the financial situation abroad had to be added those of the situation at home, the two conditions interacting. The Unemployment Fund out of which Unemployment benefits were granted and which was partially dependent upon the contributions of the employed, was bankrupt by the drains upon it and had to resort to borrowing. On 4 July 1931, the Insurance Unemployment Commission issued an Interim Report recommending economies which, though obviously inadequate, were violently opposed by the parliamentary supporters of the Government. *The Report of the MacMillan Commission* (July 13) was just as disturbing. The May report (July 31) more so.

Snowden, Chancellor of the Exchequer, sounded warnings,[1] though somewhat late in the day. Yet—doubtless under the pressure of his colleagues—he found himself unable in his 1931 spring budget to give effect to his own cautions. Morrison recognized the need for close co-operation—in a non-political sense—with the men who were actually running the country's industries and stood very pluckily by his policy when it was attacked, as it sometimes was, by the more demagogic members of the party in the private party meetings. Arthur Henderson, shrewd and able beyond most, would have done even better as a foreign minister and chairman of the Preparatory Disarmament Conference if he had not been compelled to combine those offices with virtual management of the party. The politician in him came into conflict with the statesman (as it almost inevitably does with very many Parliament men in a system like ours). MacDonald was often bitterly critical of Henderson, especially in the latter's work at Geneva. But I am inclined to think that ' Uncle Arthur ' had a better grasp of the essentials than MacDonald had. When I asked Henderson what in his view lay at the root of the disarmament failure he replied instantly : ' The failure to tackle security effectively before we started on disarmament.' That was the right reply and Henderson saw it more clearly than MacDonald.

Any leader could have been excused for confusion and puzzlement concerning the economic situation of 1929-31. But MacDonald was more oracular, more eloquent, more uplifting in his confusions than any man of his generation. The behaviour of certain others in Parliament at that time sticks out in my memory. George Lansbury (*le bon vieux papa* of the Party), who became for a short time leader of the Parliamentary party after the Great Schism, when the crash came simply chanted the party hymns. All would be solved when we had ' complete Socialism and power as well as office. Let's sing the Red Flag.' Tom Mosley had already shaken off the dust of the party and begun his Fascist experiment. What one saw of his character made one

---

[1] In Jan. 1931, on the eve of the appointment of the May Committee, Snowden as Chancellor of the Exchequer said; 'I say with all the seriousness I can command, that the national position is grave: that drastic and disagreeable measures will have to be taken if the Budget equilibrium is to be maintained and industrial recovery to be made.'

shudder; its arrogant angers and intolerances, and hint of
utter ruthlessness. I happened to sit beside him in the Chamber
when he made what was virtually his speech of resignation from
the Labour Party. It was really a tour de force. Packed full of
figures and dates, he made little if any reference to his notes,
even if he had them (of which I saw no evidence). John Strachey
flirted with the nascent Fascist organisation and seemed to
oscillate between it and the Communists. Strachey's speeches at
party gatherings were often a compound of all the Marxist in-
cantations ('Not until the oppressions of capitalism had been
swept away and that evil system utterly destroyed would the
down-trodden masses of the workers . . . and to capitalism alone
must we look for the ultimate cause of war'). His rapid rise to
high office has been as surprising as Noel-Baker's slowness in
rising. Noel-Baker probably knew more of the factual background
of the League and foreign affairs than the rest of the House put
together; yet it was Dalton who took precedence over him in
that province when it came to the distribution of offices. And
Dalton, when it came to the Schism, could talk of it all with the
best of the demagogues as just another bankers' ramp.

Indeed, the Party as a whole took the view that the financial
difficulties arose solely from the inherent defects of capitalism.
Snowden and MacDonald had to face from their ex-colleagues
the same kind of accusation which the Communists and Labour
Left Wingers bring against the present Socialist Government of
being stooges of American capitalists, of Wall Street pirates and
Detroit thugs, as one Labour member put it a year or two since.
The Party's mood and temper of 1931 is indicated in the address
of the President of the Trade Union Congress which met at
Bristol just after the formation of the coalition government.
Arthur Hayday, the president for the year, explained that
'political and financial influences of a sinister character, working
behind the scenes, have taken advantage of the difficulties arising
from the policy pursued by private banking interests, not subject
to any public control, to dictate to the British Government and
people.' The people must learn, he added, that 'until we govern
the banks, the banks will govern us, and the policy of the Labour
and Trade Union movement be brought to naught.'

Well, fifteen years later, a Socialist government with a large
parliamentary majority *had* come to power, and the Central Bank

had been nationalized, and the severest measures of financial control had been introduced; and it was then that the Socialist Government was to meet financial crises even more grave than those which Snowden and MacDonald faced in 1931; and the Socialist Chancellor of the Exchequer of 1946-7-8-9 was to use a language of warning even graver than that used by Snowden; was to refrain from even pretending that the crisis was due to a banker's ramp; and was to urge that even under Socialism such crises, due largely to world conditions, could be resolved only by sacrifice, by greater production, by restraint in the matter of wage claims.

Reference to other writing and speaking of 1931 reveals how far the party had drifted into the language and mood of the class war. Dalton kept repeating the 'bankers' ramp' jibe. Cripps—who was a member of the 1945–50 Socialist Cabinet was to use Snowden's language—insisted in 1931 that the events provided the 'clearest demonstration of the power of capitalism to overthrow a popularly elected Government by extra-parliamentary means. The ruling classes will go to almost any length to defeat parliamentary action if the issue is the continuance of their financial and political control.' And the Cripps of 1931 went on to forecast that among the measures a socialist government might have to adopt would be 'the prolongation of the life of Parliament for a further term without an election.'[1]

G. D. H. Cole at that time also took the view that it would be impossible to bring a real socialist society into being without a period of dictatorship. Most of the party spokesmen drew terrifying pictures (like those drawn by Cripps) of the power which the financiers and capitalists would be able to wield for the destruction of the socialist state when it came into being. For twenty years I had been insisting that this picture of the influence of the 'money power' was the hobgoblin of doctrinaire minds, though aware that the criticism was having very little effect on the party mythology. No one seemed to have the faintest inkling of what was shortly to be demonstrated by the event, namely, that the real danger to the socialist state would come, not from the mysterious and largely imaginary 'money power' painted in such terrifying colours, but from the very real power of Trade Unions,

[1] *Problems of a Socialist Government,* quoted by Clifford Allen in *Britain's Political Future.*

each fighting for its own interests. In the event the capitalist class, once a parliamentary majority for a socialist government was obtained, was to reveal itself as completely impotent to prevent widespread socialization and even its own pretty complete dispossession. We were to see not only the millionaire, but virtually the whole of the 'country house' opulence which had been so typical of English life, abolished, and the standard of living of the whole bourgeois order most seriously reduced, by a socialist government that had not even a clear electoral majority (as distinct from a parliamentary) behind it. This social revolution was accepted without any attempt at revolt or counter-revolution. The much publicized 'money power' proved quite impotent. The real difficulties of the Socialist Government were to come from a very different quarter: from rank and file Trade Unionists occupying strategic positions in railways, docks, mines, food markets. Far from duplicating the impotence of shareholders or other property owners, the Trade Unionists were able by their power to paralyse the life of the nation, to defy their own leaders and to jeopardize the government their own votes had created. It had never been within the power or to the interest of the capitalist to bring the railways to a sudden stop, to deprive a city of its meat, the countryside of its food, the factories of their coal or power. But organized labour was shortly to prove that it could do all these things despite all the pleas of an embarrassed Socialist Government. The dangers of such an outcome were neither discussed nor foreseen. Indeed, what was so soon actually to happen would have been regarded as demonstrably impossible, as something against nature. For a third of a century the party had been proclaiming that permanent peace could come to the world only when the nations had abolished capitalism. Any forecast that the threat of the most appalling war of recorded history, the greatest peril to free and humane society, would come from a state that *had* abolished capitalism and achieved total social revolution, would have been swept aside as plainly impossible. To have gone on to foretell that a British Socialist Government, in its efforts to defend itself from the aggression of an older socialist state, would ask for and get aid from a great capitalist power—all this would have been regarded as stark, raving lunacy.

The fact that it was thus inconceivable to the orthodox socialist of the twenties, because in flat contradiction to his dogmatic and most cherished articles of faith, was a measure of the gulf between those doctrines and reality.

The crisis of 1931 had results which were to extend beyond the immediate internal situation of the country. Preoccupation with the domestic scene obscured the significance of what was happening in Germany, where Hitler was so soon to come to power; in Japan and China; in Italy and Abyssinia, events which, within the decade, were to put Britain and the whole of Western civilization in mortal jeopardy.

I look back on my own small rôle at that time with no pride whatever. It seems to me now to have been vacillating, even pusillanimous. I had almost immediately on entering Parliament felt that we were drifting into the economic, financial and monetary chaos which I had predicted would inevitably follow on the heels of a world war. I knew also that this period of economic breakdown would in a sense be more menacing to Western civilization than war itself. In war time, faced by the threat of alien domination, we can drop our internecine differences, knowing that the things which unite us are of more worth than the things which divide us. But in peace time we let party purposes take precedence of the bigger, more universal purposes; and the peace time problems are the more complex. In war at least we know what we want, and are agreed on our purpose. In peace we do not; and are not.

I did not feel, as so many Labourites seemed to feel, that coalition would prove fatal to the future survival of the party. After all, Labour was to work with the other parties for the five fateful years of the Second War under a Conservative leader of greater personal power than any man in modern British politics; and, on the morrow of that experience to achieve its greatest party success. Yet although MacDonald pressed me very much to join with Clifford Allen, Elton, De La Warr and others who were coming over to the National side; and although he hinted that a peerage would be available if it were not practicable to work from the House of Commons—despite all this and with added pressure from Allen whom I liked and respected and with whom I had worked closely in the past, and—which weighed heavily with me—from Harold Wright, I refused finally to take the plunge. And I have felt since that it was no credit to me that I did refuse.

The motives of refusal were, I am afraid, mainly that I shrank from facing the censure of old friends in the Labour ranks—censure for 'ratting', for 'betrayal of the cause', for failing to stand by old comrades. This ought not to have weighed with me at all. But it did. Other motives were sounder.

My position at this juncture was the more difficult because I had been elected by the whole Parliamentary party as a member of the Consultative Committee, which was in the nature of being an executive of the Parliamentary party (as distinct from the Labour Party), as the general framer of policy and method. Moreover, in the election of the several members of this committee I had come out pretty near the top. It was Dalton who at this juncture came to me and in effect said : 'Your case of conscience about MacDonald's action puts us in a hole. You are a member of the Consultative Committee and as such all our plans, opinions, are discussed freely before you, and yet in a day or two you may decide to join the MacDonald end.' I found the whole suggestion offensive and told Dalton so. First of all, there were not any secrets of which MacDonald would not be entirely aware; secondly, it was quite unlikely that I would join the MacDonald push, and thirdly, I should be more than a little scrupulous to see that nothing in the way of confidential conversation was repeated to MacDonald. I don't think that Dalton saw the point, as he expressed the hope that I should not be 'pompous' about the case of conscience. Incidentally, throughout this whole episode Dalton showed in all public pronouncements a thick strain of rather crude demagogy.

Among the notes spared by the blitz there are a few with dates attached dealing with that time. Thus :

8 September 1931 :
Susan Lawrence has been urging me to throw aside all doubts. She said that the Labour Party had great need of me, and that sort of thing. I have never seen any evidence of it, but that's what Susan said. I was nominated to this Policy Committee, and I nominated Stafford Cripps to it and in the evening the Committee met, Arthur Greenwood was in the chair. There were

S

present Hugh Dalton, Stafford Cripps, Frank Wise, Molly
Hamilton, Attlee, Addison. It was held while Winston was talking.
I dined to find the dining-room full of Tories and tables full,
having in the interim had to correct an important interview for
the American Press, and thereby missed some of the discussion.

In the course of the evening Dick Denman, Strauss, and Miss
Picton-Turberville came and said they were doubtful as to the
wisdom of voting a lack of confidence. Denman left about ten
o'clock. I said I would definitely abstain.

9 September 1931 :

The Prime Minister's secretary rang up in the morning for me
to be at his room at 4.30. We had no sooner got talking than the
division bell rang; nobody knew what it was about but thought
it was a closure on the taking of private members' time. In the
lobby I ran into Tom Kennedy, who asked me why I had
abstained, I told him and he said : 'Don't you suppose that all
that was taken into consideration by the executive?' He added
he must bring the matter before the executive, I said I would
send him a statement, but didn't. On the way back to the Prime
Minister's room Strauss stopped me and said that Kennedy had
threatened to withdraw the Whip from him. Back in the Prime
Minister's room he made a long, rather rambling, detailed statement of the crisis and events, speaking from notes of cabinet
meetings. He must have talked for the best part of an hour. I had
been anxiously watching the clock as I was due at a committee
upstairs for the formulation of policy at 5 p.m. and the P.M. was
still talking at 6 p.m.

Afterwards Lovat Fraser in a formal sort of way thanked
him on behalf of those present and offered a pledge to support
him. I intervened quietly and said that in order to prevent mis-
apprehension Strauss, Picton-Turberville and myself gave no
pledges at all, that we came with open minds, having felt it was
advisable to vote against the Government the previous night, but
were keeping our hands free for future occasions. The P.M. said
he quite understood and said that so far as we were concerned
we kept our hands free. I had a talk with Gillett coming out of
the Prime Minister's room and bumped into Dalton; we walked
into Henderson's room where we found Philip Noel-Baker. Dalton
explained that the big policy committee had been split into sub-
committees and that he, Noel-Baker, and myself had been appointed to draw up a memorandum immediately on the international side of policy regarding gold, finance credit, etc. Having
disposed of that, I warned Dalton the position might be changed

somewhat in view of what Kennedy had said; that he had threatened to hoof me off the committee. This brought the conversation to my own case.

I think the determining reason for my not going over to MacDonald despite the offers he made was that I simply did not trust his judgment in foreign affairs or his ability so to influence his new colleagues as to steer that policy even approximately in the right direction. Events were to justify this misgiving.

It could be argued of course that the fear I felt about the mismanagement of foreign policy was a good reason for helping MacDonald, if I could: not for leaving him just when any support by his old colleagues would have been valued. But I knew that my chances of being able to influence him at all were extremely slim.

Looking back, I believe now that had the Labour Party as a whole gone into the coalition in 1931, as it did go into that of 1941, the result would have been sounder governments than those of the MacDonald-Baldwin-Chamberlain period of appeasement and there would have been greater chance of arresting the fatal —and fatalistic—drift to the unnecessary war. Even from the party point of view, Labour could hardly have fared worse than it did in the autumn election of 1931, producing a Parliament, it will be recalled, in which of its 615 members no fewer than 554 were pledged to support the National Government, giving it a normal majority of about 450. The socialist opposition were reduced from 265 to 52. Many of the 554 who found themselves on the Government benches never expected to be in the House at all; had no qualifications for serious politics and made up a House probably lower in moral and intellectual quality than any which has assembled there in this century—excepting only perhaps the House which resulted from the Khaki election of 1918.

There was one quality about MacDonald in which he differed greatly from certain other more successful leaders, from Lloyd George, for instance. It was related of Lloyd George that if he had to tackle (say) a budget speech, he would invite a succession of City men to breakfast, beginning with people like Montagu Norman or Huth Jackson, and say to each in turn: 'I know nothing about the City. Please regard me as your ten-year-old boy asking questions. The Treasury people are too learned for me as they would be for your ten-year-old. First please explain to me . . .' And on the delivery of the speech the men in the House would remark : ' Really, L.G. is astounding. He's never seen a bill of exchange in his life, yet he handles the subject like an old hand.'

MacDonald was congenitally incapable of such an attitude. He could not put himself in the position of a learner. Even with some of his oldest friends he had always to be the oracle. One would make a suggestion, which more often than not he would criticize somewhat contemptuously and reject. A little later, sometimes in the same conference, or it might be in one a week or two later, he himself would make the same suggestion. He had to be persuaded that it came from him. It may have been part of that strange vanity which grew on him with the years and with success; and that in its turn may have sprung from the fact that his birth was, as one biographer put it, obscure. I am quite sure that to the public as a whole, and to his opponents as well as his supporters, the circumstances of his origins—though they were generally known—did not matter two straws. But they mattered to MacDonald in the sense of having an influence on his character. He felt unconsciously perhaps that he had to offset them by pride of place, by association with the obviously great, by a vanity which reached to snobbishness.

This quality in MacDonald affected his bearing to his old Labour colleagues during the crisis and had a real effect on the party's attitude. The bearing may well have been explained in large part, of course, by the strain through which he was going. But many party members with whom he came into contact deeply resented it. One Trade Unionist gave a description of the way in which he received a number of trade union spokesmen. ' When we came in, there he stood at his desk lighting a cigarette with a lardy-da air. He hardly looked at us, just waved with his hand for us to sit down. Kept paying attention to the cigarette and not to us. When I remembered all he owed to us, I could have given him a clout over the head.'

Sir Arthur Salter, in his *Personality in Politics*, has a sketch of MacDonald which brings out very clearly the essential tragedy of success in his life. Salter points out that ' the rise from

an origin both humble and obscure to the highest office in the
State; to be a creator and leader of a great new party; to battle
for many years against the citadels of privilege and then enter
them as victor; in a grave crisis to lead not merely a party, but
a national Government; and for some years to be an outstanding
figure not only in national but world affairs '—that surely is a
record of achieved ambition with scarcely a parallel in the annals
of British politics. But ' at the climax of success to lose the friendships of earlier life; to be a renegade instead of a leader in the
eyes of those with whom success was won; to find the captured
citadel turning into a gilded prison; then to be conscious of
waning powers while still in an office which demands the best;
and at last to drift into impotence and open disrespect'—that
indeed is tragedy.

Immediately after dissolution the Bradford party strongly
urged me to stand again. Alfred Pickles—who had become Lord
Mayor of Bradford during my period in Parliament and whom
I had come to like so much—brought all the pressure of mutual
friendship to bear. But I was exceedingly unhappy at my own
rôle in this crisis; knew now that I could not do the work I was
most fitted for as a member of the House; and so stood firm in
my decision to leave that type of party politics altogether. This
did not mean that I had left the Labour Party—only that I would
not now put my main effort into purely party work; but into
work that would perhaps help to make the task of the honest
politicians a little easier.

THE SECOND FATAL DRIFT

AFTER retiring from Parliament in 1931 I was able to give more time to work in connection with the League of Nations Union, the Royal Institute of International Affairs; to do a great deal of lecturing, with frequent visits to the United States, some to France, two to Holland and Scandinavia. As I came more and more into contact with the general public I grew to feel, pretty much as I had felt in the first years of the century, that we were drifting to a disaster we refused to face. 'It is happening all over again.'

This mood was reflected in a book, published in 1933, and which I called *The Great Illusion—1933*, relating the themes of the first *Great Illusion* to the events of the later date. This was the early stage of the appeasement period and it terrified me no less than had the opposite error which marked the drift in the years before the First War. In the first decade of the century the public took the view that the trouble with Germany could be cured simply by fighting Germany and beating her; in the case of the Japanese, German and Italian aggressions of the thirties the public seemed to believe that the trouble could be cured by not fighting, by doing nothing. Both courses were to prove equally disastrous. The one course of action most clearly indicated for the Western democracies in the thirties was to make plain to the potential aggressors : 'We intend to defend your victims; if the aggression continues you will have to meet our collective power.' One recalled once more the warning of Clemenceau to Wilson in 1918 : 'Let Britain and the United States say now that they will defend France if she is again attacked and you will *not* have to fight Germany. If you don't say this now you will have to fight Germany.'

One saw that all this was coming true. And most of the public refused to listen. 'What! Commit ourselves to war! How can you, an anti-war man, make so wicked a suggestion? I thought you were against coercions, and now you want us to coerce

Japan, an old ally.' What I wanted, of course, was that we should do our best to see that Japan did not coerce China, nor Germany her neighbours. 'Commitments lead to war' was a slogan of that time, despite the fact that in 1914 we had no commitments, the United States had none, and both were drawn in. The public seemed to have forgotten the answer Lloyd George had given to the question, 'Could the war have been prevented?' He had replied instantly. 'Yes. If Germany had known beforehand that in following the course she did she would have to meet the combined power of the nations who finally took arms against her, she would not have followed that policy and there would have been no war.' I had tried during thirty years to show that there can be no defence which is not collective defence; that if each nation is left to be its own and sole defender then the nations can be picked off one by one, by any aggressor that manages to make himself stronger than the single victim of the moment; just as a bandit gang that made itself stronger than a single household could have a whole countryside at its mercy unless the organized power of the community in the shape of the police stood ultimately behind each household. If we won't defend others—by, say, paying our police rate for the defence of neighbours we may not like—then in the end we shall be unable to defend ourselves. Thus to organize the power of the community does not mean perpetuation of an unchanging status quo. It is the necessary foundation of peaceful change; the means by which the rights of the community can be asserted against individual anarchic violence; the necessary basis of law and its peaceful evolution.

The enunciation of these simplicities crops up again and again repetitively in most that I wrote in those years, more particularly in *Preface to Peace; a Guide for the Plain Man* (1935), in *Defence of the Empire* (1937), in *Peace with the Dictators?* (1938), *Must It Be War?* (1938), and in books written for the American public even after 'The Unnecessary War' had come upon Britain but not yet upon America. Those simple truths are still being challenged by certain eminent party leaders in America in this year of 1951 in which I write; and for the moment at least splitting that unity of opinion and policy in the West which is the best hope of deterring Russian aggression, as it might have deterred the German aggression of the two previous wars.

My own personal position in the fight of the interwar years

differed greatly from what it had been in the struggle before the First War. Before 1914 I carried on a one-man show in the sense that the movement described in previous pages was based upon the statement of the case which I had given it in *The Great Illusion*. During and immediately after the war I had to face the animosity meted out to a man whose position the public took to be that of having ' opposed the war.' But after about 1925 all this altered and I was welcomed into all the groups that sought rational and realistic means of preventing a second war. I became very willingly a private in a sizeable, if very scattered, army.

They were busy years, those between 1920 and 1940. During most of them I was a member of the Labour Party Advisory Committee on Foreign Affairs; a member, while in Parliament, of the controlling Consultative Committee of the Parliamentary Labour Party; for something more than ten years a member of the Council of the Royal Institute of International Affairs (Chatham House); the British member of the Presidium of the Comité Mondiale Contre la Guerre et le Fascism; an active member of the Executive of the League of Nations Union; President of the Abyssinia Association; during the first of those two decades a pretty frequent contributor to the *Daily Herald*, for a period on its staff and manager of the Trade Union Pledge Scheme described in a later chapter; a little later editor of *Foreign Affairs* (English); contributor of a monthly supplement to *Time and Tide* on Foreign Affairs; acted as chairman or Director of Studies nearly every summer at conferences of students in Geneva or Paris or in England; made a yearly visit to the United States on lecturing tours; invented some card games designed to show the nature of money and banking; farmed Northey Island, built a house there (largely with my own hands); sailed (sometimes by myself) in a little yacht in the North Sea; and, in the twenty years, wrote twenty-three books.

After the German occupation of the Rhineland, the Italian attack on Abyssinia, the German-Italian attack on the Spanish Republican government, I began to co-operate in the Popular Front movement both in Britain (where I spoke on the same platform with Stafford Cripps, and on one occasion with Lloyd George as well) and in France, where I addressed a dozen or so meetings, at one time or another. (I am probably the only Englishman who has made a political speech from the stage of the Grand Opera in Paris.) At one big meeting on the outskirts of Paris the platform was dominated by the Communists and the government seemed to fear rioting. Police were stationed all around the inside wall of the big hall. When Cachin rose to speak, there was a shout from the gallery, counter-shouts from the floor; two thousand people rose from their seats, the police drew their batons . . . But the chairman, with the help of an enormous bell, managed to restore some sort of order after an anxious twenty minutes of noise. He would take *one* question from the gallery. Would the comrade there state it in thirty seconds? The comrade said: 'The question I put to Comrade Cachin was, Will he please speak into the microphone?' The Third Republic was safe.

The constituency of Bury in Lancashire at about that time sent a delegation, composed of anxious Liberals and Labourites, to ask me if I would stand as an independent candidate. But though I felt keenly the need of energetic opposition to the policy of appeasement then being pursued by the government, I felt I could do more useful work outside parliament, and, so, after some discussion, went no further with the matter.

Another incident I recall is that at the time that Ethiopia was expelled from the League as having lost her territory, the Ethiopian Legation approached me to ask whether I would be their representative at Geneva to take up the case and to argue against expulsion. I agreed to do so, but at the last moment had flu and was not able to travel, which I have always regretted. It was true that I should have had to argue against Lord Halifax, whom I respected (and whom I got to know pretty well in Washington later on), but nevertheless it would have been an interesting thing to do, especially in view of the Emperor's final restoration. It meant, however, several interviews for me with the Emperor Haile Selassie himself, who for some years every Christmas sent me a long document in Aramaic (kindly enclosing a translation). When the Emperor arrived in London and was met by a delegation including myself at Charing Cross, he appeared in a cloak, yellow leather shoes and a billycock hat. Yet with it all, he impressed one with his innate dignity. He was only about five feet tall, with sharply-cut Semitic features, very dark, and yet every inch a chieftain. One of his letters is headed as from 'The Conquering Lion of the Tribe of Judah, Haile Selassie I., Elect of God, Emperor of Ethiopia, to Sir Norman Angell.

Peace be unto You,' and proceeds : 'We remain indebted to you
for the disinterested and wise advice which you were so good as
to give us during the preparations for the Session of the Council
of the League of Nations in May last. It is true that on that
occasion we had to lament the fact that the Spirit was willing
while the Flesh was weak. But this very fact increased our
gratitude to you. An equally critical period for the cause of our
unfortunate country is now approaching; and I venture to
express a hope that the state of your health may so improve as to
permit you to bring once again your practical support to a cause
which, I feel sure you will agree, is the same as that for which
you have so nobly and consistently struggled all your life. Written
at the City of Bath, the Second day of Nehassie, in the Year of
Grace one thousand nine hundred and thirty. (8th August 1938.)'

Alas, in the multiplicity (rather than the importance) of the
tasks which fell to my lot during those years, I was not able to
give to the Abyssinian business the attention which I do not doubt
it deserved.

I think the chief weakness of those of us in the Collective
Security ranks at that time was that we had to fight on several
fronts. We still had to struggle with the old type Nationalist
Conservative, who did not want any part in these new-fangled
' pacifist ' ideas. Dear old Blimp was far too muddle-headed to
distinguish between pacifism and internationalism ; or to see that
sufficiency or effectiveness of national arms would depend on who
was with us and who against; and that for this reason defence
was as much a political as a military problem. Then, at the
opposite end to the Blimps, were the non-resisters who were against
all force, and who perhaps did not see very clearly that the refusal
to endow law with power did not diminish the total amount of
force in the world but left it in the hands of the lawless, the most
violent; that a world of international anarchy would contain
more of such lawless violence than one which put its combined
power behind some acceptable rule of international life.

But the worst split or dissipation of energy was due to the
socialists of Marxian complexion who insisted that the greatest
hope of peace lay, not in the collective action by ' capitalist ' governments, but in the expansion of Socialism throughout the world.
Many, perhaps most, British Socialists would have denied that
they accepted the revolutionary Marxist class war theory. But

they slipped, half-consciously, into the Marxist attitudes. They insisted—as the public discussions of that time clearly show—that ' capitalism is the cause of war.' The Labour Party as a whole formally and sincerely committed itself to the support of the League, but having saluted it passed on and put the objectives of Socialism a long way ahead of foreign policy questions. Moreover, it soon became evident that the League itself could only be an effective instrument of collective defence if within it there existed an alliance of the great powers along the lines of Clemenceau's suggested Tripartite Guarantees, or of the Treaty of Mutual Assistance, the Geneva Protocol or the Locarno treaties. The first of these fell because of Wilson's failure to secure ratification by the Senate, the others because of wavering support or because they came too late. The younger and more dynamic elements among Progressives everywhere swallowed whole the amazing proposition that ' capitalism is the cause of war and is incompatible with peace.' The net result of its general acceptance was that in so many circles first things did not come first, the first thing being the co-operation of widely differing forms of national society for the purpose of common defence, since without peace there is not much chance of building up the kind of society the Socialists promise : as the last few years have shown.

When on 17 February 1951, in the New York Press I read the account of Stalin's interview with *Pravda*, I am reminded of the kind of thing we were up against in those interwar years. For Stalin said :

In the United States, in Britain and also in France there are aggressive forces thirsting for a new war. They need war to obtain super-profits, to plunder other countries. They are the billionaires and millionaires who regard war as an item of income which gives colossal profits. They, these aggressive forces, control the reactionary governments and direct them.

As the West reads this declaration from the Communist Pope himself, it can only wonder at the completeness with which the iron curtain shuts off the Kremlin from the world of reality. But what Stalin says in 1951 was said a thousand times in my hearing by Western Socialists even of the milder sort during the twenty interwar years; said with dogmatism as setting forth unquestionable truth. And it was my old friend Laski (perhaps in his generation the most distinguished philosopher of the Left, as he was certainly the most erudite) who as late as 1944, in his *Faith, Reason and Civilization*, wrote:

> The solemn truth remains that in the Soviet Union more men and women have had more opportunity of self-fulfilment than anywhere else in the world . . . it is the only nation which . . . knows without doubt that its people move to the control of their own destiny. . . . If therefore it be accepted that our own time bears a profound resemblance to the era in which Christianity was born, it seems to me that we are entitled to conclude that the regeneration of values which the new faith effected, after no doubt a long and bitter struggle, is more likely to be secured in our own age by the central idea of the Russian revolution than by any alternative principle we are in a position to choose.

It was some sense of the danger inherent in revolutionary doctrine and the temper it produces that prompted me in 1926 to write a reply to Trotsky's *Where is Britain Going?*, a book which argued the inevitability, not of gradualness, but of revolution, and was a bitter attack on British Labour leaders as 'lickspittle lackeys of the bourgeoisie.' My reply was entitled *Must Britain Travel the Moscow Road?* and was, in a publishing sense, a thumping success, getting exceedingly good reviews (including one by Ramsay MacDonald and another by J. L. Garvin) from all quarters except the extreme Left.[1] Yet reading the book after twenty-five years, I am struck by one detail of misjudgment of the trend in Russia revealed by subsequent history, which may contain a warning as to the future of Socialism in the West. At the time the book was written (in 1926) all the most acute observers agreed that since the revolution had not dislodged the peasants who were still in possession of their holdings, the economy of the country nearly ten years after the revolution was not in fact socialist at the base. Michael Farbman, who spoke Russian as his mother tongue, was making constant visits to Russia (he wanted me to accompany him on one of them), and had written two carefully documented books, which, like a dozen others equally well documented, showed that the

---

[1] However in the *New Statesman and Nation*—which has seldom since reviewed my books at all—Leonard Woolf wrote;—'If human beings were rational or reasonable animals no one could possibly read Angell and remain a Bolshevik or even a revolutionary.'

Moscow government had in fact accepted compromises and had left large fields open for private property and enterprise. In those fields all the coercions had, Farbman and others insisted, failed. That was true as of 1926. But it was a strategic retreat of Bolshevism, effected in order to make a much more decisive advance a little later on.

My book was one more protest against the dangerous class-war psychology as an instrument of social change; of presenting the struggle for peace and welfare as a war to be fought against a privileged class, instead of as a series of difficult problems to be solved by reason and patience.

As far back as 1912 I had written for the Independent Labour Party a small book, *War and the Workers*,[1] in which I crossed swords with Kautsky on the proposition that 'Capitalism is the cause of war.' Kautsky had maintained the usual socialist thesis that capitalists profited enormously from war and foreign conquest. In addition to the part of the book designed to expose that fallacy was another part answering the arguments of Chesterton that the capitalists, 'the usurers,' were plotting sordidly to avoid war at the cost of national honour. The net impression left on re-reading this argument after forty years is that the learned German Socialist and the learned English Catholic were both at astronomical distances from reality; that neither was facing the facts of the external world nor the forces within himself.

Ever since that time I have continued to ask myself how it comes about that the honest, idealistic, and often very learned folk who embraced Communism, above all priding themselves on their super-scientific approach, moved only by 'fact,' failed to foresee the one most stupendous fact which was to emerge from the Communist experiment—that the society it produced would not be free and humane, but slavish and debased. No early Communist wanted or expected what has come about. Why then the oversight of such prodigious proportions?

In the flood of recantations by Communists ('The God That Failed' kind of thing) and explanations of why they changed their minds, there is no explanation of how at the beginning they could have overlooked the likelihood of their encountering along that road precisely what they did encounter. Orwell's *Nineteen Eighty-Four*, though managing to leave an appalling picture,

[1] The National Labour Press, Ltd.

does not tell us how the British nation got there; tells us nothing of the process of the change.

I have tried at times to get it out of Zilliacus, whom I knew. But he always became foggy and inarticulate whenever we got on to the subject, as little able really to explain it as a Salvationist is able to explain his special experience. All the Salvationist can do really is to tell you that he ' came wonderfully to Jesus.' Yet Zilly calls himself an atheist. Nor are his letters (of which I possess some scores) any more enlightening.

We were, however, to do a book together consisting of an exchange of letters. Zilly writes from Geneva on 3 April 1937, that he has ' a much clearer conception now of what the book ought to be about. The title should be PEACE AND THE CONFLICT OF IDEOLOGIES, and it ought to be an attempt to bridge over the intellectual gap between Socialists and Liberals, or had I better say Marxists and non-Marxists on the issue of peace. In some ways I believe I am really well qualified to do the Socialist side of that. Because you and I are old friends; I started as your disciple and still very largely am. I have read, I think, all your books and a large proportion of your review articles. But I have gradually and reluctantly come to the conviction that the only thing that really matters in the world to-day is the class struggle.'

Well, we did confer. Yet we did not manage to do the book (the second war came too soon), and I never managed to understand how Zilly so interpreted political facts in the Britain of 1950 as to write in the *New Statesman* that 'it would be hard to exaggerate the fanaticism, folly and ferocity of our ruling class when faced with a real challenge to their power and privileges. . . . They will stop at nothing and would gladly bring down civilization about our ears in atomic dust rather than allow the world to go socialist quietly.'

The vacillating policy of the Chamberlain government—which was to lead to Munich and thence to the second war—brought men of all parties into consultation. One group called itself ' The Five Years Group ' and centred its efforts upon the creation of an agreed agenda for a five-year policy. It included most of the independent members of Parliament—Clifford Allen, Harold Macmillan, Eleanor Rathbone, Arthur Salter as the active nucleus, with much wider support among the general public. I had some hand in the drafting of their memoranda and in the production of the book which they published, *The Next Five Years*. It stated the shortcomings of the general policy of appeasement and suggested alternative lines of action. And of course Winston Churchill was active in the direction of an inter-party, or non-party movement. The nature of one part of his effort is indicated in a letter to Arthur Salter in April, 1937, in which I say: 'Winston Churchill and a few friends—Lady Violet Bonham-Carter, Wickham Steed, Walter Citrine, Philip Guedalla, the Duchess of Atholl, Archibald Sinclair, Noel-Baker, Wall—are anxious that you should come to the next of the luncheons held at longish intervals at which pressing aspects of foreign policy are discussed. They have delegated me to invite you. Do come if you can. It is a purely private affair, and they beg me to assure you that they are not a new Party, or Group, or Movement, or in competition with any existing organization whatever, " just a focus." My own interest has derived from the fact that Winston seemed disposed sometime since to join the League of Nations Union, or to persuade some of his Tory friends to do so, and it was something which at that moment the Union particularly needed.'

These meetings proved useful and became regular monthly luncheon functions. Out of them grew a series of public meetings of which Wickham Steed, I think, was the chief organizer—all being an attempt to wake up the public to the fatal drift of things in the foreign field. My papers also indicate that we made an attempt to extend that kind of inter-party consultation to France. I explain to a French correspondent that 'the condition of our meeting and lunching or dining together here is that the meetings, although not secret, are confidential; that there are no newspaper men present; that no reports are given and that we talk together as individuals, not in any way committing our parties or our organizations. It does, however, help us to see how far those of different parties can agree on a common policy, particularly in relation to foreign affairs, the League, the maintenance of peace. We want to arrange a meeting of this group with a similar group in France. We would go to Paris, say, once a month; and they would come over to London, say, once a month and at the cost of no more inconvenience create exceedingly useful contacts.' But we were never able to carry that part of the project into effect.

All these efforts had of course one purpose : Not merely to bring home to the public a sense of the way things were drifting, but to give also such means of judgment, that a government could take a decisive line without being hamstrung or shackled by demagogy and emotionalism—as for instance by the raucous isolationism of the Beaverbrook Press which was virtually against any foreign commitment and was helping to create in the Britain of the late thirties the same sort of confusion which the revival of isolationism of the McCormick order is creating for the Truman Administration of the year 1951.

Two experiments of my own in the interwar years bore on this issue of Press sensationalism, and the power of Press combines.

Already back in 1922 I had published a small book entitled *The Press and the Organization of Society*, on the problem of the Press. A new edition appeared in 1935. The problem as I saw it has already been indicated in the account of my relations with Northcliffe. The difficulty did not, I felt, arise mainly from the tendency to trustification or the influence of advertisers or the dictation of outside interests, but from the nature of public opinion, from the fact that it was more profitable in terms of circulation for a newspaper to pander to existing prejudice or error than to give the facts which would help the public to a better state of mind.

If the public was in a mood to bully the Boers and suppress the Boer republics, an editor was tempted to publish stories which tended to paint the Boers as psalm-singing scoundrels; if in a mood to fight Germany, to paint the Germans as a special sub-human ' race.' Since Anglophobia in America had deep roots, a Robert McCormick could make his Chicago *Tribune* ' the greatest newspaper in the world ' by serving out daily doses of anti-British hatred which feed isolationists of the kind which makes a consistent foreign policy for any secretary of state next to impossible. Add to this a scale of values in news in the ' popular ' as opposed to the ' serious ' Press, which consistently makes the trivial important, and the important, often matters of national life and death, so dull that no attention is given to it. Given these factors, press of competition sets up a Gresham's Law, the bad coin tending to drive out the good, so that a picture tabloid can work up a circulation of anything from two to ten times the circulation of a *Times* or a *Manchester Guardian*.

Things are a great deal better now than they were when I wrote my book on the Press in 1922. The 'serious' paper has become sometimes a more valuable property than the tabloid. But even so the Royal Commission on the Press, reporting in 1949, confirmed to a disheartening degree the general conclusions of my 1922 book.

Contrary to the general impression, the Commission found the Press to be the source of great debasement and corruption of public judgment. 'In newspapers striving for mass circulation,' the report runs, 'a sense of values based on entertainment appeal becomes second nature ... Consequently the picture is always out of focus. The continuation day after day of distortion due to these factors ... has a cumulative effect upon the reader. It results, where it is carried farthest, not only in the debasement of standards of taste, but also in the further weakening of the foundations of intelligent judgment in public affairs.' The report continues:

> The appeal (of the popular papers) is very largely to the lowest common denominator of taste and interest; some popular papers are almost entirely frivolous on nearly every subject that they handle, while others attempt to deal with serious material seriously but give little of it; and finally, we cannot accept the view that the Press is doing everything that it can reasonably be expected to do; some of the spokesmen of the Press who gave evidence appeared to us unduly complacent and deficient in the practice of self-criticism.

What the Royal Commission did was to dispose of the charges of Labour critics that the Press in England (described by one member of the Labour Cabinet as 'The most prostituted Press in the world') was the mere instrument of corrupt capitalist interests. Judging on the basis of exhaustive and carefully sifted evidence, the Commission reported, 'The public can dismiss from its mind any misgiving that the Press of this country is mysteriously financed and controlled by hidden influences.'

A year or two before I wrote my book on the Press I joined the staff of the *Daily Herald* and developed the hope that a daily paper owned by the five million workers organized into Trade

T

Unions, able to depend upon their support for circulation, would be able to dispense with the kind of competition in sensationalism and triviality to which the Royal Commission makes reference.

The Trade Unions were in a position materially to create, almost from one day to another, an enormously powerful Press of their own, co-operatively owned, and to impose upon it a code of truth-telling. If any considerable proportion of the five million Trade Union members undertook to give a preference to their own Press, that Press would from the start be assured a circulation in excess of even the most successful capitalist daily papers.

I drew up a 'Pledge Plan.' Cards were to be issued to every Trade Unionist who would sign them, promising to 'Take the Labour Daily First.' There was to be no boycott of other publications. Having taken the Labour daily, it was open to the Trade Unionist to buy any other paper that he chose. The plan was put up to the Trades Union Congress, which appointed a special committee to study the scheme. This they did in great detail and approved it. It was put into operation.

The General Council of the Trades Union Congress and the Executive Committee of the Labour Party decided to use their machinery for putting the facts individually to every Trade Union member. Millions of 'pledge cards,' with counterfoils attached, were printed; dispatched to all the Trade Union branches; distributed to members. Later on these numbered counterfoils were to be used for prize draws—scholarships, holiday tours, etc. The secretaries of the branches which returned the winning numbers were also to be awarded valuable prizes. One of the circulars employed pleads that, 'if the tiny obligation embodied in the pledge card could be made a part of Trade Union loyalty, a means of setting up a new tradition, we should have a force behind circulation for Labour papers greater than that which any stunt yet devised by capitalist proprietors for the millionaire Press can achieve. This capacity to appeal to Trade Union loyalty is an asset special to the Trade Union daily. Lord Rothermere and Lord Beaverbrook are not in a position to make this appeal. Labour alone can do it. Here the capitalist cannot follow. Let us " up and at him " at his weakest spot.'

The plan failed. It failed largely because 'the little daily disciplines' are normally so much more difficult to maintain than the occasional heroic sacrifices. Men will die gladly on the barricades to get the vote, but having got it will stay at home on election day and fail to use it—if it happens to be raining.

After the plan had been abandoned the Trade Union organization still retained a half-interest in the *Daily Herald*, still had the last word in decisions on political policy. But the administration of the paper passed into the hands of a considerable newspaper trust organized along capitalist lines; the paper adopting methods of reaching the public long used by the much abused ' capitalist ' Press. It can hardly be said that in impartiality, objectivity, and seriousness the *Herald*, whatever its merits otherwise, is better than its capitalist neighbours.

I did not suppose for a moment that a Labour Press would be entirely free from these old evils, but one was justified in hoping, I felt, that such a Press would act as a counterweight to the almost exclusively capitalist and conservative outlook of the Press as it then existed; that something like a real discussion of social problems would emerge when both sides got a roughly equal newspaper representation and that the effects of putting both sides equally to the public would be an improvement of social judgment. Whether that objective has been aided by the presence of (say) the *Daily Herald* the reader may judge.

The book on the Press made one or two constructive suggestions. One anticipated the fact that the need for governmental organs of information would necessarily grow. Since the book was written the Ministry of Information has come into being, in Britain as in nearly every country. Another forecast was that we might come to need something in the way of the *Journal Officiel* already at that date existing in France. The book urged that if such an organ did come into existence it should be managed 'not by the government but by a journalistic judiciary pledged to the impartial presentation of the facts. Such a judiciary should be independent of the Cabinet, and owe its power to a Royal Charter: should constitute a Public Concern.' The publications of the B.B.C., especially in the case of the *Listener*, are a successful example of the general method I had in view. Another suggestion was 'to make of journalism a chartered profession like that of the law and medicine, demanding a minimum standard of qualifications and adherence to a certain code of professional conduct.'

The report of the Royal Commission indicates that the ob-

jectives reflected in this last proposal could be best achieved by
the establishment of a General Council of the Press. Though it
has been criticized severely in some quarters, it has been warmly
welcomed by several practical journalists.

The other social experiment to which in those interwar years
I devoted some effort from time to time was prompted by a sense
of the enormous dangers—to which the public as a whole was
all but completely oblivious—inherent in the prevailing economic
illiteracy. Here was a society become so vulnerable in its intricate
mechanism that gross economic errors, like those which lead to
bad inflation, could bring chaos and disaster both social and
political; deprive us alike of welfare and freedom. The thing
was happening before our eyes in the post-war years of the early
twenties. In *The Great Illusion* I had tried to point out that, as a
result of the new interdependence of the nations which had grown
up since the industrial revolution, the destruction of another's
financial stability would react disastrously on our own; that the
notion of collecting ' vast indemnities ' from the defeated enemy
after a great modern war was fantasy; that such indemnities
could only be paid in the last analysis in goods and services. It
all fell on deaf ears. Yet it all began to happen after the first war.
Germany became plunged in runaway inflation, which helped
to bring on Hitler, and Hitler a new war. The efforts of the
Socialist Government of Britain in 1939 to make the beginnings
of the socialist state were frustrated by the economic blizzard
which raged through the world, a storm raised, however,
not by the action of socialist governments, but by the governments
of capitalist societies. Popular feeling in America became embittered by the failure of Britain to pay its war debts, and
resolutely closed its eyes to the fact that those debts could be
paid only in goods or services which, by its tariff actions, the
United States adamantly refused to accept. All this made it
disastrously easy for the McCormicks and the Hearsts to inflame
the sentiment for complete isolationism. That helped to lead to
the second war. And in this year of 1951 the failure on the part
of the mass of workers really to appreciate the nature of inflation, its relation to the wage problem, and its bearing on a

sound economy, has bedevilled both the tasks of government and the organization of defence against the new danger from the East, alike in the United States and in Britain.

The case for a better general understanding of (say) the nature of money and of the illusions to which misunderstanding gives rise, is overwhelming, if we are really serious in our protestations about democracy, the possibility as well as the right of the people to direct their own destiny.

For some years I had been putting all this to educators. I called their attention to the fact that our school curricula had been expanded to include some weird subjects. But of the money in our pockets, its nature, function, vulnerability, its past failures as an economic device, the untrustworthiness of governments in the matter of its control and management, the disasters its mismanagement have brought about, the illusions which provoke the mismanagement—of all this ninety-nine per cent of our youngsters will not hear one word, from the day they enter school to the day they leave. And this notwithstanding that we live in a world which would come to a full stop, in which the trains could not run, food could not be brought to our houses and life go on without the money device. Why the complete blank at this point?

The answer usually was: 'Monetary science is so complex and difficult as to be virtually unteachable below the university standard. I myself find it quite incomprehensible.' To which I would reply: 'Bridge or chess would be quite unteachable if expounded in the usual scholastic method. Try the experiment of teaching bridge to a class that had never seen a pack of cards, in the manner in which we teach economics, that is, by abstract exposition, oral or written, by lessons, text books, *without resort to visual demonstration of the processes.* The first lesson would run something like this:

> The game of Bridge is played by the distribution of fifty-two discs, divided into four classes or denominations. These separate denominations consist of discs of an ascending scale of values, the whole distributed by the players in rotation, each distributor having the right of determining . . .

At this point of the lesson, or text book, any ordinary child— or adult—has either ceased to grasp what it is all about, become completely confused, or got it all wrong. How long would it take to teach bridge by that method? Doubtless it could be done: a two years course at a university might enable a few exceptionally brilliant students to play an indifferent game of bridge.

Yet bridge, so baffling as a subject of abstract exposition, more baffling perhaps than currency itself, can, if another method is employed, become so easy of understanding that a child can learn the general principles of the thing in an hour. That method is to sit down and play it, so that the student has a visual demonstration of the processes, as they unfold, participates in them, becomes indeed part of them.

The same pedagogical truth is illustrated in another way. Try to explain abstractly any intricate piece of mechanism, the differential of a motor car, say, to someone not a mechanical specialist or expert. You will fail. Take the student into the garage and let him see the mechanism actually moving, and what was before confused becomes plain.

Assuming that money is a more intricate subject than bridge, we get this result: we adopt, as a means of teaching the more difficult subject, a method which we know would fail when applied to the less difficult. My suggestion was that we must somehow do for the understanding of money what we do for the understanding of bridge—make understanding possible by visual demonstration; by a game, for instance. Usually, the educationalist would reply that it just could not be done. No game could do it.

During some twenty years I turned at intervals—usually quite brief ones, as on Atlantic crossings—to thinking out some means by which we might do for the understanding of money what we do for the understanding of bridge; demonstrate its processes through a game, a card game, almost inevitably. But, as I detest cards, I was certainly not an ideal person for this particular job.

Nevertheless I went on with it, largely, I think, out of sheer irritation at the complacency of the educationalists who insisted that no card game clarifying the processes of currency and banking *could* be invented. I would show 'em.

After some years of trial and error—the trial being for the most part borne by long-suffering nieces and nephews and their young friends—I did produce a card game, played with special cards, which showed at least that the thing was possible. After the special apparatus had been manufactured (and that presented exasperating difficulties) I played the game a number of times with bankers, professors of economics, heads of schools, journalists, most of whom spoke of it in high terms. Among those who did so were Professor Wesley Mitchell of Columbia, Professor Maynard Krueger of the University of Pennsylvania, Walter Lippmann, Morris Markey of the *New Yorker*, Hamilton Fyfe, Professor Ernest Patterson of the Wharton School of Finance and Commerce, University of Pennsylvania, John Dewey, Evelyn Wrench, and a very considerable number of teachers.

The book and cards were published in both New York and London, in the latter case going through several editions and revisions and achieving a quite considerable sale.

Yet the experiment did not fulfil the hopes I had of it. The immediate practical difficulty as a tool of education was the fact that very few elementary teachers had read any economics, and feared that the children would confront them with questions they could not answer. The line they usually took was ' the curriculum is overcrowded now; our classes are too big; we are overworked already; this is not an easy subject; it is no use our playing the game unless we can enter pretty fully into the facts which it illustrates. We are against it.' A natural enough attitude in the circumstances; and it proved fatal to my purpose.

I knew indeed that the game was defective as entertainment— a thought too complex. In its working out it tended to fall between two stools : if it was made attractive as a game it failed in some measure to illustrate money and banking; if the illustrations were exact it became too complex as a game. But I hoped that having demonstrated that some method along those lines was at least possible, someone, more expert in card games than I am, would improve on it. Some day of course this will be done, and some improver will reap a fortune which the inventor missed. Which is what usually happens to a pioneer.

My conviction remains that we can never equip our people with the kind of understanding necessary to the democratic management of a free society unless we show more ingenuity than we have done in the tools of education, and that the ' Money

Game' is a kind of tool which we shall have to add to our educational kit-bag.[1]

Such efforts as the two experiments just described, aimed at making a contribution to finding cures for the sicknesses of our society, were of course of a very long-term kind. They could make no contribution to the urgent day-to-day crises that piled one on top of another at about the time of Munich. I wrote a great deal both in periodicals and in books. None of the books was quite a failure in a publishing sense, only three successes in terms of sales. A Penguin reprint in 1939 of *The Great Illusion*, with an introduction showing the relevance of the original theme of that book to the events of that year, sold in very large numbers. And five years later a book of mine published in America was to run to considerably over a quarter of a million (and net me royalties in excess of any other book of mine).

Of these books the one which gave me the greatest pleasure to write was *You and the Refugee* (to which Mrs. Roden Buxton contributed a couple of valuable chapters). It was a plea for accepting virtually as many of the refugees from the Hitlerian persecution as could be got out of the countries he was over-running. That book too was an attempt to destroy an illusion, the illusion that a foreigner taking a job in Britain necessarily threw a Briton out of work. These immigrants offered in fact a great opportunity to the British Commonwealth, with a largely unfilled territory, and with resources as great as those of the United States, a country which, in one life time, has multiplied its population three times and become the richest and most powerful nation in the world, indispensable to the defence of the free world. Of that more presently.

I realized as we drew near to this Second, The Unnecessary War, that the years of my own life were slipping away. I fell a good deal into the habit of taking stock: Had I used those years to the best purpose? How were the closing years to be used? I had tried to escape; had known rewards and punishment; had had friendships and enmities. How did it all add up?

I think that stock-taking might be made the subject of another section of this record. It now follows.

[1] The publishers of the 'Money Game' in England are Messrs. Dent and Sons. The game is also discussed at some length in my *The Money Mystery; An Explanation For Beginners*, also published by Dents.

Part IV

A PERSONAL BALANCE SHEET

CHAPTER I

ESCAPE TO AN ISLAND

THE first chapter of this story is largely concerned with a boy's impulse to get away from a world which he felt to be cursed with problems it could not solve; to escape from contacts which only provoked misgivings, dismay and emotional frustration. Better the 'simple life of the open spaces.' Nearly everyone, I suppose, has this desire at times. A quarter of a century after my return from the American West the same sense of being compelled helplessly to witness a descent into needless misery and hopeless folly, came over me. It was hardly astonishing in view of what the preceding few years had revealed : the Versailles Treaty, the making of which I had watched at close quarters; the 1918 khaki election in which nearly all candidates but the cleverest had promised to 'wipe Germany from the map' (whatever that might mean); also to 'make Germany pay the whole cost of the war,' when ten minutes of honest reflection would have revealed that it could not be done, and that the attempt to do it would help to bring about the economic collapse of Europe and endanger the security of Western civilization. One had to witness also the maintenance of the blockade of a starving Germany after all the fighting was over (a folly whose meaning was brought home to me by some weeks' travelling in Germany and Austria after the war); the vilification of those English people who tried to help the starving children; (in the popular Press they became 'despicable Hun-coddlers'); French policy falling under the influence of the least worthy elements in France, with the result of a foolish and bootless invasion of the Ruhr, making ever more difficult the healing of the Franco-German wound and worsening Anglo-French relations; and (on the other side of the Atlantic) the foundering of the hopes that had centred round Wilson, a rejection of all the lessons the war might have taught, reversion to the crudest isolationism.

Of what avail to struggle against *that* current?

And there was something more than nausea at the general drift of things. More than most perhaps, I had always felt the need of what someone has called a ' daily bath of solitude '. A friend sends me a letter I had written in the days of the movement before 1914 in which I say 'I find myself craving solitude as a drunkard craves gin. The social side of this business of agitation exasperates me to the last degree. I don't write or do my work easily, and just when I am hammering out a clarification of some point which the public get so muddled, I am distracted by futile social functions which I could only avoid by gross discourtesy. And with all my sins, I am not capable, with comfort, of conscious discourtesy.' This does not mean that I ever had the movie star kind of popularity, but the work I was trying to do was badly interrupted by trivial social obligations, by requests for appearance at committees and meetings which I found difficult to refuse. So I sought half-consciously for a ' way of life ' that would enable me to escape that kind of obligation *without* ill-feeling or discourtesy.

On my return from the Paris of the Treaty makers, I had purchased a small yacht—a converted ship's life-boat in excellent condition. She was about thirty feet long, about eight tons Thames measurement; clinker built, well decked; raised cabin top; a fo'castle that took two bunks quite comfortably, a main cabin that took two more; a small galley so devised that a kettle or a frying-pan could be made to stay on the primus or the boiling stove in a sea way; a smallish cockpit, but big enough to take four people comfortably.

It sounds a lot of accommodation for a thirty-footer—but then a ship's big life-boat, a double ender, is ' all boat.' She was cutter rigged, behaved extremely well in a sea, would point up well into the wind, and, a most precious quality in a cruiser intended for use among the shoals of the East Coast estuaries, would take the ground without heeling if there were but a foot of mud under her keel; and even if there wasn't she would not heel so much as to become uninhabitable.

Such a boat to-day would cost six or seven or eight hundred pounds. I paid a hundred and twenty for her.

I had a vague notion, I think, of living on her during most of the summers (by myself) and by that means getting the solitude I did not seem to manage in any other way. In the first summer after getting the boat I did manage to spend some six weeks on her alone, taking my Corona typewriter with me and doing a little work. I sailed about the Blackwater estuary a good deal; took her occasionally into the North Sea, although she proved at times a bit of a handful for single-handed sailing. On one occasion, by some confusion, I managed to walk overboard when I was by myself and came to the surface in time to see the ship calmly sailing away without me. By great good luck I did not happen to be wearing heavy sea boots at the time, and I knew that she would quickly come into the wind. But even that was not necessary because, also by good luck, the dinghy was on a long painter and I was able to grab it as the boat sailed past. That was the only occasion, touch wood, when I came near to any serious accident. In thirty years of sailing I never hit any other craft, although once or twice other craft hit me.

I found in practice that living on a boat did not leave very much time for writing. The need of going ashore in the dinghy for provisions and water; cooking the meals and washing-up; keeping the gear in order (even a small yacht needs endless attention) did not leave much time for anything else. It was all great fun—but a full-time job. One feature of the life on board I recall. I had taken on board a 'linguaphone' for brushing up my very rusty German. A passing fisherman, hearing loud German talked on board, reported to the authorities that I was secreting a spy.

Occasionally I did have flesh and blood visitors, among them my niece, Barbara, and her brother Dennis Hayes. They were at the time children of twelve and ten respectively. They were with me on the boat a week while their parents were away from home. Looking back, I have sometimes been appalled at my own temerity in taking on a responsibility of that kind, and a little astonished at the trustfulness of the parents. Neither of the children could swim, though swimming lessons with ropes and life belts were part of the week's entertainment. Perhaps the experience was accountable for some features in the subsequent

life of both: Dennis was to get part of his education on the
Worcester training ship, to become a mercantile marine appren-
tice, to secure a mate's ticket, and during the Second World
War to command a corvette. Barbara was to become my
secretary for ten years, and then build a career of her own in the
Foreign Office.

The different behaviour of the two children raised questions
in my mind I have never been able to answer concerning the
existence—or not—of such a thing as a male mind and a female
mind. The boy from the very first day became vividly interested
in the external world about him ('What's that ship? What's her
rig? How fast can she sail? When shall we let down the anchor?
When shall we pull it up?') Whereas Barbara was interested even
then mainly in the personal aspect of things ('What present shall
I take home to Daddy? When are we going to get letters? There
may be one from Mummy'). In the evenings at anchor I read the
children stories (one I recall, *True Tilda*), a chapter each night.
But I discovered that Barbara had taken the book to bed with her
and gobbled the whole of it the first night, with the result that
she did her best to substitute for the reading of *True Tilda* some
other form of entertainment. Dennis, the future naval com-
mander, had difficulty in not falling out of his bunk if the ship
at night took any kind of list.

But I had to admit that the boat as a permanent retreat had
its limitations. (You can't store many books, for instance, on a
thirty-foot cutter.) Exploring one day in the dinghy I discovered
Northey Island; and finding it was for sale, bought it.

Northey was a 'wrecked island.' Originally its sea walls had
enclosed about three hundred acres of some of the best wheat
land in England. But in the 19th century the sea walls had been
breached and the agricultural depression forbade the cost of their
restoration. What remained of the island available for farming
was about seventy acres of high land well above high-water
mark. There was a farm-house on the place, and an enormous
barn (both later to be destroyed by a bomb in the Second World
War).

The island indeed had its place in history. It is now pretty
generally agreed that it was the Danish stronghold in the 'Battle
of Maldon', the subject of perhaps the greatest Anglo-Saxon
poem left to us, 'the last great work in old English before the

Norman Conquest' as one of the best historians of the battle[1] (fought most probably in 991) puts it.

The island is situated at the head of the Blackwater, and the Blackwater, even in Roman times, was regarded as an important avenue of invasion of Great Britain. The Danes so regarded it, for, within a mile or two of the island, on the hill stands Danbury (Daneburg). The strategic importance of the estuary was emphasized by Banse, the Nazi military teacher; with uncomfortable consequences for the island's resident and owner in 1940. Jerry took great pains and, alas, to some degree successfully, to bomb the buildings on Northey. I had thought a remote Essex farm would be secure from that kind of attention, but was mistaken. The old farm cottage was virtually destroyed, although the modern part, which I had designed and constructed, stood up against the blast a good deal better. Perhaps the surrounding wall built with my own hands—buttressed by round towers in the Normandy fashion—may have given the place a military aspect from the air. Whatever the reasons, blitzed it was.[2]

I fell in love with Northey for several reasons. The thing which had fascinated me in the early years of the California experience was the delight of planning and building a home and farm. Stock-breeding, animals, horses, agricultural experiment,

[1] H. J. Rowles, B.A. *The Battle and Song of Maldon*, Benham and Company Ltd., Colchester.

The author quotes from the *Anglo-Saxon Chronicle* under the year 993 this passage;

'In this year came Anlaf with three and ninety ships to Stone and ravaged it without and went thence to Sandwich and thence to Ipswich, which he harried: and so to Maldon. And against him there came Brihtnoth the alderman with his force and fought with him, and there they slew the alderman and won the battle.'

There is a reference to the battle in some MSS. under 991, as follows;

'This year was Ipswich plundered and very soon afterwards was Alderman Brihtnoth slain at Maldon.' This entry is probably copied from the *Liber Eliensis*. The two entries have caused confusion and some writers have taken 991 for the date of the battle, others 993. The probabilities are with the earlier date.

[2] It would be a mistake of vanity perhaps to assume that this blitzing was any personal attention on the part of Hitler's people. But it did so happen that in the black list of those marked down for liquidation on the morrow of an effective German invasion of Britain (a list captured by the Allies) Norman Angell—because his name begins with A—happened to be among the first.

carpentry, brick-laying, all that is very much in my blood. I saw Northey's possibilities. It was remote, a true retreat, a 'funk hole,' to use the expression which the First World War with its trenches had given us. And then, too, I had a theory about a new kind of homesteading. I would have a married couple who would live on the farm of the island and make it at least self-supporting with stock—cows, chickens, ducks, pigs. As a by-product in their work they could manage the very simple housekeeping which I should need. In this way I would solve the problem of domestic service and devise a kind of life which would be within my income. I myself would do part of the outdoor work and I had no doubts that it would work out as a feasible economic arrangement. (In practice of course this proved largely fallacious.) The scheme was the more attractive to me at the time as income was becoming a bit of a problem. Before the war, during the time of the ' movement,' my personal income from royalties and articles was sufficient, particularly in view of the fact that, though the Garton Foundation paid me no salary, they did pay the salaries of my secretary and his assistant and most of the office expenses. But with the coming of the war and my resignation from the Garton Foundation, and with a great deal of voluntary work done for the Labour Party, the nursing of constituencies, much work with League of Nations propaganda, all defrayed out of literary earnings, I was faced with something like an economic crisis. It is true that a small block of shares which I had held in the *Daily Mail* had risen greatly in value. I had held on to them and bought a few more, to discover that the financial reorganization which had followed Northcliffe's death was making this form of property extremely insecure. In all the changes I did not come out too well. It is true (as already related) that the Rowntrees, who knew that I had for some years devoted much of my income and resources to propaganda, had delicately and very generously offered to arrange an income for me. But that was not the kind of arrangement I could accept.

I bought the island, then owned by Vere de Crespigny, who, like certain other members of his family, was, to say the least, eccentric. He had been an officer in the war, and it was commonly reported (quite erroneously in all probability) that he shot more of his own men for shirking than the Germans managed to shoot. For him, as for most men of his type, the delights of life con-

sisted in huntin', fishin', and shootin'. The 'shootin'' included
the shooting of any trespassers on the island. He had a complex
about that because he had been in the Irish 'troubles' and
evidently thought that some of the Irishry were determined to
get him. He had bought a wooden hut on wheels with iron-barred
windows, and in this hut at times he slept, having it hauled
to different parts of the island, so that he would the more easily
be able to perceive and deceive any Irishry on his track, since
they would not find him in the house if they entered it. I think
his people had helped him with the purchase of the island as a
means of putting him where he would be as little embarrassing
as possible. But he refused to stay there, took a job as game
warden in Africa, where he was trampled to death by an
elephant; the sort of end which it did not need crystal-gazing to
foretell as probable.

How even a microscopic island can develop a sort of island
patriotism was illustrated in the remark one day of a woman
visitor who had the distinction of having been born on the island.
I said to her: 'It appears that when Major de Crespigny lived
here he used to shoot at people who came on to the island.' To
which my visitor replied: 'And quite right, too.'

In the odds and ends included in the purchase was a large
barge abandoned on the beach as past its prime, half loaded with
coke. One of the first tasks was of course to have that barge
emptied of its coke, to haul it up on to the beach; to jack it up on
blocks and turn it into a large house-boat, comprising a very
large living-room, some thirty feet square, a galley, and five
separate sleeping cabins. This for some years was to provide in
summer-time housing for the children of friends and relatives.
Together with the cutter, which I moored in one of the creeks
of the island, the barge-house-boat furnished young visitors
during many summers incomparable delights. (The parents of
the Hayes children told me that if you were to ask the latter
at any period of the year how many days remained before the
beginning of the summer holidays on Northey, they could tell
you to the last hour.)

All this side of the island life was sheer delight. There were
three hundred acres, including creeks where fish could be speared,
crabs caught, nests of wild duck discovered, bathing pools where
at low tide nature had conveniently provided swimming, a hard

beach for bathing at high tide, boats, dinghies, punts, a little sailing ship anchored just off the house-boat, sailing trips down the estuary. Sometimes I would let two or three boys take the cutter out by themselves, even though they would promptly run it on to the mud and have to stay there half the night till the return of the tide.

But the farming and economic side of it was another story. Whatever the charm of an island might be for the male mind, the wife of any bailiff simply detested the place. A visit to town was possible only by the appalling danger (in their mind) of being rowed across a quarter of a mile of water or adjusting their visits to the time of low water, when the causeway would be uncovered. (People could live on the island for years without ever managing to get the arithmetic of high and low tide right.) And this difficulty of communication was at times a serious economic obstacle. If there was any work on the island which demanded help from the mainland, the difficulty of providing transport was considerable. The time wasted added appreciably to the cost of much of the work.

It had been my intention in purchasing the island virtually to give up all political activities and nearly all writing. I had spoken in this sense to Harold Wright who did not take such intention seriously. But when I wrote him one day that I was going down to Maldon to complete the purchase of Northey Island he sent me a telegram : 'You cannot do this. Please delay.' Whereupon I sent *him* a post card : 'The steward on the channel steamer told the passenger, "You can't be sick in the saloon, sir." To which the passenger replied, "Can't I?" And was.'

The theory behind the move was that I would get away from the political world altogether. 'You can't do anything about it, so why worry.' But of course in leaving political preoccupations for those associated with farming you are merely exchanging one kind of worry for another, of closer and more personal kind. If you go to bed having discovered some sign of swine fever among the pigs or a possible case of anthrax among the cattle, you don't go to bed with Virgilian calm—'at secura quies, et nescia fallere vita' . . . These problems under your roof demanding action to-morrow morning, if not to-night, are not less disturbing than a studious consideration of how to check the drift to a war which is not likely in any case to occur for ten or fifteen years.

A man must have problems, big or little, unless he is to go mad. If he has not real ones he makes his entertainment out of solving artificial ones, as in chess or bridge. The artificial ones had always seemed to me less interesting than the real ones presented by human relationships. I had plenty of these on the island—the jealousy of one workman of another; the determination of the bailiff's wife to make her husband leave a place where it was so complicated a business to get to the shops; the determination of the husband to keep the job and 'be hanged' to his wife, I coming in of course as the butt of both parties.

On one occasion I arrived at the island to find the bailiff barricaded in the cottage, around which marched two discontented workmen with shotguns, loudly proclaiming their intention to 'do in' the people inside the cottage 'even if we swing for it.' (Can any passion equal that of village hatreds?— the hatreds that flow under the surface of 'peaceful country communities' and between people who have known each other all their lives and see each other daily? It is why I have always been a little sceptical of the view that enmity between nations can be ended by more frequent contacts, 'by getting to know each other better.' The more one knows of some people, the less one likes them.) Situations like this 'investment' of the house by the men with the shot-guns provoked one day the remark to my secretary, 'It's evident we shall have to get back to London for a little peace and quiet.'

But I did not get away from the island problems merely by going to London—or even to America. In files left by the blitz I find a letter headed 'The Civic Federation of Dallas' to Ida Nielsen, then my secretary, raising questions about a bull on the island, whether it would be safe to have one about the place 'with children around.' Had the Messengers (Messenger was then bailiff) no misgivings about it? 'But if the bailiff decided it would be all right to have a bull, let it be a good one. The future of the place is cattle so it will be false economy to skimp a few pounds on a bull'. This was followed by instructions for an experiment in planting Bokhara clover ('you will find a five pound bag on one of the shelves in my room'). Something should be done to keep the poaching duck-shooters off the island—'let the word be passed around in the neighbourhood that we'll prosecute if the nuisance does not

U

cease'. As to the stealing of rock from the sea walls I would certainly prosecute. 'Get Messenger to estimate how many horned stock he thinks we can dispose of each year if the pastures are really put in order.' And there follow other details of the island economy.

The secretary herself wrote to me in America (15th October 1926):

If you want to get wholesale publicity, talk about pigs! I received nine newspaper cuttings about your farewell talk at Liverpool all headed 'Amphibious Pigs' in capitals. And as the news cutting agency was . . . there were probably many more. (By the way, as soon as the current subscription expires, I am changing to another news agency.)

This reference to pigs is explained thus: I had at some luncheon address or other made a remark about the unreliability of the 'everybody knows' type of statement; and had cited the all but universal belief of country districts that pigs could not swim, because their sharp hooves would cut their throats. I must have said that I knew that legend to be unsound having put it to the test of experiment. In this wise:

Almost immediately after taking possession of the island, I installed a fine old sow, Betsy, who soon discovered that succulent little inshore crabs were to be had for the hunting in the ditches of the marsh at low tide. One day she found herself marooned by a rapidly oncoming tide and had to make a swim for it. She lost her head entirely and we saw her swimming in circles some distance from the high land, So I got into the dinghy and shooed her in towards the beach, which she finally reached in a state of collapse. But she learned by the experience. When she got cut off by the tide again she took it much more calmly, and simply swam home. When a few weeks afterwards her family of thirteen piglets arrived she deliberately, by example, taught them to swim, entering the water with great serenity and grunting for them to follow her . . . 'The water's fine.' One day, looking from the windows of my room at the top of the new house, I saw on the now flooded meadows of the marsh what I took to be a flock of ducks. Taking the field glasses I saw that it was Betsy calmly swimming home with thirteen little piglets following up behind.

One interesting experiment which I made was the planting of spartina on the two hundred odd acres of the marsh land which

is flooded at high tide. Spartina is a grass which appeared
for the first time in Southampton Water about half a century
since, being, it would seem, a hybrid naturally produced. It grows
to the height of oats, which it vaguely resembles and will grow
even though two or three feet of salt water passes over it at
every tide. It has some value as pasture, cattle and horses going
out on to it as a change from ordinary pasture. But its chief value
is as an anti-erosion measure and as a help in reclamation of
sea-invaded land. As it will grow in liquid marine mud where
nothing else has been known to grow, it can convert huge areas of
heretofore barren mud into pasture land and is therefore of great
potential value in the reclamation of marsh. Northey Island
was one of the first places on the East Coast where the plant was
tried. It was at the suggestion of James Bryce of the Essex
Institute of Agriculture and of Professor Oliver of London
University that I obtained plants from Southampton Water a
quarter of a century ago. They now cover two hundred acres
of salt marsh.

Two things were a constant delight in island life : the coming
of the children in the summer time to camp in the barge-
house-boat (in addition to the Hayes children and their Dutch
friends from Holland there were at other times the twin girls of
Beatrice Forbes-Robertson Hale and the children of Bernard
Langdon-Davies and others). This meant sailing trips in *Ida* or in
the half-decker; hunts for oysters and mussels—with pearls in
both—and of course bathing and swimming all the time. (Sometimes the children were replaced by students who would come on
to the island for week-end discussions of the League of Nations
and similar problems. My friend Leonard Behrens even discussed
for a time the idea of making these visits of students a regular
feature of island life, converting the island into a sort of Seminary
of Internationalism. But there were too many difficulties.)

Among the queer incidents of island life during some thirty
years, one or two stand out.

After the purchase of the place I managed to get a telephone
installed, although it meant the laying of a submarine cable. The
post office people were, I think, glad enough despite the expense,
to stretch a point since it solved for them the problem of getting
telegrams to the place—they could telephone them. While at work
about the farm one day the son of the bailiff came running to

me, ' Please, sir, the post office say they have a telegram for you
which they say they can't give to my mother. They will only give
it to you personally.' Going to the telephone I heard an austere
feminine voice ask, ' Is this Sir Norman Angell? ?' ' Yes.' ' Sir
Norman Angell himself?' ' Yes.' ' We have a telegram for you
which I will read.' And the voice read this message : ' Can sleep
with you after the theatre Friday night. Love, Rosalinde '—a
message which I heard with very mixed emotions. For though
I knew the Rosalinde[1] in question those were not my relations
with her—' cross my heart,' as the children say. This sudden
shower of favours descending out of the blue left me a little
breathless. I could make neither head nor tail of it. On my return
to my chambers in the Temple a few days later, I asked the lady
to tea and showed her the telegram (which the post office had sent
me in confirmation of the telephone message). '*Will* you please
tell me what you mean by sending a telegram like that. What's
the joke? It makes things uncomfortable for me with the local
post office people—to mention only them.'

Rosalinde looked puzzled for a moment and then burst out
laughing.

' You asked me a few weeks ago if you could bring a young
playwright to lunch or supper, since you knew I did not eat
dinner—because his play had a part you thought might suit me.
I forgot about it for some time but wired you the other day,
" Can sup with you after the theatre Friday night." '

' *Sure* you wrote " sup "?'

' Quite sure.'

I was in the House of Commons at the time and knew Lees-
Smith, the then Postmaster-General, pretty well. I told him (if
not altogether seriously, then half-seriously) ' I'm going to sue
you for damages. Think of my reputation among my country
neighbours. Of course, the shocked spinster who read me the
telegram will discuss it in great secret with *all* her friends.'

' Yes. But think of the great discretion she showed in reading
it only to you.'

' Oh, that won't do. I sue. I could do with a few thousand
just now for the development of my farm.'

A day or two later he came to me : ' Nothing doing, my dear
fellow. Reflections on a man's chastity are not actionable unless

[1] Rosalinde Fuller.

he is a clergyman. You are not a clergyman. Ergo, no action lies. Go to blazes.' Just possibly he might have been bluffing. Anyhow I took no action.

One of the island occupations which I found increasingly fascinating was brick-laying. I had bought a barge load of over-burnt brick, the over-burning producing bricks of all shapes, sizes and colours. But with 'compo'—sand and cement used as mortar—these uneven, oddly shaped and beautifully coloured bricks made most excellent building material. In the course of a few summers I had built two or three hundred yards of walls for various purposes round about the place. Instead of using the usual square buttress for these walls I used small circular towers which were just as effective and far more picturesque, and the irregularity of the bricks gave the whole thing a weathered and interesting appearance. Wall and towers thus made were some-times varied by using as material the stones of demolished build-ings which I bought by the lorry load. (Visitors usually guessed the period as 'late sixteenth century.')

In a year or two it became evident that if I were to live on the island at all continuously and do work there, the old farm cottage would not suffice; it hardly indeed sufficed for the bailiff and his family. By the side of the cottage therefore I built a house completely of my own design using for much of the interior woodwork—beams, joists—the timbers of a derelict sailing barge which had been part of the property of the island. For some of the other woodwork I used trees from the island itself, shaping them with an adze. Making part of the fireplace in the large living-room on the ground floor is a monster beam supported on lesser giants, all cut and shaped by myself. The arch of the fireplace contains some gargoyles which came from the Parliament building when the buildings were being repaired in 1930 or thereabouts.

The top of the house consists of one room with large windows on every side. This was my bedroom and work-room, where I lived. The roof was flat, with a surrounding 'fence,' and it could be used for sun-bathing. Each of the five bedrooms of the new house had running water and a lavatory attached. The island being much exposed to winter gales, I installed central heating.

It sounds opulent, but it wasn't; isn't. But it is convenient and comfortable. When the blitz came the old farm-house was blown to smithereens, but the part I had designed, that looks so gimcrack at first glance, stood up and suffered virtually no damage beyond the breaking of all the windows. By the grace of God no one happened to be on the place when the bomb demolished the old part of the house. (I had taken the precaution of constructing small underground air-raid shelters.) The only serious casualties were among my papers which had been stored in an outbuilding. The place suffered quite as much from marauders and looters during the years that it had to be left to itself as it had from the attentions of 'that man.'

During the years that I had to be in America this looting was serious, as the place is so remote from any police supervision and so easily accessible by boat, that the visitor cannot be observed. Thus the police could do little to prevent this kind of loss. A whole roomful of furniture—dining-room chairs, arm-chairs—would disappear between the visits of the caretaker who looked in two or three times a week. Stephen Toulmin (son of my old and valued friends Doris and Geoffrey Toulmin) who had frequently come on to the island as a child (and is now a married don at Cambridge) paid a visit during these abandoned years and described it in a letter to his mother :

We rowed across a choppy Blackwater to Northey. The pier by the Ark [1] is down, the Ark derelict, decayed and looted. Hardly one of the partitions remains, the flooring has been ripped up, and the sink alone shows where the kitchen once was. Desolate.

We walked up to the house along a road pressed in upon by shrubs at last grown to maturity. The garden could have been rich and beautiful, but was beginning to be rank. The house and tower were mainly boarded up, the farmhouse in particular being smashed up and dilapidated. We collected a lot of burrs in the garden and farmyard, but eventually found a way in, up the stairs and into the blackness of the tower. The stairs in the tower were quite safe and we reached the study, which was good and light, its great windows only half obscured. There indeed was a cemetery of our political sins : a great variety of magazines, pamphlets, ephemeridæ, hurriedly scribbled notes, covering the whole period of inanition which culminated in the debacle of 1940 —and everywhere dyspepsia tablets. Hardly a memory was left

---

[1] The barge-house-boat referred to above.

unstirred, from China to Czechoslovakia, Abyssinia to Austria, Moscow trials, Spain, Yugoslavia, all were there, and there only the debris which remained forgotten when the mass of his library had gone. How a man's books become entwined, almost identified with his thoughts.

As Alison is an early English historian I took her to the Causeway to watch small boats sailing over the probable site of the Battle of Maldon, 991. I tried to put forward some of the reasons for that being the site, but did not get very far. Have we the book of the Lay somewhere? We let Alison row us back through the calm evening, while the lovely boats, which had spanked up, slid quietly down to Heybridge and Osea with the tide.

It was at the island, in the year preceding the last war, that I wrote *You and the Refugee* dealing with the problem of the refugees flying from the Hitlerite terror. Few of my books have given me more pleasure to write, since I had the feeling that, if it had any effect at all, that effect would express itself in the salvage of actual human beings. At the time of the writing the admission of Hitler's victims in any number was still opposed on the ground that they would worsen the problem of unemployment, and my book discussed that problem in terms as objective as I could make them.

Occasionally guests at the island would include students I had known at conference or summer schools at Geneva or in America. Among them on one occasion was a charming young Italian anti-Fascist. This was in 1938, and when he left we both knew to what he might be returning. In a letter posted from France on his way home he wrote: 'The days at the island—a site so lovely and peaceful, and yet so full with thought and work—will always be among my dearest memories. . . . Barbara to whom I shall never be able to express entirely my gratitude and my affection could not have been a better friend to me. . . . Crossing is fine to-day: all is calm and indifferent around the ship, yet Europe will probably be in flames before I arrive at home. It is almost unbelievable and there is a bitter contest of feeling within myself between love of my country and knowledge of what its end is to be.' In a year his country was at war, which, by God's grace, the boy survived.

After 1945, when it became evident that so much of the work remaining to me would have to be done in America, I felt it better to dispose of the island. This I did by transferring it to my nephew

Eric and his wife Nora. Eric Angell Lane (son of Tom of the first chapter of this narrative) is a good representative of the modern type of competent and scientific farmer to which Britain owes so much. He learned his agriculture at Cambridge (Clare) and to-day manages with great success a whole group of farms in Lincolnshire, Norfolk and now in Essex. By purchasing the neighbouring farm on the mainland he has made it possible to run Northey as part of a workable economic unit, truly self-supporting. The old farm cottage which the blitz nearly destroyed has been restored and it is there that I live and work while in England; Eric, his wife, and children—Nicholas, Tom, Judy and Alice, the last-named my godchild—occupying the adjoining modern part. Nora by her native good taste has been able to make of the house and surrounding garden an attractive, indeed a beautiful, little country home—still the resort of children, still a source of delight to them, still a retreat where, watching the last of the commercial sailing ships, the Thames sailing barge, move down the estuary, one may find relative peace; some surcease from the idiocies of a demented world, set, it would seem, upon a particularly messy suicide. Meanwhile, we make the best of this island refuge, *Après nous, le déluge.*

CHAPTER II

ENMITIES AND FRIENDSHIPS

I PUT the enmities first because the exploitation of enmities arising from conflict of opinion, or doctrine, has become a great political force in our time, and a few individual cases may not be without interest in that context.

The ideological hatreds which played so large a part in the wars of religion and in the later wars of rival nationalism, seem now to have been transferred in large part to the field of economic theory. Moscow has succeeded in giving to Marxism all the passion of fanaticism which characterized earlier religions. The catechism taught to every little boy and girl throughout the Soviet's land is extremely blunt in teaching hatred of the heretic. The Moscow power has recognized the political value of culti-vating this innate impulse to dislike those who have the impudence to disagree with us.

I put the enmities before the friendships for a more personal reason. Though few men could have been more blessed in their private friendships than I have been, not many writers could have been more cursed—in the sense of damage to the work they were trying to do—by misrepresentations springing from differ-ences of opinion.

It is not a pleasant thing, of course, to be expelled from your club like any card-sharper, or to be refused your passport when it might enable you to make at least some contribution to the solution of your generation's worst problems. But my life has been so abundantly full of warm friendships that the personal side of that sort of enmity never troubled me very much; never cost me a single night's sleep. What did touch me was the fact that the easily excited animus to the heretic—or the assumed heretic—did increase enormously the difficulty of reaching the minds of otherwise reasonable men. It made it possible, for instance, for so many to believe that a serious publicist really had taught that 'war had now become impossible.' The constant and long-continued misrepresentation which arose out of this animus—or was associated with it—diminished the effectiveness of my work as a pamphleteer by a very heavy percentage.

Hostility to those opposing, or seeming to oppose, a war in which their country is engaged, is understandable. The position which I took in 1914 would, I knew at the time, involve an unpopularity which was in the circumstances natural enough; it was something one just had to face. But what is curious is that while in 1914 those of us who were supposed to be against war with Germany, and were condemned as Pacifists, were to find ourselves, twenty years later, almost as unpopular for arguing resistance to Hitlerian Germany and were condemned as warmongers. Apart from that phenomenon I have often been puzzled at what seems to provoke these sometimes violent enmities.

Take the case of Mr. Ezra Pound, whose letter (as a literary curiosity) is here reproduced. On receiving it I thought it worth a better fate than obscure burial in my letter file, or obscure cremation on my study fire. I therefore sent it to the Editor of *Time and Tide* with this covering note :

> As the writer of the enclosed letter—whom I have never seen or communicated with in any way—would presumably like his views to have a wide publicity, I send the enclosed to you for publication if you deem it of any interest. It is addressed to me at the Bank of England (which I have never entered) in ' Needle and Thread Street.'

Time and Tide reproduced it—in facsimile.

I did not reply to Pound in any way but he continued to send me letters at intervals, all in the same strain, and to discuss them in an Italian Fascist magazine. He continued to describe me as a ' bastid ' (his spelling was peculiar) and ' louse.' In one of his letters addressing me as ' Montagu NORAMN Angell', he asked me to confess who was financing me in campaigning for a Pan-European war and suggested that if I had been begotten by the Queen of Sheba, I might as well say so.

It is perhaps a commentary on a certain prevailing worship of incomprehensibility that a committee of American and English poets should have awarded Pound, as the poet who in all the world had done the most for poetry during that year, a Congressional prize.

E. POUND   **RAPALLO**

13 April.
VIA MARSALA 12-5

Norman Aggell

       Sir / as a man who has exploited pacificm ,
who has ma_de money and a career bleating about pacifism but
contributed nothing to the knowledge of the economic causes of
war . You merit not only contempt but loathing when you bleat
publicly of things you and your accomplices have been too lazy
to s tudy.

I regret that you are too cowardly to meet me , and that
dueling in prohibited in yr/ enslaved country.

However as a banker's pipm , please consider yourself slapped.

       And may hell rot your bones.

I am glad to inform you that Nic Butler has been called a
traitor in the American House of Representatives. The lot
of you fakers will be known in due time.

       And now go lick someones' boots

       yrs Ezra Pound

Of a very different order of attack was that maintained for a considerable period at one time by a weekly review edited by Hilaire Belloc called the *Eye-witness*. The paper on one occasion stated that I was 'once more prophesying the impossibility of hostilities.' I wrote to point out (giving chapter and verse) that I had, on the contrary, been emphasizing the great likelihood of hostilities. The paper accompanied my correction by this note :

> To this we can only reply : (1) That it is a public duty of journalists to expose the harm and stupidity of stupid and harmful books, especially when they are artificially thrust upon the public as was this book—and by such money ! So earned ! (2) 'De' Bloch, the money-lender, may have said that war would linger on, but wrote to prove it ultimately impossible on account of human cowardice, which he took for granted. We fear that men like 'De' Bloch and our correspondent do not appreciate how grossly offensive their doctrines are to men who retain European lineage and tradition. (3) That if the author will satisfy us by documentary evidence that his present surname is 'Angell' we will withdraw our suggestion to the contrary.

Whereupon I wrote to point out that the 'reply' thus given was 'so far as it concerned me, a falsehood from beginning to end, alike in which it says and what it implies.' That though I should not hesitate to accept financial help in the spread of ideas I believed to be true and useful, so far none had been forthcoming, and that at that stage 'such success as the book may have had with the public it has had without outside financial help of any kind.' As to the Jew business—hinted in the reference to men who do not 'retain European lineage'—I wrote that I had no Jewish blood at all, although, unlike the editor of the *Eye-witness* I cherished no hostility to the race which gave us Jesus Christ, His apostles and His Mother. I happened to be of purely English stock.

The name under which I wrote, I went on, was part of my name, had been in my family for a very long time, and I drew attention to the fact that in the *Eye-Witness* itself pseudonyms were a commonplace. As I thought Mr. Belloc had earned a little lecture I delivered one, thus :

> An editor professing to be a serious critic, evidently with no first-hand knowledge of the work he is criticizing, makes a grossly

misleading statement concerning its author's attitude. Corrected, there is nothing in the shape of an apology; but, on the contrary, a retort that anyhow the book has not obtained recognition on its merits but through the use of ill-gotten money. And in making such a charge mere hearsay is quite sufficient, although the first injustice has been done by passing judgment at second hand. More : an attempt is made to strengthen the effect of the second falsehood by the left-handed appeal to race prejudice by the introduction of irrelevancies which would be contemptible if based on fact; beneath contempt when based on invention.

You are quite sure that I do not appreciate how ' grossly offensive are my doctrines to men of European lineage and tradition.' Which tradition? . . .

I am wondering, and I think your readers will . . . whether the *Eye-witness* in its treatment of larger issues of policy shows the same care for verification of fact, the same determination not to have its judgment coloured by temper and prejudice, the same innate attitude of good faith that it has shown in this small matter. Ex pede Herculem.

In any case, its conduct relieves me of any sort of regret or surprise that it finds the doctrines I have attempted to preach, ' offensive.'

The publication of this in the *Eye-witness* was followed by a private letter from Belloc inviting me to ' fight.' Whether the ' fight ' was to be in the form of a libel suit, fisticuffs, or duel I was too occupied with other things at the moment to find out. [1]

I deal with this little episode partly because for a good many years I was the butt of a kind of blackguardism from a few— not many—academic folk; partly because it increased my scepticism concerning the trustworthiness of a certain type of erudition, whether displayed on the Right or on the Left (and it was to become even commoner on the Left than on the Right); partly because it throws some light on the psychological difficulties of getting and keeping an intellectual climate in which reason, reasonableness, and sound judgment can thrive. And, once more, that is the chief problem of this atomic generation.

If I could have foreseen at the time of Belloc's attack that a

[1] Leonard Woolf writing in *The Nation* (17 July 1926) remarks:

'Many people whose minds are closed to reason are exasperated by *The Great Illusion*, a masterpiece of political argument so cogent that if you do not agree with it there is nothing left for you to do but lose your temper.'

quarter of a century later I should be almost as bitterly attacked, not for Pacifism but for 'warmongering' (i.e. for early notification to Hitler and Mussolini that further aggressions would be resisted) the psychological puzzle would have been deepened. The grounds of my growing scepticism of erudition of the Belloc type are pretty obvious. There was just one subject in the world about which, without any sort of doubt, I knew more than Mr. Belloc and his colleagues, namely, the background, record, purposes, motives of Norman Angell, a contemporary, a man whom they could have called up on the telephone. And on that subject I found quite abysmal disregard of things which were self-evident, or of evidence easily ascertainable. What was the likelihood of the pundits being right in conclusions dependent on the evidence of a thousand years since?

Among these academic hornets was a Cambridge mediævalist who for years continued to accuse me of something near to personal dishonesty, not for any reason connected with his province of mediæval history, but because I had at some stage opposed conscription, which he seemed to regard as the one certain cure for war. It was not on any ground of absolute principle that I opposed conscription for Great Britain before World War I, but because I felt that merely to add one more conscriptionist country to all the others of Europe would not carry us much further towards our goal of peaceful defence; and might well, of itself, carry us in the opposite direction. But my critic somehow had conceived an implacable hostility to me and meant to indulge it.

It was indeed one of the discoveries I made in nearly half a century of controversy that if a man becomes possessed by some panacea for an evil like war and you don't accept it, you are usually his enemy henceforth. In the case of the mediævalist Coulton it was conscription; in the case of others it was some monetary device like that of Major Douglas; in the case of Joseph Fels it was single tax (he apologized to me after a time for his behaviour); in another case it was Calendar Reform ('Only an unpardonable blindness prevents your accepting this remedy for the evils you fight with such futile weapons'). To some of these critics I would reply: 'Your reform may be very valuable. But why do you have to insist that it is a cure for war? Why drag that in?' But they usually would. And after all they were not much worse than some of the Marxists who, like Briand's friend referred to elsewhere, were quite ready to give you the Economic Interpretation of the Immaculate Conception and relate it with such irrefragable logic to the class war.

From first to last I was brought into some little contact with H. G. Wells. I am afraid my own estimate of him is coloured by the side of his character which made him at times an insufferable cad. I am thinking not only of his reference to MacDonald (whom I liked probably as little as he did) but to his personal attacks upon the Webbs, upon Lady Rhondda, upon Bernard Shaw. He has been described as a great teacher on the strength of his *Outline of History* and similar educational work. I can accept that. But in his dealing with some of the issues of his time a strange temper which led him to personal vilification stood in the way of sound political judgment. He violently attacked the Labour Party. Winston Churchill became for him ' the Boy Scout in politics who has refused to grow up.' I recall a talk at Chatham House where a member was discussing some modification of the League constitution, and Wells, parting company with a great deal that he himself had written and argued about constitution-making, insisted that constitutions could not be made in that abstract way at all; that men grew into law and political structures not by a formulated or formalized notion of social structure but by unpremeditated habit and custom. At least that was the general drift of the argument. I tried to point out that this was not true in every case; that the American Constitution had been the work of men who deliberately set out to create a constitution, who were quite conscious of what they were doing and why they were doing it; who had taken into account alike the experience of the ancient world, notably the Athenians, and of eighteenth-century Europe, particularly Britain; that the papers in the *Federalist* of more than a century and a half since were definite evidence that man did at times do precisely the thing which he, Wells, was arguing that men could not do. The only reaction to this line of argument was a sort of ferocious contempt, an attitude which made any rational discussion extremely difficult. Yet a little later on, Wells was to write to me in cordial terms, particularly when he became interested, after

the outbreak of the Second World War, in the formulation of a
Bill of Rights. He asked me to join the committee he had
formed and of which, if I remember rightly, Lord Sankey was
the chairman. A lot of paper work was done on this matter, but
once more I found Wells's scale of values astonishingly topsy-
turvy. I argued that one of the first things to stand for was the
thing which Milton put first : ' Give me the liberty to know, to
utter and to argue freely according to conscience, above all
liberties.' But Wells wanted to put first the right of every
individual to be guaranteed against physical mutilation, an order
of vital needs which seemed to skip most of the process by which
any such right could be guaranteed or given much hope of
security.

The changes that may occur in a man's life in the conversion
of a certain hostility into friendship were brought home to me at
a luncheon in the House of Commons on March 20, 1930, given
me by members and friends to mark the twenty-first anniversary
of the publication of *The Great Illusion*. Lord Cecil presided, and
there were altogether some two hundred members and friends
of members present. A newspaper account notes that ' The Prime
Minister sent a message and Mr. Arthur Henderson, Mr. Philip
Snowden, Lord Passfield, Mr. H. B. Lees-Smith, Lord Thomson,
Sir Charles Trevelyan, and other members of the Ministry were
present as part of a representative gathering of those who have
been associated with Mr. Angell in his work. There were present
also many Liberal and Labour members of Parliament and pub-
licists, including Mr. H. N. Brailsford, Mr. Henry Nevinson, Mr.
J. A. Hobson, Mr. J. A. Spender, Professor H. J. Laski, Mr. E.
T. Scott (Editor of the *Manchester Guardian*), Mr. Harold Wright
(Editor of the *Nation*), and Mr. Evelyn Wrench, of the *Spectator*.
Among the congratulatory messages that were read was one from
Mr. Shaw, which amused the company. He described Mr. Angell
as ' a very doughty specimen of the right type of diehard.'

The report notes that John Buchan, who proposed my health,
said :

The profound truth which he taught twenty-one years ago has
to-day the unacknowledged support of the vast mass of thinking
people. I say ' unacknowledged ' for that is the fate of true

prophets. The world accepts their teaching when it is too late to accept the teacher. The building of the prophet's tomb is a very old pastime of humanity. . . . Some of us do not forget that he was the true pioneer; that in Browning's words he has been 'doing the king's work all the dim day long' and that we hold in eternal honour his vision and his courage.

The toast was supported also by General Sir Ian Hamilton and Lady Barlow, a friend of many years.

As I sat there I could hardly forbear recalling the fact that the chairman, now become a close friend and speaking in terms of high eulogy, was the official who fifteen years previously had acted to deny me a passport to the United States in order that I should not promulgate the very ideas he was at that moment expounding; and that some at least then gathered at the luncheon would, a few years previously, have approved all the measures of restraint and censorship taken against their guest. Tempora mutantur. . . . The reflection prompted me to say on that occasion, as noted at the head of this chapter, that seldom could an author have been so lucky, so happy in his private friends, so unlucky in some of his public contacts. Yet how innaccurate are generalisations of that character apt to be. If 'public contacts' are to include treatment at the hands of reviewers, I can only describe myself as, on the whole, extremely lucky. For almost all my books—and there have been far too many of them—have had for the most part extremely generous, often very flattering reviews. Unhappily the reviews, like the books themselves, seem to have had small effect on those mass movements of opinion and feeling—especially feeling—to which politicians pander and governments bow, and which seem to oscillate between moods of blind belligerency and an isolationist inertia; both moods having proved, in the experience of this century, utterly disastrous, the prelude to wars which a little more balance and wisdom might have avoided. The newspaper report of the House of Commons luncheon gives this extract from what I said:

Few of us know our motives. The naturalist tells us that if you put a beaver into a room it will immediately begin to cut down the furniture in order to build a dam against the flood. I have so often felt impelled to build a dam against fallacy, unreason, destructive passion. The dams I have tried to help in building may not hold. The floods may sweep them utterly away. But even so, it is better to have built them.

I was to work in close co-operation with Cecil for a number of years as a fellow member of the League of Nations Union Executive and as a promoter of the Peace Ballot. In those years of co-operation with him it never occurred to me to mention that he had refused me a passport to go to America to do what I could to help promote in that country the League idea. If either of us had recalled the fact I am sure we should both have done so with amusement. Perhaps of all the men in English politics who have inspired me with respect for their probity, Robert Cecil comes very near the top.

A previous chapter has made mention of the part played by Esher in the agitation I carried on previous to the First War; his active participation in and his initiative in the creation of the Garton Foundation.

I certainly count him among my friends, and I had much opportunity of judging a strange character.

Reginald, Viscount Esher, as his son and biographer Maurice Brett truly notes, was little more than a name to the majority of his fellow-countrymen; yet was one of the most influential men of his time.

Something of his character may be judged from the offices which were offered him and he refused. In 1899 he was offered the Under-Secretaryship for War. The offer was refused. In 1900 he was offered the Governorship of Cape Colony. Refused. In 1903 he was offered the Secretaryship of State for War. Refused. In 1908 he was offered the Viceroyalty of India. Refused. (' I would rather break stones.') He refused an Earldom. As a younger man he had been offered positions of a very different order: Editorship of the *Daily News* (Dickens' old paper); Editorship of the *New Review*; a request to write the life of Disraeli—all these offers had been refused. But there were others he did not refuse. He was Secretary to the Office of Works. He was Chairman of the War Office Reconstruction Committee (1904); Hon. Secretary to the Committee for Queen

x

Victoria's Memorial; he was Lieutenant and Deputy Governor, and, later, Governor of Windsor Castle; he was co-Editor of Queen Victoria's letters; Permanent Member of the Committee of Imperial Defence; Chairman of the Committee to reorganize the Territorial Army; Governor of the Imperial College of Science; Chairman of the Committee of the Organization of the Indian Army; Royal Trustee to the British Museum; Trustee of the London Museum; of the Wallace Collection; Chairman of the Executive Committee of the British School at Rome; a Director of the Opera. And to these and other offices he added the Trusteeship of the Garton Foundation.

None of the above, of course, tells us what Esher's real work was. Several of the appointments he held brought him into close contact with the royal family of three generations and he became their intimate friend; and, in the case of King Edward, the eminence grise of Edwardian England. He acted unofficially, informally, intimately, as a link between the personalities of both parties and the monarch. He was a source of information concerning the character and views of most of those with whom the king had business of any kind.

Given Esher's antecedents, interests and offices, so very military in character, he would have been—one would suppose—the very last person to want to concern himself with a new type of peace effort. And there were plenty of my friends on the Left who insisted that Lord Esher did so for the purpose of seeing that it remained innocuous and harmless, and did nothing to interfere with the interests or dividends of Esher's armament-making friends. One or two hinted that he was probably accepting fat commissions from armament kings. This, I was told, was the realist interpretation of his attitude in the affair.

Most of this was, of course, monstrous silliness. But even if some of it had been true, it would still not affect the fact that his interest in my effort arose out of a combination of intellectual attraction to what he regarded as a new idea related to that statecraft which was his business, and a belief that a big European war, or a series of European wars, would indeed so weaken Britain as to reduce her to a second-rate position and dissolve her Empire. (The event has come near to justifying his fears.) In one of the letters which appear in his memoirs he makes a reference to his efforts to convince Balfour that this new move-

ment was not just another peace movement, that it had fundamental differences which were vitally important.

It is a curious thing that though I worked closely with Esher for
two years, saw him during that time about every week, saw
his son Maurice during that time almost daily, I never appreciated quite fully the vital part he was playing in the nation's
life and government; how greatly he influenced, within certain
limits, the course of events at home, in the Empire, and in
Europe; nor what an incomparable instrument he might have
been in happier circumstances for the promotion of a purpose
like that which I had in view. The long list of offices which he
was offered (and mostly refused) does not indicate the nature of
his power, nor indicate the most significant part of his real
work. The fact that he was, as above noted, an intimate of
King Edward, came to know most of the Ministers with whom
the King had to deal, discussed with those Ministers most of the
important appointments, particularly the military ones, was one
of the King's main informants on the political situation, became
the confidant of statesmen of all parties and a powerful force
behind the scenes of Court and political life; knew newspaper
proprietors, editors, writers—these facts constituted the source
of his influence. One of his letters contains this passage : '*Why
would you wish me to plunge into the horrid vortex of public life
once more, out of which I escaped with such joy? You can never
again feel that you are à l'abri du regard of the world? . . . And
as for " popularity " and " fame " they are tastes like any other,
racing or gambling, and they are not my tastes.*'

Despite the fact that with the coming of the First World War
we drifted apart, I had nothing but high regard for Esher's
qualities and never placed him among the 'enmities.'

From one very interesting source I used to get exceedingly
severe indictments of Esher's character. This was from the Ranee
of Sarawak, whom I had somehow come to know. As already
mentioned, one of Esher's daughters had married the 'Crown
Prince,' the heir presumptive, that is, to the throne which the
Ranee's husband had occupied. Dinners at the Ranee's (at the
house which she then had near Ascot) were an entertaining
mixture of acid evaluation of the Machiavellian wickedness of
Esher and strange stories of her life in Sarawak, of journeys
through the mountains with her husband, where she would re-

late that she had been awakened in her tent in the morning by hearing the Rajah shout to the assembled head-hunting chieftains : ' You either deliver those heads you have hidden before dinner-time to-night or I will have yours for breakfast to-morrow' ; of the petition of the executioner who prostrated himself before his queen begging with all the passion of an artist that he be permitted to hold his job until he had completed his ' century,' i.e., the collection of a hundred heads of executed criminals.

The whole history of the White Rajah of Sarawak, of the naval officer who, early in the nineteenth century, became king of a sizeable Eastern country and passed on the throne to his white heirs, is a schoolboy adventure tale of real life. I wonder Hollywood has not turned it into a movie. It would make an exceedingly good one.

One or two friendships in the course of my work have had a special quality which throws interesting light perhaps on human motive, though I find it now, at this distance of time, a little difficult to convey their special flavour.

Take the case of Harold Wright. Out of the blue a man in his thirties inheriting considerable wealth, comes to an ' agitator ', a pamphleteer, and says in effect (though not in words, for Harold was studiously unsentimental) : ' I want to place my life and my capacities, such as they are, at your disposal for the promotion of the work you have begun. Please use me as you see fit.'

That was never said ; there was never a particular point in our relationship in which it would have been said naturally; yet that came to represent the kind of relationship between us from the time Harold came down from Cambridge till his sudden death in 1933.

The background is worth a word or two. Harold was the son of Charles Wright of Lloyds, a businessman and Gladstonian Liberal of the very best type. Harold had been an invalid as a boy, suffering from a painful and serious complaint which damaged the bone of the leg and necessitated recurrent operations. He passed much of his boyhood in bed, missing school, and indeed formal instruction of any kind. But instead of formal schooling he read voraciously in politics and economics, discussing those subjects constantly with his father and other friends.

At twenty-three he went to a coach—Bernard Noel Langdon-Davies—to be crammed for Cambridge. (Langdon-Davies was, like Harold, a keen Liberal, had been President of the Cambridge Union and was to become an active member of the 'Movement' which later absorbed so much of Harold's life.) At twenty-three Harold had to begin on those subjects which others had learned at their prep. schools. A friend has painted a picture of him as a man of twenty-three with a black moustache, patiently learning very elementary Latin—'amo, amas, amat——'. But this 'backward' pupil passed the Little-go in his stride, while many of his more formally schooled fellow-pupils at the crammers came to grief in one part or another. At Cambridge (Pembroke) Harold read mainly economics; came to edit the *Granta*, to be President of the Union, and to have an influence in the intellectual life of the University. Among the close friends he made were J. M. Keynes of King's, Hubert Henderson, F. Lavington of Emmanuel, and Dennis Robertson of Trinity.

In a Memoir of Harold Wright [1] there occurs this passage :

> In achieving the editorship of the *Granta* and the Presidency of the Union, Wright had received the two highest honours that Cambridge has to bestow outside the Senate House and the playing-fields; but the most important aspect of his Union activities, in its influence on his later life, was that they brought him into personal contact with the author of *The Great Illusion*. Wright was already a strong pacifist when he came up to Cambridge; but he was too much of a rationalist and too much of a realist to find complete satisfaction in the propaganda of the peace societies. Norman Angell's argument as to the futility of armed aggression supplied him at once with a reasoned basis for his instinctive pacifism, and with a case which could be put forward as practical politics. From his first reading of *Europe's Optical Illusion*, the form in which the main arguments of *The Great Illusion* were first published, Wright became an enthusiastic adherent and a persuasive exponent of 'Norman Angellism,' and at the beginning of 1912 he had the supreme delight of introducing Norman Angell himself to Cambridge.

There follows an account of a debate at the Union and meeting of the Political Economy Club. The Union debate was a full-dress affair.

[1] *Harold Wright, A Memoir* by C. E. Fayle: George Allen and Unwin Ltd., London, 1934.

The meeting of the Political Economy Club, held under the presidency of J. M. Keynes, in Lowes Dickinson's rooms, was a much less formal but not less strenuous occasion. At this time the Garton Foundation was in process of formation, and Wright wrote me: 'If you are initiating a general movement in this country, I hope our Cambridge Society may serve as a Kinder-Garton Foundation.' I had hesitated to identify myself too closely with the proposed society and Wright wrote, on 3 June 1912: '... I am quite sure that you are mistaken in supposing that we shall get anything but good from being associated with your name. You must remember that there is always the danger of being mistaken for a Peace Society of the old type; and the only discussion of War and Peace which is not militarist and not pacifist is that of *The Great Illusion*.'

What stood out as the dominating quality in Harold's mind was that elusive thing, judgment, sagacity. As a student of international politics and economics he had no exceptional erudition; though well and widely read, he was not 'learned' in the academic sense. But he had an exceptional understanding of politics because he had an exceptional understanding of human behaviour, and that freedom from dogmatic prepossession which is so intimately related to kindliness and toleration. He realized that the science of politics consists so largely in the adaptation of institutions to living men, in unravelling the motives of conduct of men in the mass, in some understanding of the fallacies which possess them; some sympathetic appreciation of their scale of values—things which the very learned sometimes utterly lack. Had Harold's type of mind been commoner among the erudite of Germany, had a few Harold Wrights been scattered among the students and faculties of the German universities of the last generation or two, it is possible the world would not have known either war or the Nazi revolution.

The circumstances in which I learned of Harold's death were characteristic of the life we both lived. The day he died I was in the North in the midst of a series of lectures. My niece, at that time my secretary, who had known Harold since she was a child, on being notified of the death was embarrassed as to what to do: for she knew what the news would mean to me. It was an important meeting that I was to address that evening. She did not notify me of the death. The next morning I went straight to a meeting of the Executive of the League of Nations Union. Gilbert Murray was in the chair, and opened proceedings by suggesting a resolution of condolence and sympathy on the death of Harold Wright. Thus did I learn that our association—I had almost written partnership—of a quarter of a century had come to an end. On getting to my chambers I reproved my niece for not having notified me by wire to the North the day before. She said, ' It was an important meeting; you could not give it up; you could do nothing. If I had been able to ask Harold's advice, as I have asked it so often when I had to make decisions in your absence, what would he have advised? '

In a few notes that I supplied for the memoir on Wright, I wrote this:

Much of the work I have been able to do in the quarter of a century I worked with Harold would not have been done but for his friendship, particularly perhaps for the feeling that I must not let him down; must not fall short of the estimate which he had formed of the work I had to do, and might do. Without such a friendship, cynicism on my part—the feeling, after so many years of work which did not seem to show much result, that it might be simplest to let the world go to the devil in its own way, if going to the devil was what it liked—would have been fatally easy. Once I was near to ' chucking it all up in order to live on an island.' Harold's intervention stopped that. He had no objection to the island (he came and stayed there himself), but helped to draw me back to the mainland and ' get on with it.'

The getting on with it without Harold will be exceedingly difficult. But his life will have made it impossible for one at least who worked with him not to go on persistently to the end.

The memoir of Harold Wright was edited by Ernest Fayle. The latter was one of quite a number of secretaries I have had during half a century, and no account of the work I did during that period, nor any note on the friendships of my life would be complete without mention of the fact that practically all those secretaries remained warm personal friends long after they left me, the men to go to better paid work, the women usually to get married. These lifelong friendships are the more noteworthy in view of the fact that I am not naturally a ' mixer ' and do not easily get on terms of intimacy with those about me; and my work has not been sufficiently remunerative to permit of salaries at all adequate to the work my secretaries did. Moreover, they were all over-worked and their private convenience constantly disregarded. Nevertheless there resulted these life-long friendships, beginning with George Langelaan, who came to me half a century ago in Paris and left me to become Northcliffe's secretary and who still dines with me whenever I am in Paris where he lives; still shares my views and expresses them ardently to his friends. As to Ernest Fayle, surely a man never had a better assistant, but he did *not* always share my views. He was with me for some years before I discovered that his main interest in life was military science. It came out one morning as I was dictating an article to him, in which I had ventured into the realm of military strategy and tactics. For the first time he then revealed a sort of : 'I have stood a good deal of nonsense these past years, but this is the limit.' For a few minutes, Fayle let himself go and revealed all the reserves of criticism, expression of which he had bottled up during his years with me. The outburst did not make the slightest difference to our relations—indeed I only regretted he had not been freer in his criticism during the preceding years. He had been glad to remain because it was not on fundamentals that we disagreed ; only on certain military aspects. He himself was the author of several books (*The New Patriotism* and a history of shipping during the First World War) and had a charming gift for light satirical verse, which appeared regularly in the *Nation* where he was assistant to Harold Wright when the latter became the editor of that paper. When I left for America in 1915 Fayle moved on to the Garton Foundation in its new incarnation under the direction of John Hilton. He wrote a number of articles for the American Press discussing my work of which he spoke in the highest terms, and to me personally wrote every Christmas and on such occasions as my receipt of the Nobel prize, in terms of warm affection and regard.

It is now a quarter of a century since Patsy Kelley, the Philadelphia Quaker girl, joined me as secretary and remained some years and left me to marry Stephen Wilson, the civil servant whose record has been a brilliant one. I often visit their home and Patsy brings her children to the island. Doris Toulmin was also for a year or two my secretary and with her and her husband, Geoffrey, I remained on terms of affectionate friendship. They too, with their children, have been visitors to the island, and have learned to sail the Blackwater in little ships. Josephine

Robertson, who joined the Wrens at the outbreak of the second war and was invalided out (and who adopted the dog we had on the island) still comes to see me occasionally.

Without the help of Carolyn Schuyler Joy in New York, I could never have managed this last ten years to divide my work between Britain and the United States; and ' Sunny ' Lozier has taken time off from her beloved music studies in London to make work possible for me on the island.

Memories seem long. In 1949 I made a pious pilgrimage to the old office in the Rue de Sentier. Going into the entrance I noticed an old, old compositor, slowly coming along the corridor with a handful of proofs in his hand. He stopped, glanced my way a minute, then said cordially but casually, with a tone which implied we had met yesterday : ' Bon jour, Monsieur le Directeur. Ça va bien ce matin? ' After all, it was only forty years since we last met.

I have always found Lady Rhondda a delightful editor to work under. The fact that after the U.D.C. publication, *Foreign Affairs*, ceased I did a four-page separate supplement every month for *Time and Tide* may have had something to do with the fact that the *New Statesman* for many years has never reviewed a single book of mine, although Kingsley Martin, the editor, is an old friend and has, he tells me, read every book I have written. It may be true, as some other unorthodox members of the Labour Party have remarked, that if you leave or criticize a Leftist organization, you are apt to be completely damned. I would not put it quite at that. I think that many Leftists feel that a socialist who recognizes certain dangers in collectivism while admitting the desirability of applying it up to a point, is neither fish, flesh, fowl nor good red herring. They do not know where to fit you in or the attitude to take. You are likely to be damned by all sides.

Ellen Wilkinson was rather a special friend during my few years in the House of Commons. She was a generous, red-headed little spitfire, at one time obsessed with the class-war psychosis, although a great friend of Lady Rhondda's. During her pacifist period she attacked me rather bitterly for what she regarded as my apostasy in supporting the policy of collective defence—which involved, of course, commitment to fight in common resistance to aggression. But later she apologized very handsomely indeed, too handsomely perhaps. 'I was completely wrong,' she said. 'You were completely right.' Neither statement was of course true. She had not a very high opinion of her Trade Union colleagues. 'Tammany Hall could learn a lot from the British Trade Union movement,' she remarked one day after a meeting with some trade unionists. But then Ellen's dicta were never to be taken *au pied de la lettre*.

Lowes Dickinson, like Gilbert Murray and one or two more of the really big academic figures, never made on me the impression of considering me something of an outsider trespassing on their preserves. We were close friends for many years and I have always felt that 'Goldie' never had his due either during his life or after it. He was one of the great lights of English political literature. He saw the dilemma of modern politics as the best of the Greek thinkers saw the dilemma of Graeco-Roman society. Although he wrote before the coming of atomic weapons, what he wrote has especial reference to the Atomic Age.

Desmond MacCarthy wrote of Lowes Dickinson that 'he was one of the few literary men of his period who applied their talents to problems of the day—without telling lies. He was contemplative, caring more for ends than means. He might perhaps have been content to be a philosopher if the miseries of humanity had not haunted him. He wrote not for fame but to do good. He was that rare type, a truthful zealot, always preferring to be genuine rather than impressive. He was a man of peace who could not stand aside from struggles. What he aimed at was to bring into controversies, social, moral, international, the spirit of culture; its impartiality without its aloofness, its superiority without its superciliousness.'

With too much generosity MacCarthy links my own work with that of Lowes Dickinson.

It was a peculiarity of the sort of agitation in which I was engaged before World War I that it should engender warm friendships among those sharing the work and that the friends should be drawn from all political parties. It would be my lot in that 1910–14 period to come on the same day from a conference with Lord Esher, Permanent Member of the Committee of Imperial Defence, intimate of the King, to a conference with Hyde Park or open-air speakers, headed by Wilk Haycock, who had such a genius for that kind of work.

During the first war Haycock became a conscientious objector and I recall getting up at dawn and waiting five hours at the prison gates to greet him on his discharge. At our more formal conferences you would find Lady Barlow, the Quaker Aristocrat, arguing earnestly with Dr. John Mez, the German university student (who was to become a professor in an American university) or with Ernest Busvine, the ladies' tailor and keen yachtsman, all of them friends of mine during many years. As I look down the list of those who attended our conferences I see many whose friendship I enjoyed but from whom an unsettled life on both sides of the Atlantic has separated me in the course of the years. Twenty of those years have been passed in the United States, and twenty in France or Switzerland. Among those I have hailed so pleasantly were Reginald Kapp, Joseph Thorp, C. H. Rothwell, R. B. Graham of Magdalen, Frank Nixon, Cyril Rhodes, and Roland Sturgis.

Since I have known the United States for more than half a century, it is natural that some of my oldest friends (outside the newspaper and writing folk already mentioned) should be in that country. There are the Huycks—Mrs. Francis Conkling Huyck and her daughter Katharine and *her* children. Mrs. Huyck was for some years the centre of much of the intellectual life of Albany, and her country home at Rensselaerville was a refuge for me during many summer week-ends.

The Rublees, George and Juliet, who in 1915 had a house in Washington and who have been constant and unchanging friends for a period of forty years, furnished at times extremely useful links with Washington personalities. I think it was they who first brought me into touch with Colonel House and so, by memoranda and other means, with President Wilson; and it was at the house of the Rublees that I was to meet a good many Washington politicians and personalities, including Justice Oliver Wendell Holmes. The Rublees made a good team : Juliet, of quick, alert intelligence, fruitful of suggestion, George acting as a brake on Juliet's impulsiveness. It may have been at their house that I first met Norman Hapgood (at that time very close to Wilson) who wrote so often with high appreciation of my work, while Elizabeth Hapgood, who has kept a shining loveliness into grandmotherhood, and I have maintained a close friendship ever since that time. Judge Learned Hand was part of that circle and we have been friends for forty years.

The Kaltenborns managed to combine American open-handed friendliness and hospitality with European culture, between them embracing several foreign languages and literatures. At Sam and Margaret Lewisohn's one was always pretty sure to meet interesting folk of the literary and artistic world.

Gertrude Winslow is a friend of thirty years' standing. At the Winslow house I would encounter that English veteran of the American lecture platform, S. K. Ratcliffe, whose work in journalism has always had real distinction. Friendship with Max Eastman goes back just as long; his early insight into the Communist fallacies anticipated by many years the disillusionment of so many other intellectuals of his generation.

In the previous chapter I have related how, as quite a small child, my niece, Barbara Hayes, would become part of the crew of my little yacht and a constant visitor to Northey Island. By stages—almost imperceptible to me, less so I suspect to her—she became my secretary and took over more and more the management of lecture tours, elections, keeping of accounts, what not, until finally familiar with all my affairs she was able to run things in my absence in the United States (as when she managed the campaign when I stood as Labour Candidate for London University while absent in America).

As my health got steadily worse I saw that I ran the risk of allowing an able, talented young woman to drift into the position of becoming the caretaker, nurse, guardian of an ageing and ailing relative, making the kind of sacrifice I have seen among my friends, but which I have always felt no man ought to accept if he can do otherwise. I could do otherwise. Barbara having learned how to manage lecture tours for me, I suggested she could do it for others. The result, two years before the second war, was the establishment of a Lecture Agency in England which was an immediate success, and would, without doubt, have been an important commercial affair if the coming of war in 1939 had not killed it, as it killed so much else. A couple of years later she was able, however, to turn the experience she gained in the management of speakers and their tours to good account in a position in the Foreign Office where she has since remained, and has made a career, standing on her own feet. I lost an invaluable secretary, but avoided the guilty feeling that I was 'exploiting' a disinterested affection or passively accepting another's sacrifice.

MEDALS, REWARDS AND PUNISHMENT

MOST men, I suppose, at times make the reflection, looking back on a long life, ' I've been punished most of all for the good things I did, and have escaped punishment for the bad.' This is true of the public work I've tried to do, as well as of my personal life. Had the very wide criticism which my earlier work on international affairs provoked been directed at its real—and sometimes great—defects, that criticism would have helped the public to clarify ideas concerning our major problem. For where my work failed mainly was in giving a plain and simple answer to the question : 'How shall a political truth, once established, be translated into workable policy?'

It would have been a service to public understanding if this incompleteness had been criticized and exposed, and if the critics had carried on from the point up to which I was right and derived therefrom a practical conclusion in policy. Yet I cannot recall one single instance where this was done at all effectively by my many and often very severe critics.

Similarly in a private life full enough of weaknesses and errors. The old age of penury and bad health with which it ends is not a result of those weaknesses and errors, but rather of what most would regard as virtues. That is probably a very commonplace experience.

It is certainly no punishment that I should never have achieved public office. It is unlikely I should have gained it even if I had sought it (which I did not). Such indeed was once hinted to me by a colleague in the Labour Party, himself a holder of high office at the time of the formation of the 1929 government. He said : 'You are too incalculable to be altogether a safe member of a political team—likely to go off on your own and talk something which is not party doctrine. And then Ramsay MacDonald has an unconscious dislike of all who were associated with him in what one might call his pacifist period, a period he now wants to forget.'

There were, however, certain spheres in which I thought I might have been some use to a government of the Left : in the presentation of the case for the League as an instrument of defence; in re-shaping public education so as to enable the millions turned out by our schools to grasp the nature of the society they are called upon to manage, and more particularly correct the prevailing economic illiteracy.

One immediately practical project I did urge upon Mac-Donald in the early days of his second government : the building up of a marketing organization of a special type of which I drew the outline, and which, although due to government initiative, would, I am pretty sure, have been welcomed by trade and industry, and at the same time would have increased employment —the prime need at that particular moment. But I could never manage to rivet MacDonald's attention to the scheme : always was there that outer shell of unapproachability. I did not manage to break through it even when I saw some little of him—and of Ishbel, his daughter—during an Atlantic voyage. (I was a member of his party in a journalistic capacity when he visited President Hoover to talk naval agreement.)

Nor was I ever included in any official work in connection with the League—on grounds for which there was a good deal to be said. If a man has some technical knowledge, or qualification in a subject—mines, shipping, coal, colonies—he must not be appointed to deal with the subject which he understands. This rule is not as comic as it sounds. A minister is there to represent the public interest in the department he administers, coal or shipping or what not. He is not there, save in very exceptional circumstances, to contribute to the technical management, or to touch policy where technical details are involved. The permanent officials prefer it so—and that is a very important consideration in the smooth working of a competent and impartial civil service.

I think MacDonald at times did have some feeling of not having used me as he might (as, for instance, at Geneva). My own feeling in the matter was that, after all, he may have been right. It is quite likely that I was unsuitable for office, and in any case was overwhelmed with the day-to-day jobs that come up when a man has added Parliament to book-writing. However that may be, about 1930, without his having spoken to me about it, I had a communication from his office to the effect that he proposed to recommend me for a knighthood. In view of the fact that he had given no consideration to the marketing scheme, this had the effect of making me angry. I got the impression that he was throwing baubles at me instead of using me as he might have done in international affairs, the League, the possibilities of an improved popular economic education (through the Board of Education); or in threshing out with the Board of Trade some of the marketing proposals I had discussed.

Harold Wright happened to call at King's Bench Walk a couple of days after the receipt of the notification about the knighthood from the Prime Minister's office. I told Harold that I should certainly decline. He immediately protested that it would be the wrong thing to do; seemed very earnest about it and a couple of days later wrote me as follows :

It's a lordly gesture, of course, and you're feeling a hell of a fellow, refusing a knighthood. But I suggest that meantime you are forgetting your job, which you have not been doing very well of late. For you, there's only one thing which should count : the fate of the ideas you have thrown into the common pool, ideas which, if generally understood—understood with all their implications—would be useful and far-reaching. But they are *not* widely understood. For the multitude, as apart from the intelligentsia, your ideas, and you, are a jest : you are the fellow who said there never could be any more war. You have spent twenty years quite unsuccessfully, trying to destroy that myth. *Punch* had to make a joke of it only the other day : the latest book on Reparations repeats the jibe. Having begun the job, you cannot be considered to have finished it, until that sort of thing is impossible. The multitude will be impressed by an official honour. Many will decide you cannot be such a fool, that there must be something in which you have written or you would not be knighted. That particular public will be a bit more receptive. Where you now get a ten line report of a lecture, you would with a title get half a column : the difference between a useful and a useless report.

' Further,' he went on, with the freedom our old friendship allowed, ' because you have to live by your pen you sometimes do shocking bad work. In order to live, you turn out stuff hurriedly. Editors, and lecture publics, being what they are, you'll get higher

fees with a title and choose your work more and do it better.' He
concluded :

> You are offered a tool which will help you to get an idea into
> thick heads; to reach people—vulgar and snobbish people—who,
> if they are not reached, will inflict upon themselves and the
> world infinite suffering. This next few years particularly are
> crucial. And you reject the tool because you think it cheap and
> vulgar, associated with common people like successful grocers.
> So long as your fastidious soul is not offended, your job can
> remain unfinished, and the multitude go hang.

Harold sometimes talked to me like that; and I felt that on this
occasion he might be right. So, at first very much against the
grain, I notified the P.M.'s office that I would accept the knighthood. Events justified Harold's judgment; approach to the big
indifferent public *did* become a bit easier because of the possession
of this six-a-penny title.

When American friends have 'kidded' me about the acceptance of a title I have tried to put the point that a title in England
is merely a medal, a decoration, hung on to a man's name instead
of on to his coat. The whole principle of medals may be wrong,
but every society, including rather especially the Communist
society of Russia, has found medals and orders socially useful.
To very many Englishmen up to about 1930 I was a mere
'poisonous pacifist,' a crank. . . . The title did at least make it
possible to 'have my day in Court,' as Americans put it.

Harold's letter struck me as sufficiently good to justify my
sending copies of it to two or three friends to whom I felt disposed
to give some sort of explanation of accepting a title of this kind.

The real 'reward' in connection with this business was the
tone of some of the letters of congratulation. Gilbert Murray
(now, of course, a member of the far more distinguished Order
of Merit) wrote that he thought Harold's 'arguments are on the
whole convincing. Whichever decision one makes, one feels doubtful afterwards. I had the same question to settle in 1911, and
like you, wrote two letters and then read them over to see which
I liked best. On the whole, I am inclined to think my refusal
was a mistake, partly for the reasons your friend gives and partly
because I no longer approve of the old Radical-Protestant
attitude of standing defiantly superior to the ordinary standards
of society. Co-operation is the word now, not mere independence.'

Y

Gilbert added that his wife, 'who is a great radical about honours and started by thinking you were more distinguished as a plain citizen, was convinced by the arguments you quote and told me to send her congratulations.'

John Buchan, who became Lord Tweedsmuir and was soon after to be made Governor-General of Canada, and whom I had known ever since the Northcliffe days, wrote, ' I have not a doubt that you were right to accept. . . . Your friend spoke words of wisdom. In public life one has to consider other things besides one's own tastes. Your knighthood is a recognition of the great pioneering work which you have done, and continue to do, and it was important for the sake of that work that it should have this kind of imprimatur. Further, the fact that you have been knighted by your King has a very real meaning in foreign countries and will undoubtedly increase your international authority.'

Charles Trevelyan, who had resigned from the Asquith government in 1914 in protest against the war policy and had, with MacDonald, Arthur Ponsonby, Snowden and myself, been one of the five founders of the Union of Democratic Control, wrote ' how the wheel has come full cycle. How different to the time we met two days after the war had begun; both hopelessly discredited. Well, what you teach is just as badly wanted as ever, and I think even there are a few more million listeners.'

Mary Agnes Hamilton, a close friend of many years who was with me in the House of Commons, who came to front bench status when the party went into opposition, and who later was to do such invaluable work at the Foreign Office in Anglo-American relations, wrote, ' I am so very glad you have decided to say yes and glad that you appear in so generally distinguished and good a list.' She added the feminine touch, ' You have the good fortune of a name that makes a really pretty title.'

J. A. Hobson (whose work in economics, far too little appreciated, on the relation of unemployment to the proportion of consumption-spending to capital investment, preceded so usefully Keynes' work on monetary policy and unemployment) wrote approvingly, much on the lines of Harold's letter. As did S. K. Ratcliffe, whom I have known for nearly half a century.

My very old friend, Leonard Behrens, who had in the old pre-1914 days founded the Manchester Norman Angell League, and was later to do hard and patient work in the United Nations Association, wrote, also with the prejudice of friendship : ' Some of your friends, perhaps all your friends, will be surprised that you have accepted the knighthood, not because there is anything disgraceful in it, but because there is no particular honour. It is like offering twopence to a millionaire. That is why, if your friends are surprised—as some of them will be— it will be a compliment to you. . . . You have done right. There is no reason for your feeling cheap ; and it *does* concern me and all the thousands who have to thank you for more than they can ever repay.'

There were a couple of dozen letters in similar terms from those who had worked closely with me in the early days previous to the first war.

These were the real reward.

The other 'medal,' which I accepted without any of the hesitations involved in the knighthood, was the Nobel Prize for Peace, although in this case the prize is accompanied by a tip, amounting in this particular instance to some nine thousand pounds.

It may be a reflection upon the English scale of values (I think it is) that a Nobel Prize brought fewer letters of congratulation than did the knighthood. The award was genuinely a surprise to me, for I knew that I had been recommended for the prize as far back as 1912—twenty years before I received it. It would have been more logical to have awarded it at the earlier date, since the kind of work I had been doing in the intervening years was being done—often far better—by others; while what I was doing in 1912 did break new ground, in a new way, for peace ; in a way that had secured for the peace problem a worldwide attention. And after twenty years I had assumed that that prize would pass me by. So the announcement that it would be awarded me was all the more heartening ; and the more so as I could not but recall that ten years previously I had still been very much in the wilderness, the sort of person to whom passports were refused, whose books were on the index expurgatorius, to many a figure of fun, to some others a dangerous subversive revolutionary.

The letters I received, though few in number, came from those of intellectual worth who did not express opinions lightly. Arthur Salter wrote: 'I am delighted at the Nobel award, as everyone who believes in peace through the collective system must be. It is only a few books that live and transform the thought of the generation which follows their publication, but in your case, as all who are interested in the peace movement know, your most famous book has only been the precursor of many years of unremitting work in every sphere of public education. I have just been reading with great interest and complete agreement your *Unseen Assassins.*'

Robert Cecil wrote: 'It is long overdue. . . . No one in this country, or perhaps in the world, has done more for peace than you have.'

Brodetsky of the Jewish Agency for Palestine, wrote that he spoke 'for Zionists and Jews all over the world' in the congratulations which he sent.

Harold Laski wrote: 'I need not say whether I was glad I signed one of those queer nomination papers as long ago as 1916. They say it takes nineteen years for the Report of a Royal Commission to come into operation. It looks as though in the case of Nobel Prizes wisdom takes the same time to be justified of her children.'

Philip Noel-Baker: 'It is of course twenty years overdue. . . . If peace comes it will be more your doing than that of any other man alive. Other people have battered on the walls of hell, but you have undermined the foundations, and the man who does that is the man who breaks them down. My most affectionate congratulations.' Philip Snowden, who had taken some part in organizing the committee which promoted my nomination, wrote with similar warmth: 'Your vast number of friends and admirers all over the world will be delighted.'

Gilbert Murray wrote: 'It is a magnificent crown to at least twenty years of continuous and concentrated work. I think the Nobel Committee have done themselves credit in selecting a real peace-worker who is not a cabinet minister or a general or a head of a State.'

Any story of punishment should include that which comes from a general mismanagement of life. Great personal difficulty has arisen from my tendency to be dragged into work of administration instead of sticking to my last of explanation and clarification. Great organizations had been created to carry on campaigns of enlightenment in foreign affairs and I belonged to very many.

In most of these organizations I found a degree of self-sacrificing labour by men often in the forefront of politics and literature which never ceased to astound me and awaken an admiration for patience and abnegation I felt I could never equal. I have seen Robert Cecil, Gilbert Murray, Victor Lytton, Megan Lloyd-George, Philip Noel-Baker, Clifford Allen, sit through weary hours of barren discussion at the L.N.U. Executive, for instance, which produced in me actual physical pain.

It is true that during those twenty years my health got worse and worse. And in addition to that kind of work I did an immense amount of travelling and lecturing in England, France, at Geneva, and in the United States. On these travels I was in the habit of writing to my niece, now become my secretary. The fact that I had known her since she was a child gave my letters to her a very unreserved and confidential character, and thus a very frank picture of the kind of life I was then leading. One of the letters deals with a typical 'International Adult Education Conference' at which I had become 'Director of Studies'—in the midst of journalistic and unfinished book work. 'On Sunday, I got up at six or a bit before, and slaved at my " Foreign Affairs " article till lunch, immediately after which a big public meeting; immediately after which my first lecture,' the letter begins, and goes on :

It was raining cats and dogs; I got wet and when I went on to the platform there was an arctic draft which set my teeth chattering. About midnight that night I woke up with the worst headache I have had. It was all I could do to stop from shrieking and howling. (I did howl a little.) Took aspirin, no result, took more and was then deathly sick and kept on being till morning. Nevertheless, did my four hours talking and questions; prepared a précis for the Press; made a start on licking my Pelican book into shape. One Tuesday dealt with F.A. proofs, tried to read the papers to bring them up to date. (The Czecho matter is touch and go); saw newspaper men, more précis; dealt with complaints that I was not conducting the discussions fairly (there are full-blooded Nazis and Fascists here and wild Irishmen who are worse); wrote a statement for reading this morning; today, thanks to the omission of the evening lecture, have just managed to scramble the Pelican MS into the post (hours and hours checking the pages, marking the type, writing in the short heads . . .) (I swore I would keep my promise to send it ' at the end of August '.) ' And now am trying to finish the American Enclo. article and to do a Symes article. (There are good fees attached to all this work and I can't afford to miss them just now—not to speak of other considerations.) But I doubt if I shall manage to finish either before I leave. The food here is abominable, gives me vile indigestion; the bed is the kind I cannot possibly sleep in and my head gets steadily worse.

The letter goes on to discuss a proposal that I should ' take over the virtual editorship or editorial articles of *Headway*,' and another more confidential proposal for journalistic work. ' If Eden, Winston, Cranborne, Cecil, Lytton, Violet Bonham-Carter, all come into this, as they seem disposed to do; and make me as it were their spokesman, I should in some sense be very close to the centre of what may be the new government of England, if England in the next five years is going to have a government other than a Nazi-appointed one.'

A word or two as to these references to health.

About twenty years ago I began to develop a peculiar type of migraine, waking up after three or four hours' sleep with an instant and raging headache. They began by being occasional, once or twice a week. They are now nightly. There are very few days in the year which do not begin for me at three in the morning with a paroxysmic headache after three or four hours of sleep. With the help of strong coffee and strong doses of an analgesic of one kind or another the headache passes in a couple of hours. It is not a good beginning to a day of active work in the sixties and seventies. In July 1939 I wrote to my niece that, ' As these headaches get worse and worse my conscience gets worse and worse also that you should give so much of your youth to associating with someone always out-of-sorts, always on the edge of invalidism. I've tried to make up for it by seeing that you shall have an independent life of your own—lecture management as a future possibility, public work, committees, soroptimists, refugees. . . . Still, I feel a terrible burden. And I'm worrying about the immediate future. If these headaches do get worse, I shall not live more than a year or two. That is the stark truth. I would not indecently parade it but for the fact that it bears on immediate arrangements.' The letter goes on :

> I would never have mentioned it at all but for the fact that you would never know why I was suggesting this, that or the other arrangement for the future unless you were aware. It need cast no shadow over the year or two ahead of us. It's like the war : we cannot be sure that it will come but we must be prepared for it and arrange in view of its coming. I've felt of late that if I could get the thing off my chest and drag into the light a ghost I was trying to cover up, our talk and plans and companionship would be that much freer. And, of course, we can both face it with courage. An eventuality like that is only terrifying if you *don't* face it. I won't say that at times it is not bitter because I love life and there are a million things I wanted to do that I shall never do. *Mais, qu'est-ce que tu veux? C'est la vie—et la mort.*

I cite the letter as a caution against the kind of pessimism which it reflects. It was written twelve years ago. The headaches still continue, but in the eleven years I have published five books, one of them putting the British case in the war to the American public, which had a very large circulation and was a choice of the Book of the Month Club. The years may not have been entirely lost.

Part V

AT THE END

CHAPTER I

IN THE SECOND WAR

NORTHEY ISLAND is situated at the head of the Blackwater Estuary, an estuary which, as already noted in these chronicles, was an avenue of invasion even in Viking times (Northey itself having been the scene of a tenth-century battle with the Danes[1]). Banse, the Hitlerian military authority, had indicated that this same estuary would be a gateway to Britain for German invasion forces when the time came. No sooner had war been declared in September, 1939, than we farmers were warned to be ready at twenty-four hours notice to drive all stock inland so that it should not fall into the hands of invaders and would be available for the home needs. ('Thus,' remarked a neighbour, 'creating such congestion on the roads as to prevent military forces and supplies reaching the coast for the purpose of defeating the invasion forces.') On the island we took such steps as we could : got our gas masks, dug a couple of underground shelters, one of them under a small haystack, tucked away a couple of dinghies in inconspicuous creeks so as to be able to get away to the mainland if the occasion should arise, while on the mainland we noted that the sea walls had been mined in such a fashion that great areas could be flooded as a check to enemy approach. And then we waited for the bombs. But, it will be recalled, no bombs came during that period of the 'phoney' war and things soon dropped back to relative normality. The married couple who had been doing the work of the island did not relish putting in the war on a spot so out of the world and insisted on 'returning to civilization.' Among the Hitlerite refugees who had managed to reach England and whose circumstances I had come to know, were a Viennese doctor, her husband and her mother. I put it to them whether they would care to make their home on the island for a time and take charge of the house and necessary outside work. They jumped at the offer and were duly installed.

[1] See Part IV, Chapter I.

329

I was just then at work on a second edition of the Penguin book on the refugee question, so that I was able to verify certain facts from the personal experience of these people. I was busy also with other book work, with much typing, arrangement of material, proof-reading. Because of this, two secretaries remained on the island, bringing its normal population to six persons. In the early months we never used the shelters and the first Christmas of the war had a large Christmas party at the house, consisting mainly of the refugee German children Barbara was taking under her special charge. Barbara's parents came down and, despite the blackout, it was a jolly occasion. It was pleasant to think that the brilliant woman doctor who had been driven from Vienna as non-Aryan, together with her mother and husband, could find haven and sanctuary on this little morsel of England's soil.

But it was not to be such smooth going for long. The weather turned arctic and for the first time within the memory of man the estuary was virtually frozen over. Great icebergs piled up on the causeway which served normally at low tide as a road access to the island. As the ice also prevented our using a boat, we were virtually shut off from the mainland except by foot—carefully clambering along the edge of the ' icebergs.' Then the movement of the ice carried away the jetty which had proved so useful in giving access to boats when the tide was low. Then *Ida*, my old yacht, moored in one of the creeks of the island, got pinched on the ice and some of her seams opened, which would make it difficult to move her to any boat yard on the mainland if we should be obliged to leave the island. Fortunately, we did not lack fuel, partly because of the abundance of driftwood to be found along the coast.

And then, as the period of the ' phoney war' passed, and the war of movement began on the Continent, we felt the change immediately on the island. One peaceful Sunday afternoon a motor-boat moored off the beach, and two policemen landed. Was Mr. Holin, the gentleman from Vienna, at home? He was. They had instructions to convey him immediately to an internment camp: all alien enemies, whatever their race or political background, were being interned. I asked : What of Dr. Holin, the Viennese woman doctor, Holin's wife? No. She could remain. But a month or two later orders came that she and her mother must move from the coast. They would not be interned and could live in my chambers in London if they desired. This for a time they did. I pulled such strings as I could at the Home Office in an effort to secure the release of the husband from the internment camp (we did not even know where it was), on the ground that people who by origins were, first Jews, then Polish, then by training scientists, whose near relatives had perished in Hitler's death camps, were not likely to be agents of Hitler. All of which was admitted but, as Churchill put it at the time, it was not possible in the press of events to screen very carefully the friendly from the unfriendly aliens. So all had to go into internment. Happily, Barbara, with characteristic energy, was able finally to secure visas for all three of these harassed people for entrance into the United States, where Dr. Holin quickly qualified for medical practice and has done exceedingly well. The refugee children that Barbara befriended have done well either in Britain or the United States.

The second edition of the Refugees book and an American version were no sooner out of the way than I was busy on the next book, which must have been begun a few days after the Declaration of War, since by December 1939, it had been published by Hamilton in London and by Harpers in New York. Looking back on this degree of activity from the near octogenarian standpoint, I kept wondering how the devil I did it. The book, published at the end of 1939, is entitled *For What do We Fight?*, and reading it after twelve years I am struck by its relevance to the situation of 1951—and the unhappy verification which the events have given to its various warnings. In the brief introduction I wrote, ' The insistent belief that the simple destruction of Hitlerism will of itself free us from the evils for which it stands is an insidious and dangerous fallacy. We have slipped into the habit of speaking of ' freeing Europe from the menace of recurrent aggressions,' as though that would automatically be achieved by the defeat of Germany in war. Yet we know that such an assumption, far from being self-evident, as we seem to assume, is completely disproved by the plainest experience. In 1914, also, we believed that the simple defeat of Germany and the destruction of Kaiserism would free the world. Kaiserism was destroyed. We did not get something better, but something worse; more evil, more menacing.'

The underlying theme of the book was of course the one I had been elaborating ever since the beginning of the previous war: We should win allies, and thereby achieve our own security, only to the extent that we made it plain that 'in future our power will be used to resist aggression by the defence of its victim even though the aggression is not aimed directly at ourselves. Only by being clear ourselves on that point can we make it clear to the neutral—or quasi-neutral—world. In making their choice, those at present neutral will have to judge whether their security after our next victory is likely to be such as will justify them in taking the risk of standing up to totalitarian pressure, or whether it might not be better from their point of view to come to terms with totalitarianism before sharing the fate which Czechoslovakia and Poland and certain other of our past allies have had to face since our last victory. The judgment which neutral and enemy peoples form of our future conduct will determine their present conduct. What we stand for in the war may well determine (both by the degree of enemy resistance and the course of neutral— particularly American—behaviour) whether we shall win the war.'

This was written, remember, in the first two months of the war before the entrance of Italy and Japan and while yet the policy of the United States was quite undetermined. While, the book goes on, we could not and ought not to state our terms in the sense of drawing frontiers, 'we could give an earnest of our sincerity by *acts*); by initiating the federal unity of Europe, in so developing our own relations with France as to bring about a virtual Franco-British Federal Union.' Six or seven months later Winston Churchill was to offer France 'a solemn act of Union,' and five years later to stand for the beginnings of an European Union. I went on to point out that we could add enormously to the strength of any current towards unification by 'throwing our Empire open to the world on equal terms with ourselves *now*, by offering to give neutrals (e.g. Denmark, Norway, Holland, Belgium) the same economic position in the Empire as that occupied by the Dominions. This would be the best answer to the charge that we (Britain and the other Dominions) are waging war to retain imperialistic monopolies, excluding others from "living space."'

To all this I add the old warning that there is no magic in some special form of constitution; that you may have very indifferent results from good constitutions, as in the case of certain Latin American republics, or pretty good results from no written constitution at all, as in Britain. 'Whether this Western unification (which alone can meet the challenge of Russo-German Totalitarianism) comes into being, will depend, less upon the precise form of any constitution that may be drafted, than upon the degree of public wisdom that can be applied to its working; and determine whether repetition of the old errors can be avoided.'

The relevance of those errors to the tasks then confronting Britain was emphasized and an attempt made to clear up confusions which still, at the eleventh hour and fifty-ninth minute before the declaration of war in 1939, were bedevilling the public discussion of policy. The book went on to emphasize the need for a Western ideology comparable in appeal to that of the enemy. The point is even more apposite to-day in respect of Russia than it was in respect of Germany. 'To say that we need an ideology or a creed,' I wrote, 'is merely of course another way of saying that we need to have an aim, to know what we were fighting for. The enemy has his. It may be an utterly wrong and false creed, but it is one appealing to many of the fiercest instincts and most deeply-ingrained weaknesses of men, and by the younger generations at least is held with fanatical conviction. The indoctrination, the conditioning of the youth is carried out with scientific thoroughness, by methods of applied psychology, cunningly devised to excite deep feeling. It is made understandable— understandable, it is true, in terms of monstrous fallacies, of assumptions which flatter vanity, sadism, all the weaknesses of our imperfect human nature. But it is understood by the simplest, especially when it comes to foreign policy.' And the book then went on to state the case for German *lebensraum* as the Germans saw it—and as great sections of the American public saw it. (The view that the war had come because 'Britain owned too much of the world and Germany too little' was put by Lindbergh to great audiences in the United States a year or so after the appearance of my book.) If Britain allowed the belief that 'British imperialism is the enemy of human freedom' to go by default, it would hardly make for the unity of the resistance whether to Hitler or to Stalin.

When I was chatting with John Hilton one day at the Ministry
of Information, he said, 'Why don't you do a lecture tour in
America? The F.O. would welcome it and I'm sure we would at
the M.O.I.'

'Well,' I retorted, 'the Foreign Office did not precisely encourage my missions to America on the last occasion, you may
recall.'

Hilton laughed : 'You don't know how much the F.O. has
learned since then.' (Hilton had been with the Garton Foundation
from its first establishment until he left it in the twenties to
enter Government service and later become a Cambridge Don.)

For the time being I did nothing about going to America. But
after the fall of France in June, 1940, the situation of Britain
became all too clear. Hitler was master of all the European
Continent which Stalin had not already seized. Britain, having
left her armour in France, faced an armed Continent alone. If the
Western way of life was to prevail against the Satanic Hitler-
Stalin combination, then the United States would at least have
to provide the materials needed. The words we had so often used
—sometimes lightly—about the survival of Western civilization
had now taken on a real, an urgent and desperate, meaning. It
was true, as Churchill had declared in the House, that if Britain
failed, 'then the whole world, including the United States, and
all that we have known and cared for will sink into the abyss of
a new Dark Age, made more sinister and perhaps more prolonged by the lights of a perverted science.'

I had a certain audience in America; practically every book
of mine published in England had appeared also in the United
States (though not all those appearing in the United States have
appeared in England). What ought I to do? I put the question to
Harold Nicolson among others. He consulted Duff Cooper, his
immediate chief at the Ministry of Information. The reply came
quickly, 'Get off immediately. Duff Cooper feels more strongly
even than I do that you can be of most use in the United States.
We can get you a berth on a ship to Halifax in two days.'

All so very different, I reflected, from my position at the
beginning of the first war, when my passport to America was
refused, my writings put on the index, and I was listed as an
ideologically dangerous and subversive person.

In two days I made such arrangements as I could : closed the house on the island; appointed a man to visit it twice a week; kept my chambers in the Temple; gave a power of attorney to manage my affairs to a relative; nearly missed the ship at Liverpool; and when I reached it found among the passengers a number of Frenchmen whom I knew, including André Maurois. I shared a cabin with the permanent head of the French Foreign Office, who had just managed to escape the German occupation of Paris.

I was of course going to the United States entirely on my own; as a private person. I had no official mission, no assistance from the government (save as to securing passage), no instructions or even recommendations. I had no plans whatever in the United States; no lecture engagements (at sixty-seven I had thought my lecture tours in the United States were over). I had a bank balance in New York of exactly three hundred dollars, and had asked no authority to change pounds into dollars.

CHAPTER II

A SECOND DECADE IN AMERICA

When I arrived in New York in the late summer of 1940 I was thinking vaguely in terms of a prolonged lecture tour, talks with a few editors, commissions from magazines for a few articles, from publishers for a book, and then return to King's Bench Walk and the island, both of which I was keeping up. What actually happened was that I remained in America as my base for eleven years, and write these lines from New York, as the most 'fixed' address I now possess, my thirty-year tenancy of the chambers in King's Bench Walk and the ownership of Northey Island having come to an end.

It is true that practically every year since 1940 I have crossed the Atlantic to brush up my knowledge of the European situation, and spend the greater part of the summer on Northey. In the war years I flew, or travelled in troop-ships. (A calculation reveals that I have spent two years of my life altogether on the North Atlantic, travelling to and fro.) I don't like this living on both sides of the Atlantic, but it seems to be a condition of the work I can do best.

Within twelve hours of arriving in New York in 1940 I was giving a lecture; within a month, writing a book (*America's Dilemma: Alone or Allied?* published by Harpers). For already 'the great debate' of that second war was raging. President Roosevelt's policy, already revealing itself, though not yet having got as far as the Fifty-Destroyers Exchange, still less Lend-Lease, was meeting in many quarters violent opposition. The most raucously voluble was of course that of the Robert McCormick-Hearst type of rightest isolationist. But opposition was by no means confined to them. Ex-President Hoover led another group of Republican opponents, and opposition came from sections of the Left as well, both within Congress and outside. Norman Thomas, as leader of the American Socialists, led a very vocal campaign against involvement. Farther to the Left, Communists and 'fellow travellers' were still at the stage of representing the Western powers as engaged in an imperialist war waged by profit-thirsty capitalists. It was only a year later, after Hitler's attack on Russia, that the wicked imperialism of the Allies was, for Communists, transformed (in twenty-four hours) into a holy crusade for human freedom. The line-up in that debate cut curiously across the usual group and party divisions. While many Democrats were opposing Roosevelt, it was the Republican William Allen White who started the powerful 'Committee to Defend America by Aiding the Allies.' It was the radical and Leftist *Nation* under Freda Kirchwey which campaigned for American support of Britain. And emotions were as mixed as the parties. During and for a month or two after the Battle of Britain, even the professional Anglophobes became pro-British. (Always with the exception of Colonel McCormick and William Randolph Hearst, who even then expressed loudly their desire to see Britain 'soundly trounced.') One newspaper correspondent reported an Irish American politician as remarking, 'I used to have twelve good reasons for hating Britain. I wish I could remember what they were.'

It gave an Englishman a pleasant glow, all these loud cheers for the island people standing up so valiantly, and all the Bundling for Britain that went on. But one knew that that kind of enthusiasm was no adequate foundation for an American foreign policy by which victory, when it came, could be made the instrument of permanent peace. When the enthusiasm had cooled a little the old prejudices and old confusions would reappear, with the old angers at the idea of American boys being sent to die in 'foreign' wars. (Are wars indispensable to America's own security 'foreign' wars?) Certainly the President knew that he could only carry along his people slowly and gradually. Thus his assurances 'again and again and again' that American boys would not be sent to fight on foreign battlefields unless the country were directly attacked. At the time he gave these undertakings there was no certainty at all that the country would be attacked—until, that is, the one nation still resisting and fighting Hitler had been beaten and had gone the way of France, with much of Africa, including the area of the Suez Canal, occupied, and a pathway opened to the United States.

Z

It was surprising to find arising in this Second War the same questions which had arisen in the First twenty years earlier. One put it to oneself after the fall of France and all through the greater part of 1941 : Assume that, by some miracle, Britain stands up and Germany is worn down. The achievement would have, among other results, that of enormously increasing the relative power of Russia and Japan. Russia had already seized half of Poland, had extinguished the Westernized Baltic states, had sent all 'anti-democratic bourgeois deviationists' (i.e., all professional groups that retained any vestige of moral and intellectual independence) to perish in Arctic camps. Japan was already knocking at the doors of India. The preponderance of power in all the Old World was already shifting from Western into Eastern hands, and the long struggle for keeping, while bettering, the Græco-Roman way of life, with its emphasis on the quality of the individual, was gradually receding in favour of the Oriental conception of vast hordes, obedient to despotic power. Germany had become Easternized, demonstrating how difficult a task it is to maintain a free society and defend it against its ultimate and most cunning enemy, the anti-social passions which exist within each of us.

And so an Englishman in the United States during 1940–41 would ask his American friends, ' Suppose you do give us all the necessary tools and we do finish the job, and you come in at the peace, as you did at the end of the last war in 1918, for what sort of post-war world are you going to stand ? What is to be the shape of your foreign policy in general ? Are you once more going to withdraw as you did before ? '

Of course, there were all sorts of answers. Most insisted that there was no possibility of return to isolationism ; no more Neutrality Acts, or Johnson Acts. But almost all answers included this condition : British imperialism must go ; colonialism must cease. The government of one people by another is immoral, an infamy, and must stop. Such an answer—usually with anger—from the extreme Right as readily as from the extreme Left ; from readers of the Chicago *Tribune* as inevitably as from readers of the *Daily Worker*. We know now that it came from President Roosevelt and the extremely influential Mrs. Roosevelt, as much as from ex-President Hoover, and would-be President Wendell Willkie. It all provoked the famous retort of

Churchill that he had not become the King's first minister for the purpose of presiding at the liquidation of the British Empire.

So far as I was concerned, the sooner the liquidation of the Empire the better, given only one condition—that the result of its liquidation was not either savage and unmanageable chaos, or the establishment of a non-British imperialism which would be very much worse than the British, an almost certain result if the liquidation were ill-timed. It was all but in vain that in personal conversation, lectures, university courses, articles, books, I attempted to show that the instant and simple liquidation of the British Empire would not give more of freedom and self-government throughout the world, but less; the real issue lay as between forms of imperialism which provided means of development into real self-government and those which aimed at making all self-government impossible; that we could not altogether brush aside as irrelevant the fact (more than once noted in these pages) that if there had been no British Empire in 1940—no Gibraltar, Malta, troops in North Africa, in the Near East, on the Suez Canal—then without question we should have seen the triumph of Hitler and the division of most of the world between Hitlerian, Russian and Japanese Empires. Which would not have been an improvement upon a rapidly changing British Empire that had already peacefully evolved into such practically independent nations as Canada and Australia. None of this had much effect. Here, in effect, said America (the Chicago *Tribune* and the *Daily Worker* again using precisely the same language) is a simple issue of right and wrong, Empires are wrong and must go. The right of a people to have the government it prefers is an inalienable human right and must be vindicated. All this irrespective of the fact that, if one accepted literally this 'principle' that all peoples, all groups, at all times, everywhere, and in all conditions, are entitled to reject the government they dislike, then there could be no government at all; that democracy would be rendered impossible if members of a Republican party refused to accept government by Democrats; that in fact most democracies are governed for long periods by minorities, especially in those countries of multiple parties where governments can be kept going only by bargains between minorities, so that at no one moment can it be said that the majority rules.

Nor could one get much consideration for the fact that imperialism is often a means, the only available one at times in the confusion of human affairs, of setting up some sort of government without which no real freedom is possible. Without government there results, usually, not freedom, but the maximum of violence and injustice. When traffic has become hopelessly snarled, angry discussions only making it worse, a policeman, or even someone self-chosen acting as policeman, has to enforce some rule of the road in order to prevent fatal accidents. It was strange to find American capitalists, friends of the 'democratic way of life,' accepting the Marxist interpretation of British imperialism and regarding it merely as a matter of capitalist exploitation. It was still stranger to find, among even university folk, failure to consider the relation of British imperialism to the birth, growth and defence of the United States. What were the English to do when the Spanish Armada sailed up the Channel? Submit? There could have been no settlement of the Pilgrim Fathers in what is now New England, if Old England had taken that course. Nor could such settlement have grown into what is now the United States, unless (as noted previously) British power had resisted the pressure of Spain in the South and that of France in Canada and Ohio; nor, for that matter, if Britain had accepted a Napoleonic domination of Europe. For part of the Napoleonic plan had been the re-establishment of a French Empire in North America. Not merely is it true that if there had been no British Empire in 1940 Hitler would have been victorious, but if at earlier stages Britain had not been 'imperialistic,' the United States as we now know it could not have existed. Indeed the United States has shown a good deal of 'imperialism' on its own. The very religious Pilgrim Fathers came to a country which was not theirs, took possession of it, gradually ousted the original inhabitants; and the American Colonies, having become an independent state, that state, under its own steam, revealed not a little expansionism and imperialism, as in the Mexican War and the enormous additions of territory which followed it.

All this is recalled because in 1940, when I once more found myself in America, it was clear that the story was not finished, that the United States was concerned in it; and that if life was to be worth living in the future these problems of power had to be settled without world wars every twenty years or so. The previous war had demonstrated that the mere defeat of Germany would not of itself be enough. Policy, even military policy, had to take into account the situation which would face us after the surrender of the German armies. The enemy peoples would remain: seventy or eighty million Germans, an equal number of Japanese, both peoples having shown a very great capacity for military conquest; there would also be the Russians, the Chinese, the diverse populations of India, of Africa. Together they represented the preponderance of potential military power in the world.

How would the rise of such power affect the future defence of the West, the survival of its way of life? Would Moscow make of the enormous potential of the Asian and African masses an instrument for imposing upon the world that new type of society and civilization already developed in Russia, a type which found some ardent advocates among intellectuals even in the West?

Those questions would find their answer far more in the military situation which would exist at the end of the war—in the geographical distribution of the various armies, for instance—than in any detailed clauses in a peace treaty. Churchill had always had clearly in view the bearing which the military situation at the end of the war would have upon the achievement of the political purposes of the war. For two years he struggled for the acceptance by the Allies of a second front strategy which would make the invasion of the Continent through the Balkans instead of through France, in order that at the close of the war the Balkans and Eastern Europe would be occupied by Anglo-American forces and not by Russian. Stalin, obviously with political ends in view, wanted the invasion through France. This would ensure that at the close of the war Russian, not Anglo-American troops, would be in occupation of Eastern Europe. On purely military grounds, disregarding the ultimate political effects, invasion through France was the better plan, and on those grounds was favoured by American military chiefs. President Roosevelt opposed the Churchill plan on political grounds as well. The motive behind the plan seemed to him that of defending Britain's imperial interests in the Mediterranean, the Near East and in India. To agree on a strategy which could promote any British 'imperial' interest would in the prevailing American view make the war on the Allied side an imperialist one. While there was deep-rooted suspicion concerning British

imperialist motive there was no corresponding misgiving concerning Russian motive, notwithstanding what had already
happened in Poland, Estonia, Lithuania and Latvia. The
President, with much public support, particularly on the Left,
sided with Stalin against Churchill, with the result that, when
Germany surrendered, the Russians occupied most of the Balkans,
most of Eastern Europe and Germany up to and including part
of Berlin. Which is why in 1951 the United States finds itself compelled to send troops to Europe in order to prevent further
advance of the Russian armies; and probably why great American
armies are fighting in Korea.

For the prevailing American conviction that Churchill's fears
about future Russian power were merely camouflage for British
imperialistic cupidity affected also American policy in China.
Because in the American view Russian imperialism was not much
to be feared in China, and Russian support against Japan greatly
to be desired, there came about the agreement at Yalta in
February, 1945, by which Russia was given Chinese territory
and Russian Communism a leverage which contributed later to
the setting up of a Communist government in China; which, in
its turn, involved the United States in a war with the troops of
that government. How far the American belief in the harmlessness
of Russian expansion carried policy was illustrated in the
American conduct of the war a few weeks after Yalta. In April,
1945, American forces were within a hundred miles of Berlin.
They could have entered the city and occupied it. From
Washington came the order to halt so that the Russian army
should be the first to enter the city. The results are writ large in
the history of the five years which have followed the occupation
of part of Berlin and the surrounding area by Russian troops.

In this year, 1951, it seems shocking to state bluntly that as late
as 1945 there were powerful elements of American opinion, both
Right and Left, quite convinced that future peace and freedom
could be best assured by increasing the power of Russia and
diminishing the power of Britain. It is true that the Hearsts and
McCormicks did not like Russia, but they disliked Britain still
more; and, almost by habit, were disposed to give judgment in all
diplomatic and political questions against Britain. And while
the Left in the United States had supported Britain in her fight
against Hitler, they supported Russia as against any of the pre-

cautions that Churchill desired to take against undue expansion
of the Soviet power. We seem to have forgotten—so short are
memories—that a common accusation in the Progressive
American Press up to the middle forties was that Britain under
Churchill, in the interests of British imperialism, was dragging the
United States into a new war with Russia, a country upon which
the Liberal world was centring its hopes. Perhaps the most
astonishing thing about Elliott Roosevelt's description of his
father's attitude to Stalin on the one side and Churchill on the
other, was that such a picture could be drawn by the President's
son and create no astonishment. That particular reporter may be
mis-reporting when he gives us in direct quotes the President's
consistent and detailed suspicions of British perfidy, with
Churchill endlessly scheming—to the amusement of the President
and his son, runs the story—to divert the United States from the
war against Germany to the war against Russia. But we may take
it that the President's son was accurately reporting himself and
very many among whom he mixed. In recounting the talks of the
British military and naval leaders on board the *Augusta*, Elliott
Roosevelt speculated 'whether it was the British Empire's
purpose to see the Nazis and Russians cancel each other out,
while Britain grew strong.'

It is important to recall this because the time was to come when
Churchill was to be blamed for having conceded so much to
Russia, or acquiesced in Roosevelt's decision. We have to take
into account what he was up against in the forces of American
opinion. Those forces were having their effect in determining,
long before Pearl Harbour, the nature of the future 'peace.'

The foregoing indicates some of the difficulties encountered
by an Englishman in the United States in attempting to explain
the British Commonwealth and its position in the world. Yet I
had good proof that it can be done with some measure of success.
In 1942 a literary agent asked me if I would do a book to be
entitled *The People's War*. I replied that I was not at all convinced that it would yet prove to be the people's war in the sense
of giving results which would serve the interests of the people.
Whether or no that would prove to be the case would depend on
the degree of understanding the general public could manage to

bring to bear on the subject. As an alternative title I suggested *Let the People Know*, and presented once more the points upon which the public had shown itself in the past most likely to go wrong, including certain truths about the British Empire and Commonwealth. Not only was the book well reviewed but it was made a selection of the Book of the Month Club, which meant sales running into the hundreds of thousands, as already related.

The success of *Let the People Know* meant, of course, more invitations to lecture than I could manage. Wherever I could, I hammered home the danger of continually presenting Russia as the instrument of progress and Britain as the instrument of reaction. In a letter to the *New York Times* at the end of 1944 (December 7) I make a comparison, giving chapter and verse, of the treatment meted out by opinion on the one hand to Russia and to Britain on the other, showing that on a relatively trivial matter the latter had come in not merely for popular but for ' official blame more severe than that administered to any other member of the thirty-five United Nations,' while 'much of the Leftist Press of this country adds its quota of condemnation, of a violence never at any stage meted out to Russia.' I go on to point out that ' this contrast constitutes a message of encouragement to Russia; and not only to Russia but to the Communist parties, or other parties of violence which exist in every country.' This was, I added, certainly not 'the intention of the diplomatic bombing of Britain by America, but it may well be its effect— an effect hardly favourable either to the future independence of the nations of Europe or to the rapid re-establishment of those institutions of democracy which, under the strain of war, have collapsed in the territories of all the European Allies, save only in the territory of Britain.'

About a week after the appearance of this letter there was a ' Town Meeting of the Air ' debate in which I was asked to take part. The topic was ' Should the Allies Maintain a Hands-Off Policy in Liberated Countries? ' I was on the platform with Frank Kingdon, Congressman Coffee and Jay Allen. Most of the discussion centred on Greece, the implication of the three other speakers throughout being that British troops were in Greece for the single purpose of compelling the Greek people to accept a Greek monarchy they did not want, a government, as Congressman Coffee put it, 'which is pro-king, not representative of the sentiments, the aspirations and the heartbeats of the people of Greece themselves.' Britain should therefore be compelled to clear out; the Greek people (this came out in reply to a question from the audience) were being slaughtered by Churchill's troops and were no better off under British rulers than they would have been under German. Speakers and audience alike seemed to be quite sure they knew all the intricacies of Greek politics, with never the faintest hint that the British were in Greece to prevent the government being seized by a Communist minority and the country going the way which Poland, Bulgaria, Roumania, Hungary, Czechoslovakia had already gone or were shortly to go. Speeches and questions alike reflected a slant which was bitterly anti-British-imperialism, anti-Churchill. I seemed to be in a minority of one when I suggested that the future peace of Europe and the world demanded the presence of Allied troops in Greece until the danger of seizure of the government by an armed minority had passed. Howls of derision greeted my statement that order and peace in Europe was being undermined by the tendency of Liberals and the Left to subject Churchill to savage attacks while completely exonerating Russia. (Not one word of blame to Russia was uttered by the other speakers, or by the audience, throughout the whole evening.) Surely, I suggested, this tendency of the Left made Churchill's task immensely more difficult than it need have been. Stalin was in a position to say that, as between Russia and Britain, Progressive opinion in the United States public showed every tendency to prefer Russia and indict Churchill.

It is noteworthy, however, that though no single voice at the meeting was raised in defence of Britain's position in Greece, or the position generally which I took, I received from the radio audience a large number of letters supporting me. This seemed to demonstrate once more that there is a gulf between private and public opinion; that the more reasonable fail to make themselves heard and leave the stage to the violent-minded energumens. It is these latter that seem most to impress the politicians and to whom the politicians yield.

Among the letters I received after the Town Hall debate was one from Booth Tarkington, who wrote that 'Listening to you gave me the experience of seeming to hear an alertly sane mind engaged in a sort of combat of reasoning against two blind brains and a rather ignobly devious one.' He added:

> Your task seemed to be what should have been a needless one, yet was all too evidently worse than merely needed. Your arrows of truth showered upon your opponents, astoundingly not even denting their encased heads, so that here in the Middle West an 'old American' sat wondering not quite calmly what perverse devil has suddenly set flocks of parrots and herds of sheep to baa and chatter against your Prime Minister and 'the British'; suspicion comes: this devil may be more adroit than perverse. Whatever and whoever he is, he's harmful now and may be more insidiously so later; but there are many, many of us who hear you and would not have you fear that we don't see what's plain as a pikestaff and you make even plainer.
>
> Listening to so much slant-minded misinterpretation from Americans could have made the debate mortifying to an American; but you gallantly refused to let disheartenment have its way with us. In spite of fogs and new Babels we're encouraged to believe that your clarifications avail.

I quote that letter as one indication among many that the quieter undercurrents of American feeling run strongly in favour of an even closer co-operation of the English-speaking world, not as a substitute for a wider internationalism but as the first practical step towards it. If the nations of English speech cannot co-operate in order to survive, none can.

Yet the old prejudices and passions surge up dangerously at times—dangerously because, though they may be only momentary, they may delay and confuse steps which, the cause of survival demands, should be taken instantly and decisively. One such reversion to an older isolationism is occurring as I write these lines in the early months of 1951. The American Press reports that Senator Taft, who seeks the Republican nomination for the Presidency next year, 'appears firmly to have embraced substantially the Chicago *Tribune* version of foreign policy, which is of course dramatically opposed to everything Eisenhower stands for. Further, there are plenty of signs that Taft has entered into an alliance with Senator Joseph McCarthy. . . . Eisenhower at least will know what the results are likely to be if a major American party becomes committed to McCarthyism at home and the foreign policy views of Col. Robert M. McCormick abroad.'

Note some of the implications : On the very day that all these doubts and oscillations concerning America's future foreign policy are being exposed in the American Press, there are gathering in Paris the representatives of the United States, Russia, France and Britain to try once more to arrive at an accommodation between West and East, at a *modus vivendi*. We know, from experience again and again repeated, that Russia will make no accommodation, no concessions, if the evidence seems to point to the fact that the West is incapable of unity in resistance to her domination. For in that case she has only to wait, to help by intrigue in the worsening of Western disintegration, to give it perhaps a final push at the appropriate moment for the Communist world purpose to be fulfilled. Only a visibly growing unity of the West would deter the Russian purpose (as it was the only thing which might have deterred Hitler or the Germany of 1914). Yet what Russia is witnessing as her representatives gather in Paris is not merely the failure of the United States to agree with Britain and France, but the failure of one major American party to agree with the other, and the failure of groups within each party to agree. As to France, the Big Four gather in its capital at a time when that country is without a government, the various parties having failed to agree sufficiently to create one. And as to Britain—its government has not a majority of the electorate behind it, an electorate becoming ever more restive. The question is not what the situation actually is but what the Kremlin will judge it to be. It may judge wrongly that the West cannot unite and that therefore the Russian expansions can safely continue. If that provokes war it will not serve much purpose after it has started to prove to Russia that she was mistaken and that the West, for war at least, *can* unite. Our failures of political cohesion in March, 1951, may have disastrous results a year later, results we shall be unable to reverse by the easy wisdom that comes after the event.

It is difficult for an Englishman in America to take a useful part in the ' great debate ' now going on here. It is primarily a debate between Americans. And within sight of my eightieth year, with a continuation of the migraine headaches with which I am cursed every day of my life, with seldom more than four or five hours sleep even on the best nights, I find that I have not *quite* the energy I had until just recently for Continent-wide lecture tours, sleeping on trains at night and lecturing or debating during the day. So, as I prepare to leave for England this spring, which I have done for nearly every year of this last decade, to return in the autumn, the feeling grows that this time I may not return ; and that as I watch the skyscrapers fade into the distance, it may be my last look at the country where so much of my life has been spent.

The prospect suggests a certain summing-up.

CHAPTER III

IF I HAD MY TIME AGAIN

THE story just told is in part an answer to questions so familiar to the elderly: 'If you had your time again, knowing what you know now, would you have followed the course you did?' Or, in slightly different form, 'Could you, for the benefit of those who may work in the field you chose, distil into a few words any special lesson of your experience?'

To this I would, in summary, reply: The end I chose—elimination of war—I would, without any hesitation whatsoever, choose again. No other single task could be more worth the efforts of a lifetime. But I would modify some of the means I used, for reasons already outlined, and others which bear on the main lesson I would like to emphasize.

This story begins with an account of the vague restlessness of a youngster who had come to feel that Europe had entangled itself in problems it could not solve. The events of the half-century which followed showed that that guess, hunch, intuition, was pretty well founded. I have no regrets for the decision to which it led—to become a manual worker on the American frontier instead of going to Cambridge. It gave me probably a better insight than a Cambridge degree could have done, into the minds of manual workers, the class which, especially since the coming to power of the Trade Unions, has now the major part in determining the policies of the Western democracies. Nor do I regret the ten years with Northcliffe. They helped me to understand something of the rôle of the popular Press in shaping the public mind. I was also well advised to keep the movement which, before World War I, resulted from my pamphleteering, on a non-party basis. The decision to forsake that method and work through the Labour Party was a mistake into which the foregoing story enters at some length. But there

349

were errors of omission as well as of commission which call for notice in any general survey.

The reader may recall that the very first book in the list of those I have committed in half a century of writing is one with the sub-title, *A Plea for Rationalisation in Politics*, its argument being that events so apparently disparate as the American War with Spain, the anti-Semitism and Chauvinist militarism of the Dreyfus Affair, and the crude Jingoism which in Britain preceded the Boer War had common roots in an innate political irrationalism which would spell repeated disaster unless we could somehow correct it.

In joining the Labour Party I was almost unconsciously drawn into virtual repudiation of the proposition I had been at such pains to demonstrate; into assent to the theory that our troubles arose, not from the emotionally twisted thinking of the mass of men, but from the fact that power was in the wrong hands; that when it was transferred from the then 'ruling class' to 'the people,' the latter would, by some divine afflatus, know how to use it for the creation of a better society. And this, despite the fact that in almost every democracy the people are bitterly divided into rival parties so that often it is impossible to know which speaks for the people, or who 'the people' are. (In both the post-war elections which brought the Labour Party to power more people voted against the party than for it.) The emphasis on party loyalty tends to import into the domestic situation a counterpart of those passions of nationalism and partisanship which have wrought such havoc in the international situation and continue so to do to this day virtually all over the world——in Germany, France, Italy, the Near East, Africa, India, China and Asia generally. This situation is the basis of both the hope and the strategy of Communist world power.

But if political parties are a poor instrument for changes like those demanded in the international field, what remains? There are to-day of course a great number of private organizations established for the specific purpose of education in the foreign policies most calculated to produce peace: United Nations Societies, Foreign Policy Associations, and many similar societies. These are, for the most part, formed for promoting specific plans

—the United Nations, an European Federation, a Western Union. It is all to the good that such plans should be discussed. But their success will ultimately depend upon the attitude of the great politically illiterate mass. No plan, or design, or union, or federation can *of itself* save us. Its success will depend upon the way it is applied and worked. The idea that peace can be made permanent and secure by the universal signing of some document creating, say, a World Union, with every comma of every clause properly placed, is one of the great illusions of the movement with which I have been concerned. Every constitution needs constant change and modification and will prove quite ineffective unless those who have to work it possess sound social and political judgment, are guided by a certain scale of values, a certain code of political behaviour.

The world situation as it exists to-day is demonstration enough of the inadequacy of social and political judgment among the peoples of the world. That failure is the basic fact we must face. Concurrently with the exposure of specific fallacies, like those which I attacked in *The Great Illusion*, I should have gone on, by means of such organizations, Foundations, Leagues, Associations, that were available, to broaden the basis of the agitation; including, for instance, in our objectives improvement of school methods in the treatment of the social sciences, and bringing home to the public generally the need for a better grounding in what an American educationalist has called the real three r's— 'reality, relatedness and responsibility.' The aim would have been to achieve, on the part of every scholar turned out by the schools, a better understanding of our own inner natures, the way in which forces within ourselves are apt to twist our interpretation of fact; a better sense of the nature of society, its interdependence, the way in which one change must bring a multitude of changes, and above all perhaps a sense that the fate of the world depends on the individual good judgment of each of us, since the world is made up of individuals. All these three factors hang together and we have not made much advance in them in the twenty-five centuries since the heyday of Athens, where, without the printed book and all the miraculous means of inter-communication we possess and without the knowledge accumulated since their time, they managed to achieve a political wisdom not inferior, to put it mildly, to that shown by the highly educated Germans who followed Hitler, the Italians Mussolini, the Russians and the peoples of a dozen satellite states, including China, who have followed Stalin, either because the followers were captured by the totalitarian doctrines or had not sufficient cohesion for resistance.

It is true that the difficulties of broadening the basis of agitation in that way would have been, are, enormous, the main one, perhaps, being this:

You can form a society to promote a 'plan' like the United Nations, or the Federation of Europe. Its members and the public know what you propose to do. But to stand, not for a law which can be drafted, but for a 'changed way of thought,' a different scale of moral and intellectual values, a larger measure of reason and reasonableness in politics—what does that mean? We are all for reasonableness, just as we are all (including Stalin) for peace, and all, like Coolidge's parson, against sin.

Yet the thing for which I am pleading is definite enough in my own mind, and if I have not succeeded in making it clear to my generation, perhaps those who are to succeed me can be more successful in theirs.

What is most needed to save the West from war, or from the fate of Russia without war, is a keener sense of what one author has termed 'the moral obligation to be intelligent.' But 'intelligent' may mislead. We cannot be intelligent by an act of will. We can by such will observe the duties by which alone any man can hope to know the truth: keep his temper in check, listen to the evidence and to contrary opinion concerning it. We must add to our generally accepted code of individual behaviour the obligation, at present unrecognized or disregarded, to apply in the discussion of policy some at least of the dispassionate and impartial judgment we expect of judge and jury in a court of law. Such rights as the right to free speech must be paid for by such obligations as the duty to listen; a duty so seldom emphasized. Without it the right to speak has little social value.

The analogy of the law which I have drawn does, I think, help to clarify the point. The judge is aware that if justice is to be done the first task is to find out what justice is in a given case. He knows that good intention, moral indignation, a passion for righteousness, will not make the discovery for him. Indeed, he must set aside emotional prepossessions and examine with passionless intellectual rectitude the evidence of both sides. This is necessary even to pass judgment on a commonplace accusation of theft or homicide. But when it comes to the much more difficult task set for the Grand Assize of a national election, to questions involving the lives and happiness of untold millions, it is deemed a venial offence to jump casually to conclusions with no careful consideration of opposing evidence; or to give free rein to a partisanship more the characteristic of a lynching party than a court of justice. It should be noted that a lynching party is usually animated by intense moral indignation and is usually persuaded that it is executing justice.

The insistence upon the underlying obligation here emphasized, far from being a platitude, contradicts most of the common assumptions made in politics, in popular journalism, in many of the literary fashions of the day. Much of the Left insists that the cultivation of the judicial attitude in politics is both unnecessary and mischievous; that it would undermine party, class or Trade Union loyalty; that pugnacity in fighting the ' other side ' is what is most needed. The Trade Union ethic (fought unsuccessfully by the best of the Union leaders) to the effect that the Union has the right to be its own judge as to the share of the nation's income to which its members are entitled and to use its power of national paralysis to enforce its judgment, is a typical repudiation of the obligation we are discussing.

And it is repudiated most perhaps by the moralists.

In all the years of my pilgrimage I have listened to numberless moral exhortations of a certain type : Men must be less selfish, must love their neighbours, do righteousness, purge their hearts of fear and hate, do justice though the heavens fall, return to religion.

These exhortations almost always carry an implication which is a gross distortion of truth as revealed by repeated human experience. It is true that the world needs more of love and less of hate, more of justice and less of injustice, more of confidence and less of fear, more of kindliness and less of cruelty. But it is not true that the failure to secure these ends in public policy is due, as the

2A

exhortations for the most part imply, to the deliberate choice of evil over good, to selfishness, greed, conscious wickedness. The implication that it is easy to discern justice, distinguish right from wrong, betrays indispensable truth. For that discernment is at times extremely difficult and often cannot be achieved at all, unless we recognize the difficulty and accept religiously the moral obligation to apply severe intellectual disciplines. Causes like Communism, or Fascism, or Nazism could never have threatened us if millions had not revealed supreme self-sacrifice, been prepared to die on behalf of those causes. The hundreds of millions of ordinary folk who have suffered so grievously in the two wars of our generation did not enter those wars from greed. Indeed they neither wanted nor intended war. They wanted and intended peace. Yet, as these pages have abundantly shown, the people themselves generally approved or imposed the policies which produced the wars.

We are confronted, therefore, not with morally bad intention but with morally good intention which miscarried. The world has suffered certainly as much from the errors of the good as from the crimes of the wicked. It is not merely a matter of the dynamic few who may spearhead a revolution. No leader can get anywhere unless he has followers; the followers make the leaders. Why do the followers by the million consent to be led, or compel the leaders to lead, to such strange destinations?

It has happened to me once or twice that some parent, anxious as to his (or her) son's future, has by implication begged me to utter a warning concerning the sacrifices involved in attempting to set the world to rights. With the bluntness of friendship the question about having one's time again has been put in very personal terms: 'Your efforts of half a century, the two score books, the thousands of articles, have obviously had little or no effect on events. The First World War came, and brought the Second; the Second threatens to bring the Third. Would not your life have been easier and healthier, and the world not one whit the worse, if you had just gone about your business, amassed a competence, sailed your yacht or played golf with old friends, and died in peace?'

It sounds 'realistic.' But it simply ignores the way we are made. Only a very small minority can find the adequate satisfactions of life in mere physical comfort. Satisfaction comes from an interest pursued, even at the cost, it may be, of great physical discomfort. A wealthy man spends twenty pounds a day for the privilege of standing up to his waist in the ice-cold water of a Scotch or Norwegian salmon river. If men were compelled by harsh employers to do it for a livelihood we should on grounds of common humanity demand legislation to forbid it. The notion that it is a 'sacrifice' to give up a warm fireside for a day's fishing would appear to the true salmon fisher merely comic.

There are activities which can be as absorbing in themselves as fishing to the fisherman. They are apt perhaps to be more misunderstood. My own pleas to look at facts as starkly as we can are often greeted with a curiously confused comment. Some critics have attributed to me 'a great faith in reason.' If this means that I believe men to yield readily to appeals to reason, it is the exact contrary of what I do believe. It is extremely difficult to get men to look at the facts and interpret them rightly. But there are situations in which that rare and difficult thing is the only hope of salvation. This does not mean that men must be completely wise. We shall never be completely wise. But as our society becomes more complicated we must somehow manage to be a little wiser about it, to increase our understanding of it; of each other, that is.

Optimism can be as disastrous as pessimism. If the ship is drifting to the rocks and captain and crew are so optimistic that they refuse to bestir themselves, the ship will be wrecked. Equally will it be wrecked if they are so pessimistic as to believe that nothing can save it, and take to the boats.

When I'm asked whether I think that 'things will turn out all right,' I am apt to reply that it does not depend on 'things' but on men, on human understanding. We may learn too late, and find ourselves in the position of the man about to be hanged who, asked whether he would like to make a last statement, said : 'I would like to say, sir, that this will be a lesson to me.'

We may learn our lessons too late. My own attempts to accelerate the learning may not have had much effect. Others may be more successful.

2A*

A LIST OF THE AUTHOR'S WORKS

1903: Patriotism and Three Flags:
    A Plea for Rationalism in Politics
1908: Europe's Optical Illusion
1909: The Great Illusion:
    The Relation of Military Power to National Advantage
1912: America and the New World State (In U.S.)
1912: The Foundations of International Polity
1913: War and the Workers
1913: Peace Treaties and the Balkan War
1914: Prussianism and its Destruction
1915: Problems of the War and the Peace:
    A Handbook for Students
1916: The World's Highway (In U.S.)
1916: The Dangers of Half Preparedness (In U.S.)
1917: War Aims: The Need for a Parliament of the Allies
1917: Why Freedom Matters
1918: The Political Conditions of Allied Success:
    A Protective Union of the Democracies (In U.S.)
1919: The Treaties and the Economic Chaos
1919: The British Revolution and the American Democracy
1921: The Fruits of Victory
1922: The Press and the Organization of Society
1923: If Britain is to Live
1925: Foreign Policy and Human Nature
1926: Must Britain Travel the Moscow Road?
1927: The Public Mind:
    Its Disorders: Its Exploitation
1928: The Money Game:
    Card Games Illustrating Currency
1929: The Story of Money
1931: Can Governments Cure Unemployment?
    (with Harold Wright)
1932: From Chaos to Control
1932: The Unseen Assassins
1933: The Great Illusion—1933

1934: The Menace to Our National Defence
1935: Preface to Peace:
   A Guide for the Plain Man
1936: The Mystery of Money:
   An Explanation for Beginners
1936: This Have and Have Not Business:
   Political Fantasy and Economic Fact
1936: Raw Materials, Population Pressure and War (In U.S.)
1937: The Defence of the Empire
1938: Peace With the Dictators?
1938: Must it be War?
1939: The Great Illusion—Now
1939: For What do We Fight?
1939: You and the Refugee
1941: America's Dilemma (In U.S.)
1943: Let the People Know (In U.S.)
1947: The Steep Places

INDEX